REVIVALS AND ROLLER RINKS: RELIGION, LEISURE, AND IDENTITY IN LATE-NINETEENTH-CENTURY SMALL-TOWN ONTARIO

D1613437

In this examination of the social and cultural meanings of religion and leisure in nineteenth-century small-town Ontario, Lynne Marks looks inside churches, hotel bars, fraternal lodge rooms, and roller-skating rinks to discover the extent to which a particular Protestant value system and lifestyle dominated small towns of the period. In assessing the extent of Protestant cultural influence, Marks also illuminates the nature of social relations and group identity, particularly with regard to gender, class, religion, age, and marital status.

Based primarily on a study of the towns of Thorold, Campbellford, and Ingersoll – communities situated in different areas of southern Ontario and differing significantly in economic and occupational structure and religious composition – this investigation seeks as well to determine the nature of commonalities and differences in patterns of participation in religious and leisure activities within both middle- and working-class families. To further examine working-class values and beliefs, Marks moves beyond the local level to explore two popular working-class movements of the 1880s, the Knights of Labor and the Salvation Army, providing insights into the complexities of class and gender identity among working-class women and men and shedding light on the nature and meaning of working-class religious beliefs and practices.

(Studies in Gender and History)

LYNNE MARKS is an assistant professor in the Department of History at the University of Victoria.

STUDIES IN GENDER AND HISTORY

General editors: Franca Iacovetta and Craig Heron

LYNNE MARKS

Revivals and Roller Rinks: Religion, Leisure, and Identity in Late-Nineteenth-Century Small-Town Ontario

UNIVERSITY OF TORONTO PRESS
Toronto Buffalo London

Printed in Canada

ISBN 0-8020-0751-1 (cloth)
ISBN 0-8020-7800-1 (paper)

Printed on acid-free paper

Canadian Cataloguing in Publication Data

Marks, Lynne Sorrel, 1960–
    Revivals and roller rinks : religion, leisure and
    identity in late nineteenth century small town Ontario

    (Studies in gender and history series)
    Includes bibliographical references and index.
    ISBN 0-8020-0751-1 (bound) ISBN 0-8020-7800-1 (pbk.)

    1. Cities and towns – Ontario – Religious aspects – Protestant churches –
    History – 19th century.   2. Ontario – Social life and customs.   3. Ontario –
    Religion – 19th century.   4. Leisure – Ontario – History – 19th century.
    5. Sex role – Ontario – History – 19th century.   6. Thorold (Ont.) – History –
    19th century.   7. Campbellford (Ont.) – History – 19th century.
    8. Ingersoll (Ont.) – History – 19th century.   I. Title.   II. Series.

    FC3068.M3 1996   971.3'03   C96-930090-5
    F1057.M3 1996

Some of the material in chapter 6 first appeared in 'The Knights of Labor and
the Salvation Army: Religion and Working-Class Culture in Ontario, 1882–
1890,' *Labour/Le Travail* 28 (Fall 1990).

This book has been published with the help of a grant from the Humanities
and Social Sciences Federation of Canada, using funds provided by the Social
Sciences and Humanities Research Council of Canada.

University of Toronto Press acknowledges the financial assistance to its pub-
lishing program of the Canada Council and Ontario Arts Council.

To Marion and Gerald Marks
and
to Arthur Blakely and the memory of Dorothy Hale Blakely

Contents

viii   Contents

Acknowledgments

In the research and writing of this book I have received the assistance and support of many people. The research process was made possible through the help both of archivists and of those less accustomed to dealing with historical researchers. In particular I would like to acknowledge the assistance of Johanne Pelletier and Florence Curzon at Toronto's Salvation Army Archives, Kim Arnold of the Canadian Presbyterian Archives, the staff of the Canadian Baptist Archives, the United Church Archives, the Weldon Library's Regional Room, the Archives of Ontario, the Anglican Diocesan Archives for Toronto and for Niagara, and the Roman Catholic Archdiocesan Archives in Toronto. I would also like to thank Mr McCook of St Andrew's Presbyterian Church, Campbellford, and the Reverends David and Linda Whitehead of St Andrew's Presbyterian Church, Thorold. I am also pleased to acknowledge the financial support of the Social Sciences and Humanities Research Council, the IODE, and the Canadian Research Institute for the Advancement of Women.

In assisting me with the thesis that was the earlier incarnation of this work I was very lucky to have had the guidance of excellent scholars and teachers. Paul Craven provided invaluable advice about computer applications in historical research. Thesis committee members Ramsay Cook and Meg Luxton offered helpful and supportive comments. I am grateful to Craig Heron for his belief in my abilities and for his willingness both to encourage my work and to challenge me to push it further. As external reader, Joy Parr provided most insightful comments, which I hope have improved this work. Susan Houston's constant enthusiasm for this project, her valuable feedback, and her warm reassurances whenever necessary made her an exemplary supervisor.

Over my years of doctoral work I belonged to more than my share of study groups, which made the process of writing a much less isolating one. The Toronto Labour Studies Research Group provided useful and stimulating comments on several chapters of this book. Members of the Toronto Women's History Study Group read almost all of it in various forms and provided insightful and supportive comments. They also taught me more than I appreciated at the time about being a serious feminist historian who did not take herself too seriously. Members of the Toronto Gender History Group provided invaluable emotional support, as well as lots of wine and laughter.

I would like to thank the following people, who have been either members of one or more of the above study groups or friends who have supported and encouraged me over the years – or, more commonly, both: Michelle Alting-Mees, Sylvie Beaudreau, Ruth Compton Brouwer, Colin Coates, Lykke de la Cour, Karen Dubinsky, Nancy Forestell, Ruth Frager, Chad Gaffield, Mariel Grant, Christine Haggarty, Craig Heron, Franca Iacovetta, Susan Laskin, Margaret Little, Eleanor McDonald, Kathryn McPherson, Cecilia Morgan, Sue Morton, Jim Naylor, Janice Newton, Susan Prentice, Ian Radforth, Mark Rosenfeld, Carolyn Strange, Robert Storey, Shirley Tillotson, Mariana Valverde, and Cynthia Wright.

Having happily moved beyond Toronto, I would like to thank my colleagues in the Department of History at the University of Victoria for providing a very friendly and supportive working environment. I would also like to pay tribute to Thetis Lake, Beacon Hill Park, and the many other beautiful places on Vancouver Island that have made the completion of this book a more pleasant and calm if not more rapid process.

I would like to thank Sylvia Van Kirk and Donna Andrew for introducing me to women's history and for encouraging me to go on to graduate work. Thanks are owing to Mariana Valverde, who urged me to return to the study of the Salvation Army and whose support over the years has meant a lot. I also appreciate the encouragement of the late George Rawlyk. I am grateful to Ruth Underhill for some last-minute research assistance. The following people deserve special thanks for reading part or all of the manuscript (sometimes more than once) and providing most helpful comments: Peter Baskerville, John Blakely, Nancy Forestell, Ruth Frager, Gerry Hallowell, Franca Iacovetta, Sue Morton, Annalee Golz, and Elizabeth Vibert. I would also like to thank the anonymous readers of this manuscript for their valuable comments.

I am grateful to Gerry Hallowell and Rob Ferguson, of the University of Toronto Press, who have been most helpful in guiding me through the process of book publication; to Franca Iacovetta, of the Gender and History Series, for her support and enthusiasm for this project; and to Carlotta Lemieux for her excellent work as copy-editor.

While I have been very fortunate in having many supportive friends to help me through the writing process I would in particular like to thank the following: Sue Morton, for listening but not letting me take myself too seriously; Jacquie Buncel, for always being there with love and sound advice; Nancy Forestell, for her patience, warm support, and sharp historical insights; Ruth Frager, for her generous friendship, her enthusiasm for this project, and her gentle and much-appreciated encouragement about just getting it done; and Margaret Little, for sharing ideas, anxieties, and laughter and for both challenging and supporting me in many ways I would also like to thank Annalee Golz and Elizabeth Vibert, who have provided warm support, encouragement, and, where necessary, a sense of perspective in a new environment.

Some have wondered what a 'nice Jewish girl' is doing studying as foreign a culture as Protestant Ontario. I would like to thank John Blakely and Margaret Little for helping me understand (more than they might care to acknowledge) its distinctive nature. More importantly, I wish to pay special tribute here to my parents, Marion and Gerry Marks, who have provided me with a firm grounding and pride in my own religious heritage while still leaving me with enough curiosity about religion to explore its importance in the lives of others. My parents and my brother Saul deserve special thanks for their love and constant encouragement, and for their belief that I could be all I hoped to be – and more.

My last and most important thanks go to John Blakely for his patience, humour, moral clarity, warm and generous spirit, and much, much more. He has read and provided valuable comments on the many incarnations of this book, and (despite the absence of a methodology chapter) has steadfastly believed in it, and in me. His constant love and support sustain me and have been essential to the completion of this project.

New Methodist Church, Campbellford, built in the 1880s

New St Andrew's Presbyterian Church, Thorold, built in the 1880s

Women's Missionary Society, 1889, St Andrew's Presbyterian Church, Campbellford

Young ladies' society (probably church society), Campbellford, late nineteenth century

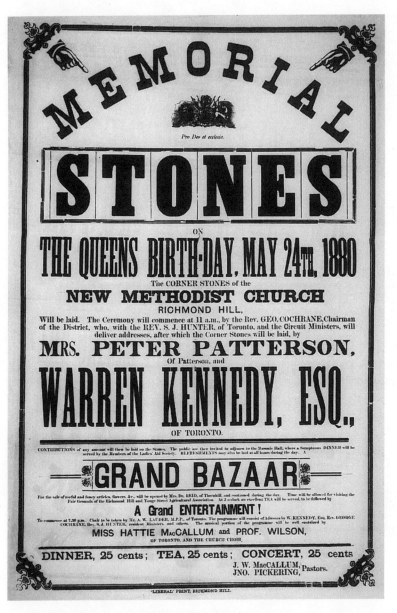

An announcement of the laying of the cornerstone of the new Methodist Church, and of the bazaar and 'entertainment' to raise money for the new church, Richmond Hill, 1880

British Hotel, Thorold, late nineteenth century

Dinner of a men's association, held at a Thorold hotel around the turn of the century

Thorold workingmen with a keg of beer, late nineteenth century

Annual march of a local fraternal order: the International Order of Oddfellows, Amherstburg, 1892

Firemen's convention, Thorold, circa 1900

Campbellford Hockey Club, 1901

First Officers' Council of the Canadian Salvation Army, early to mid 1880s

The Salvation Army in Toronto, 1884

A Salvation Army parade, Amherstburg, 1895

Abbie Thompson, who led the Salvation Army's assault on Kingston

Thomas Calhoun, a Salvationist

REVIVALS AND ROLLER RINKS

1

Introduction

What dominant images are associated with small town life in late nineteenth-century Ontario? Families setting off to church together in their Sunday best, strawberry socials, temperance campaigns, and Orange parades come to mind. These and other activities appear integrated into a seamless Protestant way of life, which not only prescribed Sunday observance but also shaped leisure activities throughout the week – a culture that linked small-town folk, rich or poor, male or female, a culture whose heritage we still struggle with today in conflicts over Sunday shopping, gambling casinos, and restrictive drinking laws.

Images of unified, temperate, churchgoing communities do not quite mesh, however, with the frequent complaints in late-nineteenth-century small-town papers of 'roughs' sexually harassing church-bound women and with reports of hundreds of men rioting over attempts to enforce prohibition legislation. Even among those who appeared most integral to this Protestant culture, consensus was elusive. Year after year small-town ministers chided the local Orangemen, those staunch defenders of Protestantism, for drinking and not attending church; they challenged 'questionable' entertainments such as the eminently respectable strawberry socials put on by the church ladies; and in an outraged chorus, they attacked Salvation Army preachers – male and female – who brought the Protestant message of salvation to the streets of the small towns with flags, drums, and tambourines, much to the delight of working-class townspeople.

Such scenes do not reflect cultural harmony. So, in reality, how dominant and how unifying was the mainstream Protestant culture? And what was this culture anyway? Were Orange parades part of it? What about the Salvation Army? This book tries to answer these questions in the context of small-town Ontario. A focus on these apparent bastions of Ontario Protestantism can tell us much about the meaning and influence of this culture both in small communities and beyond. But be warned – this study is not exclusively or even primarily a work of religious history, for it also contributes to gender history, labour history, the history of the family, and the history of leisure. But before those bewailing the fragmentation of Canadian history throw up their hands at yet another example of what they find most upsetting about social history, let me be clear: this book is intended to show the importance, indeed the necessity, of integrating subjects that have largely been studied in isolation.[1] In order to understand the meaning and impact of late-nineteenth-century Protestant culture on the lives and identities of Ontarians, it is not enough to study religion on its own. Ontario Protestantism was not just about personal belief or church attendance – though these were certainly important – for it said much, and through its practices and pronouncements implied much more, about respectability, gender, class, family, appropriate (and inappropriate) leisure behaviour, and many other issues that were central to the lives and identities of the people of the province. To understand what Ontario Protestantism was about, then, and the extent to which Ontarians accepted and lived by its values and practices, this book studies leisure as well as religion. It explores the relationship between Ontario Protestantism and concepts of respectability, gender, class, and family, and it looks at how working-class and middle-class women and men responded, both as individuals and as family members, to what we have assumed to be the dominant culture of their world.

A common culture of shared values, beliefs, and lifestyles can provide the basis of a shared sense of identity, whether of a community, a class, or a nation. Divergent ways of life, values, and beliefs, on the other hand, both reflect and reinforce distinct forms of identity. A study of the hegemonic force of late-nineteenth-century Ontario Protestantism allows us to begin to answer key questions about the nature of individual and group identity. How important was class or gender in defining the identities of small-town Ontarians? How important was age, marital status, or religious faith? How clear-cut and fixed were such identities? Did they overlap or shift in importance over time? What meaning did individuals associate with these identities? In defining themselves as women, did nineteenth-century small-town Ontario women accept the dominant ideal of women as passive, moral, and pious, or did womanhood mean something quite different to them, based in their own distinct life experiences? Did shared experiences of church and home and a common sense of femininity lead these women to feel linked to other women, or did differences in values and experience associated with class and age divide the way they saw the world and one another? Did male workers define themselves primarily as Christian men and accept the Protestant work ethic, believing it was their individual responsibility to rise out of the working class through their own ambition and hard work, or did they have a sense of group identity, a consciousness of themselves as part of a working class – as people who shared common values and needed to work together to overcome the exploitation they faced from the capitalist class?

Religion and leisure together provide a unique lens for assessing how Ontarians defined themselves and their place in the world. The workplace has been extensively studied as a central forum for the development of class identity and consciousness.[2] While class identity may have been formed primarily in the workplace, institutions such as the tavern and the church did not simply serve as barometers of group values and identities developed elsewhere. Religious and leisure activities and institutions promulgated a range of both implicit and explicit values and beliefs that were integral to how Ontarians defined themselves and one another. Religion and leisure are particularly valuable for exploring questions of identity because they were spheres in which late-nineteenth-century Ontarians had the widest latitude of choice about their lives. They could more readily choose whether to go to a bar or a church on Sunday, for example, than whether to stay away from work on Monday.

Of course, choices regarding religious and leisure options were not made completely freely. Some options were simply not available to people who worked a twelve-hour day or were a particular gender or did not have the price of admission to an entertainment. The choice of leisure activities was further restricted by campaigns against drinking and gambling. Other less material barriers also were powerful. For people who were fully integrated in a particular worldview, whether they were pious Christians or street-corner loafers, some activities simply did not appear to be options. And for all small-town Ontarians, certain possibilities were literally unthinkable in that they did not exist within the available systems of meaning. While recognizing these constraints, it remains true that participation in religious and leisure activities reflected numerous small and large choices made by ordinary small-town women and men. The study of these choices can reveal much about the values and beliefs that underlay them; by telling us about whom people felt most comfortable spending their non-work hours with, such choices reveal much about their sense of individual and group identity.

In examining how religion and leisure could both reflect and shape a range of identities in late-nineteenth-century Ontario, this book weaves together strands of historical analysis that have remained largely separate. Historians of religion have had very little to say to those who study leisure, and they have had even less to do with those who study the working class, while historians of the latter have until very recently been more than willing to return the favour. Women's historians have been more apt to cross boundaries, but much of their work remains ghettoized from the more 'mainstream' studies of religion, leisure, or the working class.[3]

While many American religious historians have defined themselves as practitioners of 'the new religious history' and have used the tools of social history to explore questions of popular religious involvement, Canadian religious history has been centred more within the field of intellectual history.[4] Canadian scholars have had a great deal to say in recent years about the position of evangelical Protestantism in the culture of late-nineteenth-century Ontario. Most have asserted the cultural dominance of Protestant values and beliefs in this period. However, these assertions have been based on the study of nineteenth-century opinion leaders,[5] who accepted and propounded the beliefs of mainstream Protestantism, not only from the pulpit but in schools, universities, newspapers, and other dominant social institutions. Although by the late nineteenth century members of this elite had begun to sound the alarm in response to emerging secularizing forces, most remained convinced that their world was and should remain defined by Christian values and beliefs.[6] We know, then, a great deal about the religious attitudes and concerns of Ontario's ministers, teachers, journalists, and professors. But what was actually happening beyond lectern and pulpit, in the pews of neighbourhood churches, and in the roller rinks and taverns that competed with the church pews for the allegiance of small-town Ontarians? It is to these and other spaces of popular religious and leisure activity that we must look if we are to understand the extent to which the Protestant belief system was not simply propounded by an elite but may in fact have been hegemonic, part of the 'common sense' worldview of most Ontarians.[7]

In recent years, North American and British labour historians have taken up the study of taverns and other leisure activities in which workers participated with considerable enthusiasm. They have argued that many of these activities formed part of a separate working-class culture and that they helped to nurture an oppositional working-class consciousness, or at a minimum a sense of working-class separateness from the dominant culture.[8] This study accepts the culturalist paradigm in recognizing that class cannot be defined only in objective terms in relation to the kind of paid work one does or one's family members do. It must also be understood in the more subjective sense of group identity, or consciousness, in which workers identify themselves as part of a distinct working class, with shared class values and interests.[9] This book, however, moves beyond the focus of most culturalist historians, who recognize that a sense of working-class identity can be nurtured on the baseball diamond or in the tavern, but who ignore the role religion may have played in fostering or retarding working-class consciousness. Perhaps because of their secular outlook, most culturalist labour historians, while proud to follow in E.P. Thompson's footsteps in other respects, have not followed up on his early recognition of the potential significance of religion to working-class culture.[10]

Religion is not the only category of identity to be largely invisible in the work of many labour historians. By privileging class over other forms of identity, these scholars can miss out on variations in experience within the working class. While there is a flourishing literature on women's labour history, both in Canada and the United States, the labour historians who look specifically at male workers often define the men's experience as that of the working class as a whole. This lack of sensitivity to gender not only ignores women's particular experience, but it can overlook the extent to which gender has affected the values and behaviour of the working-class men who are the (unacknowledged) focus of many labour historians' efforts. While some historians have begun to examine the extent to which masculine ideals have shaped the experience of nineteenth-century men, most have focused on middle-class rather than working-class men.[11]

These omissions in the work of culturalist labour historians have their mirror images in studies of women and religion. Gender is certainly not ignored in these studies, but it refers almost exclusively to women. For example, the overrepresentation of women in nineteenth-century churches is seen to require explanation, while the underrepresentation of men remains largely unproblematized. For some scholars of women and religion, class does not exist as a category.[12] In other studies, the experience of working-class women is either assumed to have paralleled that of the middle class or is invisible.[13] Scholars who explore the experience of working-class women emerge from a labour history tradition, so it is not surprising that most ignore the religious dimensions of these women's lives, focusing primarily on work, home, leisure, and sexuality.[14] One recent American study does point to the possibilities – and rewards – of integrating the study of gender, class, and religion. Teresa Anne Murphy sheds new light on the topic of labour reform in early-nineteenth-century New England by exploring the contested use of Christianity by different classes. She also deftly reveals the gendered meanings of the religious language of labour reform – and its very real implications for the participation of working-class women and men in the movement.[15]

In her study of the gendered meaning of language and the response of both men and women to such language, Murphy's work is situated very much within the new field of gender history. While many women's historians have long recognized the need to study women's lives in the larger context of gender relations, gender historians have more explicitly argued that women's roles and behaviour cannot be understood in isolation from those of men, and vice versa. They assert that to understand the basis of women's oppression, it is essential to understand the nature and meaning(s) of both masculinity and femininity. Some, most notably Joan Scott, have also argued that if we are really to understand women's inequality, we must pay attention to the way gendered meanings embedded in language can play a powerful role in limiting women's lives.[16] Certain women's historians have attacked the field of gender history, arguing that a focus on masculinity as well as femininity – men as well as women – serves to depoliticize women's history and move it away from the study of women's oppression. Some have decried what they see as the influence of poststructuralism on gender history, arguing against the dangers of a single-minded, overly theoretical focus on language to the exclusion of the material experience – and sufferings – of real women in the past. Others have denounced the way in which the study of discourse and what they view as a poststructuralist focus on the shifting nature of identities obscure the realities of oppressive power structures.[17] While the debate between women's historians and gender historians can be useful, some contributions have shed more heat than light, oversimplifying the positions on either side and not fully acknowledging that the majority of both women's and gender historians have been and continue to be part of a shared feminist project to understand women's lives and women's oppression.

This work was begun over ten years ago as a study of working-class women's involvement in religion. But during the research, I again and again came up against the reality that in exploring this question I could not fully understand these women's experience – and the narrowness of the options available to them – unless I also studied men's lives, both in the churches and in the alternative nonwork opportunities that were open to them. At the same time, working-class women's religious experiences remained incomprehensible if they were not studied in relation to the dominant middle-class ideals of feminine piety, and also in relation to the actual religious practices of middle-class women. Pushed by empiricism, then, rather than pulled by theory, this book is very much a work of gender history. However, my call for integration goes beyond the need to study women's and men's experience together. As with gender, in many historical contexts the study of working-class or middle-class patterns requires a comparative approach. To understand how distinct working-class behaviour and consciousness may have been, one needs a clear understanding of middle-class ideals and practices. I am not arguing here that 'good' historical studies will always give equal time to the study of men and women or to both the middle and the working class. Although this is necessary in certain contexts, in answering other historical questions a primary focus on women or men, or on the working or middle class, may be more appropriate. Even here, however, I believe that most historians would agree that an understanding of the larger context of gender and class relations remains essential.

When turning to the influence of poststructuralism on gender history, I would argue that the analysis of systems of meanings, or discourses, for implicit gendered or class meanings – whether found in sermons, fraternal rituals, or in the structuring of church interiors – is a valuable tool in helping us understand historical behaviour, which unfolds within such systems of meaning. As many historians have argued, an exclusive focus on discourse is limiting; it can ignore material realities and deny agency to historical actors. Recently, however, certain scholars have noted that the material and the discursive need not be mutually exclusive historical approaches. They have also argued that discourses do not simply shape consciousness and behaviour; as Ava Baron has noted, they 'compete with each other for the allegiance of human agents.'[18] While this study focuses considerable attention on unearthing basic 'facts' about who was and was not involved in the churches and various leisure activities in late-nineteenth-century small-town Ontario, it also seeks to understand the forces that shaped these patterns of participation – and here it must explore an intersection of both the material and the discursive. In this study we see, for example, how the increasing material wealth of many Ontario Protestants led to the emergence of new, more class-based definitions of who was a good Christian, definitions that subtly but powerfully discouraged poorer workers from being involved in the churches. Workers were not simply passively marginalized by such discourses, however. Many of them joined working-class movements that articulated powerful counter-discourses around the meaning of 'true' Christianity, critiquing the materialistic hypocrisy of middle-class Christians.

Those shaping or resisting new definitions of what it meant to be a Christian did not exist simply as members of the middle or working class. They were also gendered beings, and they were members of families. Some of the best work on gender and religion has focused on the family. Idealized notions of a particular form of heterosexual family life have been central to religious discourses, whether in the late-eighteenth- and early-nineteenth-century period that was so ably studied by Leonore Davidoff and Catherine Hall, or in late-nineteenth-century Ontario.[19] The churches were very clear about the cosy Christian domesticity expected of the model Christian family – and of the gender roles appropriate within these families. These roles were to be played not simply by men and women, but more particularly by husbands and wives, mothers and fathers, sons and daughters, each with their own domestic and Christian obligations, to be either fulfilled or resisted. The family is thus a valuable forum for comparing the behaviour not only of men and women but of individuals at different stages of the life cycle. While there is some recognition among historians that the various stages in the life cycle were of major importance in defining values, behaviour, and consciousness, most scholars have studied one phase, such as youth, in isolation. However, as Suzanne Morton has recently shown, a comparative approach is essential if we are truly to understand each stage in context.[20] By unravelling the complexity of a range of intersecting and overlapping experiences among family members, this study explores the nature and impact of Christian domesticity in late-nineteenth-century Ontario, points to the significance of age and marital status in defining behaviour and identity, and contributes to recent work by feminist scholars that challenges assumptions about the family as a monolithic entity in which all members share common interests and values.[21]

This book seeks to do three things: to explore the meaning(s) of Ontario's Protestant culture – not just, or indeed even primarily, from the pulpit but far beyond it; to examine how dominant this culture actually was in people's lives – in the choices they made to attend church, fraternal order meetings, or local cockfights; and to look at these choices as a prism through which to explore the nature of individual and group identity in Ontario society. To do this, it is necessary to integrate much that has often been studied separately. For instance, in studying Protestant culture, I have generally grouped together the four main Protestant denominations of late-nineteenth-century Ontario. Theological differences were becoming increasingly less divisive in this period, particularly among the three evangelical denominations – the Methodists, Presbyterians, and Baptists. I do note, however, where the Anglicans differed significantly from evangelical patterns.[22] As well as grouping together denominations that have often been studied in isolation, I have drawn together more discrete topics: religion and leisure, the lives of men and women, the middle and working classes, the young and old, the single and married. The study of small communities, in which people of different classes live, work, worship, and play in close proximity makes this integration more feasible. In this study I look closely at life in three small Ontario towns: Thorold, Campbellford, and Ingersoll. Because working-class activities and beliefs can sometimes be less than fully visible at the small-town level, I also look at two popular working-class movements of the 1880s: the Salvation Army and the Knights of Labor. Both reveal much about working-class identity and the relationship of Ontario workers to the dominant discourses of gender and Christianity. The Knights and the Army are explored in a range of settings, though the small-town experience remains the primary focus.

Despite the need for integration, the chapters that follow necessarily focus on different aspects of a complex subject. It will therefore be helpful if I briefly pull together the major strands of the story before pulling them apart, chapter by chapter, in order to give the story in more detail. Not surprisingly, efforts to explore a range of categories in the study of such complex and messy concepts as culture and identity do not produce tight and clearly packaged answers. However, some things become clearer, while others are at least revealed in their complexity and multidimensionality. The meaning of the dominant Protestant culture certainly becomes more complex when explored where it was lived in small Ontario communities. As other scholars have argued, piety permeated late-nineteenth-century Protestant culture.[23] Then as now, religious belief was of central importance to decisions about that most visible symbol of religious involvement, church participation. Studies of individuals can most readily explore the spiritual dimensions of church involvement, although even in such cases the nature of personal belief can prove elusive.[24] In a study such as this, which seeks to explore religious involvement among large groups, it is next to impossible to make definitive statements about the shape and meaning of belief. It is nonetheless essential to recognize the significance of the profoundly unquantifiable dimension of religious faith, both for those within the churches and perhaps for many beyond them. However, it is equally true that in the late nineteenth century a range of social and cultural motivations – and barriers – also influenced decisions about church participation, just as they do today.

We may define certain barriers as concrete, such as the lack of money to afford Sunday clothes or pew rent. But these material barriers are also linked to the cultural meanings associated with being a good Christian at a particular time. By the late nineteenth century, having the financial resources to afford decent Sunday clothes and the money to pay pew rent were part of being a good Protestant. The church-building craze of the late nineteenth century, which allowed wealthy Christians to demonstrate their religious commitment in bricks and mortar while making the poor feel less a part of the churches they did not pay for, was only the most visible of many ways in which the socio-economic pressures of the world entered into definitions of true Christianity. While we still need to learn more about early-nineteenth-century evangelical Protestantism, it appears that in this period, church members defined themselves primarily by religious faith and saw themselves as separate from the world – or, in Curtis Johnson's term, as 'islands of holiness' in a surrounding world of sin.[25] By the late nineteenth century the situation had changed dramatically for most Protestants, who now saw themselves far more as part of the world. This transition did not only affect church members; it also affected the world, as definitions of respectability in the larger community increasingly came to require worship at a mainstream Protestant church. The link between churchgoing and respectability did not preclude the continuing importance of piety among churchgoers, though it no doubt brought some people into the churches for reasons that had as much to do with community acceptance and material advancement as with faith.

The fact that the socio-economic pressures of the world had entered the churches did not keep all workers away. In small communities many working-class inhabitants joined local churches, though they were less likely to be church members than their middle-class counterparts. However, the fact that the material distinctions of the world were increasingly embedded in definitions of respectable Christianity was challenged by many workers, who felt marginalized or excluded by these definitions. Both the Salvation Army and the Knights of Labor articulated a working-class critique of the mainstream Protestant denominations. Appropriating the language of 'true' Christianity for themselves, in related but distinct ways each movement attacked the churches for accepting materialistic values and abandoning the authentic message of Christ.

True Christian respectability was not only defined in material terms. Race was also key. Although white Canadians considered churchgoing African Canadians and Native Canadians more respectable than their nonchurchgoing counterparts, the racism of Canadian society meant that even a complete adherence to dominant religious practices could never make African Canadians and Native Canadians fully respectable.[26] The almost complete ethnic and racial homogeneity of small-town Ontario and the fact that this study focuses primarily on the differences among Anglo-Celtic Ontario Protestants has meant that race figures less prominently in this work than certain other categories. Nonetheless, the attitude towards the small nonwhite congregations that existed in some Ontario communities starkly illustrates the racism of nineteenth-century Ontario. The whiteness and Anglo-Celtic identity of most small-town Ontario Protestants was integral to their construction of their respectability and indeed superiority both at home and in the larger world, whether in working through missionary societies to save the souls of the 'heathen' abroad or by donating used books to the Sunday school of a local African-Canadian church.

In small-town Ontario religion could define one as 'other' almost as effectively as race could. Roman Catholics, the largest minority group, could never aspire to full respectability in the dominant Protestant culture. While the virulence of anti-Catholicism varied considerably over this period, it remained a constant in the self-definition of Ontario Protestants. Although this study focuses primarily on the Protestants, a comparative examination of Catholic activities points to some of the 'small differences' that underlay – though they certainly did not justify – Protestant bigotry.[27] Since the nature of the Catholics' religious participation was in many ways similar to that of their Protestant neighbours, it provides a valuable comparative framework for understanding Protestant patterns.

One such similarity was the predominance of female worshippers in both Catholic and Protestant churches. Among Protestants at least, the feminization of church congregations reflected not only feminine piety but the reluctance of many men to join the churches. Their reluctance stemmed from many sources, including the particularly gendered nature of Protestant culture in this period. Although the mainstream Protestant denominations proscribed female leadership, late-nineteenth-century Protestant discourse was imbued with feminine imagery. The close fit between notions of the ideal woman and the ideal Christian – in piety, gentleness, morality, and submission to the will of God – could not help but make the upright Christian man uneasy. This uneasiness could lead to what might otherwise appear to be a rather irrational over-reaction to innocuous feminine efforts, such as organizing strawberry socials to raise money for church projects – for these activities could be viewed as feminine efforts to gain a further foothold in church space.

Despite the feminization of church congregations and Protestant discourse, many men did join the churches. For married men, church involvement was integral to definitions of responsible manhood. Most single men, however, stayed away, rejecting ideals of respectable masculinity for an alternative 'rough' masculinity of street corner and hotel bar, which defined itself in opposition to the more feminized world of home and church. Most Protestant families thus attended church without their younger male members, a fact that challenged the idealized images of Christian domesticity and family togetherness. These images were further challenged by most working-class families, whose members were far more likely to make separate, individual decisions about church membership than their middle-class counterparts.

The decisions made by working-class family members about leisure activities reflected a similar lack of concern for family unanimity. Some working-class people participated in the leisure activities that were most closely associated with the dominant Protestant culture – church socials, Sunday school picnics, and other respectable entertainments – while other members of the same family might be found pursuing activities that were either more questionable or, in some cases, completely antithetical to the ideals of respectable Protestantism – for instance, cock-fights, drinking, and brawling. Not surprisingly, these divisions were usually based on gender and age, with the men (particularly the young men) involved in the 'rougher' pursuits. Although less extreme, these divisions were also evident in middle-class families. The lives of married middle-class women were centred on home and church, but single middle-class women, like their working-class counterparts, did have further leisure options, such as 'wholesome recreation' at the local roller

or ice rink, or the somewhat more suspect activity of going to the theatre
or to a local dance. Middle-class men had access to a far greater range of
leisure pursuits. Many married middle-class men were involved in the
Mechanics' Institute or a sports club – activities that were intended to
foster the industry and self-improvement integral to respectable Protestant culture. Other leisure pursuits of middle-class men, especially single men, were more removed from the dictates of Protestant orthodoxy,
overlapping with the pursuits of working-class men and pointing to the
existence of a shared masculine leisure world in small-town Ontario.
Although this world did fracture somewhat along lines of class, marital
status, and levels of 'roughness,' it shared many common characteristics,
the foremost being an exclusion of women and an ambivalent relationship towards definitions of Protestant respectability.

The dominant Protestant culture was not as dominant at the local
level as might appear from the pulpit. It also had more appeal to some
groups than to others. The gender and class meanings embedded in
Protestant discourse provide some explanation here, as does the existence (or nonexistence) of alternative ways of spending one's nonwork
hours. Middle-class women were the most active in local churches, a fact
that reflects both the reality that most leisure and associational options
of small-town Ontario were open to men only, and the 'fit' between
dominant notions of the ideal woman and the ideal Christian. While
many working-class women were church members, social unease and
limited financial resources restricted their involvement. The popularity
among working-class women of the Salvation Army with its alternative,
more active, vision of Christian femininity also suggests that the dominant Christian ideal of passive, pious femininity did not fully mesh with
the reality of working-class women's active and arduous lives. Men had
their own varying and complex relations with the churches. Married
men were most likely to adhere to a more respectable churchgoing
vision of masculinity, but even the most respectable married middle-
class men played some role in the rich cross-class masculine leisure culture of small-town Ontario. This culture reflected an ambivalence
towards feminized religious culture, an ambivalence which in the
'rougher' young male version of this culture was transformed into out-
right hostility.

The differing responses to religious and leisure participation tell us
much about the power of the Protestant culture. They also show us that in
small-town Ontario identity was cross-cut by a variety of competing categories. Class, gender, age, marital status, and religious faith all played a

significant role in how these people saw themselves. While scholars have often preferred to prioritize one category, such as gender or class, this misses the reality as well as the messiness of the actual historical experience. As Joy Parr has recently argued, the various categories were lived 'simultaneously.'[28] The complex relationship that working-class women and middle-class men had with the churches points to a particular fusion in each case of class and gender identity. The relative force of different categories of identity could, however, shift over time. The presence of the Knights of Labor or the Salvation Army in various Ontario communities in the 1880s reinforced the significance of class-consciousness among working-class inhabitants, and in Thorold in 1893 a major revival temporarily overcame class divisions, eased gender concerns, and brought the townsfolk together in a common Protestant faith.

Before delving further into the intricacies of cross-cutting and shifting identities, I would like to introduce the communities in which all of this complexity will be explored. Thorold, Campbellford, and Ingersoll were among the seventy-eight Ontario urban centres that reported populations of between 1,500 and 5,000 in the 1891 census; the inhabitants of these centres represented more than one-third of Ontario's urban population. Ingersoll, with 4,191 inhabitants, was one of the twenty-six towns with a population of more than 3,000, while Thorold with 2,273 inhabitants and Campbellford with 2,424 were among the fifty-two towns and villages that had a population of between 1,500 and 3,000.[29] As in the majority of smaller centres, the economies of these communities were at least partially based on factories fuelled by local water power. The percentage of the population employed in industrial workplaces in Ingersoll and Thorold was about average for towns of their size, while Campbellford's inhabitants were more likely to work in local industry than was the norm.[30] While these communities all included an industrial working class, they differed from one another in geographic location, historical development, economic and occupational structure, religious make-up, and patterns of labour activism. And while they certainly do not span the range of diversity to be found among smaller Ontario towns, they do exemplify some of the differences that could exist.

Thorold, as a local poet celebrated, 'rules in regal splendor/ Queen upon her granite crest'.[31] Perched on the edge of the Niagara escarpment, looking down at Lake Ontario, Thorold saw itself as a proud community in its own right, though it had close links with the neighbouring city of St Catharines, especially after regular streetcar service was instituted between the communities in 1882. Many Thoroldites took the streetcar to the 'northern suburb,' as the local newspaper editor liked to call St Catharines, to take in its entertainments. Alongside the more pleasure-seeking travellers, Thorold Baptists took the regular Sunday streetcars down to the city for church services until they founded their own church in 1887. Besides the Baptist congregation, which was always a struggling one, Thorold was able to support substantial churches of other Christian denominations. Two of these stood on either side of the Welland Canal, which served both to divide and to sustain the town. By the early 1890s, the impressive new Church of the Holy Rosary domi- nated the area west of the canal, providing a visible reminder of Thorold's large Irish Catholic community.[32] The majority of Catholics, most of whom were working class, lived on the west side – the 'wrong' side of the canal – as did the Methodists, whose church was also located here. On the more prosperous east side were the Anglican and Presbyte- rian churches, as well as Front Street, the commercial sector, which ran alongside the canal.[33]

Thorold's origins were closely associated with the building of the first Welland Canal in the 1820s. This work attracted large numbers of Irish labourers, both Catholic and Protestant, many of whom settled in the new community.[34] The rebuilding and widening of the canal brought both prosperity and conflict to the town several times thereafter, notably in the late 1870s, when the 'new' canal was built, and in 1886–7, when it was deepened. When the public works associated with the canal ended in 1887, Thorold was certainly quieter, but it was much less prosperous. The canal did, however, continue to offer steady work for about thirty- five lock-keepers who were based in or near Thorold, as well as providing water power for the many factories along its banks. While neighbouring Merritton boasted large cotton and paper factories that employed hundreds of workers, including some Thoroldites, Thorold's own factories were comparatively modest. The larger ones, such as the knitting mill, the basket factory, the casket factory and the silver-plating factory, each employed between forty and sixty workers during the 1880s and 1890s, while the nearby quarries employed at least some of Thorold's many stonemasons, most of whom had been drawn to the community by work on the canal.

The long history of wage labour and class conflict that had been part of the building of the canals left a legacy of labour activism among Thorold workers. The factory workers and the quarrymen were willing to strike when necessary to attain their ends.[35] The small town of Thorold had three assemblies of the Knights of Labor in the 1880s, more than many towns four times its size. What is particularly unusual is that one of these assemblies was a women's assembly, probably drawing on the women employed in the knitting and paper factories.

Campbellford was in many ways very different from Thorold. Lying in the rolling hills of Northumberland County about halfway between Peterborough and Belleville, it was more isolated from larger urban influences. Campbellford merchants and professionals provided services for the surrounding farming community, but the village's economy was based primarily on the factories that lined the banks of the Trent River. The local industries included a pulp mill and a lumber mill, but it was the two woollen factories that were of central importance; the larger of these, the Trent Valley Woollen Mills, employed more than a hundred workers, primarily women. As a result of employment opportunities in the woollen mills, women made up one-quarter of the labour force, a higher proportion than in Thorold and far higher than the Canadian average.[36]

The Trent Valley Woollen Mills, which lay along the west side of the river near the centre of the village, competed in size with the nearby Methodist church, overwhelming the old stone Anglican church to the north and the nearby Baptist church. On the other side of the river, the large Presbyterian and Roman Catholic churches looked down from the hill on the riverside mills.[37] Some prosperous Campbellford Presbyterians lived in large houses on the hill near their church, though there were also many large homes on the east side of the river, which suggests that social divisions were less spatially obvious than in Thorold.

Class divisions also appear to have been somewhat blurred in Campbellford's mills, where labour relations were characterized by personal ties and paternalism. Gifts were distributed to the workers at Christmas, and presentations were often made by workers to foremen and managers. For example, at Christmas 1885, the spinners at the Trent Valley Woollen Mills presented a silver cake basket to their overseer, apparently in appreciation of the 'invariably kind and impartial manner' in which he had discharged his duties.[38] While such presentations did occur at Thorold workplaces, they were far less common. The more personal nature of labour relations in Campbellford is reflected most clearly in the absence of any labour strife or any labour organization, even the Knights of Labor. This can be explained in part by the relative newness of large-scale wage labour to Campbellford. The surrounding township was not even settled until the 1830s, and Campbellford did not become incorporated as a village until 1876. The community gained more than a thousand inhabitants over the 1880s, a growth fuelled primarily by the founding of new factories and the expansion of existing ones.[39]

Ingersoll, on the other hand, was a more stable community by the late nineteenth century. This southwestern Ontario town, situated near London on the River Thames, experienced little growth after the 1870s. The bulk of Ingersoll's population was located south of the river, where most of its Protestant churches and principal businesses were found. While some respectable families lived north of the Thames on the other side of the railway tracks, this area was the source of numerous complaints about 'roughs.' The Roman Catholic church lay just north of the tracks, and the members of Ingersoll's tiny African-Canadian community also lived here, near their small British Methodist Episcopal church.[40] Ingersoll was the most Protestant of the three communities; the Catholico made up only 12 per cent of its population.[41] With its larger size, it could sustain more than one Protestant church of each denomination, at least among Methodists and Presbyterians. Even after the Methodist union in 1884, there continued to be two successful Methodist churches in town. While the Methodists seemed to get on fairly amicably, the constant unions and divisions between the town's two Presbyterian congregations suggest stormier relations.

All three communities provided services for the surrounding farmers, but in Ingersoll, which was in a prime agricultural area, the impact of the farming community is most evident. Ingersoll is probably still most famous for its Giant Cheese, which was produced and exhibited by the town's cheesemakers. Other industries included a large pork-packing plant and several agricultural implements factories. The largest, Noxon Bros., employed more than two hundred men in this period and exported its products far beyond the immediate area. Most of the other local industries, including furniture factories and a screw and nut factory, employed only men, leaving few options for women who were seeking employment. The fairly large industrial working class of the community demonstrated only limited interest in organization. The Knights of Labor did have one assembly here, but in other respects the record of labour activism is spotty at best.[42]

Exploring the religious and leisure activities in these three quite different communities makes it easier to assess the impact of distinct social, geographic, and economic factors on the patterns of involvement in these activities. While the patterns were not identical in each town, the commonalities stand out clearly. There has been an ongoing discussion in the historical literature about the potential dangers of generalizing from local studies.[43] Given the social and economic variation among these three communities, I believe that the shared patterns found here can be extended, cautiously, beyond these specific towns to permit broader generalizations to be made about religious and leisure activities and the nature of individual and group identity in small-town Ontario as a whole.

This study incorporates a variety of quantitative and qualitative source material. In order to determine the background of the people who were active in the various religious and leisure activities, I have linked individual-level data from the manuscript census and assessment rolls (which provide this type of personal information) with a range of church and associational membership records. Such quantitative analysis was undertaken primarily for Thorold and Campbellford. (For a more complete discussion of quantitative sources and methodology, see appendix A. Tables are grouped in appendix C.) Quantitative records take us only so far, however. In order to explore not only who participated in the various religious and leisure activities but the values and beliefs associated with their involvement, I consulted a range of qualitative sources, including local newspapers, religious and labour papers, church and associational minutes and reports, and private manuscripts. The names of all of those found in church manuscript sources have been changed in order to protect their anonymity.[44]

This study thus combines the use of quantitative and qualitative sources at the local level and, in the case of the Salvation Army and the Knights of Labor, from across Ontario. Chapters 2 to 5 explore the nature and cultural meanings of religious and leisure activities in Thorold, Campbellford, and Ingersoll; they assess the patterns of popular participation in these activities and examine the implications of these patterns for the nature of identity in the three communities. Chapter 2 focuses on the nature and meaning of religious participation and examines the range of religious options, from free thought to church membership. Chapter 3 assesses the activities of those townspeople whose church commitment extended beyond attending Sunday services, looking both at church leaders and at members of the various church associations, particularly the women's associations. The gender and class implications of the church-building craze, which occupied most of the energy of both male and female associations, is a central focus here. Chapter 4 moves beyond the churches to examine the extremes of 'rough' and respectable at the local level, exploring what it meant to be rough in these communities, who was associated with this lifestyle, and the extent of the social distance that existed between rough and respectable. Chapter 5 shifts away from these apparent extremes to survey the range of leisure and associational life that fell somewhere in between and to assess the relationship of these activities to mainstream Protestant culture. Chapters 6 and 7 move beyond Thorold, Campbellford, and Ingersoll to assess which Ontarians chose to join the Knights of Labor and the Salvation Army, and then to explore the intersecting meanings of gender, class, and Christianity within these two working-class movements. Finally, chapter 8 returns to the local level to take a close look at the social implications of Thorold's 'Great Revival' of 1893.

This study seeks to understand both the meaning and the popular 'reach' of a certain Protestant culture in late-nineteenth-century small-town Ontario; an examination of the extent to which this culture was indeed hegemonic also illuminates the nature of identity at the small-town level. We still know far too little about what it meant to be a working-class woman – or even a middle-class man – in these small communities. Studies of the workplace and detailed examinations of sermons have taken us only so far. Let us see where a look inside the churches, hotel bars, and roller-skating rinks can take us.

2

Church Ladies, Young Men, and Freethinkers: Church Involvement and Beyond

The predominance of church spires in the nineteenth-century landscape has often been commented on.[1] The physical dominance of the churches has led to general assumptions about their cultural centrality. Nowhere has the hegemony of religious values been assumed to be stronger than in the small towns of southern Ontario. People moving to the big city might lose their faith and drift away from religion, but those remaining in the smaller communities have been characterized as sharing a strong Christian lifestyle and belief system. In fact, small-town realities were considerably more complex. In these small communities, as in the largest cities, religious patterns varied from the most fervent orthodoxy to an equally passionate commitment to the latest secularist heresy. Ranged between these extremes were an indeterminate number of regular and occasional churchgoers, whose presence at Sunday services could be explained by some combination of religious belief, concern with social standing, and the desire to see and be seen by their neighbours.

These and other motivations were no doubt present in some combination among most late-nineteenth-century churchgoers. For the empirically minded historian, it is unfortunate that their relative significance is not something that can be precisely measured and tabulated. It does, however, seem reasonable to assume that religious belief played a significant role in most decisions to attend church. Many churchgoers found solace in prayer and in the promise of an afterlife, and they derived guidance and inspiration from the church's moral teachings. Even those who had abandoned doctrinal orthodoxy, like the well-known author L.M. Montgomery, may have found that 'all the associations of church ... make for good and bring the best that is in me to the surface ... aspirations for the beautiful and sacred.'[2]

The sacred no doubt figured largely in individual decisions about church involvement, but more secular concerns were also significant for many churchgoers. As we seek to determine just how dominant the Protestant culture was in this society, on one level at least its social dominance is evident, for church involvement was an integral part of what it meant to be respectable.[3] In different historical contexts, different qualities are necessary preconditions for social acceptance. In late-nineteenth-century Ontario, the vaguely defined but clearly understood category of respectability was key. Sara Jeannette Duncan may have been going a bit far when, in *The Imperialist*, her novel of life in turn-of-the-century small-town Ontario, she asserted that 'the habit of church attendance was not only a basis of respectability, but practically the only one.' Nevertheless, she identified an important dimension of the culture of her day. Similarly, while L.M. Montgomery recognized the spiritual dimensions of her decision to attend church, she also noted that in her small Prince Edward Island community it was 'the respectable thing to do ... and I would be branded black sheep if I didn't go.' In the 1882 anniversary sermon in Ingersoll's Canada Methodist church, the minister complained that many attended for appearances' sake, since 'being a pew holder in the house of God gives a man a distinction both socially and politically,' and in Stratford a letter writer to the local paper argued that 'Christianity is not now what it used to be. It is now considered respectable, and even fashionable, to belong to an orthodox church.'[4]

While Duncan recognized the important role that church attendance played in defining respectability, she also understood that for the inhabitants of small-town Ontario it meant much more than this, since it was 'for many the intellectual exercise, for more the emotional lift, and for all the unfailing [social] distraction of the week.' Montgomery too understood the social significance of church involvement, pointing out that 'in this quiet uneventful land, church is really a social function and the only regular one we have. We get out, see our friends and are seen of them, and air our best clothes.' More cynically, the Toronto reformer C.S. Clark argued that Protestant churches were places 'to go for enjoyment and [to] display millinery.'[5] Churchgoing did indeed provide a social outlet for the respectable folk of small-town Ontario, and so did the many church-sponsored activities, including concerts, lectures, picnics, and socials. Both on Sundays and throughout the week, the churches were the central focus of local respectable culture.

Going to church, then, did not just reflect religious commitment; it could also indicate a willingness to adhere to the dominant norms of respectability, as well as a social identification with others who shared these norms. Conversely, nonattendance did not necessarily reflect a lack of belief; it might simply point to a rejection of or indifference to the tenets of respectability that were embodied in the churches, or to the social groups or classes who identified with this church-centred definition of respectability.

Two empirically measurable indices of religious involvement are church membership and financial contributions to the churches. While both can reflect either piety or an adherence to the norms of church-centred respectability – or, more usually, some combination of the two – church membership provides the clearer measure of religious commitment.[6] In the Presbyterian, Methodist, and Baptist churches, one could participate in the church-based culture of respectability by attending church and donating money without actually becoming a church member.[7] Prospective members made a formal undertaking to adhere to the religious and moral teachings of the denomination. Although the extent to which members supervised one another's adherence to these teachings had lessened significantly in the course of the century, some vestiges of this practice remained. In all churches, members were expected to attend regularly and to be present at communion services. Nonattenders were dropped from the membership rolls.

In the evangelical churches (the Baptist, Methodist, and Presbyterian) some form of conversion experience was an essential precondition for church membership. The exact nature of the experience differed between denominations, but there were significant commonalities. Through this experience, one came to a strong recognition of one's sinful nature and felt a willingness to submit to the Lord, to give oneself to Christ. Among Methodists, this was defined as 'one experimental crisis of religious life, from which a consciously new life dated its beginning.'[8] The experience was not always sudden. For Nathaniel Burwash, a prominent Methodist professor, the conversion process was drawn out and troubled, but the following experience was an important part of the process. Burwash attended a revival meeting in 1852 and 'in a moment like a flash of light I saw that God was declared to be gracious and merciful through Christ, forgiving iniquity, transgression and sin and I began to claim that mercy as mine.'[9] As is clear from the memoirs of ministers recalling their agonizing doubt and anxiety, and the peace and certainty that followed their conversion experience, the spiritual and emotional force of the experience cannot be reduced to concerns with respectability. Nonetheless, we continue to know more about the nature of this experience among the clergy than among the majority of Ontarians.

We do know, however, that even among clergy from the mainstream denominations, the centrality of an emotional conversion experience had begun to decline by the late nineteenth century.[10] By then, the conversion experience may have become as much scripted as spontaneous for many of those raised in the evangelical tradition. Many others, who continued to have strong spiritual beliefs, may not have experienced the requisite conversion experience, or they may have felt alienated from the self-proclaimed respectability of the churchgoing classes and thus have chosen not to express their beliefs through church membership. We are left, then, with the caution that while church membership no doubt indicated at least some level of belief among most members, it could also have reflected other, more worldly, concerns. Conversely, nonmembership cannot be equated with a rejection of Christian belief.

This study examines the church membership records of all the Protestant churches in Campbellford and Thorold. By linking these records to census and assessment records, it is possible to differentiate clearly between church members and nonmembers in these communities.[11] Since financial records are not available for all churches it has not been possible to gain as global a view of financial contributors. Also, while church membership was at least in principle available to all people above a certain minimum age, the records of financial contributions are skewed towards those most able to pay, that is, towards the more prosperous men. Despite these problems, the financial records provide a valuable supplement to the view of church involvement available through church membership records.

Church Involvement

Who, then, went to church in late-nineteenth-century small-town Ontario? Certainly not the entire community. In the early 1880s the editor of the *Campbellford Herald* claimed that no more than one-fifth of the inhabitants of the village could be found in church on a Sunday morning. If true, this would put Campbellford's religious participation lower than Toronto's, since the *Globe*'s 1882 survey found 45 per cent of Torontonians in church at least once on a given Sunday.[12] The *Herald*'s estimate may have been unreasonably low, but other evidence suggests that churchgoing was a far from universal practice in small communities. For example, in Ingersoll in the mid-1880s, local ministers 'called attention to the numbers who walked the streets on the Sabbath day, seemingly going to no place of worship,' and the *Thorold Post*'s editor was similarly troubled by the large number of nonchurchgoers found on Thorold's streets on Sundays.[13]

In these communities many families lacked even a single church member. In Campbellford, only 50 per cent of Protestant families included church members, and the percentage dropped to 41 per cent in Thorold (see tables 1 and 2).[14] Even when one includes families in which individuals donated money without becoming members, only 59 per cent of Thorold's Protestant families could be linked to the churches.[15]

Geographical Mobility

Were nonchurchgoers less likely to be an integral part of the small-town community and more likely to be 'men in motion' – part of the constant geographical mobility of nineteenth-century Ontario society? To a certain extent, this was the case. The men who remained in Thorold between 1886 and 1891 were more than three times as likely to be members of a local Protestant church than those who did not stay.[16] Despite this, one must be careful not to create a rigid distinction between 'rootless' drifters, who had no commitment to organized religion, and solidly rooted small-town folk, who attended the same churches their parents had attended and who saw church involvement as part of their participation in the larger community.

Many church members were on the move, as the high rates of turnover in the church membership rolls testify. Although some names were dropped for nonattendance, far more were listed as 'removed,' meaning that they had moved elsewhere, generally requesting a letter to take to their new church to demonstrate church membership. The rolls of Thorold's Presbyterian church, for example, list James Pond, a blacksmith, and his wife who came to Thorold from Orillia in 1883, bringing with them their certificates of membership in an Orillia Presbyterian church. The Ponds did not stay long in Thorold. They moved in 1884 to the greater economic opportunities of St Catharines, taking with them the certificates of membership issued by the Thorold church. Another Thorold Presbyterian, Harold Jackson, left Thorold in 1886 for Saratoga, New York, seeking his fortune in the United States, as did many other Thoroldites. Jackson arrived in Saratoga with his certificate of church membership issued by the Thorold church, and when he returned to

Thorold two years later he carried with him a certificate of membership from the Presbyterian church at Sandhill, New York, obviously the last American community in which he had sought to improve his fortunes. While most of the more geographically mobile people may have had only tenuous links with their local churches or avoided them altogether, a minority regarded church membership as significant. Even though religious faith may have been central with them, the desire for community probably played a role too. Those carrying certificates of membership knew that they would find the comfort of familiar rituals and a welcome into the 'fellowship of the church' in their new community.

Mobility among church members had implications for those remaining behind as well as for those who left. The high annual turnover rates meant that the membership of these small-town churches was certainly not stable.[17] A core of members, consisting largely of farmers from the surrounding region, remained in some churches for decades, but this was not the common pattern. Although, in most communities, the majority of those leaving were replaced by others, churches in communities that faced economic difficulties had particular problems. For instance, as Thorold's economic prospects dimmed in the late 1880s and early 1890s, the various 'pillars' of the small Baptist church left town. The church minutes reflect how increasingly difficult it was for the remaining members to find anyone to take up leadership positions in the church.

Class and Gender

Thorold's Baptist church had a higher proportion of working-class members than any other Protestant church in town. The same was true of Campbellford's small Baptist church (see tables 1 and 2). In both communities, working-class people were also members of the Methodist and Presbyterian churches and took communion at the Anglican churches. In larger towns and cities, workers could choose to worship in predominantly working-class congregations, and many did, but in the small communities where there was only one church of each denomination, workers who wished to participate in public worship had little choice but to do so in the company of their middle-class neighbours.[18]

How common was working-class church involvement in these communities? The middle-class townspeople were more likely to be church members than were members of the local working class. In both Thorold and Campbellford approximately 40 per cent of all working-class Protestant families included at least one church member. But although church membership was more common among middle-class families, it was far from universal, ranging from about half of all middle-class families in Thorold to just under 70 per cent in Campbellford (see tables 1 and 2). At the same time, many workers did belong to local churches.[19] Approximately half of all the families involved in the Thorold and Campbellford churches were working class, though workers were more likely to join some churches than others.

The differences in church membership patterns in the working class are not as clear-cut as images of 'respectable' churchgoing skilled workers and 'rough' unskilled ones would suggest. In both communities the families of skilled working-class men were slightly more likely to be church members than was the case among the unskilled. However, this pattern was not consistent across denominations. Members of semi-skilled and unskilled working-class families were more likely to be Anglican communicants than people who came from skilled working-class families, but the reverse was true among Methodist and Presbyterian workers. The most striking patterns are apparent among servants, who very rarely became church members in any denomination, and among wealthy skilled workers, whose church membership rates were higher than those of most middle-class families.[20]

Religious involvement and a concern with the respectability conferred by church involvement were not just middle-class phenomena. Some wealthy skilled workers, especially those living in small towns, may have considered themselves among the prominent respectable citizens of the community, a prominence that was reinforced through church involvement. In small communities, some workers had family links with churchgoing farm families, and their church involvement may have reflected family commitments and traditions. Many other working-class families, who were neither particularly wealthy nor particularly well connected in the community, also chose to become members and worship together with middle-class townsfolk. This appears to point to the strength of Christian beliefs among all classes in these small communities. For working women and men who faced lives of endless toil and economic uncertainty, religious faith no doubt provided solace, a sense of meaning and hope for the future, either in this world or the next. Working-class church membership may also suggest that many workers, like their middle-class neighbours, sought the respectability conferred by church involvement. The relatively small difference between middle- and working-class involvement in Thorold shows that conflict in the workplace did not prevent the different classes from worshipping together on Sundays and sharing in a common culture based on Christian faith and social respectability.

At the same time, the workers were less likely to join a church than the middle-class people were, a fact that points to a degree of religious indifference coupled with a sense of social distance from church-centred respectability among many small town working-class families. The relative absence of servants from the church membership rolls is particularly striking, suggesting a major social gulf between mistress and servant, a gulf which the servants had no interest in bridging even on Sundays. The apparent unwillingness of servants, most of whom were female, to become church members is of interest given the general predominance of women in nineteenth-century congregations in both Canada and the United States.[21] The Thorold and Campbellford congregations were no exception to this pattern. Women were much more likely to be church members than men were; they made up about two-thirds of all church members.[22] The sex ratios differed between denominations, however, with the Baptists consistently demonstrating the lowest levels of feminization, though even among the Baptists approximately 60 per cent of the members were women.[23]

Historians have argued that women's greater propensity to become involved in the churches reflected the contemporary perceptions of their nature. Women were assumed to be more moral, more spiritual, and thus more religious than men, and they were certainly taught that this was true. For evangelical women, the religious submission to the Lord that was integral to the conversion experience was congruent with the dominant ideals of feminine submission and self-abnegation. American scholars have argued that during the late nineteenth century the image of Jesus, and thus of the ideal Christian, was particularly closely associated with the feminine qualities of tenderness, love, and forgiveness.[24] While the Canadian churches were distinct from their counterparts in the eastern United States, there do appear to have been certain parallels.[25] It is certainly telling that when praising Christian men, small-town ministers did not hesitate to identify among these men's ideal Christian qualities the fact that they revealed 'the tenderness of a woman.'[26]

While the 'feminized' nature of Christian faith in this period may help explain women's high levels of church involvement, it is also true that women had few other options beyond home and church. Alice Chown, an early-twentieth-century Kingston feminist, noted that for her pious Methodist mother, who had no outlet for her aspirations beyond church and home, 'her religion was the poetry of her life.'[27] Marguerite Van Die has similarly argued that for many evangelical women, Christianity provided a spiritual sense of fulfilment that was not available through the narrow daily round of domestic work. Women such as Anna Bellamy of eastern Ontario found that taking communion on Sunday provided a time of 'consolation' and 'improvement.' Many such women also found that with conversion they entered into a sisterhood of shared belief that extended beyond the bounds of home and family.[28] While religion may not have been as spiritually significant for all women, church attendance and related activities probably provided welcome social opportunities for many.

Within the Family

Although there has been considerable discussion, at least in the American context, about the feminization of religion, there has been little effort to understand the precise nature of feminization, for both women and men, at the level of family and household.[29] A finer analysis is needed here, one that moves beyond simple gender categories. Which women were most likely to attend church – young or old, single or married? And how did male church involvement break down? Were men generally more indifferent to the churches, or did their behaviour change over their life cycle? Another issue, of course, is the relationship between class and gender, age and marital status. Can we discuss working-class or middle-class attitudes towards religion without looking more closely at the behaviour of individual family members? In studying the history of immigration, family economies, and family violence, feminist historians have increasingly recognized the dangers and limitations of studying the 'family' as a unified construct without looking more closely at the behaviour and interests of different family members.[30] This insight has rarely been taken up by social historians of religion. We have not moved far beyond Bruce Laurie's division of the working class into 'revivalists,' who took religion very seriously, and other groups who did not – an approach which assumed that members of the working-class family shared common religious values.[31]

This approach risks missing or misunderstanding significant dimensions of the relationship between gender, class, and religious involvement. How, for example, are we to characterize the Craigs of Thorold? There is no evidence that the widower father, who worked as a lockkeeper, ever went near a church, but his unmarried daughters, who were employed in the local knitting mill, were extremely active in the town's small Baptist church. Or what about Anne Crane of Campbellford, an active member of the village's Methodist church whose husband John, a carder at the woollen mill, had no visible links to the church? Can these families be characterized as examples of working-class irreligion on the basis of the behaviour of the male head of the household?

The religious behaviour of these families was at least as common as a complete rejection of the church by the entire family, or the cosy Victorian picture of father, mother, and children walking to church together on Sunday mornings. Women were likely to be active in church regardless of age and marital status.[32] In both Campbellford and Thorold, the difference between married and single women's church membership rates was minimal. Working-class women were somewhat less likely to be church members than their middle-class counterparts, but in most cases the class-based differences were fairly small (see tables 3 and 4).

The dominant ideal of pious spiritual womanhood was thus not confined to the middle-class women with whom it is usually associated; it also influenced many working-class women, and it appears to have been an equally powerful ideal for both married and single women. Among men, however, marriage made a major difference in church membership status. Very few single men were church members. In both communities, unmarried women were approximately three times as likely to be church members as unmarried men.[33] In some occupational groups – for example, the workers in Campbellford's factories – the differences are even more striking. Almost half of the 'mill girls' were church members, compared with less than 10 per cent of the single men working in the mills (see tables 5 and 6). Middle-class single men differed little from their working-class counterparts when it came to church membership. For example, in Thorold, 10 per cent of single middle-class men were church members, compared with 7 per cent of single working-class men. Marriage was the significant turning point here. In the two communities, married men were between two and three times as likely to be church members as single men were. Married men were less likely to be church members than married women, but the differences were generally not large[34] (see tables 3 and 4).

Women predominated in the churches not because all men stayed away but because single men were not there, or at least would not become church members. Some middle-class single men who were not members were willing to donate money, which suggests at least occasional church attendance (see table 7), but church membership remained the exception among the unmarried men of both communities. This pattern was not unique to Campbellford and Thorold; it has been identified in a recent study of Methodists in St Stephen, New Brunswick, in the same period.[35] Marriage clearly made a major difference to men's religious involvement. Why was this so? Perhaps women, who were assumed to be more moral and more religious than men, were able to 'tame' their new husbands and bring them into the churches. Given the power and authority of men within marriage in this period it is unlikely, however, that even the combination of saintly feminine moral suasion and plain nagging would in itself have brought most husbands into the churches.

To understand men's willingness to become church members, we must look not only at the concepts of ideal femininity but at the concepts of ideal masculinity. In late-nineteenth-century Ontario, as today, there was no single masculine ideal but a number of competing and overlapping images. Certainly, most men of the period aspired to the 'manly' qualities of strength, independence, and self-assertion. These qualities are certainly some distance from the more feminized qualities of the ideal late-nineteenth-century Christian, and particularly from the emphasis on submission to the Lord that was integral to the evangelical conversion experience. The distance between ideals of strong, autonomous, and virile manhood and Christian tenderness, love, and submission may have helped to keep many young men away from the churches.[36] However, while such images may have made church involvement a complex adjustment for many married men, other ideals of masculinity had the power to draw them into a church-centred world.

An important contemporary masculine ideal was that of family provider, the man who worked hard to support his family financially. For married men the ideal of being a good provider or breadwinner was an inherent part of respectability.[37] The solid respectability expected of the family provider was strengthened by church involvement. While the head of household reinforced his respectability by being seen in the family pew on Sundays, what he heard there was intended to strengthen his commitment to the role of family breadwinner. For example, in 1890 the minister of Thorold's Baptist church told his congregation that providing for one's family was a divine command and that 'he who failed to do so was worse than Voltaire, or Hume or Ingersoll' (all infamous freethinkers).[38]

The married man's presence in church, surrounded by wife and children, reinforced his role as respectable family provider, but it did more; it also reflected a particularly Christian masculinity that incorporated a commitment to domestic life.[39] Victorian family scenes were generally centred in the private space of home, women's role being to make the home a warm and welcoming place where men would rest from the battles of the public world. Here men could enjoy domestic life and at the same time be influenced by women's higher moral and spiritual values. The churches preached of the value of family life for men as well as for women, and frequently bemoaned the decline of family prayer, which was considered a centrepiece of ideal Christian domesticity.[40] But while family life in the home was important, family church attendance extended this almost sanctified togetherness of the ideal Victorian family into a public yet sacred space. Among the various ideals of masculinity competing in Victorian society, E. Anthony Rotundo has identified the powerful ideal of the 'Christian gentleman,' for whom Christian belief and church involvement were central and were closely linked to a deep commitment to family life.[41] Although Rotundo does not differentiate between single and married men, the link between religious involvement and domesticity appears to have had a particular resonance for married men.

Did these masculine ideals of respectable breadwinner and Christian family man extend across class boundaries? Certainly, for many church-going working-class men they had considerable significance. However, middle-class married men were more likely to be church members than their working-class counterparts. This suggests that for some working-class men the particularly working-class masculine ideals of toughness and physical strength were incompatible with a feminized Christian faith.[42] Working-class men also appear to have been less concerned with the respectability conferred by church attendance. Many middle-class men who were not willing to become church members supported the churches financially. This suggests at least some level of church attendance among these men, as well as a desire to assert their respectability visibly through church contributions. Married working-class men who were church members contributed to the churches – often quite generously, considering their incomes – but working-class men who were not church members rarely contributed at all (see tables 3 and 7). This no doubt reflected the limited financial resources of working-class men, but it also suggests that working-class men who had not made a formal religious commitment to the churches were unwilling to spend their scarce financial resources to support them. These men may have attended church, at least occasionally, but they did not feel sufficient commitment to rent a pew, make a regular weekly contribution, or donate to mission-

ary funds. Working-class men who had not made the religious commitment of church membership may have been less interested in 'buying'
respectability in the community through financial support to the
churches than middle-class men who were not church members.

In Thorold, some working-class married men may in fact have been
actively hostile to Christianity and to church-based respectability.
Although in Campbellford working-class married men followed the
middle-class pattern in that they were only slightly less likely to be
church members than working-class married women, in Thorold the difference was far more significant. Among families of skilled, semi-skilled,
and unskilled men, the women were approximately twice as likely to be
church members as their husbands (see table 3). The labour activism
among Thorold's working class did not keep working-class families out
of the churches, since many working-class wives and daughters were
members. However, for at least some men, conflict in the workplace
may have heightened class-consciousness and led to a reluctance to worship with employers and other middle-class townspeople.

Class-consciousness among Thorold men may explain the divergence
in church membership patterns between married working-class men
and women in that community. However, different conceptions of the
family and of domesticity are also relevant here. In both communities,
working-class family members more readily went their own way on
Sundays than members of middle-class families. In middle-class families
in both Thorold and Campbellford, if one partner belonged to the
church, the other was very likely to be a member too. If only one partner
was a member, it was more often the wife than the husband (which is
not surprising, given the contemporary gender ideals). Nonetheless, the
middle-class norm was the church membership of both partners (see
tables 8 and 9). The Blain family of Campbellford, of which the physician father, his wife, and daughters were all members of the local Presbyterian church, is typical here.

The Crandalls of Campbellford represent a different pattern. Paul
Crandall, a labourer, and his son, John, a fireman, appear to have had no
links with the Anglican church, where Paul's wife Jane was a regular
communicant. The Crandalls' approach to church involvement was
fairly common among working-class families. In just over half of Campbellford's working-class churchgoing families and in considerably less
than half such families in Thorold, both husband and wife were church
members. In both communities, working-class wives were more frequently the only church member in the family than husbands were, and

in fact in Thorold wives more often belonged to the church without their husbands than with them (see tables 8 and 9). Dominant notions of women's particularly spiritual nature seem to have had a cross-class appeal. However, something else was also going on here. While working-class wives were more likely than their husbands to be the only church member in the family, the reverse was also possible. In fact, working-class men were more commonly the only church member in the family than middle-class men were. In both communities there were also some working-class families where daughters were the only church members.[43] So what we are seeing here is not only the piety of working-class wives but also a willingness among many working-class family members to go their own way on Sundays.

Intermarriage patterns also suggest an acceptance of variations in religious behaviour in working-class families. The middle-class families of both communities included very few spouses who were of different Protestant denominations and only one Catholic-Protestant couple.[44] This reflects either a very low rate of intermarriage or the regular adoption by one spouse of the other's religion. Either possibility points to an emphasis on familial religious unanimity, suggesting both the importance of religion in middle-class homes and an emphasis on family 'togetherness,' or domesticity. Among working-class families, the percentage of couples that had spouses of different denominations was approximately three times as great as among middle-class families, with almost one-third of these marriages being between Catholics and Protestants.[45] This suggests an indifference to religious issues in at least some working-class families, though in other families it points to a willingness to take different paths, as we see in the case of Mary Danforth of Thorold, wife of a prominent Roman Catholic moulder. She was very active in the local Presbyterian church, while he appears to have remained completely aloof from its activities.

The differences between middle- and working-class patterns of church involvement should not be overstated. In many working-class families both husband and wife were church members and led their family into church on Sundays motivated by a similar mix of religious faith, the desire to appear respectable, and a commitment to family togetherness as their middle-class neighbours. However, the religious discourse of Christian domesticity – in home and church – does appear to have had less influence on working-class families. They were less likely than middle-class families to attend church together. This suggests religious indifference, or some level of class hostility, particularly among working-class men, who were less likely to join churches than their wives or daughters. In at least some working-class families, a willingness to go different ways on Sundays may also have reflected a tendency to do the same during the week. Such evidence alone cannot prove that domesticity was less important in working-class households than in middle-class ones. What we are seeing among the middle class may be more the public display of domesticity than domesticity itself. Nonetheless, the pattern is suggestive. The tendency of many family members to make their own decisions about church involvement also points to the danger of making assumptions about the religious behaviour of a particular class or gender without looking more closely into the 'black box' of the family to find out what the individual family members were actually doing.

The 'Problem' of Young Men

When speaking of families attending church together, it is important to remember that when unmarried men of all classes reached the age to decide for themselves, they were very unlikely to be part of the family circle on Sundays. Most unmarried men were under thirty, so the fact that unmarried men stayed away from the churches was viewed primarily as a problem of young men. There were a few serious young male churchgoers, such as Donald Mills, the son of a prominent Thorold merchant. Mills was a member of the local Methodist church, as were his parents and sisters, and in a diary he kept when he was seventeen he recorded his regular attendance at church with the rest of his family, as well as his attendance at Gospel temperance meetings, prayer meetings, and missionary lectures.[46] Mills was a clerk in his father's store, and it is true that in both communities clerks were more likely to be church members than other young men – a fact that suggests a greater concern with respectability, or with the upward mobility which they hoped respectability would confer.

However, the majority of clerks and the vast majority of Donald Mills's contemporaries were not church members. But this does not mean that they stayed completely away from the churches. The *Ingersoll Chronicle* noted that many young men stood outside the churches during Sunday evening services, hoping to see and possibly walk home young women attending the services.[47] The *Thorold Post* complained about young men who did attend church on Sunday evening but seemed to go 'for no other purpose than to make remarks about all who pass in or out and during the services, no respect is paid to the place or speaker.'[48] Other young men attended occasionally, when a service was of particular interest to them. For example, an exceptionally large number of young men were present in the Thorold Methodist church to hear a sermon on gambling.[49]

This sermon and others like it were not intended for the entertainment of young men. Ministers were very concerned about their absence from the churches. No greater praise could be bestowed on a clergyman than that given to Thorold's new Presbyterian minister, who in his previous station had apparently drawn in 'many ... young men who had formerly stood aloof from the communion of the church.'[50] Few ministers were as successful, though many tried to be. Sermons to young men were a common occurrence in Thorold, Ingersoll, and Campbellford, as they were in towns and cities across Canada. Some of these sermons focused explicitly on religious belief, while others ranged more broadly, setting out the Protestant standards of appropriate manhood. Some ministers focused on explicitly moral issues, trying to steer young men away from the evils of drink, gambling, and sexual 'impurity.'[51]

In many other cases, ministers revealed the convergence within Protestant discourse of sacred issues and what we might view as a more 'secular' concern with material success. They preached that true Christian men exhibited the qualities of self-mastery, hard work, and ambition. These attributes were identified not simply as Christian virtues that would lead to rewards in the next world, but were shown to have concrete material payoffs here and now. While the majority of young men appear to have believed that the ideals of appropriate masculinity and religious faith were not compatible, the ministers preached that there was in fact an integral relationship between being a respectable and materially successful man and being a churchgoing Christian. Donald Mills recorded in his diary that on 8 December 1878, 'Rev. Mr. Sellery preached a sermon to young men ... His points were Industry, Economy, Perseverance, a good Moral Character, Fidelity, Truthfulness, Charity and Religion.'[52]

Catholic Church Involvement: Small Differences?

Thorold, Campbellford, and Ingersoll were predominantly Protestant in the late nineteenth century, but certainly not exclusively so. So what was the situation of the Catholics in these small communities? Was their relationship to their churches similar to or different from that of their

Protestant neighbours? Did the similarities or differences emerge from religious differences, or did the position of Catholics as a small minority in a Protestant community and Protestant province more directly explain their religious practices? And what about the role of ethnicity, given that Irish Catholics predominated among English-Canadian Catholics at this time?

The religious meaning of Catholic church involvement did differ somewhat from Protestant patterns, since among Catholics no distinction was made between church members and nonmembers. All Catholics were expected to attend mass regularly and, at a minimum, to take communion each Easter. Visible piety was intensified in Ontario in the second half of the nineteenth century through the Catholic hierarchy's promotion of a range of devotional practices that provided spiritual solace for many.[53] Church attendance may also have signalled social respectability.[54] Piety and respectability were no doubt important to many Catholic churchgoers, as they were to Protestants. Among Ontario's Irish Catholics, however, churchgoing served the additional function of reinforcing their sense of ethnic identity. Murray Nicholson has argued that in Canada the church became 'the receptacle of Irish culture and the embodiment of the Irish soul, a national institution.'[55] Brian Clarke has demonstrated the shifting links between Irish nationalism and the Ontario church, but there is no doubt that although the nature of the relationship changed during the second half of the nineteenth century, for most Ontario Catholics of Irish origin churchgoing reinforced a complex blend of ethnic and religious identity.

In this period the vast majority of Catholics in Thorold, and indeed in the entire Niagara area, were of Irish origin.[56] St Patrick's Day was always a major holiday among Thorold's Catholics, and the local priest, the Irish-born Timothy Sullivan, had no difficulty raising money in the parish for the cause of Irish Home Rule.[57] For Thorold Catholics the links between church involvement and the affirmation of ethnic identity were clear. The social climate of nineteenth-century Ontario made the affirmation of ethnic/religious identity through church involvement particularly significant. Being an Irish Catholic meant more than minority status; it meant being part of an embattled Catholic minority within a hostile Protestant culture. It is true that by the late nineteenth century, Catholic-Protestant riots were largely a thing of the past, and that on a day-to-day basis Catholics and Protestants lived together fairly peacefully. Many Protestants were willing to make gestures towards toleration. For example, in Ingersoll some Protestants attended the annual

St Patrick's Day banquet in a spirit of 'liberality and good feeling.'[58] Thorold's Orange Lodge, that bastion of Protestantism, even made the noble gesture of lending chairs to the Catholics for the consecration services of their new church. On this occasion, Father Sullivan also thanked the Thorold Protestants for contributing financially towards the new church.[59]

Despite such gestures, anti-Catholicism ran deep in Victorian Canada.[60] School controversies were not restricted to the national or provincial level; they revealed the existence of strong anti-Catholic feeling in various local communities. In Campbellford, which lacked a separate school, the omission of school prayer in deference to Catholic sensibilities elicited considerable hostility from the Protestant townsfolk, many of whom were also outraged when the schools were closed for a Catholic picnic.[61] In Campbellford and other communities, anti-Catholic feeling was reinforced by the sermons of various evangelical Protestant ministers. For example, one Sunday in January 1887, the Reverend Mr Ross of St Andrew's Presbyterian Church in Ingersoll contrasted 'true' and 'false' religions – Catholicism, of course, being castigated as the religion of ritualism and Pharaseeism.[62]

In these small communities, anti-Catholicism was most evident in the late 1880s and early 1890s, a time of considerable Catholic-Protestant tension in the national political arena. Itinerant anti-Catholic speakers were particularly popular at this time. In Thorold and Campbellford, branches of the Protestant Protective Association, a 'viciously discriminatory' anti-Catholic secret society, sponsored lectures by self-proclaimed ex-nuns and ex-priests who denounced the evils of Catholicism.[63] These speakers featured men-only and women-only talks, whose central attraction appears to have been the promise to 'reveal all' about the sexual depravities of priests and of convent life.[64] In Campbellford, Margaret L. Shepherd, who billed herself as the former Sister Magdalene Adelaide of Arnos Court Nunnery, Bristol, spoke to 'ladies only' on 'The Priest and Woman in the Confessional.' Shepherd's talk was well attended, as were similar lectures in other towns.[65] Father Sullivan of Thorold charged that 'a large number of ladies, from the stripling entering up her teens to the aged maiden and even to the grandmother' attended such a lecture in that community in the expectation of hearing 'some of the "awful disclosures and revelations" of convent life.' Certainly, as J.R. Miller and others have argued, sexual prurience attracted many to these lectures. The focus on the supposed sexual dangers of Catholicism suggests that at this time anti-Catholicism may have assumed elements of a moral panic, in which fears of sexuality were used as a scapegoat for deeper social fears.[66]

Catholic priests were not silent in the face of these attacks. When writing to the *Thorold Post* to attack the local Protestant women for their interest in these lectures, Father Sullivan decried the general popularity of those who were spreading 'filth and calumny' and expressed regret that the anti-Catholic lectures were announced from the pulpits of Protestant churches. The local Baptist minister, the Reverend John Irvine, was 'much amused to see the injured air assumed by Rev. Sullivan, when he advises Catholics to pray for those persecuting them,' and he asked, 'Who who used the inquisition with its horrors, the bloody stake ... and every imaginable persecution?' The Methodist minister, though slightly less hostile, also called up the memory of the Inquisition to mock Sullivan's claims of persecution.[67]

While the anti-Catholicism of the late 1880s and early 1890s was particularly virulent, it reveals a current of feeling, whether active or subterranean, that Catholics were habitually forced to live with. For Irish Catholics, the attacks strengthened their links to the church, which provided an affirmation of identity in a hostile culture. The church was not, however, simply a passive institution which the Irish Catholics used for their own cultural purposes. As Brian Clarke has shown, in the second half of the nineteenth century the Ontario church worked assiduously to teach Irish Catholic immigrants the importance of disciplined, devout, regular churchgoing – a practice that appears to have been relatively rare among pre-1850 immigrants, despite their emotional attachment to Catholicism. By the last decades of the century, the efforts of the church hierarchy had paid off, all statistics pointing to the embarrassing (for Protestants) fact that church involvement among Catholics far exceeded that of Protestants. The 1882 *Globe* survey of church attendance revealed that more than 70 per cent of Catholics attended church on Sunday, compared with an average of 45 per cent of all Torontonians.[68] The Thorold Catholics appear to have been particularly devout.[69] During the 1880s the proportion of Thorold Catholics taking communion at Easter was more than 90 per cent. This was an even higher percentage than in neighbouring St Catharines and was probably a reflection of the greater cohesiveness of a small parish as well as the firm hold which the forceful and long-serving Father Sullivan had over his parishioners.[70]

The Thorold Catholics differed from their Protestant neighbours, then, in that they were much more likely to attend church. Despite this, class, gender, and marital status could still affect decisions about church attendance, so it seems that the social and cultural forces shaping Protestant church involvement also touched the Catholic community. Given the high levels of church involvement and the predominantly working-class character of the Catholic community in Thorold, it is obvious that a high proportion of Catholic workers attended church. The majority also contributed financially, often with surprising generosity in view of their limited means. Between paying pew rents, church envelopes, pastor's support, and Christmas or Easter offerings, almost half of Thorold's working-class Catholic families donated more than $10 a year to the church. Many of these families had a total yearly income of less than $360 (see tables 10 and 11). Not surprisingly, however, some of the poorer unskilled workers were less likely than other parishioners to contribute to or participate in church activities, both in Thorold and in neighbouring St Catharines.[71]

The dominant womanly ideal of morality and piety affected Catholic women at least as much as their Protestant counterparts. In fact, for Catholic women, gender ideals took a particularly powerful sacred form in the image of the Virgin Mary, who, as Brian Clarke has noted, 'personified the idealization of womanhood, and a very particular type of womanhood at that: woman as the repository and embodiment of self-sacrificing virtue, purity and motherhood.'[72] At the same time, the church provided Catholic women with one of their few acceptable social and emotional outlets beyond the home, just as it did for Protestant women. It is thus not surprising that Catholic women had a particularly high churchgoing rate, even among a people known for their piety. For example, in St Catharines, 90 per cent of the women attended mass regularly, compared with 70 per cent of the men.[73]

On any given Sunday, churchgoing women and the husbands and sons who accompanied them might, like their Protestant neighbours, expect to hear a sermon attacking the lack of devotion and piety of young men. Certainly, given the higher overall Catholic church involvement figures, young single Catholic men were far more likely to have some links to the church than the young Protestant men were. Nonetheless, among a highly devout population, young men, once again, were the 'problem.'[74] In Thorold, for example, young single men were far more likely to fail to honour their pledges to make regular church contributions than other groups in the parish (see table 12).

Ideologies, values, and patterns of behaviour associated with a particular gender, class, or marital status in Protestant congregations thus crossed boundaries to the religiously 'other' of nineteenth-century

Ontario. In at least some Catholic families, wives and daughters were more likely to be in church than other family members, and unmarried men were the least likely to be there. But the experience of being 'other' did make a difference. Among Irish Catholics, church involvement was more commonly the majority experience for all family members and all classes than it was among Protestants. The fact that this strongly nationalist minority culture defined itself very much in terms of its Catholicism, which it saw as being under attack, added a significant ethnic/ cultural element to the meaning of church involvement. This may have lessened the significance of class distinctions within the church while providing an additional appeal for those who were less likely to be seeking either the stamp of respectability or the solace of belief.

Christianity at the Margins

Even after marriage, many Protestant men and women never joined a church or donated money to one. Does this mean that these people did not have any relationship at all with institutional Christianity? Canadian and British studies have suggested that many who did not join the churches, particularly among the working classes, did retain some links through their children by having them baptized and by sending them to Sunday school. Available Sunday school records indicate that there were some echoes of this pattern in small-town Ontario.[75] The records of Anglican baptisms in both Thorold and Campbellford also show that working-class parents were more likely than middle-class parents to have no other visible link with the churches beyond having had their children baptized.[76]

The act of having one's child baptized suggests some basis of faith as well as a potential claim to respectability within the community. Some of these marginal Anglicans probably also attended services at least at Christmas and Easter, when the religious force and solemnity of the occasion and the beauty of the elaborately decorated churches attracted far more worshippers than the number listed as communicants and contributors. For example, the *Thorold Post* noted at Christmas 1887 that the services of St John's Anglican Church were 'attended by large congregations and marked by bright, joyful music ... Among the special musical parts may be particularly mentioned the anthem, "Behold, I bring you good tidings of great joy" ... Over the window in the chancel there has been placed the word "Emmanuel" in large letters of gold. The walls and pillars have been adorned with wreathing of evergreen. Altogether the appearance is pleasing and attractive.'[77]

Even the townspeople who did not attend the Christmas services and had never been to Sunday school lived in a society in which Christianity, especially Protestantism, was integral to the dominant culture. Anyone who had attended a public school had been exposed to the basic Christian teachings, and weddings and funerals also created a general familiarity with Christian rituals.[78] Some small-town people who remained outside the churches were clearly committed to the basic beliefs of Christianity. In the British context, Jeffrey Cox has identified a 'diffusive Christianity' among most nonchurchgoers, which he argues included 'a general belief in God, a conviction that this God was both just and benevolent,' and a 'certain confidence that "good people" would be taken care of in the life to come.'[79] This belief system was certainly different from the more complex theological issues that divided the various Christian denominations. When Hugh Crossley and John Hunter, the famous Canadian revivalists, conducted a major revival in Thorold in 1893, some of their converts refused to join a church. They seem to have had no use for the division of Protestantism into denominations, each with its own minute theological distinctions, and maintained that they could be as good Christians outside the churches as within them – a claim hotly contested by the revivalists.[80]

Intriguing evidence indicates that for a small minority of Thorold inhabitants, Christianity itself was largely irrelevant. The Thorold assessment roll of 1886 lists eleven ratepayers whose religious affiliation was marked with an X. They were primarily labourers and poor widows, though a few were skilled workers. None owned their homes. The majority appear to have been nominal Catholics. Like widow Ann O'Leary, who occasionally received relief from the town council and otherwise supported five children by taking in washing, most of these people may in their poverty have felt far removed from organized religion, and perhaps from God.[81] One must, however, be careful here. Annie Foulds, another relief recipient, was not a church member, but religion did play a role in her life: having her children properly baptized in the Anglican church was obviously important to her, although unlike other Thorold parents she had to sponsor them alone, without the support of her drunkard husband. So while Christianity may have seemed irrelevant to some of the most poverty-stricken, for others it provided spiritual comfort and may have permitted the assertion of some shred of respectability.

Active Opposition: The Local Infidels

The handful of desperately poor townsfolk were not the only Thoroldites who did not claim any denominational affiliation on the 1886
assessment roll. However, unlike those whose X's suggest a poverty-
induced indifference to religion, there were a few ratepayers who
proudly identified themselves as freethinkers, or secularists. Secularists
claimed that the world functioned on the basis of scientific, rational principles. In their view, these principles left no room for belief in God or
other theological 'superstitions.' Secularism was a full-scale challenge to
the legitimacy of religious belief, and although it was not a new phenomenon, it gained currency among a small but vocal minority in the late
nineteenth century as new theories, such as those advanced by Charles
Darwin, undermined the theological foundations of religious faith.[82]

Thorold's assessment roll listed ten freethinkers, though a few other
townspeople appear to have been associated with the cause. The ten
men listed were not among the town's poor. Thorold's freethinkers
included two merchants, a manufacturer, and a hotel keeper, as well as a
few skilled workers and one sailor. Most owned their homes, and some
owned considerable local real estate as well. Free thought obviously ran
in certain families, for two McDonalds and two McAlpines were listed
as freethinkers, and so were the Tay brothers, Martin and John. These
men do not appear to have formed an official association, as local freethinkers did in some Ontario towns. They may, however, have been
influenced by the association in neighbouring Welland, and they were
clearly linked to the broader North American secularist movement.[83] In
September 1883 the *Thorold Post* reported, 'Mr. John McGill has returned
from the Free-Thinker's Convention at Rochester, and is quite enthusiastic over the gathering.'[84]

Like secularists in other communities, the Thorold freethinkers
brought in speakers to popularize their cause, one being Charles Watts,
a transplanted Englishman who edited the Canadian journal *Secular
Thought* in Toronto. R.B. McAlpine, a manufacturer and leading local
freethinker, chaired the Watts lecture, 'Wherein Is Secularism Superior
to Christianity,' which was given in the Oddfellows Hall to a large audience. The *Post* of 9 January 1885 noted that 'while very many in the hall
differed from the speaker in what he said and knew that he was making
statements which were totally at variance with their own knowledge,
yet few would not admit but that Mr. Watts is a clever debater ... and
possesses to a high degree the faculty of making "the worse appear the
better reason."'

The Christians listened politely to Watts but lost no time in organizing a defence of the true faith. The week after the lecture, the general superintendent of the Methodist church preached a sermon at the local Methodist missionary anniversary which 'contained a succession of irresistible arguments in favour of Christ as the true and only Saviour of men.' He argued that 'Christ is the only cure of the moral troubles of the race,' while 'skepticism is as coldly cruel as it is fatally false.'[85] A few months after Watts's talk, the local churchmen imported the Reverend Dr Sexton, 'a man who once was an infidel, but who having renounced infidelity, has since been a most fearless and faithful defender of the Christian religion.' Sexton had previously spoken in St Catharines, and many Thoroldites had gone there to hear him, but there was still a crowded house in the Oddfellows Hall for his lecture, which was titled 'Secularism Deficient as a Moral Guide, and Incapable of Meeting the Demands of the Intellect or of Satisfying the Wants of the Heart.'[86]

Thorold's debate between the secularists and true believers was aired not only on the public stage but in the columns of the local newspaper. The Methodist minister, John Kay, was horrified by a lecture given by an American ex-minister, C.B. Reynolds, who was brought in by the town's freethinkers. Kay wrote a lengthy letter to the *Post* denouncing Reynolds in particular and 'infidelity' in general. R.B. McAlpine responded, airing many of the secularist arguments of the period. He attacked the Bible as irrational and as advocating violence, charged that Christianity was the very antithesis of rationality and science, and denied that it was essential to morality, arguing that the prisons were full of Christian criminals and that infidels were certainly more moral than preachers.[87] Kay responded with another lengthy epistle, which proclaimed the moral and spiritual value of the Bible and affirmed the integral relationship between science, rationality, morality, and Christianity. He countered McAlpine's argument that most crimes are committed by Christians by suggesting that many freethinkers had falsely identified themselves as Christians for the census and had thus saddled Christianity 'with the crimes of infidelity.' Kay accused the local freethinkers of hypocrisy, stating that he had 'heard of one or two persons whose interest would be materially affected if the public knew they were tinctured with the poisons of the infidel sect, who should have the manliness to record themselves under their own true colors.'[88]

It is likely that we have the Reverend Mr Kay to thank for the fact that Thorold's assessment roll the following year recorded at least some of the secularists under their 'true colors.' Moreover, his comment is interesting for what it suggests about the relationship between the freethinkers and respectable society. In a material sense, most of Thorold's freethinkers could be counted as respectable: the majority were solidly middle class, most of the remainder being prosperous skilled workers. However, could a man attack the dominant religious faith and still be considered part of the respectable community? R.B. McAlpine's letter makes it clear that he viewed himself as an eminently moral and respectable businessman, more in tune with the progressive rationality of the age than those who clung to outworn creeds and superstitions. Kay's letter, however, implies that it was not only the local ministers who thought otherwise and that at least a public profession of Christianity was essential for acceptance in the community. The link between public respectability and church involvement is suggested by the fact that during the 1880s more than 80 per cent of the municipal councillors elected in Thorold were active church members.[89] However, at least three prominent freethinkers – John Tay, John McDonald, and William Charles – were elected to municipal office, Charles being continually re-elected during the 1880s. The unhappiness that Donald Mills recorded in his diary over the election of these men indicates that for a core of churchgoing townsfolk, such men were beyond the pale.[90]

Even Thorold's most respectable Christians could not totally ignore the town's freethinkers, for these men did not exist only as individuals; they were also part of families. Most of their families had very close links to the churches. The wives of John Tay, John McDonald, and R.D. McAlpine were all active members of St Andrew's Presbyterian Church. Martin Tay's wife was a communicant at St John's Anglican Church, and Mrs William Charles was active in Thorold's Methodist Church. Similarly, most of the other freethinkers had close relatives who were church members. None, however, appears to have had any links to the Roman Catholic Church.

How do we explain the presence of the wives of freethinkers in the churches? Certainly, this is one of the clearest examples of a lack of family 'togetherness' in religious practice. The women may have thought they were upholding the respectability of their families in the small-town community. We may also speculate that the coldly scientific language and approach of free thought, which meshed with the masculine ideals of reason and logic, had little appeal to women, who were taught that they were naturally more religious, emotional, and spiritual than men. To embrace free thought would be to deny their nature and also to deny their claim to moral and spiritual superiority. Some of the women may also have been influenced by the arguments of ministers who asserted that 'infidel' cultures had oppressed women and that only Christianity offered them liberty and respect. An article reprinted in the *Ingersoll Chronicle* typifies these arguments. It stated that without Christianity, women would suffer under polygamy and that 'Bible Christianity alone gives to the gentler sex the true dignity of womanhood.' All true women 'in the domestic circle,' it said, 'owe their liberty, influence, and general comfort to the Bible of God.'[91]

While it was certainly not unknown for there to be different religious beliefs in Thorold families, the divergence between secularist and Christian beliefs must have created particularly bitter family tensions. This may have been especially true in middle-class families, who viewed the observance of common religious rituals as an extension of much-valued family togetherness. Religious rituals with strong emotional significance would have offered particular potential for discord. For instance, it is not difficult to imagine the feelings of John McDonald's wife, a staunch Presbyterian, when at the funeral of their son, McDonald insisted that no minister officiate and that there be no prayers or hymns. Instead, a local freethinker, Dr J.R. Johnstone, offered a secularist address that focused on 'the ennobling feelings of humanity, love for the family, love for our neighbours, love for mankind.' No mention was made of an afterlife, and although Johnstone did mention Jesus, it was only to call on those present to try to emulate his moral example.[92]

In other families, secularists were not as successful in imposing their beliefs. In a will made only two months before his death, R.B. McAlpine stated, 'As I have no faith or belief in the dogmas of Christianity I wish that the Executor Dr. Robert J. Johnstone be permitted to officiate at my obsequies instead of any of the Sky D.D.s.' (the secularists' contemptuous term for ministers).[93] McAlpine was a widower, so did not have a wife to object to this will, but his wishes were unacceptable to other members of his predominantly Presbyterian family. The local Presbyterian minister, the Reverend C.D. McDonald, officiated at the funeral, as the *Post* noted, 'at the special request of the family.'[94] The funeral was 'largely attended by leading men of the town, and many from a distance' – men whose respect for McAlpine's commercial success clearly overcame any concern over his religious unorthodoxy.

Free thought was not the only unorthodox movement to touch Thorold in this period. In 1889 a major crisis erupted in St Andrew's Presbyterian Church when the elders objected to fellow elder Robert

Maxwell's belief in Christian Science. The minister, C.D. McDonald, had questioned Maxwell on his beliefs and ruled that they were compatible with Maxwell's retaining his position as elder and clerk of session, but the other elders disagreed. The fracas precipitated the resignation of Maxwell and ultimately resulted in the departure of McDonald for a new position in Manitoba. Most of the congregation supported their minister in this dispute and were very upset about his resignation. The conflict created long-lasting bitterness within the congregation, with many members refusing to attend services for almost two years. This incident points both to the influence of unorthodox beliefs among those active in mainstream churches and to a significant willingness to accept such unorthodoxy at the local level.[95] Robert Maxwell left Thorold soon after this dispute, but others in town remained faithful to Christian Science. In 1893 they gathered together to hold regular Sunday services in a local hall, complete with Sunday school. Christian Science services were still being held in Thorold two years later. The new faith was clearly unacceptable to some members of Thorold's elite. In 1896 the executive of the Mechanics' Institute declined a local enthusiast's offer of a Christian Science text, *Science and Health*, for the library, and also refused to receive the Christian Science journal.[96]

By the early 1890s, there was considerable interest in yet another contemporary heresy in Thorold. In 1893 the *Post* noted, 'Spiritualism is rapidly gaining ground in town. Where a year or so ago you might count all the spiritualists upon your fingers, there is now quite a band of believers ... and their meetings are usually pretty well attended.'[97] Spiritualism, which first became popular in the United States and Britain at midcentury, involves a belief in various psychic phenomena. A central tenet is the belief in the possibility of communicating with the spirits of the dead through mediums – individuals who claim to have the ability to make contact with the spirit world. In Thorold, as elsewhere, many Christians incorporated the tenets of spiritualism into their more orthodox belief systems. The new Presbyterian minister, the Reverend Mr Mitchell, took it upon himself to point out the error of these efforts, preaching a sermon which denounced spiritualism as a snare of Satan that was completely incompatible with Christianity. Interestingly, he noted in his sermon that several former secularists had taken up spiritualism. For Mitchell, such a shift in allegiances merely 'substitut[ed] one error for another,' but in fact the Thorold freethinkers were following a fairly well-trodden path among contemporary secularists.[98] While many of the local spiritualists were men, it seems probable that the movement would have attracted women too. This was certainly true in other cities and towns across North America and in England. Unlike secularism, with its association with masculine rationality, spiritualism could appeal to women's supposedly more emotional and spiritual nature. In fact, women's more spiritual and passive nature was said to make them particularly suited to the important role of medium.[99] The first spiritualist speaker to come to town was a female medium, Ann L. Robinson. She was one of very few women to give a public lecture in Thorold in this period.

Thorold may have been unusually influenced by various unorthodox spiritual currents of the age because of its close proximity to the city of St Catharines as well as to the larger American city of Buffalo. It is certainly true that in Campbellford, which was more isolated from urban influences, there is only limited evidence of flirtations with free thought, spiritualism, and other new beliefs. But given the high levels of geographic mobility and the relatively sophisticated transportation and communication networks of the period, even towns like Campbellford could not avoid some exposure to new ideas. At least one Campbellford minister was clearly worried about the potential influence of secularism on that most wayward of groups, young men. In the spring of 1895 the Reverend Mr Jolliffe of Campbellford directed a sermon at the local young men, denouncing free thought and giving 'conclusive proof that the Bible was the language of inspiration and ... should be the guide to every man's faith.'[100]

Small towns were not necessarily bastions of Christian orthodoxy, no matter what their location. Napanee, Aylmer, and Gananoque, for instance, all had active secularist societies in this period.[101] Both spiritualism and secularism had their adherents in Ingersoll, though spiritualism was clearly the more popular, with many townspeople flocking to seances in the early 1880s.[102] There is no evidence of a major secularist presence in the town, but in the mid-1880s the Ingersoll Chronicle's letters column was devoted to an acrimonious correspondence between the town ministers and W. Hunt, an 'infidel' from the neighbouring hamlet of Beachville. Hunt claimed to believe in God but challenged biblical authority, the concept of eternal damnation, and other central Christian beliefs. One defender of orthodoxy declared Hunt's arguments to be 'as old and as rotten as the bones of Tom Payne [sic].'[103]

In late-nineteenth-century small-town Ontario, a number of intersecting, overlapping, and sometimes contradictory meanings adhered to the

apparently straightforward practice of belonging to a mainstream Protestant church. Faith was clearly important, but the clumsy tools of the
social historian do not allow us to say much more about its relative significance among churchgoers. Church involvement was also about demonstrating respectability in the larger community, and for many people
it was an important part of their social life, both on Sunday and throughout the week. The churches had taken on various feminine connotations
in this period, but the gendering of church involvement was not
straightforward. Male heads of families bolstered their manly breadwin-
ning role through church membership and signalled their support for
the values of Christian domesticity.

The response of small-town people to the complexity of meaning surrounding church membership was itself less than clear-cut – reflecting
the various divisions of small-town life but also blurring them. The fact
that, at most, only half of the Protestant families in Thorold and Campbellford included even one church member undermines arguments
about small towns being bastions of Protestant culture. Certain groups
were even less likely to be seen in church, a fact that further challenges
the claims of Protestant hegemony. Class was an important category
here, but Thorold working-class men were far more likely to stay away
from the churches than their Campbellford counterparts. This points to
the importance of local context in defining levels of class-consciousness
and the subsequent willingness (or refusal) of members of a town's
working class to worship with the middle class.

Gender was important in determining levels of church involvement.
Working-class women were slightly less likely to join the churches than
middle-class women but were certainly more involved than working-
class men. For both groups of women, the appeal of church involvement
(and perhaps the lack of alternative options) crossed boundaries of age
and marital status, whereas marital status and age were key dividing
lines for men. For ardent churchgoers, young men of all classes were a
problem, which suggests that there were at least two distinct ideals of
masculinity in small-town Ontario – one linked to respectable Christian
manliness, the other defined in opposition to the feminized churches.
These masculine ideals crossed boundaries separating Catholic and
Protestant, since young male Catholics were the most reluctant churchgoers, even though Catholics as a whole were highly observant in their
attendance.

Gender could also serve to divide that minority of small-town people
who actively embraced a variety of heretical new ideas. While spiritual-

ism appealed to both women and men, the more coldly rational secularism primarily attracted men. The wives of secularist men remained firmly within the churches – providing the most glaring example of how religion could divide families. For the wives of middle-class secularists, these divisions may have been particularly difficult, given the more general acceptance in this class of the values of family togetherness, both in home and church. In the working class, family members seemed more accustomed to going their own way.

The nature of religious involvement was truly heterogeneous, even in the smaller communities. Studies of church participation can explain only so much, however. To deepen our understanding of the meaning of religious participation in these communities, we need to explore the myriad of church-based associations and, moving beyond the churches, to trace the conflicts and commonalities between the churches and other community activities and institutions.

3

Gender, Class, and Power: Church Associations and Church Improvements

In 1894 the Ontario Baptists sent out a survey to 'discover the inner life of our churches.' The results were not pleasing – they revealed that the majority of church members were at best minimally involved in church-based organizations. The Baptists wondered how they might 'organize different classes in the church into organizations of their own, and get the whole church harnessed for work.'[1] In the late nineteenth century, most churches dramatically increased their efforts to found associations for various 'classes' of members, by which they meant groupings by gender, age, and marital status as much if not more than they meant divisions by social class. The Baptist report noted the existence of active women's mission circles and young people's societies, but lamented the fact that more churchgoers did not become involved in these or other groups.

This problem was not unique to the Baptists. In all denominations some combination of apathy, lack of free time, more appealing alternatives, social unease, and material barriers kept many church members away from church-based associations. Faith, social responsibility, personal ambition, and a desire for community drew others into active involvement in their churches. For some, particularly middle-class men, this involvement offered the opportunity to exercise considerable power. For women, and at the margins of associational life even for working-class women, certain church organizations could offer at least limited scope for power and activism.

What use did the men and women who were active in the churches make of their power? While sacred concerns were important to them, their activities also reveal a weaving together of more secular class and gender interests and anxieties. The late-nineteenth-century craze for church building and church improvements shows most clearly how the inequalities of the world had entered the churches as the definition of what it meant to be a respectable Protestant increasingly included some ability to contribute financially to the imposing new buildings. These churches were not built only by the male church leaders; they also depended on the fund-raising efforts of women's church associations. Women's groups thus contributed to a deepening of class inequality within the churches, while at the same time their initiatives served to domesticate and feminize church interiors. While the women's efforts were welcomed by the male leaders, fears of feminization remained strong, leading to attempts to suppress the innocuous strawberry social, which was viewed as a threat to male-controlled sacred space.

Lay Leadership and Male Power

Patriarchal control in the churches was epitomized by the figure of the ordained religious leader. In the late nineteenth century, these leaders were exclusively male.[2] Ministerial power and the extent to which it was limited by central bodies or local lay leadership varied considerably between denominations. Catholic priests had the most local power and were responsible primarily to their bishops, not their congregations. As a result, there was limited scope for Catholic lay leadership, but in Presbyterian and Baptist congregations the lay leaders had considerable power over both financial and spiritual matters. The Anglicans leaned closer to the Catholic model, though local vestries did exercise considerable power, particularly over financial matters. Methodism combined a strong centralized control over ministers with considerable opportunity for lay leadership at the local level.[3]

Who were the lay leaders of the churches? First, they were predominantly – though not exclusively – male. Although all those holding executive positions were men, there were some limited opportunities available for women to participate in the administration of the churches. Among Methodists, a few women became class leaders, though they generally led classes of women or young people.[4] Among the Presbyterians and Anglicans, all the office holders were male, but women did attend annual congregational meetings, and in at least some small-town congregations they spoke out and were able to move and second motions.[5] Female participation in the monthly congregational meetings was common in Baptist congregations across the province, though it was the smaller churches that provided the most opportunities for female leadership. For example, from the founding of Thorold's Baptist church in 1887, women had served on committees that dealt with baptism and church membership; but it was not until 1893, after several of the male 'pillars' of the community had left town, that women were able to act as delegates to Baptist conventions and meetings.[6] Judith Colwell has noted that in other small Ontario communities where tiny Baptist congregations included few male church members, women took on a variety of church offices that were usually reserved for men.[7] In small communities, then, structural factors could sometimes provide church women with more opportunities than those available in the larger cities. Nonetheless, it remains true that in urban, rural, and small-town churches, formal power lay largely with men.

Not surprisingly, most of the men who exercised this power were married. The few single men who held church positions generally acted as ushers or in other junior roles.[8] Why did married men take on the more senior positions and in many cases serve for years as trustees, stewards, deacons, or elders? Most would probably have said that they took on these responsibilities as part of their Christian duty as respectable breadwinners and Christian heads of households. Joy Parr's term 'social fathering,' which she uses to characterize married men's leadership in the community, is relevant here.[9] By attending church with their families, married men affirmed their role as head of a Christian household. By taking on leadership roles in the churches, they took up the broader responsibility of church father.

While the dominant ethos of Christian manhood no doubt played a role in the men's decision to become involved in church leadership, these positions could also contribute to secular success. In Thorold, half of the men serving on the municipal council also held leadership positions in the churches.[10] This pattern may simply reflect the close relationship between a sense of civic and Christian responsibility, between Christian 'fathering' and community 'fathering,' but it is also likely that the public profile and respectable image of church leader would be sought by those with political ambitions. The contemporary social commentator C.S. Clark asserted that in Toronto 'aspiring politicians used offices in the church as ammunition in election campaigns.'[11] Men who began as church leaders could go far. For example, William McCleary, a Thorold manufacturer who for years held a variety of leadership positions in the town's Methodist church, became mayor and later a member of Parliament.

For most men the motivations leading to church leadership were no doubt a complex mix of religious and secular concerns, but in some cases self-interest was paramount. Murray, an Ingersoll grocer who was discovered to have been forging notes for some time, had held positions in the local Presbyterian church as well as being active in the YMCA. As the *Ingersoll Chronicle* noted bitterly, 'He might have been seen any Sabbath taking up collection in the leading Presbyterian church here, and at the same time his forged notes were running in the bank.' The editor concluded, no doubt accurately, that Murray's criminal acts could only have gone undisclosed for so long because of 'his persistent profession of religion.'[12]

A letter writer to the *Stratford Beacon* declared that for many other men, church office provided a convenient avenue to more legal forms of commercial success. 'Men of the world regard it as a "paying matter" to be called "a Christian,"' the letter writer observed. He argued that by getting themselves elected to church office, ambitious merchants and professional men benefited financially, since 'the pastor speaks of the professional man as a good Christian and an eminent authority on law or medicine as the case may be. His good wife speaks of [the merchant], and his groceries or dry goods as the best in town. This is just the use [they] desire to make of pastor and wife, and the church too. They lack the saving knowledge of God's grace in the heart, but manage to use their position in the church to further their unhallowed purposes.'[13]

How common or how undiluted by more religious motivations such behaviour may have been remains unclear, but for at least some church members these were real issues. For example, in 1892 a major battle erupted in Campbellford's Baptist church when the Sunday school superintendent, Walter Flagg, who was a cabinet maker by profession, was accused of complaining that another church member had bought furniture elsewhere rather than purchasing it from him.[14] Economic and social motivations for church leadership may have been particularly significant in smaller communities, where competition for local customers was fierce and personal, where the endorsement of the town's ministers could count for much, and where church leadership readily translated into local prominence.

Church leadership could clearly benefit middle-class men such as small masters, merchants, and professionals. It may also have been viewed in an instrumental way by at least some working-class church-goers, for they may have regarded it as a means of upward mobility or, at a minimum, as a way of strengthening relationships with employers who were also active in the church.[15] Whether such motivations were involved or not, how many working-class church members actually played an active role in the administration of these churches? Did most of them worship in churches organized and controlled by the middle class? This varied by denomination. In both Thorold and Campbellford, the people who were active in the Anglican church were almost exclusively middle class. Among other Protestant denominations, middle class men were overrepresented in leadership roles[16] (see tables 13 and 14). Nonetheless, working-class men also took on leadership positions. These men were almost all skilled workers, and many were fairly prosperous. In some churches, such as Campbellford's Methodist church and Thorold's Presbyterian church, the proportion of skilled workers in lay leadership positions was similar to the proportion of skilled working-class families in the congregations (tables 13 and 14). These men may have played these roles in part for the same structural reasons that women were able to take on some leadership roles in small-town churches – that there were not enough middle-class men available.

The changing class position of the deacon of Thorold's Baptist church is instructive here. At the founding of the church, the deacon was a bank manager. On his departure, and with the dwindling of the congregation, he was replaced by a factory foreman; and when the foreman left, he was replaced by a tailor. This pattern does not, however, tell the whole story of working-class church leadership. In the late 1880s and early 1890s, two of the five elders of session of Thorold's Presbyterian church were George Grant, a millwright, and James Place, a machinist. Both men had been members of the Thorold church for many years. Grant had in fact been one of the founders of the church.[17] Both men clearly saw themselves as part of a respected and respectable churchgoing community. Teamsters and factory workers may also have been members of this community, but even in small-town churches the social distinctions were firm enough to keep them out of positions of power. On the other hand, the distinctions between middle-class members and skilled workers, particularly those with roots in the community, were far more blurred.

Poor Funds and Building Funds

Lay church leaders were responsible for a wide range of activities, which varied by denomination. In all denominations they were involved in the management of the routine financial affairs of the congregation, which included paying the minister, heating and cleaning the church, and so on. Among Baptists, Methodists, and Presbyterians the church leaders played an important role in the admission of new members. They might also be involved in the supervision of the personal behaviour of church members in order to ensure that these people lived up to the denomination's religious and moral code. Church supervision of a wide range of personal behaviour had been common in the first half of the nineteenth century, at a time when evangelical congregations saw themselves as separate communities of believers, or 'islands of holiness,' surrounded by worldliness and sin. At that time, church members accepted what they viewed as the biblically ordained responsibility of ensuring that their brothers and sisters in Christ did not stray from the path of righteousness.[18] By the late nineteenth century, the scope of this supervision had narrowed considerably, at least among Methodists and Presbyterians. In some small-town churches the members were still censured for drunkenness or for conflict with another member, but the primary basis of expulsion was nonattendance at services, particularly at communion.[19]

The Baptists were also moving away from enforcing church discipline, but in small communities the church retained some control over a range of personal behaviour. Baptist women could play an active role here, interviewing female members regarding the truth of gossip concerning their sexual morality or honesty. In the spring of 1896, Thorold's Baptist church heard a report from two female members who had been appointed as a committee to investigate rumours about a Mrs Potter. They reported that she had been 'closely questioned and the committee was satisfied there was no foundation in fact for the rumours, but that Mrs. Potter's situation was such as to give evil talkers opportunity to voice their suspicions.'[20] Historians have argued that the churches' supervision of personal behaviour became less common in the late nineteenth century as a growing distinction between public and private life made individuals less willing to accept church censure for what was now defined as private behaviour, and as increasing class distinctions made more affluent Christians reluctant to have their moral behaviour judged by working-class fellow members.[21] It is perhaps no accident that those cited for moral lapses in the records of Thorold's Baptist and Presbyterian churches were all working class.

While the evangelical churches had traditionally supervised the moral and spiritual health of their members, all churches had taken some responsibility for the physical health and well-being of members and parishioners. Some elements of this concern lingered on into the 1880s and 1890s. For example, in November 1892 the session of St Andrew's

Presbyterian Church, Campbellford, moved that the clerk of session 'write Mr. T. Carpenter of Warkworth regarding the state Mrs. Moore is in and urge on him the necessity of having her removed, if possible, to some place where she would be properly treated and cared for.' In August 1889 the elders of Thorold's Presbyterian church noted that two widows and one family in the congregation were in financial difficulties.[22] Some churches, including Thorold's and Ingersoll's Baptist churches and Ingersoll's Anglican church, had 'poor funds,' which provided some assistance to poverty-stricken members or parishioners. Others, such as Campbellford's Methodist church, made occasional donations for local charity. Among Thorold's Catholics, the only evidence of disbursements for the poor are found in the account book of the Sisters of St Joseph.[23] Many churches probably assisted members more informally, though evidence of this cannot be found in their financial records and reports. Common assumptions about the charitable role of the churches are evident in the distribution of the proceeds of benefit concerts held in Thorold in the late 1880s: the money was divided among the local churches, which were to use it to assist the 'most needy and deserving in [each] community.'[24] This form of distribution, of course, also makes it clear that only those affiliated with the churches were assumed to be deserving of poor relief.

James Pitsula demonstrates that in Toronto, where the problems of poverty were more visible, 'almost every congregation ... had a poor fund of some sort' at this time. He also notes that the amount spent on the poor varied widely but was generally quite modest.[25] This was certainly the case in small-town Ontario. The poor funds were not large, where they existed at all. In 1890 the poor fund of St Paul's Presbyterian Church of Ingersoll totalled $22.23 out of the church's total receipts of $2,993.00, and only $9.85 of the fund was actually spent that year. Ingersoll's larger Anglican church was somewhat more generous, raising $109.12 for the local poor in 1885. Thorold's Anglican church does not appear to have had a poor fund, but a bequest from a former bishop provided $22.00 a year for 'needy members of the parish.' The only Protestant church in Thorold that seems to have had a poor fund was the struggling Baptist congregation. In 1890 its poor fund contained a respectable $12.00 out of total receipts of $369.51, but by 1893 the Baptists were taking money from the poor fund for general expenses, 'the General Fund being in need and there being no calls on the Poor Fund.' Although the Sisters of St Joseph provided some assistance to Thorold's Catholic poor, it was very limited. They gave out between one and two dollars a month in the early 1890s, as well as providing other small amounts as loans.[26]

In small communities, some individual Christians assisted the poor, considering it their religious duty to do so.[27] However, in most cases, the churches themselves appear to have played a minor role. They were content to leave most of the disbursement of relief to the town or village council, which like the churches assisted only the 'deserving poor,' primarily widows. Church involvement probably made it easier to obtain relief, since ministers could request assistance from the local council on behalf of needy church members, and municipal councillors often vouched for the 'deserving' nature of applicants from their own churches. As well, being a church member made the applicant seem more respectable and thus more deserving of assistance from the council. The relief provided by municipal councils varied from relatively generous to extremely tight-fisted, depending on the political proclivities of the councillors and on the strength of popular sentiment for economy and lower taxes.[28]

While small-town churches were reluctant to direct more than a small fraction of their resources towards poor relief, most were willing to spend considerable sums on church building or church 'improvement.' The latter part of the nineteenth century saw a major increase in the building of churches in Ontario. Since the building of new churches far outstripped the growth in church membership, church leaders were not constructing these new edifices simply to house more adherents.[29] They were building them to replace churches that in some cases may have been too small but were certainly considered inadequate in a number of other respects.

The early 1880s saw the building of new Methodist and Presbyterian churches in Campbellford, while both the Presbyterians and Catholics erected new churches in Thorold in the 1880s and early 1890s. Although Thorold's Methodists did not build a new church, they spent $3,000 on 'improvements' in the early 1880s. These improvements included handsome new pews, a new pulpit desk, and a number of other changes, as described in the *Thorold Post*: 'The walls of the church have been panelled in oil, while the roof has been papered with paper of beautiful tints ... Instead of the old fashioned windows with small panes, there are handsome ones, divided in two by a large centre of mullion, with a stained border and diamond at top ... The floor is carpeted with a handsome, all wool carpet, while the platform and the altar are covered with tapestry carpet ... The building is lighted by several chandeliers.'[30] Similarly, St John's Anglican Church in Thorold was constantly concerned with church improvements, which included painting and graining the church interior, building a church spire, and enlarging the rectory.[31]

William Westfall has argued that in this period the construction of new churches, especially in the popular Gothic style, was intended 'to proclaim the reality and power of the sacred as a force in a secular world.'[32] No doubt spiritual motivations played a part in the decisions to build new churches. However, more secular social and economic concerns were becoming increasingly integrated into the churches. As scholars have noted, the mainstream churches had adopted the progressive ethos of the age. Theologians may have focused on spiritual progress, but, at the local level, congregations were probably more influenced by the contemporary focus on material progress.[33] New and better railways, new and better factories, new and better homes were the watchwords of the day, so it is not surprising that congregations also sought new and better churches. Like the Reverend Mr McDonald of Thorold's Presbyterian church, Ontarians 'saw no reason why the church should not be made as beautiful as our homes.' Many reflected the sentiments of Merritton's Presbyterian churchgoers who, according to the *Thorold Post*, 'have caught the improvement fever and have determined to be fully abreast of the times in the way of having a comfortable edifice in which to worship.'[34]

Impressive new churches may have symbolized the power of the sacred in a more secular age, but the self-interest of church members of wealth and social position was clearly involved in the building of beautiful new churches or in the improvement of old ones. As discussed in the previous chapter, churchgoing demonstrated one's social respectability. For the rich and socially prominent, this respectability was reinforced through worship in larger and more elaborate churches. However, the large and beautiful churches did not only reflect the social position of the individual church members; they also provided physical evidence of denominational status and could fuel interdenominational rivalry. In speaking at the opening of Thorold's newly renovated Methodist church, the Presbyterian minister hoped that the Methodists' efforts would 'stir up' the Presbyterians to do likewise. Indeed they did. The Presbyterians erected a handsome new church only a few years later.[35]

Church Improvements and Accessibility

Not everyone was pleased with the proliferation of new and improved churches. Although evangelicals had by this period moved some distance from the belief that all church decoration was 'Romish' (i.e., too Catholic), a minority remained unhappy with the church-building craze. These critics argued that the money spent on church improvements should have been devoted to saving souls. An article in the *Canadian Presbyterian* challenged the 'useless decorating of our churches with costly and needless luxuries ... while 856 millions have never heard that there is a Christ.' A poem entitled 'The Church Walking with the World' similarly attacked the churches for focusing on worldly adornment to the neglect of the salvation of souls.[36] These critics were increasingly uneasy about the growing acceptance of worldliness in the evangelical churches. Their unease had its parallel in the American context, where Mark Schantz has identified a concern among certain middle-class churchgoers about the impact of increasing material prosperity on the purity of Christian faith.[37]

Some of these critics had additional concerns about the impact of worldliness. For instance, the author of 'The Church Walking with the World' warned that as the churches became more elaborate, there would be no place for the poor within them.[38] With the growing emphasis on church building, the definition of what it meant to be a proper Christian did appear to be shifting. Neil Semple argues that by the 1880s, in the Methodist church 'systematic benevolence had been transformed from a symbol of faithfulness to an act of worship and a possible sign of salvation.'[39] Piety and belief remained important, but a certain standard of material prosperity increasingly became part of what it meant to be a good Christian – at least, it did if some of the prosperity was shared with one's church. Such meanings could not help but be inscribed in the very walls of the new brick and stone churches that were rising across the province. Architecturally, the newer churches were more 'democratic,' avoiding the pattern of boxes for the rich and benches for the poor, which had been common earlier, at least in Anglican and Presbyterian churches.[40] Nonetheless, as Stephen Yeo has noted in regard to church building in England, 'the more elaborate the plant, even though designed precisely to avoid restriction, the less it could be the property, in the fullest sense, of anyone other than that class of persons who could afford it.'[41]

Church membership had always carried with it financial obligations, which limited the ability of the poor to participate. The 1864 session minutes of Ingersoll's Erskine Presbyterian Church record the case of Walter Brown, who stopped attending services because he was unable to pay his church dues. The members of the session who visited him assured him that 'if he could not pay the church door would not be shut against him, members would not frown on him (as he seemed to fear).'[42] Despite such assurances, Brown and others like him knew that while the church door might not literally be shut against them, failure to contribute to the church would indeed make things uncomfortable. This may have always been true, but the emphasis on church building in the latter part of the nineteenth century increased the financial pressures on congregations. The minutes of large and small churches of all denominations reveal a constant concern about paying the bills for improvements to existing churches or paying the mortgages of elaborate new churches.[43]

Among Protestants and Catholics alike, the need to raise money for such purposes sometimes seemed to overshadow spiritual concerns. Father Sullivan of Thorold, who devoted considerable energy to building a new church, wrote to his bishop in the spring of 1886 requesting the services of an assistant priest for six or eight months so that Sullivan could devote himself to raising money for the new church. Sullivan noted, 'The improvements that are to be made this summer on the Canal will bring a large number of men to the place and I must take advantage of the opportunity to collect for the Church.'[44] Sullivan was certainly not shy in his efforts to raise money in his congregation. In the 1890s he published an annual financial statement for the parish, listing all the parishioners and the amounts they had contributed. Those who had contributed nothing were also listed. Each year the statement included admonitions to his flock to do better in supporting their church. He castigated the '*large* number of the *wage-earners* and *adult* members of our small congregation [who] continue to *shirk* their duty – that is, not to contribute *honestly* and *conscientiously*, according to their income ... to the support of religion.' Sullivan went on to instruct his parishioners not to sit in rented pews, noting that 'the *ushers*, if applied to, will show you to a free seat, if you cannot *afford* to rent one, which costs only a *trifle* in a year.'[45]

Sullivan was not unusual among Irish Catholic priests in his direct approach to raising money from his parishioners. A priest in Gananoque published, in the local newspaper, the names of those who had failed to pay the amounts promised to the church, while other priests roped off the pews of those who had not paid their pew rents.[46] The Protestants' efforts to raise money from church members may have been less direct, but they relied on the same mechanisms of community pressure. In their annual reports, churches regularly listed the names of contributors and the amounts contributed. Some of them, such as Campbellford's Methodist church, listed the amounts promised as well as the amounts actually paid. In annual reports of Protestant churches noncontributors were not listed, but in small communities they would certainly not have been unknown.

What impact would these pressures have had on those who could not afford to contribute? No doubt many workers, Catholic and Protestant alike, enjoyed worshipping in the beautiful new churches that were built in this period. The churches would have provided a welcome respite from a cramped and drab home environment.[47] Sunday attendance in impressive Gothic-style churches may have strengthened faith through an association of the sacred with the grandeur and beauty of its surroundings. At the same time, for many poorer workers, any sense of holiness may have been undermined by a disturbing feeling that they had no place in these impressive edifices if they had not contributed financially to the beauty around them.

Any feelings of marginalization would have been reinforced by the system of pew rents, a central means of financing churches at this time. Paying pew rent was not beyond the means of many workers. Skilled workers and even some semi-skilled and unskilled workers paid pew rents in various Thorold and Campbellford churches. However, even these payments did not guarantee full inclusion. While church boxes for the wealthy may have been a thing of the past, the ordering of pews clearly indicated local class distinctions. Pews towards the back of the churches and in the galleries were rented for less than those towards the front. For example, the board of trustees of Thorold's Methodist church fixed the rent for the first ten pews at nine dollars each a year, the next four at eight dollars each, and the next three at six dollars each.[48] In all churches, the free seats available for those not paying pew rents were either at the back or in the gallery. Both the elaborate new churches themselves and the organization of interior church space clearly indicated how the social and economic distinctions of the world were embedded in definitions of respectable Christianity.

The extent to which pew rents limited church accessibility – or, at best, created a two-tier system of church involvement by limiting the poor to the back or the galleries – was recognized at the time, and the issue was in fact hotly debated in a number of denominations. Some churches abolished pew rents, replacing them with the weekly envelope system. In Campbellford's Methodist church, an attempt to impose fixed rather than voluntary payments for pew rents was one of several causes of a temporary split in the congregation. The Gospel Hall set up by the seceders boasted free seats.[49] Other churches, such as Thorold's St John's Anglican, periodically discussed bringing in a system of free seats but ultimately did nothing. The ongoing discussions about the problems of financing church improvements explain the reluctance of the members of St John's vestry to abandon pew rents.[50] The majority of churches, including Thorold's Methodist and Presbyterian churches and Campbellford's Anglican church, never even discussed abolishing pew rents in this period, though the two Thorold churches also had a weekly envelope system for raising money.

Every church needs money to continue its work. However, the church building and 'improvement fever' of late-nineteenth-century Ontario greatly increased the financial pressure on congregations. This pressure further skewed the power imbalance within congregations towards the rich. Many of the wealthier men could buy respectability by donating to the churches, often without becoming a church member. The publication of annual reports meant that everyone knew who was donating the largest sums, and those donating money for specific objects (new stained glass windows, for instance, or a new pulpit) were immortalized with plaques that can still be found on church walls throughout the province.

Neil Semple has argued that in the Methodist Church an increasing focus on the importance of financial donations influenced the denomination's Christian message. He asserts that John Wesley's warning about the spiritual dangers of riches was replaced by a willingness to give a religious quality to wealth, at least if some of it was used to support the church. Semple argues that in return for the support of the business elite, 'the church bolstered the respectability and virtue of the business ethic and re-emphasized the traditional link between sin and poverty.'[51] The church-building 'craze' of the late nineteenth century could only have reinforced this process. Certainly, the new churches did more than create symbols of the sacred in an increasingly secular world. They were also symbols of the secular ambitions of many of their members, and the far from symbolic cost of these edifices brought the secular social and economic distinctions of the world more firmly into the churches.

Women's Associations: Power and Control

It is probably no coincidence that the second half of the nineteenth century, which saw an increasing emphasis on church building, also saw the growth of church-based women's groups, particularly in the Protestant churches. There were two kinds of groups. One, usually called the Ladies' Aid or Ladies' Auxiliary, was locally organized and was directly involved in raising money for the local church. While these associations occasionally provided money or clothing for poor church members, their fund-raising efforts focused primarily on projects related to church building or church improvement. The other type of women's organization was the missionary society, which raised money for home and foreign missions and was affiliated with a denomination-wide women's missionary society. Involvement in a missionary society reflected the women's piety while also serving to affirm their superiority to the non-Christian and generally non-white peoples whom they sought to convert.[52]

Scholars have argued that the ladies' aids and women's missionary societies provided many nineteenth-century women with their first opportunity to move beyond the home and work together with other women in organized groups. Through these associations many women learned the skills of public speaking, running a meeting, organizing special events, and raising money. These groups are often viewed as stepping stones towards the formation of more overtly political women's organizations, such as those that struggled for reform and women's rights.[53] However, the reality is that most women never moved beyond involvement in the church societies attached to their congregation. How much power were they able to wield here, at the local level? Officially, their power was very limited. Since male trustees or boards of managers controlled all church property, the ladies' aids had to ask permission for every project they wished to initiate. For example, in December 1895 the Ladies Mite Society of Thorold's Presbyterian church sought permission from the elders to carpet and fix up the session room.[54] These organizations were also expected to accede to all requests from male church leaders. If the local trustees or board of managers sought canvassers to raise money, they called on the women. If the men decided that a social would be appropriate at a particular church event, they appointed the ladies as a committee to organize it. At all socials organized by women, whether initiated by them or not, a man took the chair.

Despite a lack of official power, in practice women were able to exert at least some autonomy and control.[55] In particular, involvement in missionary societies provided them with freedom from the control of local male leaders, since the women had to adhere to the rules and procedures of the national organization to which they were affiliated. This could create tensions when the missionary society was the only women's organization at the local level. For example, in the case of St John's Anglican Church in Thorold, the women organized themselves as a branch of the Anglican women's missionary organization, the Women's Auxiliary (WA). They then focused their energies on sending clothing to home missions in the West and were only occasionally willing to act as collectors for St John's, since this was not part of their official mandate.[56] When they agreed in the spring of 1895 to a request from the church wardens to organize a strawberry social for the church, their president threatened to resign, stating that organizing such local events was contrary to the constitution of the WA. The membership then backed down, passing the following motion: 'Having considered more carefully the Constitution of the Woman's Auxiliary we feel that entertainments are more within the province of the Musical and Literary Society and beg leave to transfer the management of the Strawberry Festival to that body.'[57]

Anglican clergy and lay leaders objected to their loss of control over women's activities, not just at St John's but in the entire Diocese of Niagara. In 1895 the tensions were such that the bishop of Niagara noted a 'feeling which has possession of some of the clergy that Parochial and Diocesan interests are suffering because the energies of the women in this Diocese are largely absorbed by the WA in their devotion to Domestic and Foreign Missions.' The bishop sought to have the WA widen its focus to local as well as missionary concerns so that 'the members of the WA may so aid in keeping up the contributions for all the purposes of the Parish ... that the vexatious arrears may come to be unknown amongst us and the condition of our churches and parsonages may be a source of pleasurable and proper pride to all of us.'[58] He suggested that if the WA took on these tasks, it would receive support from the local clergy.

In responding to the bishop's concerns, the executive of the WA noted the opposition and hostility of 'some of the clergy and the laity also' and agreed to amend their constitution to include work at the parish and diocesan level. In this way they hoped that 'at no very distant date a branch of the WA might be established in each Parish.' They concluded by proclaiming that they were 'loyal Churchwomen [who were] at all times willing to assist the clergy in any way when called upon, and to undertake if desired, the collection of funds either for Parochial or Diocesan purposes.'[59] This little episode clearly indicates, first, the essential nature of women's church work at the local level, particularly in raising money for church funds and the increasingly popular church 'improvements'; second, the fact that their involvement in this work could not be taken for granted; and third, the ultimate reality of male power in the churches.

Women's financial contributions were not just important among Anglicans. Funds raised by the Thorold Baptist Ladies Aid kept the struggling church afloat, since the women raised money to pay the interest on the mortgage and were occasionally able to pay off some of the principal. Similarly, the Ladies Mite Society of Thorold's Presbyterian church raised major sums towards paying off the mortgage on the congregation's elaborate new church. Between 1883 and 1886 the society donated more than $911 to the church, and between 1888 and 1896 it paid $950 towards the church mortgage of $4,000.[60]

The women's organizations generally spent the money they raised as the male leadership desired, though the men often sought permission from the women's organization before spending it.[61] Marilyn Whiteley has noted that Methodist ladies' aids sometimes resorted to the 'conditional gift' as a way of retaining control over how their money was spent. For example, some ladies' aids would donate money only on condition that it be used to build a new church or to paint the church, or on condition that the trustees raise additional money themselves for a specified purpose.[62]

Certain women's societies demonstrated considerable independence from the church leadership. For example, although Thorold's Presbyterian Ladies Mite Society often acceded to the request of the board of managers to canvass for funds or to organize a tea meeting to raise money, the society also frequently refused. In 1882 a member of the board of managers, who 'wait[ed] upon the Ladies Aid Society for the purpose of getting up a social to liquidate debts reported no success.' In 1887 the members of the society rejected the suggestion of the board that they organize either a tea meeting or an oyster supper, and again in 1893 they refused to organize a series of socials which the board thought would be a good way of raising money for the church's general fund. In 1895 the men, apparently tired of these refusals, agreed to hold 'an entertainment and social to be gotten up and conducted by the gentlemen only.' The women were also sometimes reluctant to take on other traditional female tasks. At the 1896 congregational meeting, the women present agreed that $300 was needed for church purposes, but they voted down a motion that, as usual, the women would canvass for the money. Instead, it was moved by Mrs McPherson, seconded by Mrs McCrae, that 'the gentlemen collect,' and this motion was carried.[63]

The ladies of Thorold's Presbyterian church raised a great deal of money for their church, but they clearly did not do so simply as obedient handmaidens to the male church leaders. They had considerable discretion in deciding when and how they would raise the money. These women may have been more assertive than the members of other women's church organizations. It does appear, however, that although men deprived women of any share in the spiritual leadership of the churches and relegated them to a secondary position in their work of sustaining the material/financial basis of the church, many women did at a minimum attempt to gain a voice in how they performed their hand-maidenly role.

Women's Associations and Church Improvements

Women's church groups were not simply money machines that funded church improvement schemes dreamed up by the male church leadership, for the women often had their own ideas not only about how to raise money but about what to spend it on. Thus, the 'improvement fever' of late-nineteenth-century Ontario cannot be understood only in class terms any more than it can be seen as a purely religious impulse. It was also a gendered phenomenon.

In some communities the ladies' aids pressured male lay leaders to build both new churches and new parsonages.[64] In other cases the women sought to increase the comfort and beauty of the existing churches. This emphasis on internal beauty and comfort had been frowned on in the evangelical Protestant churches earlier in the century, but by this period women's groups of all denominations were actively initiating such improvements. During the 1880s and 1890s the Ladies Mite Society of Thorold's Presbyterian church took on a number of projects intended to beautify the church. They had it painted and grained, bought carpets for the pulpit and choir stand, and furnished a room for the church societies as well as initiating various unspecified projects that were a 'valued addition to the comfort of the church.' In 1882 the ladies' aid of Campbellford's Methodist church raised $500 to furnish the new church. The Ladies Sodality, the Catholic women's organization of Thorold, raised money to furnish their new church and also donated money for church windows and various religious statues. The records of Campbellford's Anglican church include a list of 'improvements made to church ... 1891–1901.' Most of the items listed that were not donated by individual bequests were funded by the local women's organization. These included a red altar cloth, a white altar frontal, white hangings, a font and platform, and various church windows. Other projects undertaken by women's groups included the laying of carpets in churches and the upholstering of pews.[65]

All of these projects suggest a domestic emphasis. They reflect Sara Jeannette Duncan's observation that 'the religious interest had also the strongest domestic character ... Threadbare carpet in the [church] aisles was almost as personal a reproach as a hole under the dining room table; and self-respect was barely possible to a congregation that sat in faded pews.'[66] Women were responsible for maintaining the beauty and comfort of their homes, and it seemed appropriate that they should extend this concern to the churches.[67] Such projects may have been viewed as suitable by the ministers or lay male leaders who occasionally suggested them. However, although the projects required male permission, many were initiated by the women themselves. This work, as part of the larger 'church improvement fever,' certainly had class implications, but at the same time these women's efforts brought a strongly feminine and even domestic emphasis into the churches. While the building of Gothic-style churches has been viewed as representing a separation between secular and sacred in late-Victorian society, the smaller improvements inside the churches tell a different story. Largely initiated and funded by women, they made the churches more beautiful, more comfortable, and as the Reverend C.D. McDonald of Thorold pointed out, more like 'our homes.'[68] The evangelical theology of the period portrayed the ideal Christian in terms that had much resonance with contemporary feminine ideals. In a parallel process, women's efforts physically to transform the interior of churches with cushions, carpets, paint, and paper can be viewed as a feminization and perhaps even domestication of sacred space.

Women's Associations and Women's Culture

If church interiors were being domesticated in the image of comfortable middle-class homes, did the women involved in these efforts all come from such homes as some scholars have argued?[69] Many working-class women were active church members, which suggests that they shared with their middle-class sisters a common commitment to organized religion. But did this commitment extend to the women's Protestant church associations in small-town Ontario? Did middle- and working-class women come together in these organizations, reinforcing a common religiosity and reflecting the existence of a cross-class women's culture or at least a shared sense of identity based on the values of Christian womanhood? Or did the associations include only women from the town's more prosperous families?[70] Contemporaries often noted that there were many female church members who did not become involved in the women's church-based organizations. The records of Thorold's Presbyterian Ladies Mite Society, for instance, reveal the efforts of the members of the society to involve all the 'ladies of the congregation.' Similarly, with the Anglicans, the president of the Niagara Diocesan Women's Auxiliary wondered, 'Why are our ranks so small? Why do so few women join us? I would like to see every woman in our churches become a member of our Auxiliary!'[71]

Undoubtedly, some of the women who stayed away from these organizations were middle class, but they were more likely to be working class. Nevertheless, some working-class women were actively involved. Their participation ranged from approximately one-quarter of the membership in the Anglican and Methodist associations in Thorold and in the Anglican association in Campbellford to up to two-thirds of the membership in Thorold's Baptist women's associations (see tables 15 and 16). Nonetheless, working-class women were underrepresented in most of the associations compared with their representation in the congregation as a whole. The wives or daughters of unskilled workers rarely belonged to these associations; the vast majority of working-class women who did join were the wives or daughters of skilled workers. In fact, the representation of the wives of skilled workers in the leadership of these associations was approximately the same as their representation among the membership (tables 15 and 16). Many of the wives of skilled workers who were active in the associations had been church members for years and had husbands who were church leaders. These women no doubt saw themselves as part of a common community of respectable Christian women. Other working-class women, particularly the wives and daughters of unskilled workers, may have felt uncomfortable working alongside their middle-class sisters. The social gulf may have been too large or the values and interests too different.

Brian Clarke has argued that among Toronto's Catholics at this time such class barriers were overcome, for women from the middle class and from the various strata of the working class all joined women's devotional societies.[72] The greater inclusiveness of minority Irish Catholic communities helps explain this difference, but the divergent purposes of Catholic and Protestant women's associations may also be significant here. While the Catholic devotional societies did raise funds for local parishes, their primary focus was to encourage devotional practices among their female membership. This emphasis on spiritual concerns may have attracted more working-class members than an organization devoted almost exclusively to fund raising. Certainly, the fund-raising focus of the Protestant women's organizations posed significant barriers to working-class involvement.

Poorer working-class women, particularly the wives and daughters of the unskilled, may have had no interest in joining ladies's aids to work for church improvements to which they could not afford to contribute and which would only make them feel more marginalized in the church. More concrete barriers also served to keep these women away from both ladies' aids and missionary societies. The nature of these barriers is evident in the divergent ways in which the different women's associations sought to raise money. The Thorold Baptist Ladies Aid, which was primarily working class, decided in the fall of 1894 that it could not afford to start a local branch of the Baptist women's missionary society, since this would cost each member one dollar a year. At the same meeting, the women voted to reduce their monthly membership fee from ten cents to five – a motion proposed by Alice Crane, a factory worker, and seconded by Mrs West, the wife of a labourer. This tiny group, which had only four to six members who regularly attended, may have been concerned about their own ability to pay, but they may also have sought to broaden access to their group. It is probably no coincidence that there were two new members at the next meeting.[73] Beyond the small monthly fee, these women were clearly unable to raise money through personal donations. So instead they made quilts and organized socials.

Thorold's Anglican Women's Auxiliary provides an interesting contrast to the Thorold Baptist Ladies Aid. A meeting in January 1893 was typical of their fund-raising efforts. The treasurer reported that the association owed money to a diocesan missionary fund, and the secretary noted, 'It is pleasing to be able to state that before the meeting adjourned the whole sum of $8.45 was contributed.' Since there were only thirteen members at this meeting, at least some of these women clearly had access to money. Those who could not produce money on request may have been reluctant to attend meetings where they would be pressured to contribute. This may explain the frequent complaints at Women's Auxiliary meetings that 'the support of the Auxiliary falls chiefly on the few who attend the meetings regularly.'[74] The varying financial resources of women are also evident in Thorold's Presbyterian Ladies

Mite Society. The society raised much of its money through various social events. However, a few of its members were also able to make individual donations. For instance, when the society decided to paint the church in the summer of 1895, Mrs Draper donated two dollars towards the project and Mrs Hall donated one dollar.[75]

Clearly, some women were more able than others to donate money. For women struggling to survive, even the smallest monthly fees posed a major barrier to involvement. This probably largely explains the virtual absence of the wives and daughters of the unskilled from church-based women's associations. Other women may have joined but been reluctant to attend if further donations were constantly solicited. Among the regular participants, the fact that some women could afford to make personal financial donations no doubt affected the power dynamics within the association.[76] Organizing socials or making quilts was often an alternative to personal donations, but even these activities posed material barriers for some women.[77] The poorer women would not have been able to afford to bring sewing supplies for quilting, or cakes to socials. There was also the problem that many of the church socials took place at the homes of association members, and the majority of working-class women would not have been able to offer their homes for this purpose.

Other less tangible barriers also kept many working-class women away. In May 1890 a meeting of Campbellford's Methodist Women's Missionary Society drew only a small turnout. In commenting on why more women had not come, an organizer asked, 'How few cannot take an hour from visiting, entertaining, reading or fancy work?'[78] Such a comment assumes a middle-class membership and ignores the fact that, of necessity, most working-class women spent their days in an unending round of domestic toil. This left little time for attending church association meetings. Even those working-class women who might have found an hour somewhere in the day discovered that the meeting times did not reflect the realities of their lives. Most women's church associations met during the day on the assumption that potential members had considerable leisure time and perhaps even a servant with whom to leave the children. Some associations, however, were aware that their meeting times could limit access. For example, the president of Ingersoll's Baptist Foreign Mission Circle noted that the association had had a very small membership in 1880 but that when they changed their meeting time from the afternoon to the evening, attendance increased significantly.[79]

The Catholic women's associations were divided between single and married women, but this was not the case among Protestant groups.

However, married women predominated among the membership of Protestant missionary societies and ladies' aids (see tables 15 and 16). Working-class participants were particularly likely to be married, since afternoon meeting times would have been most difficult for single working-class women, many of whom worked for wages.

Other Church Organizations

Although working-class single women were not active in the middle-class-dominated women's associations, some found other niches for themselves in the churches. The Sunday schools were one such option. The Sunday school superintendents were all male, but the vast majority of Sunday school teachers were female. In the senior classes of the Sunday schools, most of the students were female, and the more committed went on to become teachers.[80] Women teachers generally taught either the younger students or the older girls. The majority of these women teachers in Thorold's Baptist and Methodist Sunday schools were working class.[81] Most were the unmarried daughters of skilled workers, though a few were wives or daughters of unskilled men. Sunday school teaching was more feasible for these women than involvement in the ladies' aid or the missionary association, since it took place on Sundays and did not require the payment of monthly fees.

Some of these working-class women served on the executive of their Sunday schools, though here they were outnumbered by men.[82] All teachers could apparently attend the Sunday school meetings, and at those of Thorold's Baptist and Methodist churches the women teachers predominated, moving and seconding motions, and making decisions about such things as what form the Christmas entertainment would take that year, which books should be bought for the Sunday school library, and who would be sent as a delegate to the county Sunday school convention. The Sunday schools provided a small space within the churches where working-class women could make decisions and exercise at least a little power. For the men who ran the churches, this was very petty power indeed, but for a woman such as Mrs Potter, the wife of a labourer, her position as librarian of the Baptist Sunday school was probably the only opportunity available to her to play an active role outside her own home.

In the late 1880s and 1890s some working-class women, primarily young single ones, were also involved in a new form of Protestant church organization. These were the Christian youth organizations, which were known in the 1880s as Christian Endeavour and by the 1890s had a variety of denominational aliases. These organizations were founded in the hope of retaining young people in the church after they completed Sunday school. They had committees for a range of activities, again in an effort to keep young people active and involved. There were committees to organize social events, to visit the sick, to recruit new members, to organize regular prayer meetings, and to evangelize the 'unchurched.' Fund raising was not a focus of their work. The Young People's Society of Christian Endeavour (YPSCE) affiliated with Campbellford's Presbyterian church advertised church services to attract non-churchgoers and held cottage prayer meetings in the homes of poor villagers.[83] Thorold's Presbyterian YPSCE made some attempts at house-to-house evangelizing but spent more time visiting the sick and organizing public prayer meetings.

The range of activities offered did not have a wide appeal. The minutes of Ingersoll's Methodist Epworth League and Thorold's Presbyterian Society of Christian Endeavour show that most of their committees had little (or, more often, nothing) to report from meeting to meeting.[84] A Thorold association meeting that focused on the question 'How can YPSCE reach young men?' revealed the core of the problem. Although young men made up about one-third of the membership in both the Thorold and Ingersoll associations, only a few played an active role at the meetings. Once they reached their late teens, young men were reluctant to remain involved in these associations.[85]

The few active young men generally ended up on the executive of the local young people's association, but their small numbers left much of the power in the hands of young women. Middle-class women no doubt predominated in some of these associations, but in others working-class women composed the majority of the female membership. This was certainly true of Thorold's Presbyterian YPSCE, where more than 70 per cent of the membership was working class and where working-class young women made up the majority of executive members. While the majority of the working-class female members were the daughters of skilled workers, the daughters of factory workers and unskilled workers were also represented, both in the membership and on the executive (see table 17). Working-class women also became involved in less formal church activities. Although female factory workers from the local woollen mills were well represented in the congregation of Campbellford's Methodist church, only one can be found on the roll of the local Methodist Women's Missionary Society; but these women found other active roles to play in the church, as can be seen from a report of a successful Methodist 'young ladies' social' in which the majority of participants listed were 'factory girls.'[86]

Sunday school teaching, the local Christian Endeavour society, and other less formal church-centred activities thus provided young working-class women with a public space for social interaction and perhaps even for the exercise of some power. Nonetheless, their involvement does not necessarily point to the existence of a distinct working-class women's culture in the churches, for middle-class women and a few young men were usually involved in the activities too. Sunday schools and Christian Endeavour shared with the church-based women's organizations a common focus on Christian service and a shared vision of Christian womanhood. The involvement of working-class women in these organizations in greater numbers than in the women's associations was probably based mainly on a practical preference for organizations that did not pose the financial barriers associated with fund-raising activities and that did not meet during the working day. Many of these women, particularly the wives and daughters of unskilled workers, may have been socially uncomfortable in organizations dominated by middle-class women, and may have avoided the women's organizations for this reason. But the younger working-class women, at least, may also have preferred to associate with those of their own age and marital status in Sunday school teaching and young people's societies.

Strawberry Socials and Sacred Space

Some church activities, rather than dividing church members and adherents by age, class, or gender, were intended to bring them together. The columns of the small-town papers of the period were not complete without announcements and reports of an array of the latest church socials. These took a variety of forms. The Sunday schools organized summer picnics as well as Christmas treats, complete with a present-laden tree and refreshments. The women's organizations arranged most other church socials. While a few were free and were organized to strengthen sociability within a congregation, most were intended to raise money for the church. The events ranged from large 'tea meetings,' which were often associated with church anniversaries, to a diverse array of socials and concerts. Most socials took a standard form, providing refreshments as well as a program of musical selections and recitations. The strawberry social was the most common of this type. Spring was not complete without one church association, and sometimes several, getting the strawberries, ice cream, and cake together for such an event. Raspberry, peach, and pumpkin pie socials followed over the course of the summer and early autumn. The frequency of these events, as well as 'pink teas' and 'necktie socials,' suggests that ideas for the get-togethers were drawn from well-subscribed church papers. Some women's associations did, however, try to be more imaginative. In Ingersoll a women's association held a Pullman car supper that drew three hundred people, 'the novelty of the thing ... attracting a very large number.'[87]

Barring bad weather or an alternative attraction, the socials (both the novel ones and the more traditional) generally drew a reasonable crowd. While people obviously patronized the events of their own church, the socials also attracted church members and nonmembers of other denominations. Some of the more respectable townsfolk sought in this way to support their fellow Christians, but the limited social options of small-town Ontario ensured that many came just for a good time. The *Campbellford Herald* noted that at the 'bazaar and promenade concert' put on by the Anglican women's association, 'the audience were apparently bent on the enjoyment of such pleasures as ... ice cream etc., promenading, gossip and flirtation.' These events provided a respectable space for courtship as well as a general opportunity for social intercourse.[88] The entrance fees were apparently intended to keep out 'roughs' as well as to raise money, but this was not always effective. The newspapers sometimes noted 'ungentlemanly' behaviour or the presence of a 'hoodlum element.'[89]

While Protestant church socials were relatively popular, their appeal was limited by the restrictions of the evangelical moral code, which prohibited dancing or any form of gambling. The Protestants looked askance at the Catholics' church entertainments, which generally featured dancing as well as raffles, lotteries, and other activities that seemed perilously close to gambling. The use of such 'morally dubious' methods ensured that the money raised at Catholic events put the Protestants' efforts to shame. Father Sullivan of Thorold spent several months organizing a huge bazaar that was advertised all over the United States and Canada. Held in the spring of 1882, it netted more than $6,000 for the building of Thorold's new Catholic church. A similar Catholic bazaar held in Ingersoll a few years later made more than $3,000.[90]

Although the Catholic fund-raising socials generated feelings of both envy and moral superiority among their Protestant neighbours, they were not completely beyond the pale of the respectable community. The same could not be said when the division was race rather than religion – for instance, when members of the small African-Canadian congregations sought to raise money for their churches in the same way as their white neighbours. In Ingersoll the local newspaper at best treated such entertainments with patronizing condescension, and the general public often behaved far worse. In the spring of 1887 an outraged inhabitant of Ingersoll wrote to the paper to complain of the audience's behaviour at a recent fund-raising entertainment put on by the African-Canadian church. This entertainment, like those of other Ingersoll churches, featured recitations, songs, and dialogues. But, it was not received as other such events would have been. The writer noted: 'The coloured people ... following in the footsteps of the other denominations of the town, got up a public entertainment   The mob insulted with impunity the coloured people, who did their part with propriety and decorum ... The noisy element ... included young men and boys from Christian homes ... [who] seemed to think coloured people were fair game for rude and insulting remarks and noises ... showing that the prevailing sentiment in even Christian homes ... [is] that God is a respector of persons.'[91] Such events reveal that while being a middle-class Protestant represented the ideal standard of religious respectability, whiteness was an absolutely essential precondition.

Thus, only church socials put on by white Christians could possibly be respectable. In fact, even they could be suspect. In the late nineteenth century, Ontario's evangelical Protestant churches debated the question of whether the socials were acceptable in any circumstances. This debate raised questions about the relationship between the sacred and the secular in mainstream Protestant denominations and reflected ministerial unease over the role of women in the churches. In the 1891 minutes of the Niagara Conference of the Methodist Church, one finds the following warning: 'We would again call the attention of ministers and people to the undignified and inappropriate character of all methods of raising money for God other than by direct giving ... It would not comport with the dignity of the Niagara Conference that one of its ecclesiastical documents should even mention such things as tea-meetings, strawberry festivals, bread and butter socials, pumpkin pie socials, neck-tie parties, rainbow socials and other similar means of financing the church of Jesus Christ, were they not real evils against which our people must be warned.'[92]

Such comments reflected a belief that the sacred nature of the churches was being sullied by the use of worldly means to raise money for them. Fund-raising socials were seen as taking away from the real meaning of Christianity. David Marshall suggests that by the turn of the century many ministers reluctantly accepted these and other church-sponsored social events as necessary to counter more secular attractions. However, in the 1880s and 1890s many remained hostile. One correspondent to a Presbyterian paper attacked church socials as worldly and unnecessary and proclaimed that the church 'was not ... to be a social institution for aiding the matrimonial projects of the young people.' In listing the vast array of church socials taking place in the spring of 1888, the *Welland Tribune* noted, 'The question in the minds of many is this: Are not the churches going rather far in this matter of amusements? Are they not leaving their own proper sphere?' The Toronto ministerial association also debated the issue, most of the ministers maintaining that 'it was in no sense a part of church work to provide amusements for their people.' Church socials simply cultivated 'a taste for worldly frivolities.'[93]

It is interesting to see what was defined as worldly and what was not. While a few voices were raised against the worldliness of spending vast sums on elaborate new churches and the way the 'building craze' was bringing the social divisions of the world more firmly into the churches, most ministers had no concerns here. The beautiful new churches may have been 'feminized' with new carpets and upholstered pews, but church improvements, large and small, could only reflect well on the status of the denomination and the local ministers. So why did ministers attack the church socials, which funded so many of these improvements? Was 'worldliness' the central concern here, or did the gender of those organizing church socials influence ministerial attitudes?

Ministers had learned to live with the almost feminine sensibility that imbued Protestant ideals of the sacred, and with the awkward fact that they ministered primarily to women. As many scholars have noted, these issues could potentially undermine the manliness of the minister, but his sense of manhood was reinforced by the fact that regardless of the feminine overtones of the 'sacred,' this was a sphere in which he had complete control and in which the female worshippers were required to be passively pious. However, the use of the churches as centres of respectable leisure provided an increasingly popular and more secular space within the realm of the sacred. The fact that this space was organized by women did not necessarily give them more formal power. Nonetheless, the socials symbolized an increasing and interconnected process of secularization and feminization within the churches. As such, they could not help but pose a subtle challenge to ministerial control. This helps us understand what otherwise appears to be a rather excessive response to the seemingly innocuous strawberry social.[94]

People of different genders, ages, and classes worshipped together in small-town Ontario churches, but they did not work together on an equal basis within these churches. The barriers and inequities of the world were brought into the churches. Men – primarily though not exclusively middle-class men – officially had a monopoly on power within the churches. This was not always true in practice, however, since a shortage of men could give women access to at least junior leadership positions in certain denominations. Women's power over the money they raised also gave them some leverage, and official male power could be further limited by women's refusal to cooperate when they did not agree with or had no interest in male proposals.

While the women's associations remained subordinated to a male church leadership, they also reflected divisions among women church members. In most churches, middle-class women were overrepresented on these associations, and the wives and daughters of unskilled workers were almost entirely absent. Some working-class women, particularly young unmarried ones, found other places for themselves in the associational life of the churches, primarily as Sunday school teachers and in the young people's societies. Social unease may have kept some working-class women away from the women's organizations, but the financial demands of membership were a more potent barrier. Financial barriers were not a major concern either in the women's associations or among the male church leadership, and both groups cooperated in the building of imposing and costly churches. In concrete terms, these churches limited the access of the poor as well as further skewing the power imbalance towards those who could donate to such projects. More subtly, the new edifices symbolized a redefinition of what it meant to be a good Christian. Piety could be the sole determinant of Christian faith outside the churches, but acceptance as a fully respected member of a mainstream church increasingly entailed a certain level of material affluence in the secular world.

While the new churches reflected the material success of the middle-class male church members as much as the glory of God, they were also shaped by women's particular interests. The interiors of the churches, with their carpets and upholstered pews, financed through innumerable strawberry socials, suggest a certain feminization and domestication of sacred space, while the strawberry socials themselves and the women who organized them were viewed as a secularizing threat in the realm of the sacred.

4

Rough and Respectable: Loafers, Drinkers, and Temperance Workers

Moralistic editors and indignant letter writers filled the columns of late nineteenth-century small-town newspapers with frequent complaints about the problem of 'loafers,' men who spent much of their time 'hanging around' on street corners. John Thompson, editor of the *Thorold Post*, was particularly vocal here. In the fall of 1894 he noted the problem once again, commenting, 'Sunday evenings it is most odious, because the people are bent on church and thoughts gained in attendance there; and there are just two classes on the streets – the loafers and the church goers.' He went on to complain that on a recent Sunday evening, three 'ladies' had to go to church the long way round to avoid 'the gauntlet of tobacco spitters and starers.'[1] Thompson's comments graphically depict the division between rough and respectable in the small-town community. Respectable townsfolk were closely associated with the local churches, while 'roughs' represented the antithesis of church-based values and particularly the values of the evangelical Protestant moral code.

Dominant rhetoric, then, would place rough and respectable subcultures at the two extremes of small-town life. Certainly, the behaviour associated with each culture was quite distinct. Loafing was of concern to the respectable community, but the use of alcohol, and particularly public drinking, was the most potent symbol of division. Like most apparent opposites, however, the rough and the respectable were interconnected in many complex ways. Certainly, the participants of each culture cannot be divided neatly into clear-cut categories. Class was not irrelevant in these divisions, but it was cross-cut by a range of other considerations, including age, gender, marital status, religious affiliation, and perceptions of personal self-interest. Both middle- and working-class young men were to be found drinking in the local hotels. And although women (and many men) of different classes worked for temperance, they did not all work together or with the same motivation. Many temperance supporters were part of Protestant church communities, but some – particularly in the working class – were not. Participation on either side of the 'great divide' between rough and respectable was thus more complex than moralistic stereotypes might suggest. And it was made even more complex by the fact that many men (but no women) wandered back and forth across this divide, and in many cases both rough and respectable coexisted (although not always happily) in individual families.[2]

Loafing: Just Hanging Out or Sexual Harassment?

The most visible symbols of rough culture in small-town Ontario were the groups of 'loafers' who congregated on street corners, apparently oblivious to the constant attacks in the newspapers, where they were vilified as a disgrace to the community. The tone of these comments suggests that the loafers were working-class men who were far beyond the pale of the respectable community. An indignant letter writer referred to Ingersoll's loafers as 'filthy creatures,' and a Campbellford correspondent was outraged that 'such a class' had the liberty to lounge on street corners. It seems that most loafers were young men and boys. In Ingersoll and Thorold, there is no mention of women spending their leisure time on the public streets. On the other hand, a visitor to Campbellford condemned 'the number of young girls who parade your streets, particularly on Saturday nights, up and down, up and down, by the hour, apparently with no aim but to see and be seen.'[3] Most of these young women were probably employed in Campbellford's woollen mills. Factory employment provided them with a modicum of freedom and a shared camaraderie, which was less likely to be available to the women of Thorold or Ingersoll. For the outraged letter writer, the very presence of young women on the public streets was a problem. Whatever the realities of women's lives might require, ideally they were to be in the home.

Men, however, were expected to inhabit the public sphere. Respectable townsfolk made clear distinctions between the use of public space by different kinds of men. Not everyone who congregated on street corners was branded a loafer. John Vosper, editor of the *Campbellford Herald*, campaigned to have loafers arrested but was very upset when 'two gentlemen who stopped to talk were put on trial.' As far as he was concerned, 'there should be discrimination made between gentlemen engaged in business chat and street corner loafers.' The *Thorold Post* made similar distinctions. In the fall of 1889 the editor noted that the police chief had 'scattered' a group of young men who had been standing at the corner and that the group included 'some who certainly could not be called loungers and with whom it was doubtless more thoughtlessness than otherwise.' So who was a 'loafer' or a 'lounger'? For many respectable villagers, loafing was associated with idleness. Some loafers were branded as able-bodied men who were too lazy to work, while others were boys who should have been in school. However, many so-called loafers must have attended school or work, since the 'problem' was most obvious in the evenings and on Sundays.[4]

Young men in small-town Ontario, with few alternative amusements, little money, and often no comfortable home to relax in, clearly enjoyed 'hanging out' with their friends, gossiping, and observing local street life. The respectable community saw this as an improper use of leisure time. Nonwork hours were best devoted to self-improvement at the local Mechanics' Institute or should be spent in the domestic circle or at church-related activities.[5] However, as we know, church was the last place most young men were to be found. Both British and American scholars have suggested that young men viewed Christianity as sissified and unmanly. Certainly, the feminine associations of the late-nineteenth-century Protestant churches in Ontario did not attract young men. At least some elements of the young male street culture were actively hostile to churchgoing and to expressions of piety. The police court proceedings of the period regularly included reports of young men and boys who had been arrested and fined for disturbing public worship.[6] Even young men who were not overtly hostile to the churches would have been made aware that churchgoing was not the 'manly' thing to do. Thorold's Anglican minister noted in 1884 how difficult it was for the young 'to persevere in the Christian life in consequence of the sneers of the ungodly and the jests of the profane.' The prevalence of such attitudes among street-corner socializers was commonly noted in the papers. According to Vosper, the editor of the *Campbellford Herald*, people on their way to church were exposed to a 'torrent of filthy words' from loafers. Many young men also 'hung around' outside the churches but refused to enter them.[7]

Middle-class hostility to idle youth congregating in public places was linked to fears of public disorder in towns and cities throughout the province. General outrage over the 'disgrace' of street-corner loafing or specific complaints about stone-throwing gangs or about rowdies who 'made the night hideous with their howlings' were accompanied by calls for police action to make the streets safer for respectable people.[8] Much of this concern was a self-interested middle-class effort to reclaim public space and to impose respectable ideals on all townsfolk. However, there was also a commonly overlooked gender dimension.

A frequent complaint against street-corner loafers was their treatment of 'ladies.' The editor of the *Campbellford Herald* was outraged that loafers had 'been allowed to insult ladies at their pleasure on the street corners.' Similarly, a 'Ratepayer' denounced the fact that 'ladies are rudely molested on the street with impunity.' The *Thorold Post* gave prominence to the complaints of Mrs Hitchcock, a female temperance lecturer, who denounced the extent to which 'ladies could not walk the main street without having to pass through such crowds of corner loungers ... and submit to such staring and remarks.'[9] Such comments, which focused on the plight of 'ladies,' clearly reflected class as well as gender concerns. Other comments, however, make it clear that this behaviour was not simply aimed at 'ladies.' For example, the editor of the *Ingersoll Chronicle* argued that the 'women of our town cannot go out of an evening without being subject to the rivalry and unsavory epithets of loafers'; and in Thorold, street-corner loafers were said to 'ogle every pretty lass that has to pass the corner.'[10]

This behaviour looks very much like the kind of unwanted sexual attention that today would be called sexual harassment. However, since we are viewing this behaviour through the eyes of outraged middle-class townspeople, we may be missing the possibility that, in some cases at least, a more reciprocal form of flirtation was going on. Karen Dubinsky has shown that in small-town Ontario much heterosexual courtship took place on the streets and that 'a pickup on the street ... often was the evening's entertainment.'[11] It is thus probable that outraged moralism, led 'respectable' folk to miss elements of mutual flirtation. Nonetheless, it is true that some of what men consider flirtation women experience as harassment, both then and now. At least some of the behaviour described in the papers was clearly sexual harassment. In some cases it may have included elements of class hostility, for the loafers harassed 'respectable' churchgoing ladies, who clearly disapproved of these young men's way of life and sometimes organized campaigns against their leisure practices. However, all women could face harassment. In the summer of 1892, in Thorold, when 'two grown youths ... grossly insult[ed] females whose duties required them to walk along the tow path,' there is little doubt that the working women involved experienced this behaviour as unwanted sexual attention.[12] The fact that insults to 'ladies' were more commonly featured in the pages of small-town newspapers reflects the class bias of the editors, who were outraged that respectable and refined middle-class ladies had their movements restricted and faced insults from those considered their social inferiors. The editors clearly expected respectable men to share this outrage and often focused their concern on the fact that the wives and daughters of these men could not walk the streets unmolested.[13] Chivalric concern was less commonly extended to the supposedly less delicate working-class women, who also faced sexual harassment – as well as opportunities for more mutual interchanges – on the streets and tow paths.

Drink and Disorder

Even more objectionable than the loafers' insults to ladies was the fact that they were often drunk. While drinking was linked to middle-class concerns about loafing, it clearly took priority. For example, a Thorold minister worried that laws prohibiting loafing on the streets would simply 'drive [young men] into the barrooms.'[14] The hotel bars certainly attracted large numbers of men. Hotel proprietors spent considerable resources furnishing their bars to make them appealing and innovative and to give them a very masculine aesthetic. The editor of the *Thorold Post*, though no fan of alcohol, duly noted a range of such improvements. He admired the 'beautiful array of novel bottles displayed' at the bar of the British Hotel, including huge bottles shaped like soldiers, violins, and other like instruments, 'the whole present[ing] a brilliant appearance.' The Welland House received praise for its 'handsome bar cabinet [which] stands twelve feet in height and twelve in length being made of walnut ... the carving being especially handsome ... Two large British plate mirrors add beauty to the whole.' Other hotels tried to attract customers by such novelties as the 'genuine Indian war club' on display at Franklin's Hotel in the early 1890s.[15] The hotel bars clearly provided an appealing masculine space, very different from home or church, where men could relax after work.

In the American context, Roy Rosenzweig has identified the distinct sociability of saloon life as reflecting the existence of an 'alternative culture' among the American working-class men of this period. In small-town Ontario the male sociability of the bars was particularly attractive to young men.[16] Alex Bolton, who later joined the Salvation Army, provides what may be a somewhat jaundiced description of the young men's tavern culture in late-nineteenth-century Ingersoll. Bolton was a blacksmith who boarded at a local hotel, the Carroll House, and apparently spent his leisure time, including Sundays, 'in the bar-room drinking, swearing, and telling yarns and sometimes fighting.'[17]

Whether or not such a lifestyle was completely distinct from that of the respectable community, it was certainly seen that way by the reformers, who viewed the drinking that went on in local hotels as the root of much that was wrong with their communities. Vosper, editor of the *Campbellford Herald*, condemned the existence of 'deep undercurrents of drunkenness ... in a community which calls itself Christian.'[18] By this period, drinking was considered a sin by evangelical Protestants. It had no place in a respectable Christian life, in which success was to be achieved through hard work, frugality, self-denial, and self-improvement. However, drinking in the home, an option available only to middle-class townsfolk who had comfortable homes in which to relax with a drink, was less commonly addressed by temperance advocates. It was the public drinking in hotel bars, and the disorder that was assumed to accompany it, that provoked the most outrage from the respectable community. In the winter of 1885 the respectable townsfolk in Ingersoll were horrified to lose control over public space as 'nightly the streets [were] taken possession of by scores of intoxicated young men.'[19]

Fights apparently caused by alcohol were duly noted in the local papers, as were frequent arrests on 'drunk and disorderly' charges. For example, in January 1886, David Eli of Ingersoll was arrested 'while intoxicated' after he had 'created a disturbance on the street and in the grocery of Messrs Dundas and Menhinnick.'[20] While the newspaper editors wished to see men such as Eli as quite separate from the respectable community, an analysis of the backgrounds of those arrested in Thorold on 'drunk and disorderly' charges reveals that this 'alternative' culture of the hotel bars, though separate, was not quite as separate as the reformers may have assumed.[21] Most of those arrested on these charges were working-class men, both skilled and unskilled. Single men were considerably overrepresented.[22] Whether single or married, most of those arrested who could be traced to assessment rolls or census records lived with their families. Few were lodgers. However, many of those arrested during the boom created by the deepening of the Welland Canal in 1887 could not be traced in local records. While stereotypes suggest that such 'men in motion' were particularly likely to be part of a 'drunk and disorderly' lifestyle, the data make it clear that a significant number of men who lived with their families were also part of this world.

Women and 'Rough' Culture

Almost all those arrested for being drunk and disorderly were men. Only three women were arrested on this charge in Thorold during the late 1880s and early 1890s. Drinking was clearly perceived as a masculine pursuit. Yet as Cheryl Krasnick Warsh has shown, the reality was somewhat different: a significant minority of women from all classes did drink. However, because female drinking was considered so deviant, and indeed was associated with a form of 'bastardized masculinity,' most women who drank did so not only privately but, if possible, secretly. Public drinking was confined to a small minority of women who were considered completely beyond the pale.[23]

The few Thorold women who came before the magistrate in this period were as likely to have been arrested on charges of using abusive language (usually in an argument with another woman) as for being drunk and disorderly. Of all the men arrested, only one was charged with using abusive language. Perhaps women were more quickly punished when they went beyond the bounds of 'appropriate' feminine speech. Women may have also been more likely to attack each other verbally than physically, though the occasional physical fight between women is recorded.[24] In either case, it is clear that not all women in small-town Ontario adhered to the dominant standard of passive, fragile, respectable womanhood. These standards were clearly of little relevance to working-class women such as Mrs Nellie Baker, who physically attacked her neighbour Mrs Putland in a dispute over the loan of a gander, or Mrs Betty Gunning, who commonly resorted to 'abusive language' to defend against attacks on her family's honour. These women do, however, appear to have been a small minority among small-town working-class women.

Sexuality was another – and perhaps the most significant – sphere in which women could transgress the dominant womanly norms. Like female drinkers, those violating sexual standards were seen as 'other' than true women. Once fallen from the sexual purity expected of Victorian womanhood, they could not be redeemed.[25] In these communities there is little evidence of women's involvement in the sex trade, the ultimate transgression. The Thorold paper was silent on the issue, while the Campbellford paper noted only a few brief appearances of 'soiled doves.' Ingersoll had at least one small brothel in the early 1880s, though it was apparently staffed by women from larger communities nearby.[26] While the existence of sex trade workers is noted, there is no evidence of any public anxiety about local young women who may have transgressed sexual bounds less fundamentally. Certainly, some small-town young women were sexually active before marriage, regardless of the contemporary moral proscriptions, but they would have been condemned on an individual basis. At the level of public discourse, the middle-class moral concerns about young women's sexuality focused on the young women living 'adrift' from their families in big cities.[27]

'Rough Culture': Class, Gender, and Age

Although a few women drank, assaulted one another, or became involved in the sex trade, in the eyes of the respectable community local 'rough' behaviour was identified primarily with masculinity. The majority of those arrested on charges of being drunk and disorderly were young working-class men, which suggests that at the extremes, the problem of rough behaviour was largely confined to this group. However, other men, particularly other young men, also drank. Local constables may have been reluctant to arrest drinkers from more prominent families, and some of these young men may have been more careful than others not to cross the line into the kind of disorder that would attract police attention. It was understood in Thorold, for example, that different hotels had different clienteles. As a correspondent to the *Post* noted, 'It is a well known fact that it was always the roughest crowd that was found' at the Osborne House.[28] However, drinking, like participation in other 'rough' leisure pursuits, drew men from a range of backgrounds.

While team sports were widely accepted by this period, certain outlawed blood sports remained popular, at least in some circles. Cockfights were covertly organized on a fairly regular basis, usually taking place in the nearby countryside. Although condemned by respectable folk, they attracted a large and varied male audience. A series of cockfights involving fourteen birds held near Thorold in early 1889 drew 'no less than three hundred ... young and old, genteel and rough, tender and hardened, all bent on seeing the brutal exhibition which had been secretly arranged.' The following year another series of cockfights was held at the same location, and as a scandalized correspondent noted, it took place, in 'violation of all law and decency,' just as a nearby church was holding special revival services. The cockfights were denounced not simply because of their brutality but because they encouraged gambling. At an 1892 cockfight 'the betting was fast from start to finish, a very large amount of money changing hands. One young Thoroldite dropped $100 in cold cash and another $60.'[29]

The *Post* and other small-town newspapers also denounced the many other forms of gambling found in these communities. There were dark references in the *Post* to the existence of 'gambling hells,' illegal gambling houses in town where 'young men do nightly congregate ... to engage in games of chance for money.' Various other comments and complaints make it clear that gambling was part of the lifestyle of many men, particularly young men. It certainly took place at races, both horse races and running or skating races, as well as in various other venues. The proprietor of the Mansion House in Thorold was fined for 'allowing the shaking of dice over his bar'; dice throwing for tobacco or cigars was also common in local barber shops.[30]

In a sermon attacking gambling, the Reverend Mr Wakefield of Thorold's Methodist church noted that the practice was particularly popular among young men and that it permeated 'every class of society.' The Reverend Marcus Scott of Campbellford's Presbyterian church also denounced gambling, especially among those 'persons calling themselves members of the church.'[31] Evangelicals condemned gambling as a sin. Although they were less ambivalent about acquiring wealth than they had been earlier in the century, the wealth was to be gained through the Christian virtues of hard work and self-denial. To evangelicals, the appeal of easy winnings – the hallmark of any form of gambling – lured young men away from the respectable Christian path to material success and spiritual salvation. Not everyone agreed, however. It will be recalled that Catholics permitted gambling in the form of raffles and lotteries at church events. Furthermore, debates over the licensing of billiard parlours in Ingersoll and Thorold pitted the evangelical councillors, who denounced such places as dens of iniquity, against the Catholic, Anglican, and secularist councillors, who were willing to encourage billiards and would even admit to enjoying the game themselves.[32]

The lines between rough and respectable were therefore not always clear-cut. The respectable community could unite in condemning rowdy drunken men loafing on the streets, the majority of whom appear to have been working-class, but beyond this things got murkier. Most young men of all classes were not actively involved in local churches. Some were no doubt dragooned into occasional church attendance by mothers or sisters, or were attracted by the social opportunities of particular church entertainments. However, they preferred more masculine activities to the more feminized church environment. Most young men would not have been arrested for being drunk and disorderly, but many frequented the hotels, 'gambling hells,' cockfights, and other less than respectable activities that were part of a certain masculine culture, predominantly a youth culture, which to some extent crossed class lines. Many elements of this culture were not new and not unique to late-nineteenth-century Ontario. Scholars have identified a form of masculinity that valued physical strength, recourse to violence, danger, and a certain wildness among youth in ante-bellum America, Upper Canada, and late-nineteenth-century Britain and the United States. Few scholars, however, have noted the cross-class appeal of this culture.[33]

Middle-class parents certainly recognized (and worried) that their sons could become involved in this subculture. James Sturgis has chronicled the sad story of the three sons of the Reverend John Rennie, a small-town minister in late-nineteenth-century Ontario. On leaving their home community, all three young men were caught up in the masculine drinking lifestyle of hotel bars and were sooner or later destroyed by alcoholism. For other young men, rough culture had less dire consequences. Fred Fawkes, the son of an Ingersoll temperance activist, was no doubt not the only middle-class young man to spend much of his time 'loafing around the streets ... getting into scrapes.' Like many other young men, Fawkes mended his ways. This occurred when he and his father moved to Saginaw, Michigan, and he was put to work in the family store, which left him no time for 'monkeying around.' Other young men undoubtedly mended their ways on marriage – when, as we have seen, many men, both middle- and working-class, became church members as part of taking on the solid respected masculine role of family breadwinner.[34] For women, the transformation from rough to respectable was not so easy. Once a woman was defined as having transgressed the bounds of respectable womanhood – especially in sexual terms but also by drinking and other 'rough' behaviour – she was beyond the pale and could never be fully redeemed.

For men, the boundaries could be crossed much more easily, and the distance between rough and respectable was not that great. Many of the rowdiest and most drunken men in small-town Ontario were not all that far from the respectable church-based culture. None of the Thorold men who were arrested for being drunk and disorderly were church members themselves, but the majority were members of churchgoing families.[35] Some of these working-class men were the sons of churchgoing parents; others were married men who had not abandoned the rough masculinity of the hotel bar for the churches to which their wives belonged. The fact that the two apparent extremes of rough and respectable – the man arrested for drunkenness and the church member – often belonged to the same family blurs hard-and-fast distinctions between rough and respectable. At the same time, these realities reinforce the fact that in some working-class families, domesticity or family togetherness was not the norm. Individual family members went their own way, sometimes inhabiting quite different worlds.

Temperance: Gender, Class, and Marital Status

By attending church on Sunday with her middle-class neighbours, Mary West and her daughter may have inhabited a different world from her labourer husband Thomas, who at the same time was drinking in the back of a local hotel with his friends; but the two worlds obviously intersected in the Wests' home. In this case they did not intersect happily. In the spring of 1889, Thomas West was brought before the magistrate and charged with wife beating.[36] Not all wife abuse was linked to drink, despite the arguments of temperance reformers. Certainly, as Linda Gordon has argued, the ultimate basis of wife abuse is male dominance.[37] Nonetheless, while living in a society defined by male dominance allowed men to feel that they had the ultimate right to beat women, drinking could certainly loosen any inhibitions they had about such violence.

Male drinking could cause or exacerbate other problems for women. These included the worries of working-class wives whose husbands had drunk up the money needed for daily subsistence; and the anxieties of middle-class mothers that their sons were risking their souls and ruining their 'prospects' through drink. The tensions created in such cases are indicated by comments such as those of Mayor McCleary of Thorold, who noted that he had 'poor weeping wives and mothers come to him ... for hours at a time, in regard to besotted husbands and sons, who spent their money for liquor in some of the holes that had existed in town.' Other municipal officials echoed McCleary's sentiments.[38] Even though such comments were used as temperance propaganda, this does not negate the real impact that male drinking could have on women's lives.

While all women did not support temperance, support did come from all classes of women. An analysis of an 1890 Campbellford petition to end the licensing of liquor establishments and billiard halls reveals that married working-class women were as likely to sign the petition as married middle-class women, and that the majority of single women who signed it worked in the local woollen mills (see table 18). As with church membership, the predominance of women's names on the petition reflects the noninvolvement of single men rather than a generalized male hostility towards temperance. Married men were in fact slightly more likely than married women to sign the petition, and married working-class men, particularly skilled workers, were as willing to sign as their middle-class counterparts. However, of the 195 names identified on the petition, only 6 belonged to single men (table 18).

The fact that so few single men signed the petition points yet again to the existence of a distinct male youth culture centred around pursuits that were anathema to respectable churchgoers. But the presence of numerous working-class names on the petition does not necessarily reveal a united cross-class church-based opposition to drink. While most middle-class signatories were from churchgoing families, a significant minority of working-class petitioners were not (see table 19). Some may have attended church at least occasionally, but others may have had no links to the local churches. They may have supported temperance for their own reasons, which probably bore some relationship to the world of church-based respectability but were linked more closely to a distinct working-class pride and self-respect. In the case of working-class women, the motivation probably included a clear recognition of the potential effects of alcohol on their homes and families.

Sons of Temperance: Self-Help and Women's Help

Some working-class men and women demonstrated their support for temperance by joining temperance lodges. The three most popular in late-nineteenth-century Ontario were the Sons of Temperance, the Royal Templars of Temperance, and the Independent Order of Good Templars. The Sons of Temperance, on which other lodges were partially modelled, was founded in the United States in 1842. It was originally intended as a self-help organization to keep men away from alcohol by providing an alternative social world, and it had the ranks, ritual, and financial benefits of a fraternal order and held numerous 'dry' social events. Scholars have shown that in the early years in the United States, the Sons of Temperance attracted a primarily working-class membership, which was all male, since the Sons did not admit women until 1866. Jack Blocker, an American temperance scholar, has argued that when the Sons moved away from a voluntarist approach and endorsed the campaign for legally enforced prohibition, 'the result was a narrowing of its base to the middle class and those workers who aspired to middle-class status.'[39]

In late-nineteenth-century Thorold and Campbellford this does not appear to have happened, since at least half the executive members of the local temperance lodges were from working-class families.[40] Working-class participation varied by gender, with about two-thirds of the female officers being working class (see tables 20 and 21). The age and marital status of officers also varied significantly by gender. The female executive members were almost all young and single, but the male officers tended to be older and married. This difference was particularly striking in Thorold's Royal Templars of Temperance lodge, where fewer than 15 per cent of the men were single, compared with almost 90 per cent of the women.[41] At a Sons of Temperance meeting held in Welland in 1890, Thorold's Methodist minister proclaimed, 'Men no longer jeer at temperance men, but their acts are taken note of. Young men are no longer ashamed to wear the temperance badge.'[42] The Reverend Mr Brethour was being a trifle optimistic here, particularly regarding younger single men. For most young men, temperance did not have the same manly associations as the drinking culture of the hotel bars.

These young men may have linked temperance with a feminized churchgoing respectability and rejected both as a package. However, not all temperance supporters made the same link. By the late nineteenth century, although all members of the evangelical churches may have at least officially supported temperance, not all temperance advocates were part of a church community. This was even more true of those belonging to temperance lodges than of those signing temperance petitions. Sharon Cook has suggested that religious faith was not central to the temperance lodges, arguing that they 'espoused an indeterminate Christianity.'[43] One had to state a belief in God to join a temperance lodge, and lodge membership was almost exclusively Protestant, but the advocacy of temperance in the lodges was not closely linked to evangelical Christianity as it was in the churches. Some lodge members were church members who may have brought with them into the lodges their belief in the interconnection between temperance, evangelical faith, and churchgoing respectability. Church membership was particularly common among female and middle-class officers (see table 22). However, many working-class members, particularly working-class men, were not church members and had only peripheral links to evangelical Christianity and churchgoing respectability. The fact that, in the lodges, these men worked and socialized with middle- and working-class church-goers implies that there was at least some common ground here. However, for these men, support for temperance may have reflected distinct class-based values and concepts of respectable manhood rather than full adherence to the dominant church-based ethos.

The Ontario temperance lodges actively campaigned for prohibition locally, provincially, and federally. However, the male members were not only concerned with imposing prohibition on others: many struggled to remain temperate themselves. A common feature of lodge meetings was the expulsion of members who had violated their pledges by taking a drink. Erring but penitent members were generally readmitted.[44] The centrality of self-help in the temperance lodges certainly qualifies our image of the prohibitionists as dour respectable people who would never take a drink themselves and who wanted to prevent others from doing so.

While many men joined the temperance lodges to help keep themselves away from drink, this would not have been the primary motivation for female members, since drinking was viewed as a male vice in this period. Female drinkers were considered so deviant that women seeking to overcome alcoholism would have done so privately.[45] Why, then, did women join the lodges? For the working-class single women, who made up a large part of the membership, the lodges provided one of the few respectable social spaces available to them in small-town Ontario. The rough culture of the streets, billiard halls, and hotels was almost exclusively masculine and was not an option for any woman who wished to be considered respectable. The temperance lodges may also have been more socially appealing than the churches and church associations, which were the only other respectable social outlets available to working-class women. Working-class women and men were better represented on temperance lodge executives than they were on church membership rolls. In Thorold, single working-class women were far more likely to be executive members of the local temperance lodges than they were to be members of a church ladies' aid or missionary society.[46] The temperance lodges provided single women, both middle and working class, with a chance to take on leadership roles in a respectable mixed-gender organization. Even at the local level, however, women could not hold the top executive positions. In the Sons of Temperance, women filled the positions created specifically for them: associate patriarch (sic), lady conductor, and lady sentinel. Beyond the local level, officers in the temperance lodges were almost exclusively male.[47]

Lodge social life was a central drawing card for both women and men. The men were provided with a social environment removed from the drinking culture of the hotels and were given encouragement to remain temperate. At the various entertainments they could have a good time singing songs with choruses such as 'We never will drink any more.' The local lodges organized a range of social events. For example, the Thorold Sons of Temperance often drove out as a group to visit the Sons of Temperance lodges in nearby communities for an evening of songs, recitations, and refreshments. As the *Post* noted in reporting on one such event, the lodge demonstrated 'both going and coming that it is quite easy "to be merry without the aid of wine."' The relative youth of the members of the Sons of Temperance and the fact that unlike most temperance lodges this association included single young men led to suggestions that it was primarily a 'sparking school.' Lodge entertainments did provide space for heterosexual courtship and the opportunity to find a respectable partner. Given the havoc that male drinking could wreak on families, the significance of the lodges for single young women seeking future husbands cannot be dismissed. However, the alternative attractions of hotel bars and billiard halls did mean that there were never as many abstaining single men as women. This problem was illustrated at a Thorold Sons of Temperance box social, held in the spring of 1890. George Turner, the reeve who occupied the chair, was disappointed to note how few men were present 'to show co-operation.' Their absence, he said, created some difficulties at an event of this sort, since 'there were not enough men to go around.'[48]

Woman's Christian Temperance Union

The other major temperance organization was the all-female Woman's Christian Temperance Union (WCTU). In some communities, the WCTU organized the younger single women into a separate Young Woman's Christian Temperance Union (YWCTU). In Ontario the WCTU attracted fewer members than the temperance lodges, but it was nonetheless the largest nondenominational women's organization of the period. At the higher levels of the organization it was exclusively middle class, and in the small towns of Ontario it attracted more middle-class members than the temperance lodges.[49] In Campbellford's WCTU less than one-quarter of the executive members were working class, and they were wives of skilled workers.[50] A similar pattern emerges for Thorold, where only one-third of the executive members were working class, these women also being the wives of skilled workers.[51] The majority of middle-class women in the WCTU appear to have been the wives or daughters of doctors, ministers, and merchants. There was little overlap between it and the more working-class temperance lodges, though a few members of the Thorold YWCTU were also active in the youthful Sons of Temperance. This suggests that the lack of overlap between the other temperance organizations may have been an age as well as a class issue. In all three communities the husbands of certain WCTU activists were involved in the temperance lodges, particularly the Royal Templars of Temperance. Their wives may have found the all-female WCTU more congenial, both in class composition and in the leadership opportunities provided for women, which were certainly greater than those available in the temperance lodges or the churches. For middle-class male temperance advocates, however, there were no alternatives to the more mixed-class temperance lodges.

Sharon Cook has argued that evangelical Christianity provided a central focus for WCTU reform efforts. This religious focus is reflected in the close links between WCTU members and the churches. In Campbellford more than three-quarters of the WCTU officers were church members, while in Thorold all the officers were church members and at least 70 per cent of the members and officers of the YWCTU also belonged to local churches.[52] As well as attending Sunday services, the members of the WCTU were active in women's church associations. At least half of the WCTU and YWCTU officers in Thorold were involved in church ladies' aids or missionary societies.[53]

The WCTU viewed female church members as its primary constituency and was concerned at its inability to mobilize more of these women. In 1891 the president of the Ontario WCTU noted, 'In many of our towns where there are, shall we say, a thousand women members of churches, there will be only 40 or 50, possibly less, who belong to the WCTU. Now in all probability, the majority of these thousand are temperance women, and in sympathy with every effort that is made to further the temperance cause. Why is it that they do not belong to our Unions?' Class differences were not seen as a problem here, except for an occasional expression of concern that the WCTU did not interest upper-class women, or 'the upper tendom.' The WCTU recognized that many of its members were also involved in women's church societies, and they generally viewed this work as competition to their own efforts. Around the turn of the century the president of the Ontario WCTU decried the time women spent on missionary society work and went on to challenge the ladies' aids, attacking 'the ridiculous custom of allowing the busy women to raise money for organs and church cushions [which] takes ... more time of the same women.'[54]

Some women may have felt more comfortable raising money for their churches or missionary societies than joining the WCTU because there was the potential for denominational conflicts in an organization that included women from various Protestant churches. Local WCTU unions tried to minimize conflicts and rivalries by trying to elect a vice-president from each of the evangelical churches. However, in an organization centred so strongly around evangelical Christianity, denominational tensions were more likely to emerge than in the more secular temperance lodges. For example, in the Thorold YWCTU, short prayer meetings at the beginning of business meetings apparently created 'a feeling of constraint among members of different churches.'[55]

Despite such constraints, the WCTU members were usually able to find issues around which to organize. Unlike the temperance lodges, the WCTU was not concerned with self-help. It focused almost exclusively on efforts to reform others through legislation, education, and other means. But although temperance was a central concern, a wide range of other issues vied for the members' attention. While various issues gained or lost vogue during the period, the 'departments of work' could be extremely diverse. For example, in 1894 the departments of work taken up by the Oxford County Union, of which Ingersoll was a member, included the following: Press (sending temperance articles to the local press); Railroad (providing tracts at railroad stations and religious literature and 'comfort bags' to railroad workers); Evangelistic (holding evangelistic meetings at hospitals, prisons, etc.); Flower Mission (providing food and flowers to the poor and sick); Literature (distributing temperance literature); Social Purity; Scientific Temperance Instruction (lobbying that it be taught in the schools); Unfermented Wine (encouraging its use for communion wine); Lumbermen (sending religious literature and 'comfort bags' to them); Fair (serving temperance refreshments at fairs); Juvenile (Band of Hope, etc.); Legislation, Petition, and Curfew Bell; Prisoners' Aid; Narcotics; Parlour Meetings (social events for members and potential members); and Parliamentary Usages. Even this list does not include all the possible departments of work that a county or local union could take up.[56]

Nevertheless, the unions in the smaller towns tended to be less ambitious. Most seem to have pursued temperance as the central focus of their work. This was certainly true of the Ingersoll, Campbellford, and

Thorold unions, all of which presented petitions to their municipal councils, requesting a reduction in the number of liquor licenses. They also petitioned against the licensing of billiard parlours, but although they were successful in Thorold and Ingersoll, the local men then created private clubs where billiards could be played. In Thorold the WCTU women had more success in limiting the number of liquor licenses granted. They fought for years against the granting of a license to a hotel near a school. To cement their victory in this case the 'WCTU and YWCTU ... rented ... the very room originally intended as a bar-room, to be used as headquarters for both unions.' Other efforts included canvassing the newly enfranchised women voters (single and widowed women with property received the municipal franchise in 1884) regarding temperance issues, and working on campaigns to bring prohibition to their communities. Most of the latter work centered on the Scott Act, which permitted the imposition of a limited form of prohibition at the local level if it was supported by a majority of voters.[57]

The WCTU also emphasized the importance of education in promoting temperance. Both the Campbellford and Thorold unions ran Bands of Hope, in which groups of children pledged never to drink liquor, use tobacco, or swear; the children received appropriate education intended to strengthen their resolve to keep the pledge. At its height, the Thorold Band of Hope included 140 members, the majority of whom appear to have been girls. The Thorold WCTU also distributed prizes to the local schools for students studying temperance, and the Ingersoll WCTU attempted to pressure county schools to bring in temperance instruction.[58] The Thorold and Ingersoll unions also sponsored a number of lectures by prominent temperance advocates. For example, in November 1884, the Ingersoll WCTU brought in Mrs Marion Baxter of Charlotte, Michigan, to lecture on 'Nemesis, or the Will of the People.' The following year, Ingersoll audiences apparently appreciated the 'eloquent and practical' address of Colonel Bain of Kentucky, who dwelt on 'the desolation and misery that intemperance entails.'[59] Temperance lectures were usually well attended, perhaps in part because, unlike most lectures and other local entertainments, they were generally free.

Some WCTUs performed some charity work in their communities. In Ingersoll, the WCTU was ambitious enough to organize a part-time industrial school for children 'of the very poorest class.' In Campbellford, the WCTU acted as a charity society, arranging to have 'deserving' cases receive relief from the municipal council and keeping an eye on poverty-stricken families.[60] In Thorold, the YWCTU sent flowers to the sick and may have briefly taught domestic science to poor girls; but beyond this, neither local union had much to do with poor relief. The differences between the three communities illustrate the ad hoc nature of relief in this period as well as the different roles that WCTU members could choose to play at the local level.

While WCTU interest in charity work clearly varied, the willingness to organize socials was consistently high. WCTU social events were intended both to raise money and to popularize the temperance cause. Thorold's YWCTU was particularly active in this regard, and in the early years of the union it apparently was '*the style* for young women to be Y's.' The YWCTU events included the popular Quaker social, in which members dressed and spoke like Quakers, and the 'chocolataire,' in which 'the regular concert programme is rendered with an essay on chocolate, and chocolate refreshments served in every possible form.' This twenty-five-member group was able to sign up sixteen men as honorary members, and they held some socials that were open only to members and honorary members. Despite the women-only nature of the WCTU, then, this organization clearly provided a respectable space for heterosexual courtship.[61]

In the Canadian context, the WCTU has been studied less in relation to its social activities or temperance efforts and more for its contribution to the first-wave women's movement. As Wendy Mitchinson has noted, the WCTU was the first major women's organization to endorse suffrage. Its support for suffrage emerged from a maternal feminist position – that women should receive the vote because they were more moral than men and would vote to end the liquor traffic and to bring in other reforms. Despite its centrality in the Canadian historiography, however, interest in the franchise does not appear to have been a central feature of local WCTUs. Although the Thorold WCTU submitted a petition on the subject to the legislature and although the Ingersoll union sponsored a lecture by the Reverend Anna Shaw on the 'Enfranchisement of Women,' other issues were of more interest to both unions. The frequent complaints from the provincial level about the reluctance of many local unions to deal with the franchise question reveals that other unions were even less enthusiastic. For example, in 1891 the Ontario superintendent of franchise work complained, 'It has come to me again and again, our Union is not in sympathy with this work and in some instances, the President of the Union has refused to circulate the [franchise] petitions or give them to the members to circulate ... I am more than sorry that all our women are not in hearty sympathy with this department of our work.' In the Thorold YWCTU, even the suggestion of canvassing women voters on the subject of temperance was met with 'a shower of proprieties, Biblical quotations and domestic infelicities.' Clearly, many of the members remained wedded to the traditional definition of dominant gender roles. These women would not support the struggle for the ballot, despite the efforts of their leaders to redefine it into respectability as the Home Protection Ballot.[62]

The reluctance of many WCTU women to do franchise work does not reflect any lack of interest in defending the home. The organization saw its efforts – whether in agitating for prohibition or against gambling or 'white slavery' – as an attempt to defend the traditional heterosexual nuclear family.[63] Historians have suggested that, in defending the family, the predominantly middle-class WCTU women were not primarily concerned with their own vulnerability to male drinking or other 'rough' leisure pursuits, because middle-class husbands were less likely to drink than working-class men, and they were more likely to spend their leisure in the home. It is true that the social and family problems created by the drinking habits of the working-class husband were featured much more often in WCTU literature than any concern over the drinking habits of middle-class husbands.[64] Some historians have seen the WCTU women as members of a middle class that was trying to retain control in a society that was increasingly characterized by a distinct and, to middle-class eyes, disorderly working-class lifestyle.[65] Others focus less on class than on gender. Barbara Epstein, for example, argues that the WCTU women saw male drinking not as a personal threat but as a larger symbol, both of female economic and physical vulnerability and of women's exclusion from the male spheres of public sociability.[66]

While larger class and gender issues no doubt drew many women into the WCTU, more personal reasons may also have been an influence. The majority of middle-class women who attended church on Sundays with their husbands may not have been concerned about the possibility of their husbands' drinking, but many of them may have been concerned for their sons – Mary Fawkes, for instance, the WCTU leader whose son loafed on the streets of Ingersoll, and Ann Rennie, whose three sons were destroyed by alcohol. While the WCTU literature seldom featured the destruction of a middle-class home through a husband's drinking, stories about middle-class mothers devastated by the ruin of a beloved son through a fatal weakness for drink vied with stories of cheerless working-class homes destroyed by a drunken breadwinner.[67] In attempting to recruit new members in the 1880s and early 1890s, the WCTU appealed as much to middle-class women's self-interest as mothers as to their Christian altruism. For example, in 'A Word to Mothers,' the WCTU journal pointed to 'the dangers which beset their children and more especially their boys.' This article went on to exhort: 'Oh! mothers, can you face that thought? Some one's boys must be the victims [of alcohol]. Will yours be among them? Surely not, at least not without your having done your utmost to avert the danger ... Mothers, will you not come into our Union ... for the sake first of your own boys then for God and Home and Humanity.'[68]

For the respectable churchgoing people of small-town Ontario, young men of all classes were considered a problem. Few had joined the 'feminized' church, preferring the pursuits of a more masculine youth culture. Some elements of this culture may have been rougher than others, but to anxious parents and ministers it was all part of an unacceptable lifestyle beyond the bounds of church, home, and family, a lifestyle in which each step led inexorably downward. This attitude helps to explain the WCTU's consistent opposition to the granting of billiard licenses. When receiving such petitions, some municipal councillors protested that billiards was a harmless sport. But others, who were more in sympathy with the WCTU, argued that these places had a very bad effect on young men, keeping them away from home until late at night and encouraging the development of dangerous habits. For the WCTU and their ministerial spokesmen, such as the Reverend Mr McDonald of Thorold's Presbyterian church, billiard rooms were places 'where gambling was taught and drinking habits fostered.'[69] The middle-class women of the WCTU may have sought to control the habits of working-class men in the interests of their own class and in what they perceived as the common gender interests of all women, but by challenging rough male culture, many also believed that they were safeguarding their own sons.

Other Temperance Efforts

The WCTU and the temperance lodges sometimes joined together for a specific purpose, although such unity could not be assumed. In agitating for the Scott Act, men from Thorold's temperance lodges originally tried to work without the WCTU; but perhaps because most lodge members were more interested in self-help than in legislative solutions, only a small number of men became involved. As a result, the activist lodge members enlisted the WCTU women, who, they noted, 'are a great help.'[70] In Ingersoll the WCTU was part of joint Scott Act committees from the beginning. In Thorold in the early to mid-1880s the temperance lodges, WCTU, and local evangelical clergymen joined together in organizing monthly Gospel Temperance meetings in which speakers, generally ministers, were brought to town to speak on temperance subjects. As the name Gospel Temperance implies, these meetings linked the cause of temperance to evangelical Christianity. For example, at the meeting in March 1882, the usual 'devotional exercises' were followed by an address by the Reverend Mr Wetherall, of St Catharines Congregational Church, who lectured on 'the duty of Christians in regard to the total suppression of the liquor traffic.'[71]

Scholars have argued that throughout most of the nineteenth century the evangelical churches held themselves aloof from active involvement in the temperance movement, but in late-nineteenth-century small-town Ontario they were major players in temperance work.[72] Ministers frequently spoke at the temperance meetings and were usually involved in presenting petitions to town councils requesting reductions in the number of liquor licenses. The temperance meetings were often held in churches. Just before the 1894 Ontario plebiscite on prohibition, Campbellford's temperance supporters held a series of meetings in the town's Methodist and Presbyterian churches. The meetings included speeches by local ministers as well as music by the combined Methodist and Presbyterian choirs. A few months later, the WCTU and Royal Templars of Temperance organized a temperance meeting in Campbellford's Baptist church, featuring music by the local Methodist choir. The ministers frequently preached temperance sermons as part of their Sunday services. They preached in general terms against drinking as a sin and as something that was damaging both to the family and the economy, but they were particularly concerned about the influence of liquor on young men. In the mid-1890s the Campbellford ministers even spoke of trying to organize a temperance hotel in town. While regretting 'that so few of our young men were christians [sic],' they hoped that through such an institution 'the young men could be brought under better influences.'[73]

The evangelical ministers in these communities focused considerable energy on temperance but still had some left for sabbatarianism, another popular issue among religious reformers. Thorold's ministers occasionally attacked the Sunday streetcars to St Catharines, and they organized against Sunday labour on the Welland Canal, while Ingersoll's ministers tried to stop the selling of Sunday papers.[74] Ministers and newspaper editors in all three towns condemned young boys for playing baseball on Sunday. Leisure pursuits that were unacceptable during the week were particularly so on Sunday, of course, and the editor of the *Campbellford Herald* sorrowfully noted in October 1892 that 'three once bright and promising youth spent a portion of Sabbath afternoon last, playing cards near the base of the hill.'[75] The strongest condemnations were reserved for the illegal selling of liquor on Sunday, which seems to have gone on in all three communities in defiance of all efforts of the respectable churchgoing townsfolk.[76]

While the loudest condemnations of drunkenness and Sabbath breaking came from the evangelical churches, the Anglicans and Catholics also spoke out on these issues. The Anglicans' Reverend Mr Spencer, was involved in the ministerial efforts to end Sunday labour on the Welland Canal, and he also founded a branch of the Church of England Temperance Society in Thorold. This organization was particularly active in Campbellford, where it had more than eighty members. However, its efforts to join forces with other Campbellford temperance groups ran into problems because of different definitions of temperance. At a public meeting organized by Campbellford's Church of England Temperance Society, the Reverend Mr Hinds, the local rector, apparently said that 'he was a moderate drinker, and that moderate drinking was temperance.' A shocked participant accused Mr Hinds of giving 'respectability to moderate drinking' before an audience that included many impressionable young people from denominations where such teachings were completely unacceptable.[77]

The Catholics could present the evangelical Protestants with even more of a problem. M.T. Buchanan, who became mayor of Ingersoll in 1887 despite the intense opposition of the local evangelical elite, had considerable Catholic support and – from the evangelicals' perspective – a not coincidental fondness for certain aspects of rough male culture. Their dire predictions were fulfilled when he proceeded to permit the licensing of billiard parlours and refused to enforce the liquor laws.[78] Other Catholics were more pro-temperance even though most did not go so far as to advocate prohibition. However, these men, like Councillor James Battle of Thorold, found that it was assumed that they would oppose any temperance efforts.[79] Because these men were Catholics, the Protestant voters labelled them anti-temperance, no matter what their personal position may have been on the subject.

In fact, the Roman Catholic Church tried to encourage temperance among its parishioners. The church hierarchy was particularly concerned about keeping young men away from the temptations of rough culture.[80] Not all priests were willing to participate in such efforts, however. An outraged Campbellford parishioner wrote to the local paper attacking his priest, Father Casey, for being on the side of 'those that sold whiskey and those that used it,' and for being completely unconcerned that among Campbellford Catholics 'quite a few of the young men as they grow up were learning to drink.'[81]

While drunken priests did not exist only in the imagination of bigoted Protestants, many small-town priests took an active role in promoting temperance. In Thorold, Father Sullivan established a temperance society in the 1870s. Although, like many other such societies, it was fairly short-lived, Sullivan remained vigilant in his efforts to keep his parishioners away from the temptations of rough leisure. In 1884 he formed a branch of the Catholic Mutual Improvement Society for young men in an attempt to counteract 'the dangers [young men] incurred by having so much idle time on their hands during the winter which could be profitably spent in improving their mental condition.' Sullivan also organized a young people's dramatic society. Although it may have been anathema to the local evangelicals, it too was intended to keep the young men out of the hotel bars. The society presented 'a grand temperance drama' to an appreciative audience. Sullivan also brought in Catholic speakers to give lectures on temperance. One such speaker, Father McCann, seemed 'at first to manifest a sort of sympathy for moderate drinkers,' but to the relief of the Baptist editor of the *Post*, 'before concluding ... sat upon them very heavily.'[82] Local folklore has it that Sullivan also had more informal methods of dealing with the tendency of his young male parishioners to indulge in pastimes of which he disapproved. Those who went drinking in St Catharines could apparently expect to 'find Father Sullivan waiting with tongue and horny walking cane to belabour them for their folly. It was in the same manner he would greet and chastise them when coming through a certain barn door after an evening of cards.'[83]

Opposition, Conflict, and Violence

Sharon Cook points to the popularity of WCTU-organized demonstrations and entertainments to argue that the WCTU's reform platform, including its demands for prohibition, reflected mainstream attitudes in late-nineteenth-century Ontario. Some elements of the WCTU's position, particularly on prohibition, may indeed reflect the dominant ideology of the time insofar as this ideology was defined by evangelical Protestant-ism, but other aspects of the WCTU reform platform, such as its position on sexuality and women's suffrage, were neither dominant nor main-stream. Even on the issue of prohibition, one must be careful not to over-state popular support. Prohibition was opposed by most Catholics of all classes, by a large number of Anglicans, and probably by many others who at least nominally identified themselves with an evangelical Protes-tant denomination.[84] While some temperance events were well attended, others were not. The passage of the Scott Act in many Ontario counties in the 1880s certainly indicates considerable support for prohi-bition, but it is also true that these were hard-fought battles that were often lost.

The opposition to temperance could be strong and bitter. Businesses that endorsed prohibition might be threatened with boycotts. In areas where the Scott Act was in place, it was regularly flouted. The difficulty of gaining a conviction in such cases reflected a solidarity within the masculine drinking culture, for witnesses routinely lied, claiming that they had been served nothing but beef tea or 'pop' in hotel bars.[85] Informers risked violent retaliation. For example, two Ingersoll men who gave evidence in Scott Act trials had their homes broken into and were beaten up. In January 1886, when several Ingersoll hoteliers were to be charged with violating the Scott Act, the town council swore in six special constables because the councillors expected a riot. A year later there was a riot in nearby Woodstock when two men who had testified at Scott Act trials were attacked by a crowd of two hundred 'rowdies' and were prevented from leaving town.[86] The battles over hotel licens-ing, while not quite so violent, could be equally bitter. Men who sought to protect their lifestyle from the attacks of the temperance reformers knew who their enemy was. When Campbellford's reformers attempted to raise hotel licence fees, they received an 'ill spelled letter' threatening, 'We will make a hot nest for you all and a bond-fire of you[r] church.'[87]

Local rough culture was perceived as the antithesis of churchgoing respectability, and a frank hostility to 'feminized' churchgoing piety was certainly associated with the masculinity of hotel bars and street corners. Nonetheless, the apparently clear-cut opposition between these two dis-tinct cultures was complicated on a number of levels. While the evangel-ical churches were viewed as the primary opponents of the intemperate rough male culture of small-town Ontario, the churchgoers were not the only people to challenge the drinking that was central to rough culture.

Many nonchurch members, most of whom were working class, were willing to sign temperance petitions and join temperance lodges. Some of these men and women may have felt uncomfortable in the churches on either social or theological grounds, but they had their own reasons for supporting temperance. While the hotel bar could provide comradeship and conviviality, many married working-class men found that it could threaten economic security and self-respect and was not consistent with the masculine respectability expected of a household head. For working-class women, both single and married, support for temperance sprang from their hope for a respectable and happy family life. The temperance lodges similarly provided one of the few respectable social options available to single working-class women, and they were particularly appealing in view of the domination of women's church organizations and the WCTU by middle-class married women.

Looking inside families further complicates the picture, revealing clear divisions but also close links between the apparent social extremes of small-town life. Certainly, the distance between hotel bar and church pew was not always that great. The majority of those frequenting the bars were the brothers and husbands and, most commonly, the sons of members of the churchgoing community. At least some of the young men would return to this community when they married. Concepts of masculinity were flexible enough to allow for the ready movement from rough to respectable, in sharp contrast to the more constricting contemporary norms of femininity. While men did have much greater flexibility here, the fears that young men would be lost forever were very real. In the cities, reformers and parents alike may have been as concerned about the dangers facing young women as they were about those facing young men. But in the small towns it was the young men who were the problem. Concern about their ultimate fate fuelled a commitment to temperance among the anxious middle-class mothers of the WCTU and also, no doubt, among male and female temperance supporters of all classes.

5

Mostly Male Worlds:
Leisure and Associational Life

In April 1891 the people of Thorold were shocked and saddened to learn of the death of Emerson and Joseph Peart, father and son, who died within a week of each other. Both men had worked in local factories and, as their funerals demonstrated, both had been active participants in Thorold's associational life. Joseph Peart had been a member of Thorold's Orange Young Briton Band. As the *Post* noted, 'The O.Y.B. band attended [the funeral], and the solemn dirges played to the memory of their departed comrade seemed to speak the sadness that pervaded all ... There was also a very large attendance of members of the various [Orange] lodges of Thorold, Merritton and St. Catharines.' Emerson Peart's funeral five days later 'was attended in full force by Protection Hose Co., and by Summit lodge [of the Ancient Order of United Workmen], to both of which [the] deceased belonged.' Mrs Peart was a member of Thorold's Methodist church, though her husband had not been. The Methodist minister conducted the funeral, and 'at the grave the funeral service of the A.O.U.W. was performed' by officials of the order.[1]

The grieving family received messages of sympathy from various local associations. The Sons of Temperance, to which Emerson's daughter Minnie and son James belonged, sent a resolution hoping that 'Brother and Sister Peart may have grace from above to bear up under their trial and may be enabled in their time of need to feel that ... the God of all grace will give them strength sufficient to their day.' The Orange Young Briton Lodge sent a similar resolution of comfort to Mrs Peart, noting, 'Our time is short here below, and we are taught that we should spend it in such a way as to meet with the approbation of the Grand Master on high. May you not mourn your son as lost but be encouraged by the hope that when you have finished your earthly course you will meet him in Heaven above.'[2]

While the deaths of father and son in one week were unusually tragic, the funerals of Joseph and Emerson Peart were of a familiar type, demonstrating common social patterns of life as well as of death. They point to the importance of fraternal and other associations in the lives of these men, as in the lives of most male townsfolk. They highlight the very real but at the same time exceedingly ambiguous interaction between these respectable but firmly masculine associations and a more feminized Christianity. The associational patterns of members of the Peart family, both the deceased and the surviving, also hint at the range of associational and leisure activities that could exist within a family. The different activities of various family members were based in part on their divergent interests, but even in a family, age, marital status, and especially gender could close off a whole range of leisure and associational options. Many of the activities, from fraternal orders to sports, were available only to men. Women were not completely shut out of organized leisure, but their options, ranging from skating rinks to theatre and dancing, could be further constrained by their class and their religious belief. Class and religion, as well as age, marital status, and ethnicity, were certainly not irrelevant in shaping men's options, but their leisure and associational worlds were defined first and foremost by masculinity.

Men in Groups: Fraternal Orders

The most popular form of voluntary association in late-nineteenth-century Ontario was the fraternal order. These orders differed among themselves. Some, like the Sons of England, were based on ethnic ties; a few, like the Royal Templars of Temperance, were centred on temperance principles. The majority were open to all white men, though because of the Catholic Church's hostility to 'secret societies,' most lodge members were Protestant.[3] Many lodges provided a range of financial benefits, an increasing number offering life insurance.[4] Others had no organized benefit plans, though they preached the virtue of assisting lodge brothers in distress. All lodges were centred on some form of secret ritual, and most contained a series of degrees by which a member could ascend within the lodge hierarchy.

There has been considerable historiographical debate on the subject of fraternal orders. In his early work, Bryan Palmer argued that the lodges had a primarily working-class membership and that the mutuality and brotherhood of these associations reflected working-class culture and fostered working-class bonds.[5] Other historians, in both Canada and the United States, have argued that the lodges' cross-class membership, support for individualism, respectability, and upward mobility retarded the development of class-consciousness among working-class members.[6] Mary Ann Clawson has added a gender dimension to this analysis, arguing that the male-only nature of the lodges provided men with a popular alternative to a woman-centred domesticity and encouraged them to define themselves primarily in terms of gender rather than class.[7]

In late-nineteenth-century small-town Ontario, the fraternal orders were cross-class bastions of masculinity. The male inhabitants of Campbellford, Thorold, and Ingersoll could choose from a wide range of orders, including the Orange Lodge, the Ancient Order of United Workmen, the Masons, the Oddfellows, the Foresters, the Sons of England, the Sons of Scotland, and various temperance lodges. Thorold and Ingersoll also had branches of the Catholic Mutual Benefit Association, a society created to provide Catholics with the fellowship and financial benefits of a fraternal order while keeping them away from the 'secret societies' denounced by the church.[8] An analysis of the officers of the fraternal associations in Campbellford and Thorold reveals that approximately 40 per cent of them were working class. This proportion varied between associations, the Orange Lodge having the highest proportion of working-class officers, and the Masons the lowest. However, both orders included middle- and working-class men as officers and members. Most of the other orders, from the Oddfellows to the Foresters, included a more even mix of classes. Christopher Anstead found similar class-based patterns in his study of fraternalism in nineteenth-century Ingersoll and Woodstock[9] (see tables 23 and 24).

All fraternal brothers, regardless of class, lived in a shared masculine world. As Mark Carnes has shown, the fraternal rituals affirmed explicitly masculine virtues such as bravery, brotherhood, and independence. As well, for young men, the initiation into fraternal orders served as a significant rite of passage into manhood.[10] Darryl Newbury has demonstrated that the fraternal mottoes (which ranged from the Knights of Pythias's 'Be Generous, Brave and True' to the Independent Order of Foresters' motto 'Moral Courage, Physical Fitness and Stability of Character') reflected the values of respectable manhood in nineteenth-century Ontario.[11]

Social life among lodge brothers served to reinforce masculine bonds. Oyster suppers and other men-only banquets were commonly reported in the press. After the election of their officers in December 1889, the Thorold Oddfellows 'adjourned to the Welland house, where a sumptuous oyster supper had been prepared by host Winslow to which full justice was done. Toast and sentiment, song and story, all united to form an evening's unalloyed pleasure.'[12] The lodge suppers were often held in hotels. Although the fraternal orders were trying to move towards more temperate forms of socializing, alcohol continued to play a part in the conviviality of many lodge dinners.[13] Perhaps surprisingly, given the force of temperance sentiment in the evangelical Protestant community, there was no public concern expressed about this drinking. Although working-class men attended the lodge suppers, many of those making the toasts were respectable married middle-class men. After many toasts, they may have become a little rowdy at the table, but not on the streets.[14] Their drinking appears to have been publicly accepted as part of the masculine homosocial culture of the lodge. It was only at social events of the Orange Order, with its high proportion of working-class officers and members, that middle-class newspaper editors perceived alcohol consumption as producing not conviviality but public drunkenness and disorder. The annual Orange procession on 12 July seldom passed without local editors commenting on the extent to which Orangemen 'were found unruly or under the influence of liquor.'[15]

Men who saw themselves as fully respectable members of the community appear to have had no difficulty accepting some of the 'roughness,' including the consumption of alcohol, that was part of the masculine sociability of the mixed-class fraternal orders, though they may have stayed away from the rowdier Orange Order. A number of scholars have noted, however, that women of all classes shared a hostility to the lodges, since these associations took men away from the home, providing them with an alternative, all-male sphere of sociability. Various jokes and stories in small-town papers affirm this feminine opposition to the men's use of the lodge as a form of escape from the home. Women knew that lodge events were not always held on strictly temperance principles. The *Ingersoll Chronicle* joked that 'when coming home from "lodge,"' the 'thickest thing [was] your tongue ... [and] the thinnest thing – [was] the story you tell your wife the next morning.'[16]

The fraternal orders clearly provided space for male bonding and socializing away from the domestic sphere. However, the barriers between this all-male sphere and the world of home and family were not impermeable. In Thorold, almost all the officers of the fraternal orders were married. These men may have joined the lodges in part to get away from the domestic sphere. However, by providing the opportunity to take out life insurance, the lodges reinforced the masculine role of respectable breadwinner – of the man who took his family responsibilities seriously in death as in life. In December 1886 the editor of the *Thorold Post* noted that the formation of a lodge of the Independent Foresters and the increase in membership in similar lodges was 'an indication of the wisdom and foresight of the people in moderate as well as affluent circumstances, in protecting their families by a membership that secures beyond a doubt a protection in case the breadwinner and protector is removed by the hand of death.'[17] The listing of widows who received benefits from the lodges, and sometimes even letters of thanks from the widows themselves, can be found in the pages of the local papers. This underlines the fact that while lodges were male bastions, they were not completely divorced from the sphere of home and family.[18]

The masculine ramparts were also breached at the wide array of mixed-gender social events organized by small-town lodges. The fraternal orders held dances and socials for members and their wives as well as organizing public socials, concerts, dances, and other entertainments to raise money for their branch of the order. The Thorold Oddfellows were particularly active in this regard. For example, in March 1884 they held a public concert, complete with singing, tableaux, and recitations; in June they organized a concert and a dance, and in November a piano recital and temperance lecture.[19]

The lodges also regularly ventured into another mixed-gender forum, one that was more commonly associated with women. Once a year, on a Sunday of particular relevance to their order, lodges such as the Oddfellows, Masons, Orange Lodge, and Ancient Order of United Workmen dressed up in their finery and marched in a body to a local Protestant church to worship in the company of the regular congregation. For example, on 14 October 1886 the *Campbellford Herald* reported: 'The members of the Oddfellow lodge, Campbellford, 48 in number, clothed in their regalia, marched in a body to the Methodist Church on Sunday morning last, and occupied the front seats in the centre of the building. Rev. Mr. Clarke, the pastor, preached an appropriate sermon on "Friendship."'[20] Many of the leaders of the lodges regularly attended Protestant churches. The officers of the Thorold lodges, most of whom were married, were as likely to be church members as any other Protestant married men, while in Campbellford the lodge officers had a higher than average church membership rate (see tables 25 and 26). Even so, many of the officers and members did not belong to a church. Some may have rarely seen the inside of one except during their lodge's annual service.

Religion was important to the fraternal orders. Most of them required potential members to believe in God and included various religious references in their ritual. Some, such as the Orange Order, incorporated explicitly Protestant prayers into their ritual. However, as Mark Carnes has shown, the rituals of many lodges were not explicitly Christian, and even those that were Christian reflected a theology very different from that of late-nineteenth-century liberal Protestantism. Many of the rituals included overtones of paganism, and there were references to a supreme being rather than to the Christian God. The references to God often focused on the stern, powerful, and supremely masculine God of the Old Testament, rather than the more feminized Christ of the late-nineteenth-century churches.[21]

While some form of religion was integral to the rituals of most fraternal orders, the annual collective march into church was about more than religious belief. It asserted the position of the fraternal orders in the respectable culture of the town, which was most clearly symbolized by the institution of the church and the dominant Protestant ideology. The sermons lodge members listened to on these special days sometimes praised their order. For example, in June 1885 the Ingersoll Masons heard a sermon by the Anglican clergyman, the Reverend Mr Hastings, which paid 'a high tribute to the noble order of Free Masons.' Ministers were particularly willing to praise the brotherly bonds valorized by the orders, for they were in keeping with Protestant teachings.[22] The ministers also celebrated the insurance provided by the lodges in religious terms. For example, when the Thorold branch of the Order of Canadian Home Circles joined the St Catharines branch in a special service at a Baptist church in St Catharines, they were told that providing for one's family was 'a divine command' and that life insurance was therefore part of God's plan. Similarly, when Archbishop Walsh visited Thorold's Catholic church for confirmation services, he commended the local branch of the Catholic Mutual Benefit Association as 'a means of prudent provision for the families of Catholic men.' The role of responsible breadwinner was clearly central to both Protestant and Catholic conceptions of true Christian manhood.[23]

Since the ideal Christian man's primary allegiance was to his home and family, ministers did have some doubts about lodge membership. In preaching to members of the Order of Canadian Home Circles, the St Catharines minister not only lauded their provision for insurance but noted that unlike most lodges, they were 'breaking through the old lines ... [and] have admitted their wives, recognizing that "it is not good for man to be alone" and it was no longer found necessary to be shut up in the lodge room away from the family circle, until all hours in the morning.' The fact that most lodges had not 'broken through the old lines' was unacceptable to many Protestant ministers. In a sermon to the Ingersoll Oddfellows, a local minister challenged them to admit 'mothers, sisters and daughters.'[24]

Support for a unified, Christian family life helps to explain the ministerial campaigns to bring women into the lodges. At the same time, of course, the ministers assumed that women would add a purer, more moral, and more Christian tone to the masculine and more secular space of the lodges. As Carnes has argued, the churchmen's concern that the lodges lured men away from the family circle was linked to a deeper fear that these masculine preserves would act as potent counter-attractions to the churches. In religious terms, the fraternal orders certainly offered a more masculine version of God than the churches did. Perhaps more importantly, membership in a fraternal order (which was transferable as one moved from town to town, and which assumed that fraternal lodge brothers would patronize one another in business and in supplying jobs) provided a compelling counter-community, offering many similar social attractions to the churches – but in an all-male environment. Ministers clearly feared losing both members and financial contributors to the lodges. For example, one paper argued that the ministers' opposition to the lodges was rooted in the fact that 'so many men attach themselves to the societies who care little about the churches. The money spent in doing the work of the societies might otherwise be applied to the payment of pew rent or the maintenance of church organizations.'[25] Even though the ministers may have felt secure about the allegiance of wives and mothers, they knew that it was husbands and fathers who controlled most of the family income.

The men's divided allegiance was apparent in death as in life. Emerson Peart's funeral mirrored that of other lodge members; the church service was at best only part of the ceremony, which concluded with the impressive graveside service of the fraternal order conducted by lodge officials. In the United States, the Protestant churches' hostility to the lodges dated back to the Anti-Masonry agitation of the 1820s and 1830s, in which evangelical churchmen linked the Masons to deism and secularism. Over the course of the century, many Protestant churchmen had remained concerned that the quasi-religious rituals of the 'secret societies' represented a threat to Christianity.[26] Such fears were still evident in certain late-nineteenth-century small town Ontario churches. An Ingersoll minister warned that the secrecy of these orders could have 'dangerous elements,' leading to 'Jesuitism and Nihilism.' The elders of Campbellford's Presbyterian church were similarly concerned; in June 1891 they discussed the 'propriety of using the church for special services for the use of secret societies.'[27] Other churches may have had similar discussions, yet the fraternal orders generally received permission to hold services in local churches. The overlap between lodge and church leadership no doubt played a role here, as did ministerial membership in many of the lodges.[28] Moreover, the ministers may have found it difficult to resist the opportunity to remind the lodges' many nonchurch members of their Christian responsibilities.

In their sermons to the fraternal lodges, the ministers often praised particular orders for requiring potential members to proclaim their belief in God. However, this was inadequate in itself. Lodge members were told that they should focus more of their attention on explicitly Christian spiritual concerns. Ingersoll's Anglican clergyman, while praising the charitable work of the Oddfellows, informed them that 'working just for humanity's sake is not good enough' and that they must do this work for Christ's sake, since 'to him is owed your eternity.' Similarly, the members of the Order of Canadian Home Circles were told that charitable work should not take the place of Jesus Christ. The minister stressed that 'while they were insuring their lives,' they should also 'insure their souls.'[29] Although lodge members listened politely to the various sermons, and although those who were church members probably gained inspiration from them, they do not appear to have had much impact on the beliefs and behaviour of the majority of lodge members. Special services were a part of lodge ritual. They asserted the lodges' respectability by demonstrating their links to the central arbiter of respectability in their communities. However, most fraternal brothers saw no need to take on the entire package of Christian behaviour promulgated by the Protestant churches. The meeting of the Grand Lodge of the Young Men's Protestant Benevolent Association in Ingersoll in February 1883 illustrates the place of special services in the larger framework of lodge practices. During this three-day meeting, the daylight hours were devoted to lodge business. On the first evening, the members attended a banquet at a local hotel, where they no doubt enjoyed much liquid refreshment with their dinner. The second evening was spent at a special service at the Methodist Episcopalian church. On the final evening, the lodge members enjoyed themselves at a grand ball, an activity which the Methodist minister they had heard the previous night would have found scarcely more pleasing than the drinking at the first night's banquet.

Of all the fraternal orders, the Orange Lodge had the most difficult relationship with the churches. Ministers were particularly likely to chide members of the order for their religious shortcomings. At their annual services, Orangemen were frequently reminded that 'to be a true Orangeman a man should be a Christian.' Thorold's Presbyterian minister, the Reverend Mr McDonald, urged the local Orangemen 'to enroll themselves as followers of King Jesus, as well as of King William.'[30] Since the Orangemen claimed to be the defenders of Protestantism, they were particularly open to such challenges. However, the frequent admonitions from the pulpits were linked less to the fact that much was expected of them as an explicitly Protestant body and more to the particular reluctance of Orangemen to become church members[31] (see tables 25 and 26). This reluctance was no doubt linked to the particularly high proportion of working-class members in the Orange Order (see tables 23 and 24).

The fact that Orangemen were more likely to be working class than the members of other lodges does not mean that the Orange Lodge was a bastion of working-class culture.[32] Clergymen, merchants, and other middle-class men joined the order, no doubt attracted by its loyalism and ultra-Protestantism. These men, like the many middle-class men who chose not to become Orangemen, would have recognized that the predominately working-class nature of the order did shape lodge culture. Those joining the Orange Lodge had to be ready to accept or at least tolerate a rougher culture than members of other lodges.[33]

A reluctance to take up church membership was part of this culture. This does not mean that Christianity was unimportant to Orangemen.[34] But most of them did not accept the demands of evangelical churchmen that they adopt a temperate, church-centred domestic lifestyle in order to be good Christians. They believed that they could fulfil their role as defenders of Protestantism by participating in the convivial masculine atmosphere of lodge meetings and Orange parades. Thorold's Orange Young Britons had no more interest in church membership than other young men of the time. Nonetheless, when Joseph Peart, a fraternal brother, died they consoled his mother with the hope that she would meet him in Heaven, while also noting, 'Our time is short here below, and we are taught that we should spend it in such a way as to meet with the approbation of the Grand Master on high.' The Orange Young Britons were familiar with the basic tenets of their faith, and they valued its pre-eminent religious symbols, though not always in a way guaranteed to please local ministers. For example, when organizing a series of games in August 1885, they announced that the prize for the tug of war was to be 'a bible valued at ten dollars.'[35]

For the Orangemen, the Bible was not just of theological importance. It was a symbol of Protestant religious freedom against Catholic tyranny. They may not have been willing to support their religion by attending church, but over the years they had often proved more than willing to defend it against 'papists' on the streets. Although incidents of Orange-Catholic violence had declined by the late nineteenth century, the order remained in the forefront of anti-Catholic agitation. Orangemen still pledged never to marry a Catholic and never to allow their children to be educated in the Roman Catholic faith. The religious bigotry of the Orange Order may have been stronger than that of other lodges, but ethnic orders such as the St George's Society and the St Andrew's Society also fostered ethnic as well as gender exclusion. As Newbury has noted, such traditions were not particularly positive ones for Ontario's emerging working class. While the fraternal orders, from the Masons to the Orange Lodge, may have taught working-class members the values of fraternity and mutuality, they also instilled less positive lessons. They taught that brotherhood included only men and that often it did not cross ethnic or religious boundaries.[36]

Men in Other Groups: Fire Companies, Militia, Bands, and Sports

While the various fraternal lodges provided the most popular male-only associational forums, there were many other organizations that gave small-town men the chance to enjoy homosocial leisure and associational life. As in the case of the fraternal orders, two masculine ideals coexisted in these associations: the responsible, respectable breadwinner and the rowdy rough. Class and age differences in membership determined which facet of masculinity was uppermost in each association – or at least which was allowed to be more visible and public. Again, the levels of roughness shaped the response of Protestant churchgoers, who saw themselves as the central arbiters of respectable behaviour in their communities, even if other townsfolk contested their definitions of what was and was not respectable.

The fire brigade was a popular option for many men. In small Ontario communities, these brigades were largely volunteer, though they received some payment from the municipal councils and were responsible to the councils. They were expected to respond to all fires, but since most communities still lacked waterworks and since some fire companies even lacked horses to pull their equipment to the fire, their success rate was not overly high. Working-class historians have identified the fire companies as an important element of rough working-class culture in larger communities.[37] This was also the case in Ingersoll, where the firemen were castigated for the same 'want of discipline and lack of respect for officers' that was common in larger cities. The property owners of the area were not willing to accept such traits in those they depended on to protect their property from fire, and in 1885 Ingersoll's municipal council went so far as to dismiss all the town's firemen and to hire only 'first class' men. A year later, however, the councillors were still complaining about the inefficiency of the local firemen.[38]

In Thorold, the firemen were considered more respectable, probably because middle-class men and – not coincidentally – regular churchgoers made up a significant minority of the members and officers of the fire company.[39] Even so, the Thorold firemen, like those in other communities, revelled in the opportunities available through involvement in the fire company to celebrate their masculinity apart from the spheres of home and church. They spent considerable time socializing together in their well-equipped and tastefully furnished fire hall. Fighting fires, of course, gave them the opportunity to demonstrate their masculine strength and bravery. But although this was no doubt satisfying, the firemen were at least equally interested in demonstrating their abilities in the frequent tournaments that brought together fire companies from across the province to compete at laying hose, drilling, and other firefighting skills.[40] The Thorold firemen had frequent battles with the municipal council over their need for new uniforms and a more elaborate engine – not necessarily so that they could do their jobs better but so that they would look better at these competitions. In the spring of 1883 a supporter of the firemen attacked the council for its refusal to pay for 'decent' uniforms. He said this would prevent the Thorold firemen from appearing at a St Catharines tournament, since they would not 'disgrace themselves and their town by appearing in their present shabby [uniforms].' A petition from Thorold citizens pressured the council into providing $200 for the uniforms, and at the St Catharines tournament the *Post* noted: 'Our firemen made a splendid appearance ... The new uniform of scarlet tunics, striped pants and shining helmets gave them a brilliant appearance ... They went to St. Kitts ... carrying bouquets of flowers and other evidence of the favour in which they are viewed by our townspeople.'[41]

The popular support for the firemen, as well as their support from the town council, was no doubt linked not only to their skill in extinguishing fires but to their ability to act as suitable representatives of the town at intercommunity events such as firemen's competitions. Small towns like Thorold had few institutions that could serve as the focus of local pride and community boosterism. The fire company was a significant vehicle for such sentiments. The opportunity to act as popular representatives of their community was no doubt a further incentive to men who were considering involvement in a fire company. For working-class men in particular, a fire company provided unprecedented public prominence as well as the glamour of fine uniforms and impressive machines. In the smaller towns, the opportunity to serve as the focus of community pride may have drawn in more 'respectable' middle-class men than was the case in larger communities, where fire companies were less central to community pride and civic boosterism.

Community pride and a desire to parade in an impressive uniform would also have been among the reasons that motivated young men to volunteer for the militia. Those who volunteered spent some time drilling in the local community and took twelve days every year or two to attend a regional military training camp. Although the militia helped to put down the Northwest Rebellion, its major role was as an 'aid to the civil power,' which included quelling Catholic-Protestant riots and protecting strikebreakers.[42] In the local community militia companies provided an additional all-male associational space as well as playing a role in the town's heterosocial life by sponsoring dances, concerts, and other social events.

In larger communities, involvement in the volunteer militia companies was a sign of social status or a route to increased status, and the volunteers were middle or upper class.[43] Given the more limited pool of volunteers in small towns, although the officers came from upper-middle-class backgrounds, the rank and file represented a broader social spectrum, though the need to take off twelve days to drill would obviously have discouraged many potential working-class volunteers.

The popularity of the local militia varied significantly. In both Ingersoll and Campbellford, the commanding officers appear to have had no difficulty recruiting volunteers, and the social events organized by the militia companies were well attended.[44] In 1885, Campbellford held a festive reception for its militiamen on their return from the Northwest Rebellion. It included an address at a Campbellford church and presentations from the church ladies, followed by an all-male dinner at one of the town's hotels.[45] In Thorold, however, the young men were reluctant to volunteer for the militia, even at the height of the patriotic fervour created by the rebellion. Social events put on by Thorold's militia were very poorly attended, in contrast to the popularity of similar events organized by the town's firemen and other voluntary associations. The role of the militia in quelling the canal workers' riots and the attitude of Thorold's large Catholic community to the rebellion probably explains this unpopularity.[46]

Even in towns where the militia companies were popular, the patriotism of the respectable community was tempered by a hostility to the rough culture of the annual military camps. In 1883 Mr Vosper, the editor of the *Campbellford Herald*, claimed that 'volunteer camping is at the present day very little better than a season of drunkenness for both officers and men.' When the local militia officer wrote to the *Herald* to defend his behaviour and that of his men, Vosper responded, 'At Kingston, Niagara and Cobourg we have seen commissioned and non-commissioned officers so beastly drunk as to be unfit for active duty.' Vosper went on to quote the *Cobourg World*, which decried the behaviour of volunteers at a camp that had recently been held in that town. The *World* argued that the volunteers would never behave so roughly in their own communities: 'The moment some men get away from home they seem to imagine they have a legal and moral right to indulge in excesses in which they do not indulge among their own friends.' The article concluded by blaming 'many a young man's first lapse from propriety' on camp life. Such concerns were widely shared by temperance supporters. The WCTU viewed the militia camps as a threat to the sobriety and respectability of young men, and campaigned to prohibit the selling of liquor at the camps.[47] Concern about the militia's drinking extended beyond the strict temperance community because the drinking was apparently both excessive and publicly so. As a result, it was much less acceptable than the drinking that accompanied so many lodge dinners. Young men thus received mixed messages about their involvement in the militia. Patriotism and a sense of local pride could create cross-class support for the militia in many communities. But for respectable

Christian small-town folk, the all-male hard-drinking culture of the militia camps challenged the values they held dear and, more particularly, threatened young men who were already perceived to be at risk.

Another all-male voluntary association with an ambivalent relationship to the respectable community was the local band. Most small towns had some form of band. In some cases it was an independent organization, while in others it was linked to one of the men's associations. For example, the Thorold band was affiliated with the Orange Young Britons, whereas in Ingersoll the band members were Oddfellows. Not surprisingly, the class make-up of the bands varied. In Thorold the band was almost exclusively working class; in Campbellford a mix of clerks, shoemakers, tinsmiths, and merchants all played together.[48]

In small towns the bands clearly viewed themselves as community institutions. They played at a wide range of events, which included temperance meetings, church strawberry socials, and dances and concerts sponsored by the various voluntary societies. They also organized their own social events, such as dances and theatrical performances, to raise money for new uniforms and instruments. In the summer, the Ingersoll and Thorold bands also put on a series of concerts. Unlike most local entertainments, the concerts were free and were thus available to the entire community. Newlyweds were sometimes favoured with a serenade from the band, and wealthier townsfolk might be similarly visited in the expectation that they would make a financial donation.[49]

The band's role as a community organization was reinforced by its involvement in intercommunity competitions. Like the firemen, the bandsmen not only provided a service to their community but acted as a vehicle of community pride and boosterism.[50] In return, a band would expect financial support – from the municipal council as well as from private individuals. The town councils were usually willing to come up with a grant, though the amount provided could vary widely. In 1888 Thorold's council granted the band $75 'to aid them in their endeavours to make their band one that will be a credit to the town.' The bands could also give a boost to a town's prosperity. When the Thorold municipal council reduced the band's grant, the local merchants petitioned that it be increased, since band concerts were good for business.[51] In some cases, a band's affiliation with other associations made it more difficult to get municipal funding. In Thorold, for instance, the Catholic councillors sometimes objected to funding the Orange Young Briton band since it was open only to Protestants.[52]

The Catholic councillors were not the only ones to object to Thorold's

Orange Young Briton band. Although the band played at various church socials and organized a few temperance entertainments, there was significant tension between the churchgoing community and the band, whose members were primarily single working-class men. The churchgoers complained that the band disregarded their concerns by holding concerts on prayer-meeting nights. 'An interested one' who wrote to the *Post* on this matter was clearly concerned not only that the band would disrupt church services but that its concerts would provide a more appealing alternative for many church members. The letter writer assumed that since the band was funded by the community, it should not disrupt church services in the community. The response from band members reveals that they did not view churchgoers as synonymous with the larger community. They refused to change the night of their concerts, arguing: 'The writer speaks of our band looking to the public for support. We may say, in reply to this, that we think it unnecessary to look to our good friends the church goers for any financial support ... We are unable to give credit to those who are so interested in their church affairs ... We circulated a subscription list for the purpose of purchasing new instruments, and we know who are our supporters.'[53]

This exchange suggests that the hegemony of respectable church-based Protestantism was far from complete in small-town Ontario. Church people tended to divide the community into rough and respectable, mainstream and 'other,' young men being most readily identified with rough activities. Some young men, at least the working-class young men of Thorold's band, also divided the community into churchgoers and nonchurchgoers, but from a rather different perspective. The churchgoers were denigrated for their narrow church-focused interests, whereas the other townsfolk were respected for their willingness to patronize broader community-based leisure initiatives.

Another ostensibly broad-based leisure activity – which had a closer but still somewhat ambivalent relationship with Protestant culture – was team sport. Unlike blood sports such as cockfighting, team sports were eminently respectable activities, but only for men and only in certainly contexts. Women who became involved in most sports were seen as freaks or oddities who were breaching the bounds of appropriate feminine behaviour. Men who played sports for money were suspect, and those who failed to abide by other 'rules of the game' (for instance, by betting or by playing games on Sunday) could be branded barbarians.[54]

As historians of sport have noted, by the late nineteenth century, involvement in amateur team sport was viewed as an integral part of the proper character development of young men. Team sports allowed them to develop the qualities of sportsmanship, competition, and team spirit that were considered so essential to definitions of true manhood. As a result, these sports were sanctioned and encouraged by middle-class opinion leaders, including Protestant ministers.[55] Sporting activities also provided young men with a 'rational,' organized, and supervised way of spending their leisure time, which, it was hoped, would keep them off the street corners, away from hotels, and away from the rough sports that were condemned by the respectable Christian community.[56] Those seeking to encourage young men's involvement in amateur sports formed clubs for lacrosse, football, cricket, baseball, curling, and so on. The particular sports played depended on the interests of the local enthusiasts and on their ethnic background. For example, cricket was most popular among English immigrants.

The ideal of the amateur sportsman, who never played for money but valued sport for its character-building nature, was clearly a middle-class one. Not surprisingly, the officers of local sports clubs were almost exclusively middle-class men, and many were church members. These men were eminently respectable Christian community leaders who sought, through sports clubs, to shape young men's characters in the ways advocated in the many sermons directed at the youths by local ministers – sermons that most young men were usually not there to hear. The club leaders especially hoped to shape the leisure time and ultimately the characters of middle-class young men, who made up the vast majority of players in these clubs and who were a major concern of the small-town Christian community (see tables 27 and 28).

At the same time, some Christians wanted to ensure that the young men would not take a good thing too far. For example, in December 1886, at Ingersoll's St Andrew's Church, the active churchman and lawyer J. Hale, who had been involved in organizing the lacrosse club, warned young men not to overindulge in sports, since 'when so abused they often draw to extremes and sap our very disposition ... for useful or remunerative employment.'[57] Christians could be ambivalent about sports for other reasons too. Many of the club leaders were also officers in local fraternal orders. Like the fraternal brothers, members of sports clubs sometimes indulged in activities that pushed at the bounds of respectable Protestant behaviour. In June 1884, Campbellford's middle-class-dominated cricket club was attacked in the local paper for indulging 'in beer drinking and using profane language.' In response, 'a member of the Campbellford Cricket Club' denied the charge of profanity and claimed that at the match he 'did not see the slightest excess in beer drinking.' He went on to suggest that the next time 'your very respectable and too sensitive and fastidious informant' attended a cricket match, he 'should provide himself with a glass case large enough for him to sit comfortably in ... so that he might not hear the profanity, and he might have that side of it next [to] the beer frosted, so that he would not see them drinking beer.'[58] Definitions of manly respectability were contested, and even the most middle-class sports clubs, like their counterparts among the fraternal orders, were part of a larger masculine leisure culture and as such accepted a certain level of manly roughness. This did not mesh completely with the evangelical Protestant ideals espoused by ministers and accepted by many female church members – but by fewer male ones.

The development of organized intertown league competition brought more clear-cut challenges to the respectability and character-building nature of small-town team sports. Nancy Bouchier has demonstrated that the eminently respectable 'games build character' focus of the small-town amateur sports clubs was undermined by the same small-town boosterism that supported the band and firemen's competitions. As middle-class sporting clubs, whose amateur ethic and often high fees had excluded most working-class players, came to focus on 'winning over playing the game,' professionalism became more acceptable. As a result, certain clubs welcomed working-class players, who were paid for their sporting skills. Christian advocates of rational, self-improving sports were very unhappy with this growing professionalism, which they associated with betting and increased rowdiness among larger and more working-class audiences.[59]

Not all sports moved in this direction. For a number of reasons, curling remained resolutely amateur. Unlike other sports, it mainly attracted married men.[60] These men were the solid core of the respectable community. Not only were they more likely to be middle class than members of other sports clubs, but they were also more likely to be church members.[61] While intercommunity competition was not irrelevant to these men, curling seemed untainted by the growing professionalism of other sports. A curling match, either with a neighbouring community or another local rink, was as much an excuse for a convivial oyster supper at a nearby hotel as it was an opportunity to defeat an opponent.[62] These matches and the oyster suppers provided respectable middle-class Christian men with one of their few opportunities to socialize in an environment that was not only all male but was almost exclusively middle class. The convivial dinners, complete with alcoholic toasts, paralleled those of the cross-class fraternal orders and the predominately working-class firemen, but the relatively high fees for club membership and perhaps the class-specific ethic of amateurism limited the membership of small-town curling clubs to the middle class and a few prosperous skilled workers who identified with this group.[63] As a result, curling clubs seem to have provided the closest thing to a business and professional men's social club that was available in small-town Ontario.

Class divisions remained relevant even in less formally organized sports. Bouchier has noted that in Ingersoll and Woodstock, although both middle- and working-class men enjoyed playing baseball during the summer months, the teams were formed along class lines and tended to play against teams of the same class. Colin Howell has found similar patterns in late-nineteenth-century Halifax.[64] In Thorold, teams from local factories often played against one another on Saturday afternoons. Thorold was too small, however, to sustain complete class segregation, and clerks occasionally played factory teams, as did the middle-class-dominated baseball club.[65]

The preference for playing with or against those of a similar class may have been based partly on the different hours of leisure time available to middle- and working-class men. However, these preferences also show that occupational and class identities remained significant beyond working hours.[66] The relevance of these identities clearly did not prevent cross-class mingling in the masculine worlds of the fraternal orders, the militia, or the fire company. Indeed, in small-towns, men from various classes were particularly likely to interact in a range of associations. This was not so prevalent in the larger cities where, although many fraternal lodges had a cross-class membership, organizations such as fire companies and the militia were more class-specific. However, even in small communities the class-specific ethic of amateurism kept sports clubs predominantly middle class, except where small-town boosterism 'corrupted' the amateur ethic. Even in playing less formally organized baseball games, middle- and working-class men preferred to exercise their shared interest in the sport in separate forums, thus reminding us that even in small communities class identities remained relevant.

Class also played a role in defining whether a particular leisure pursuit was acceptable in the larger community. Pastimes such as drinking – which at cross-class lodge dinners or middle-class cricket club matches may have caused a few raised eyebrows (particularly female evangelical Protestant ones) – resulted in much more large-scale public censure when they went on at the Orange Parade or at rowdy working-class baseball games. Despite such class differences, masculinity was more central than class in defining the leisure world of late-nineteenth-century small-town Ontario. Men of all classes had far more opportunities to engage in organized leisure than women did. Many of the activities that have been identified by labour historians as part of a working-class leisure culture were, at least in the small-town context, cross-class male activities. Even activities that were largely working class did not define working-class culture; rather, they were options available only to working-class men.[67]

Class may have made a difference in the level of decorum expected at male leisure events, but the male associational world had the flexibility to incorporate both the rough and the respectable elements of masculinity within it. The middle-class Masons could indulge in a few rowdy toasts – behind closed doors – and the members of the Orange Order could assert their respectability as upright manly defenders of Protestantism. At both ends of the male associational continuum, there were certain direct ties to the values of home and church – as well as many more ambiguous and contradictory associations with these more feminized worlds.

Self-Improvement and the Improvement of Others

One largely masculine institution – the Mechanics' Institute – was particularly congruent with the values preached by the Protestant churches. Many Mechanics' Institute officers also sat on the executives of local sports clubs. In both capacities, these men saw themselves as providing opportunities for young men to make something of themselves, as the self-improving ethic of the age demanded. Young men could improve their moral character on the local playing fields and could accumulate intellectual capital in the Mechanics' Institute library.

In Campbellford, the officials of the Mechanics' Institute were described as 'men whose ability has placed them in the highest business, professional and civic position in the village.'[68] The same could be said of the men on the executive of Thorold's Mechanics' Institute. Most of these men were also regular churchgoers.[69] Links to the churches were reinforced by the roles played by local clergy. In Campbellford, the Baptist minister was the driving force behind the founding of the Mechanics' Institute, and two other clergymen sat on its board of directors. As part of an effort to revive interest in Thorold's Mechanics' Institute, all the town's ministers were made honorary members. In addition, it was agreed that 'all lists of new books to be purchased should be submitted to the different ministers, to receive suggestions about culling or adding.'[70] While Protestant ministers supported sports – if played in an appropriately character-building, nonprofessional way, and not on Sundays – the path to self-improvement offered by the Mechanics' Institute was particularly congruent with the Protestant ethic of hard work and self-improvement that the ministers preached. As already noted, most young men largely ignored such sermons, if they heard them at all. Not surprisingly, they were equally unlikely to seek self-improvement in the Mechanics' Institutes.

Scholars have recognized that these institutes rarely served the group – mechanics – for which they were originally intended.[71] The contemporary newspaper editors and Mechanics' Institute officials also noted the absence of workers, but they were more concerned by the fact that young men of any class were reluctant to spend their evenings improving their minds at the institute's library. An analysis of those joining Thorold's Mechanics' Institute reveals the accuracy of such concerns. Not only were the vast majority of new members middle class, but almost all (95 per cent) were married or widowed men.[72]

Young men were willing to get involved in 'character-building' sports because sports were exciting and fun. They were far less willing to spend their free time in 'musty reading rooms' improving their minds. As the editor of the *Ingersoll Chronicle* noted, 'Those persons who expect that the young men of the town are going to tie themselves down to a paper or book every night of their lives with no recreation, after working all day, may just as well give up the idea.'[73]

Although the discussion about Mechanics' Institutes centred around young men, women were also eligible to use the institute's library. It seems that not many of them made use of this opportunity. Women were, however, actively involved in another form of organized intellectual self-improvement – the local literary society. In these societies, people had the chance to read and discuss works of literature and to hear members of the group give papers on various literary topics. Most literary societies were fairly eclectic in their tastes, although some, like Thorold's Dickens Club, focused on a particular author. In small-town Ontario, most of these societies were not particularly long lasting, but the demise of one generally saw the rise of another. While a few such societies were for men only, most admitted both sexes. As well as offering intellectual self-improvement, they gave women a space in which to socialize with men and with each other beyond home and church. The small number of members who could be identified make it difficult to generalize about involvement in these societies. However, existing information suggests that, like the temperance societies, these associations attracted primarily single women and married men.[74]

Once again, the young men revealed their lack of enthusiasm for intellectual self-improvement. While working-class married men also were largely absent, half of the women involved came from working-class homes, most being the daughters of skilled workers.[75] Since the many cross-class or working-class associational avenues available to their brothers were closed to them, it is not surprising that some young women from more prosperous working-class homes were willing to participate in this more middle-class cultural world of intellectual self-improvement that provided some space for them.

Men, Women, and Rinks

Were there small-town leisure activities available to women beyond the limited and ultra-respectable space of the churches and literary and temperance societies? Team sports were for men only, since the character to be developed through these sports was a competitive yet 'sportsman-like' masculine one. There was, however, some space for women in a few non-team sports, particularly ice skating and roller skating. Recreational skating was not competitive, and unlike swimming, which was largely the preserve of boys and young men (who were frequently castigated for swimming naked in the rivers and canals), skaters were always fully and modestly clothed.

In small-town Ontario skating rinks were often the only existing sports facility. Most team sports could be played in the neighbouring fields, but skating rinks involved some kind of a structure, which in larger communities such as Ingersoll was often roofed and contained separate dressing rooms. While municipal councils could occasionally, after long debate, be persuaded to purchase land for a town park, they were certainly not willing to move any further into the recreation business. As a result, rinks were generally private ventures. In some communities, including Campbellford, the ice rink was owned by a single local businessmen, who entered into the venture to make a profit. In other communities, including Ingersoll and Thorold, the rinks were owned and managed by a joint stock company of respectable churchgoing middle-class male citizens.[76] These men certainly hoped to see some return on their investment. In urging more townspeople to become shareholders in the Thorold rink, the editor of the *Post* nevertheless implied that they should not do so primarily to make money. Since the rink, he said, 'had offered a source of innocent amusement' it had 'proven a first class antidote to barroom and corner loafing [and] as such is deserving of the patronage of the community at large.'[77] Although ice skating may not have been as character building as team sports, it was advocated as a 'rational recreation' that drew young men away from rougher activities. This, at any rate, was the view of the kind of middle-class churchgoing married men (and in many cases the same men) who organized sports clubs for young men and ran the Mechanics' Institutes.

It is not surprising, then, that ice skaters were subject to a series of rules intended to keep the rinks respectable and orderly. The rules were particularly in evidence at the carnivals, or masquerades, held monthly or even more frequently during the winter. In Thorold potential masqueraders were informed: 'The Committee of Management desire to say that they are determined to suppress anything in the way of disorderly or rough conduct at the Rink, and for that object a Policeman will be always in attendance on carnival nights.' Clearly, some townspeople had in the past hidden behind carnival disguises to engage in 'disorderly' conduct, which perhaps included the type of mockery of established figures that was common at other nineteenth-century masquerade events.[78] However, the prevalence of snowflakes, gypsies, and princesses at small-town ice carnivals suggests that the strict rules ensured that these events remained the innocent fancy-dress balls on ice that they were intended to be. The rules also assured anxious parents that young women could safely attend both carnivals and the more regular skating evenings on the rink. These events provided another respectable space for courtship, as well as being among the few sanctioned opportunities women had to partake in physical exercise and recreation.

Most of these young women would have been middle class, given the cost of ice skating. Season tickets to the rink at a price of $4.00 for a family and $2.50 for an individual would have been prohibitive for most workers at a time when the average labourer's wage was dollar a day.[79] Many, however, could probably have afforded an occasional ten or fifteen cents to attend a regular skating evening or a carnival, though the availability of free ice on the local ponds and rivers probably meant that working-class youth were only attracted to the rinks by the carnivals.

Working-class young people were, however, drawn to a new kind of

rink – the roller rink – which began to appear in small Ontario towns in
the early to mid-1880s. The roller-skating 'craze,' as it was known by
sceptical small-town editors, was not underwritten by the proponents of
rational recreation but was a strictly commercial venture. In some towns
the local businessmen built roller rinks or adapted existing structures,
while in others this was done by out-of-town businessmen who owned
rinks in a number of communities.[80]

Roller rinks attracted both middle- and working-class youth. Admission prices varied from ten to fifteen cents, including the rental of skates,
and this brought them within the reach of many working-class families.
Advertisements for Thorold's main roller rink featured illustrations of
an obviously working-class couple. While ice rinks had provided an
occasional display of fancy skating, roller rink owners offered an array
of attractions. In addition to masquerade carnivals, they regularly
advertised the roller-skating exploits of a variety of touring performers.
These performances were not for elite audiences but had a broad appeal,
usually attracting large crowds. The performers included Miss Jessie
Wartz, 'the celebrated child skater'; Miss Melrose and Roziskey, who
could 'contort himself into all manner of positions'; and Professor J.F.
Malone, 'King of the Wheels,' who gave an exhibition of 'fancy and trick
skating.' There were also performers who skated on stilts, jumped over
chairs, and exhibited a variety of other exploits. Such performances
would have attracted both men and women, whereas another attraction,
the exhibition roller-skating races, may have appealed primarily to
men.[81]

These exhibitions of roller-skating speed and virtuosity brought in the
crowds, but for small-town youth the opportunity to go skating oneself,
especially with a favourite female or male companion, was also popular.
Various stories and satirical poems in the papers reveal that the rinks
provided a space for heterosexual courtship. For some townsfolk, they
may even have temporarily eclipsed the churches and church social
events, as suggested by the following poem, which was published in the
Thorold Post at the height of the roller-skating fever:

'Are you a member of church?'
He asked, on skates, beside her,
'Oh, yes,' she slipped, 'I used to be
I'm now a poor back-slider.'[82]

Although the roller rinks provided a space for courtship, it was certainly a supervised space. The rinks had as many rules prohibiting 'disorderly' or unrespectable behaviour as the ice-skating rinks. The effectiveness of these rules can be gauged from the fact that despite their more mixed-class clientele, the roller-skating rinks were generally judged acceptable by respectable small-town middle-class Christians. The editor of the *Petrolia Advertiser* was most impressed with roller skating, arguing that 'it is upheld by clergymen as an innocent recreation which has a tendency to keep our young men from disreputable resorts and bring them under the refining influences of young ladies without the objectionable features of the ball room.'[83] Clergymen and other opinion leaders in the larger cities were not so impressed with the moral qualities of the rinks. For example, ministers in Rochester, New York, denounced them as 'nurseries of hell,' while another prominent big-city minister attacked them for encouraging flirtation.[84]

This divergence in attitudes may be explained by the different focus of social concern between cities and small towns. In the smaller communities, young men were the primary problem, so any activity that drew them out of the bar rooms could only be a good thing. In these communities, young women generally lived at home. As Karen Dubinsky has shown, living at home in small-town Ontario was no guarantee of sexual innocence, but contemporary discourse ignored such realities. Young women who lived under the supervision of family and community were considered safe and pure; they were not viewed as a moral problem. Indeed, it was believed that they could help to 'elevate' young men. In cities, however, large numbers of young women lived away from their families and thus were the target of considerable concern over their moral status.[85] Commercial entertainments such as roller rinks, which allowed young people of both sexes to mix freely, were threatening to middle-class Christian moralizers, since in the big-city context even roller skating could raise the spectre of unregulated sexuality.

Contested Leisure: Theatre and Dance

While ice and roller skating were commonly accepted recreations among all strata and denominations in the small towns, this was much less true of two other popular forms of recreation: theatre and dancing. These activities were regularly attacked from the pulpits of evangelical Protestant churches. For example, in April 1883 the Reverend Mr McDonald of Thorold's Presbyterian church preached on the subject of 'questionable amusements,' denouncing both theatregoing and dancing 'for what they lead to.' The fact that such sermons were considered necessary suggests that many church members did indulge in both theatre and dance. These activities were certainly popular with the majority of small-town dwellers who were not involved in the evangelical churches.[86]

Not all theatrical offerings were equally popular. Amateur dramatic societies, often organized through the local Catholic or Anglican church, put on occasional performances of uneven quality, which were often patronized at least in part because of loyalty to the family members or friends who were in the cast or because of the worthiness of the cause for which the performance was being held. In addition to the various amateur endeavours, small-town Ontarians were exposed to the efforts of a variety of travelling troupes with a wide range of skill and professionalism. Some were brought to town by local associations – by the firemen, perhaps, or a fraternal order as a part of a fund-raising event. Other troupes, such as the Emma Wells Co. and the Josie Mills Co., simply toured the smaller communities of the province, performing for a few days or sometimes for a week in the local hall.[87] Admission prices could range from ten to fifteen cents for seats in the gallery or the back of the hall to thirty-five cents or more for reserved seats. Many of the working-class townsfolk purchased theatre tickets despite the disapproval of such middle-class critics as the editor of the *Campbellford Herald*, who was fond of noting that the theatre companies 'carried away quite a number of dollars ... which should have been given to merchants to meet overdue grocery and clothing accounts.'[88]

One of the favourite forms of theatre was melodrama. This genre, which included plays such as the ever-popular *Uncle Tom's Cabin*, echoed dominant Christian moral values. As Doris O'Dell has noted, 'Melodrama was built upon faith in a universe in which moral laws ruled. After trials and tribulations for the good characters, this ideal was achieved with a happy ending in which justice won over chance and evil, and the hand of providence was clearly seen.'[89] Even theatre with a moral message remained suspect to most ministers. However, when *Hazel Kirke*, a popular melodrama, was performed in Ingersoll, it was advertised as 'endorsed by the ministry.' This endorsement, whether accurate or not, doubtless soothed the consciences of theatregoing church members. The performance was also described as 'pure and refined in sentiment,' as were many that lacked ministerial endorsement. Such comments signalled that the performance was considered suitable for women. While not all shows were so pure that 'a vestal could go through the whole programme untainted,' women did attend shows advertised as suitable family entertainment.[90]

While melodrama, with its morally elevating message, was generally judged the most suitable form of theatre, women also attended many of the variety shows that passed through the community. For example, the Iroquois Indian Medicine Company, which visited Thorold in December 1890, provided a variety show that included rifle shooting, 'sketches ... of Indian life in the wilds, and vocal and instrumental music.' As the *Thorold Post* noted, 'There was a fair sprinkling of ladies in the audience and not the slightest thing on the platform to prove offensive.' On the other hand, the Maud Revelle Speciality Show, which 'sang and danced and joked in the [Campbellford] Music Hall' in January 1886, was judged 'not only not refined, but unworthy of any respectable person's attendance.'[91]

Another form of entertainment often deemed morally suspect was the minstrel show, which featured black performers or white men dressed up as blacks. These shows featured singing, dancing, and a racist form of humour that was often somewhat risqué. It was for the latter not the former reason that 'low minstrelsy' was often denounced. Some minstrel shows, particularly those produced by local amateurs, were pronounced suitable family entertainment. However, even in this case, the fact that the shows were particularly popular among working-class audiences limited their appeal among the self-proclaimed elite. For example, in describing an amateur concert put on by the Thorold Catholic Mutual Benefit Association, the *Post* noted that in the minstrel show section of the performance the 'humor was very good, but no doubt the more intellectual part of the audience got tired of it before the back seats.' Similarly, the Ingersoll elite was mortified that their community had 'the name of preferring Christy Minstrels to Prima Donnas.'[92] This elite was no happier with a popular form of entertainment that closely resembled modern circuses. In 1886 Campbellford was visited by Lewis and Wardrobe's Hippolympian, which performed 'songs and choruses, acrobatic and gymnastic feats, contortions, etc.' The *Herald* reported that 'they form themselves into a brass band and play upon the streets wherever they go.'[93]

Small-town newspaper editors were also very unhappy with the theatregoing behaviour of some sections of the audience. At most Thorold performances, young men apparently sat at the back of the hall heckling the entertainers and shouting and whistling throughout the show.[94] These young men were part of the masculine youth culture that was visible on the street corners and in the hotels. The *Thorold Post* maintained that their heckling was a particularly acute problem in the town, but historians have demonstrated that working-class theatregoers in the larger cities had the same tradition of exhibiting an active and vocal response to theatrical performances.[95]

Roughs also made their presence felt at local dances – the leisure pursuit that was attacked even more vigorously from evangelical pulpits than theatregoing but was enjoyed nonetheless by many who considered themselves respectable. Middle-class townsfolk were not usually subjected to the 'uncivilized' behaviour of roughs at their dances because, unlike theatre, which often attracted a mixed-class audience, dances were generally segregated along class lines. Certainly, in Thorold, predominantly working-class organizations such as the band or the firemen occasionally organized 'hops,' as they were known, which were open to all who had the price of admission. Some of those attending did not behave up to middle-class standards. A band boys' hop in Merritton was considered unusual by the *Post* because 'there was a lack of the rough element so frequently seen at public dances.'[96] In Thorold, Ingersoll, and other communities, middle- and upper-middle-class youth avoided the working-class rough element entirely by organizing themselves into 'assembly clubs' and 'young men's clubs' and holding dances by invitation only.[97]

Community Leisure? Public Holidays

While even in small communities many leisure pursuits were divided by class, gender or age, it was traditionally assumed that the public holidays – Victoria Day, Dominion Day, and the civic holiday in August – provided an opportunity for a community celebration. This may have been true in earlier days if the nostalgic comments of newspaper editors can be trusted,[98] but by the 1880s and 1890s, at least in small communities such as Thorold and Campbellford, many holidays passed by without the staging of a celebration at all. The editor of the *Thorold Post* noted just before Victoria Day 1891, as he often did on public holidays, that 'the average Thoroldite will, as usual hie himself out of town on Monday next, to spend his time and his spare shekels in enjoying himself.'[99]

The improved transportation networks – and in particular the cheap excursions offered by the railways on public holidays – made it possible for most small-town people to seek entertainment out of town on these days. They did not leave en masse to seek the public holiday festivities in a nearby town; rather, they scattered to different destinations and pursuits. The choices made by Thoroldites on Victoria Day 1891 and on the civic holiday in 1893 give some sense of this diversity. On Victoria Day 1891 many went to Niagara Falls to cheer on the Thorold firemen at the firemen's tournament there. In 1891 and 1893 a number of other excursions were also available – to Buffalo, Toronto, or Queenston. Other Thoroldites went to Welland to watch a cricket game or to St Catharines to see lacrosse, while a more religiously minded minority went to hear a famous preacher at the Grimsby campgrounds. Some enjoyed more informal activities, as the *Post* noted: 'The primitive picnic, with its attendant weak lemonade and kissing games, is of course, sure to be the way a number of the young folks will celebrate ... A certain number of their elders will find solace from the cares of life by a day at Port Dalhousie, accompanied by a lunch basket and a fishing rod ... The young man, with a flash horse and buggy, will enjoy a long spin over the splendid condition country roads in company with his sister, or some other fellow's sister.'[100]

Class, gender, and age, as well as budget and personal taste clearly shaped the leisure choices made on public holidays, just as they did throughout the year. Class certainly limited leisure options. Whereas many middle-class Ontarians took two- or three-week summer vacations, the public holidays were usually the only days off granted to employed working-class men and women, apart from Christmas and Good Friday. Some did not even have all three days off. While Victoria Day and Dominion Day were regularly granted as holidays to all, some factories continued to operate on the August civic holiday. Even on Victoria Day and Dominion Day, many people lacked the material resources for a trip out of town. So although employed skilled workers could take advantage of the cheap excursions, many of the unskilled workers probably could not afford to leave town.[101]

These workers and their families were no doubt pleased when holiday events were organized in the local community. However, the events were not organized primarily for their benefit. Even though middle-class townsfolk were less interested than formerly in organizing and participating in community-wide celebrations, preferring to enjoy the holidays in more personal and private ways,[102] pragmatism could sometimes cause them to organize local celebrations. For instance, when Thoroldites went off seeking amusement in other towns, the *Post*'s constant refrain was that they would be spending money elsewhere rather than at home. The holding of the Thorold civic holiday in 1892 provides the clearest example of local efforts to avoid this danger. Thorold was economically hard pressed in the early 1890s, and the committee of businessmen who organized the event clearly hoped, as the editor of the *Post* put it, that the celebration would 'bring people to Thorold, money to merchants and advertise the town to outsiders.'[103]

While it was acceptable to organize public holidays to benefit the business community as a group, this was much less true of celebrations organized for individual profit. In 1884, when Mr Little, the Campbellford merchant who owned the ice rink, was in charge of the Victoria Day celebrations, there was general dissatisfaction with his efforts. He charged fifteen cents instead of the customary ten for the games; the sports started late, and there were accusations that he was much more interested in taking money in from gate receipts than in giving it out in prizes for sports events. Little claimed credit for getting 'young men to celebrate their Queen's Birthday,' arguing that he had in fact provided all the expected recreations and that 'the only thing that I failed to do was make the money that a man should have made.'[104] While most nineteenth-century Ontarians would not dispute that men had a right to make money, some ambivalence clearly remained over whether public holidays, supposedly a symbol of patriotism and community spirit, should be overtly commercialized.

In most communities the holidays were arranged by committees of prominent men or by voluntary organizations such as the firemen or the band. The Ingersoll firemen claimed that they organized such events not to make money but to provide entertainment for all and, of course, to 'boost' the town. Boosterism was also a primary motivation of the middle-class Ingersoll Amateur Athletic Association, which organized the town's Dominion Day celebrations in the late 1880s.[105]

The central events of public holiday celebrations were clearly designed to boost the community, large processions being particularly popular. The civic holiday parade organized by Thorold's firemen in 1885 included a trades procession that was 'said to be even bigger than a similar one in Hamilton of the previous year.'[106] The workers who took part in the processions marched very much as employees of a particular business and were often portrayed performing workday tasks for a local employer. For example, the 1885 procession included a wagon representing a local blacksmith's shop, with workers shoeing horses, and a float on which workers operated sewing machines.[107] In these processions the workers advertised their community's manufacturing strength, not their own class power.

Celebrations organized by the band or the firemen usually included a competition with visiting bands or fire companies, designed to demonstrate local skill and glory. Sport was increasingly featured as well, a central attraction being a game between a local sports club and a competitor. Nancy Bouchier has argued that these matches, as well as explicitly amateur track-and-field events, often replaced more traditional sports such as three-legged races, sack races, chasing greased pigs, and tugs of war. The latter events provided more opportunity for participation by community members, but middle-class proponents of rational recreation viewed chasing greased pigs and other such events as frivolous and potentially disorderly.[108] Some organizations, notable Ingersoll's middle-class Amateur Athletic Association, banished these activities, replacing them with more character-building 'improving' sports events, but most organizers of public holiday celebrations were not interested in transforming leisure practices.

The more working-class fire companies continued to arrange celebrations in both Thorold and Ingersoll that included sack races, tugs of war, and other traditional sports. The firemen also demonstrated some sensitivity to the range of leisure interests in the community. The midday processions of workers, businessmen, and municipal leaders reflected only the public – and exclusively male – face of these communities,[109] and the afternoon sports events would also have appealed primarily to men, though of all classes; but the evening events included torchlit processions, fireworks, and dances, and thus attracted working-class people of both sexes. Since these evening entertainments would have had less appeal to serious churchgoers, the firemen occasionally tried to provide for their tastes with festivals or concerts.[110] Thus, even public holidays, which were intended to demonstrate a shared sense of community, reveal the continued fracturing of leisure interests by class, gender, and religious affiliation.

The failure of middle-class reformers to transform public holidays into rational and orderly events is seen most clearly in the continuing reports of drunkenness on these days. At Thorold's civic holiday in 1892 (one of the few in that community organized by middle-class reformers) the Sons of Temperance provided a Temperance Lunch Room that served 'hot tea, hot coffee, sandwiches and pure lemonade.' Despite a large turnout for the holiday, the Sons of Temperance sadly reported that at their lunch room 'trade was not up to their expectations.' On the other hand, the hotels, which provided the largest subscriptions towards the organization of the holiday, did very well.[111]

Social commentators in late-nineteenth-century Ontario were concerned that the lack of excitement in small towns and rural areas was fuelling the move of young people to the bright lights of the city. However, there was a wide range of leisure activities in small communities. Indeed, the preceding discussion may suggest an almost bewildering and infinitely fragmented array of such activities. A closer look reveals some clear patterns. Remember the unfortunate Peart family, which sustained the loss of father and son in one week. The mother and daughter were almost invisible in the local records, appearing only in the church and temperance society membership rolls. And these women were more active than many others. Despite all the associational options of small-town Ontario, most were not available to everyone. Many leisure activities were segregated by gender and were open only to men.

Women such as the Pearts were no doubt involved in home-based leisure activities that cannot be traced in the available sources, whereas for middle-class women there are at least newspaper accounts to indicate that visiting friends and family was a frequent way of breaking up the monotony of home life.[112] However, beyond church, temperance lodges, and a few literary societies, the rich associational life of small-town Ontario was closed to women of all classes. Indeed, since female participation in the temperance lodges and literary societies seems to have been confined largely to single women, the churches provided virtually the only organized activities available to married women in these communities. Women's limited options underline the power of men in late-nineteenth-century Ontario society. As John Tosh has noted, 'All-male associations ... embody men's privileged access to the public sphere, while simultaneously reinforcing women's confinement to household and neighbourhood.'[113]

In small-town Ontario both single and married men took advantage of their privilege to join a range of associations, from the Masons to the band. Involvement in these masculine associations was cross-cut by class. Merchants and professionals who belonged to the Masons, the Mechanics' Institute, and the curling club would have considered themselves superior to many of the more working-class 'boys' in the band, the fire company, and the Orange Order. However, small-town realities made it difficult to fashion a class-specific associational life. Both middle- and working-class men could be found in the Masonic temple and the fire hall, while cross-class patterns were most clear in organizations of intermediate social status such as the Oddfellows and the temperance lodges.

While class divisions did in part shape male associational life, these divisions were mediated by a shared masculine leisure world. The social activities that had been enjoyed by Emerson Peart in the mixed-class Ancient Order of United Workmen would not have looked very different from those his son Joseph participated in through the more working-class Orange Young Briton Band. Both men may have seen themselves as respectable members of the community, as did many other men, including the firemen and sportsmen who gloried in the opportunities available to them to boost their town through parades and competitions. However, definitions of respectability varied. The masculine associational world had at best an ambivalent relationship to the more feminized churchgoing culture, which viewed itself as the epitome of respectability in these towns. Many male associational members were of course active churchgoers, and some elements of male associational life did fit nicely with the dominant Protestant values – for instance, fraternal attendance at church services, insurance provision for families, and the masculine self-improvement inculcated in the sports clubs. However, within both the rowdiest and the most refined male associations, some elements of two contrasting ideals of manhood coexisted – the ideal of the respectable family man and the rough. Their coexistence points to the fact that contemporary concepts of masculinity had greater flexibility than concepts of femininity. But this also meant that even the more middle-class fraternal orders and sports clubs could be rendered at least slightly suspect by their acceptance of convivial drinking, though they were not subject to the same censure as the rougher working-class Orange Order and the youthful militia.

Not only were public leisure activities largely dominated by men, but there were few opportunities for mixed-gender recreation. However, both middle- and working-class single women sought fun, exercise, and male companionship on the rinks. The roller rinks were an early example of what was to become a more commercialized leisure world that would offer young women far more options than the largely male associational life of small-town Ontario. Meanwhile, serious evangelical young women had few options beyond the rinks. But many other young women, who also listened to strictures against dance and theatre on Sundays, participated in these activities during the week, as did Anglican and Catholic women, who did not have to deal with religious scruples in these matters. While dancing brought men and women together, it separated people by class; working-class couples 'tripped the light fantastic' at public hops, while their middle-class counterparts attended more elaborate and exclusive assembly dances.

Public holidays, which on the surface presented the public face of a united community celebration, also reflected class and gender differences in leisure interests, as well as less than successful efforts to mold the community into the respectable image that was sought by Protestant reformers and community boosters. The way townsfolk scattered in all directions on most public holidays reveals the limitations of small-town Protestant hegemony. Although a minority of the people chose to travel to hear a famous preacher, most had other interests, which ranged from watching a firemen's exhibition in a nearby town to chasing a greased pig at a neighbouring celebration.

6

The Salvation Army and the Knights of Labor: Religion and Working-Class Culture

In 1884 the Salvation Army marched on Thorold. In the first few months after their arrival, they preached to crowded houses at the Oddfellows Hall. As was the case in towns and cities across Ontario, most of the men and women who flocked to the Salvation Army's tumultuous all-night meetings and rowdy parades were working class. One of the many local converts was a labourer, George Doherty, who played a cornet in the Salvation Army band as it marched through the streets of Thorold. For Doherty, as for many other Thorold converts, involvement in the Salvation Army was fairly brief. Two years later, he and more than three hundred other Thoroldites joined a very different working-class movement, the Knights of Labor. When Doherty died in the spring of 1887, all three assemblies of the local Knights turned out to march in his funeral cortege. They were accompanied by the Thorold fire company, to which Doherty had also belonged. The local papers reported that Doherty had been popular and 'highly esteemed by all his brethren of both societies.'[1]

The firemen, the Knights of Labor, and the Salvation Army were all predominantly working-class organizations. For George Doherty and many other working-class Ontarians, was there any difference between joining the local fire company and the Salvation Army or the Knights of Labor? The Salvation Army and the Knights of Labor did differ from other largely working-class associations examined thus far. Both admitted women as well as men, thus avoiding an exclusively masculine focus. They were not part of the masculine associational world, though the Knights did have links to this world. Both movements were, however, defined far more centrally by class than by gender. Both the Knights of Labor, a major labor organization, and the Salvation Army, which in this period was an exclusively revivalistic movement, were mass working-class movements, which over the course of the 1880s drew support from working-class Ontarians in small towns and large cities across the province.

From what we have seen thus far, working-class identity in small-town Ontario was fragmented, being cross-cut by a range of other identities, including those of gender, age, religion, ethnicity, and community. These identities were manifested and reinforced in the fraternal orders, the churches, the hotels, the roller rinks, and a range of other public and more private spaces. Working-class identity may have been cross-cut by other identities, but that does not mean that it did not exist. At certain times it could take centre stage, and for many Ontario workers the mid-1880s was such a time, and the Salvation Army and Knights of Labor were the institutions through which it was made manifest. However, even in a period when working-class identity came to the fore, the workers did not shed the values of the larger culture in which they remained embedded. In *Dreaming of What Might Be,* Greg Kealey and Bryan Palmer's major study of the Knights of Labor in Ontario, the authors argue that the Knights provided Ontario workers, if only fleetingly, with a distinct 'movement culture,' which drew on working-class values and beliefs.[2] Both the Knights and the Salvation Army did indeed reflect the existence of distinct working-class cultural beliefs, but they also drew on dominant practices and values. In this chapter, the complex relationship between working-class and dominant values will be examined in relation to issues of leisure, masculinity, and, most particularly, Christianity. The links between religion and the Knights of Labor have been largely ignored by students of the order, and the Salvation Army has received little attention of any kind from Canadian historians.

This chapter will be followed by a chapter that looks more closely at working-class women and at the nature and meaning of femininity in the Salvation Army. The fact that the Knights and the Army were less locally rooted than most organizations studied thus far, and that both were working class in nature, means that they tended to leave few traces at the local level. In order to gain as full an understanding of them as possible, the scope of both chapters therefore extends beyond Ingersoll, Thorold, and Campbellford. While the small-town experience remains the primary focus, we shall follow the Knights and the Army into the large centres as well as the smaller communities of Ontario.

The Army and the Knights: Origins and Membership

The Salvation Army was founded in London, England, in 1878 by Catherine Booth and her husband William Booth, a former Methodist preacher.[3] The Booths sought to reach the unchurched poor and were willing to use a variety of unconventional methods to do so. A key method was the adoption of military trappings and military organization, including a firmly hierarchical structure. Supreme power was vested in William Booth, who as general commanded an 'army,' which by the 1880s had spread around the world. The Salvation Army's military style extended to brass bands and uniforms as well as a distinctive vocabulary, in which prayer services were called 'knee drills' and saying 'Amen' was known as 'firing a volley.' Those who joined the movement after conversion were known as soldiers. Preachers were called officers, and congregations were corps. In the 1880s, although the British Salvation Army had already entered into social work, the Canadian Salvation Army was very different from the present-day 'Sally Ann' in that it remained almost exclusively a revivalistic movement.[4]

The origins of the Knights of Labor are better known. This organization, which combined the effort to improve workers' conditions at the local level with a broader critique of industrial capitalist society, was founded in 1869 in Philadelphia. Within the Knights, workers were organized into local assemblies either by trade or in mixed assemblies. The meetings of local assemblies incorporated ritual similar to that of the numerous fraternal orders, but the assemblies also provided various educational and social activities for their members.

The Knights organized a secret assembly in Hamilton in 1875, and both movements arrived publicly in Canada in 1882. It is difficult to compare the popular impact of the two movements, given their very different natures. Newspaper reports make it clear that when the Army first entered many Ontario towns, hundreds and sometimes thousands of people would flock to its meetings.[5] Often the majority in the audience were simply there out of curiosity. However, at least some of those 'who came to scoff remained to pray,' and the Army made large numbers of converts. Many of the converts returned to the mainstream churches, but many others became soldiers, the Army's equivalent of church members. The most conservative estimates of Salvation Army impact would therefore be based on the number of soldiers. Measurement of the Knights of Labor's popularity has been based on membership numbers.

Membership in both organizations was extremely volatile. Although Salvation Army officers were instructed not to enrol converts as members until they were sure of the seriousness of an individual's conversion, the limited local evidence suggests that the majority of soldiers did not remain in the Army for more than three or four years and that many 'backslid' much sooner; but this was a common pattern in revival movements that focused on conversion. Membership in the Knights was at least as unstable, many remaining in the order only during the peak 1886-7 period. Kealey and Palmer argue that, in Ontario, 'over the course of their history the Knights organized a minimum of 21,800 members.' An opponent of the Army recognized that at its height in 1885-6 it had 25,000 soldiers, mainly in Ontario, but that by 1889 it had only 9,000 soldiers across the country.[6]

Both the Knights of Labor and the Salvation Army were successful in large cities. Each movement also had a major following in various smaller centres throughout Ontario, though the Army was more likely to attract support in the smaller and less industrialized communities than the Knights were.[7] In some places where the Knights were strong, the Army appears to have had little success. For instance, the Army was initially popular in Thorold but soon died out there, and it appears to have had little success in the Niagara area (apart from St Catharines). A similar pattern can be seen in the communities around Ottawa. However, in other areas where the Knights of Labor attracted a large proportion of the town's workforce, the Salvation Army also did very well. This was particularly true of the region immediately east of Toronto and in western Ontario. In Ingersoll the Salvation Army claimed to have converted almost seven hundred people in 1883, and hundreds more attended its parades and services. The Knights of Labor, which had arrived in town a year earlier, also developed a significant presence in the community over the next few years. In the oil-producing town of Petrolia the crowds flocked to Salvation Army meetings in 1884, with more than two hundred becoming soldiers in the Army's first year, while only a year later five hundred townspeople joined the local Knights of Labor assembly. In other Knights of Labor towns – for instance, Woodstock, Seaforth, Chatham, Lindsay, and Belleville – the Army attracted large crowds, and in each town many of the soldiers were sufficiently committed to become full-time officers.[8]

How much overlap was there between the membership of the Knights and the Army? Was Thorold's George Doherty, who played in the Salvation Army band and was buried by the Knights of Labor, an exception? Or was he representative of larger patterns? Given the almost complete lack of local membership lists, this question is very difficult to answer directly, but it does seem that the basis of support for the two movements was not completely distinct. For example, workers in Kingston's three largest factories became actively involved in both organizations, setting up Salvation Army prayer meetings for themselves in 1883 and going on strike as members of Knights of Labor assemblies four years later. Ironworkers in nearby Belleville who belonged to a local assembly of the Knights also appear to have attended Army meetings.[9] A closer look at the class basis of these movements provides further clues on the probable extent of overlap in membership.

Although some small merchants and employers joined the Knights of Labor, the order was primarily a working-class organization. Skilled workers appear to have dominated the leadership even at the local level, and many assemblies were organized on the basis of craft skills. Nevertheless, the Knights was the first major labour organization to attempt to include all workers regardless of skill level. Unlike earlier trade unions, the Knights was also open to women, who organized both in mixed assemblies and in separate women's locals. Kealey and Palmer have estimated that women were involved in at least 10 per cent of Ontario's Knights of Labor locals.[10]

The Salvation Army was also primarily a working-class movement. The *Toronto Mail*, for instance, noted that Salvation Army soldiers were 'chiefly working people, who give what little leisure they have to helping the cause.'[11] The few surviving converts' rolls for 1886–1900 reflect the gender make-up of the mainstream churches, for more than half of all the converts were women; but there was a dramatic difference in class terms, for more than half of these women were domestic servants. The majority of male converts were labourers, the remainder working in various skilled or semi-skilled jobs.[12]

An examination of the occupations of the 1,228 officers who entered the Army in Ontario between 1882 and 1890 reinforces this working-class picture of the movement, since officers were recruited from the membership, and in the early years there appear to have been few barriers to soldiers becoming officers. As was the case with converts, more than half (55 per cent) of all officers were female. These women, almost all of whom were single, were far more likely to be employed than the average single women.[13] Almost 40 per cent had been domestic servants before entering the Army, and most of the rest were employed in traditionally feminine working-class jobs (see table 29). More than 40 per cent of the male officers had been skilled workers before entering the Army, about one-quarter had been employed in other working-class occupations, and the remaining third were mainly farmers, though there were also a few businessmen and a more significant representation of clerks (table 29). Clearly, it was not only the Army's followers who were working class; the leadership was predominantly working class too.

The difference in occupational background between converts and officers suggests that the officers may have come from a slightly higher working-class stratum than the converts. The rolls of converts that have survived may not, however, be representative of Army membership across Ontario. In any event, the Salvation Army appears to have drawn in more unskilled and nonindustrial workers than the Knights of Labor. Certainly, it attracted many more women and was popular in a large number of small communities that were untouched by the Knights. At the level of leadership, the Knights and the Army seem to have drawn on somewhat different age groups. Almost 80 per cent of Salvationist officers of both sexes were less than twenty-five years old when they began their Army careers (see table 30), whereas leaders of the Knights seem more likely to have been older married men. The rank-and-file membership of both movements was more mixed in age, though the Salvation Army was particularly popular among younger people.[14]

We see, then, that although the Salvation Army and the Knights attracted somewhat different working-class groups, both movements included skilled and unskilled workers, women and men, young and old. Thorold's George Doherty was probably only one of a number of working men and women who became involved in both movements. In the American context, Kenneth Fones-Wolf has noted that the strong Christian faith of the majority of American workers caused many of them to see no contradiction between union membership – even union activism – and involvement in fundamentalist Christianity.[15] It is not unreasonable to assume that this may have been true in Canada too.

The volatility of membership in the Knights and the Army means that even if few workers were simultaneously Knights and soldiers, many more would have been touched by both movements during the course of the 1880s. In towns such as Woodstock, Petrolia, and Gananoque, where the Army was strong and a high proportion of the workforce was involved in the Knights, this is particularly likely. In these small communities, many Knights or potential Knights would have been attracted to the popular Salvation Army services, and some may have then been converted and made the decision to join the Army.

Respectability, Manliness, Leisure, and the Knights

The fact that most members of the Salvation Army and the Knights were working class does not necessarily mean that their values, beliefs, and consciousness were distinct from those of their middle-class neighbours. In some respects, membership in the Knights would certainly seem to demonstrate a distinct working-class consciousness. The Knights provided a trenchant critique of the dominant social and economic system that treated workers as cogs in capitalist industry, with no human dignity or respect, and ground them down into poverty. They saw themselves as struggling towards a more just, egalitarian, and cooperative social system for both male and female workers. In this struggle, however, they did not reject the culture of which they were a part. Instead, they used and reinterpreted ideas associated with a number of dominant discourses – including the discourses of respectability, manliness, and Christianity – to assert working people's rightful place in society in the face of declining working-class living standards and increasing middle-class pretensions. Leon Fink has shown how the Knights embraced key elements of respectability, while reinterpreting them in a class-conscious manner. For example, he has argued that the Knights did not view temperance as a means of quelling social disorder: they supported temperance because it strengthened workers' self-respect and gave them the energy and resources necessary for organizing to battle social injustice.[16]

The Knights' use of mainstream leisure and fraternal forms reflects this complex interplay between acceptance and reinterpretation of dominant notions of respectability. In Thorold, the majority of Knights leaders who could be identified were married skilled workers, many of whom also held leadership positions in local fraternal orders.[17] Various scholars have pointed to the parallels between the Knights and other fraternal orders. The fraternal ritual so central to the lodges was also important to the Knights, though in their case it stressed the centrality of working-class pride and solidarity. As Robert Kristofferson has shown, the assertions of masculine brotherhood common to other fraternal orders were certainly not absent from the Knights.[18] However, these affirmations of shared manhood were scarcely appropriate in the minority of locals that included women. More generally, the inclusion of women in the order reflected and perhaps reinforced a Knightly vision of masculinity that did not simply mirror that of the all-male lodges.

Although the lodges affirmed men's responsibilities as breadwinners, they celebrated an all-male world that accepted a certain roughness and was clearly distinct from home and family. The Knights' vision of class unity precluded such an all male world, but their vision of unity did not simply create an egalitarian brother- and sisterhood. The Knights' idealization of dominant forms of the family led them to valorize a most respectable, family-centred manhood. As Karen Dubinsky has shown, the Knights believed that in an ideal world, women would not have to work outside the home but could rely on a responsible family breadwinner. In the current world, the Knights realized that this was not possible. So, chivalrously, as true Knights, they extended assistance to their sister Knights, helping them organize and improve their pitiable situation in a brutal capitalist world.[19]

The Knights thus eschewed the roughness of the all-male leisure activities and tried to integrate women into their social events, demonstrating more concern with respectable, domestic manhood than many of the middle class married men who spent much of their leisure time in the all-male world of the fraternal order. Rather than meeting or socializing in hotels, where women would feel unwelcome, the Knights met in halls and organized leisure activities which they hoped would attract women. For example, they do not seem to have held the all-male oyster suppers that were so popular with the fraternal orders and sports clubs. When the Petrolia assembly organized an oyster supper, it was attended by Knights of both sexes.[20]

Dances, an obvious mixed-sex social event, were also popular with the Knights. In Thorold, dances put on by the two male assemblies were followed by one organized by Advance Assembly, the women's assembly. However, the recognition of female modesty, combined with masculine protectiveness, meant that the public organizers of the latter were male Knights. Their acceptance of the dominant gender ideology was even more evident at a Knights of Labor parade in St Catharines, where the 'lady Knights' rode in carriages while their brothers marched beside them.[21] The social events organized by female Knights displayed a similar emphasis on respectable femininity. For example, Advance Assembly in Thorold organized both a strawberry social and a concert, complete with recitals and musical selections by members.[22]

The Knights' leaders, many of whom were married men, sought to inculcate appropriate gender roles in the younger men. Taking a similar stand to many home-centred middle-class men of small-town Ontario, the Knights' publication, the *Palladium of Labor*, opposed permitting billiards in Hamilton's new Mechanics' Institute, arguing that billiards inculcated bad moral, physical, and intellectual habits in young men. The editor preferred that a gymnasium be provided, since it would teach better lessons in masculinity: 'We want our young men to learn everything that is manly.' In the same vein, a Knights of Labor speaker who visited Ingersoll in December 1883 'advised young people to avoid the drink shops and to devote their time to self-improvement.'[23]

At first glance, the leisure activities organized and advocated by the Knights seem strikingly similar to those of the respectable mainstream culture, if perhaps more than usually committed to a domestic and 'improving' mode of manhood. However, class-consciousness was pervasive, and to some extent it transformed the meaning of leisure activities and the gendered values associated with them. Young men were to stay out of drink shops so that they would have the energy to challenge the inequalities of the economic system. The manly character to be developed in the gymnasium was not to be devoted simply or even primarily to self-improvement; it was to be used in the struggle for working-class rights. At the St Catharines parade in which the 'lady Knights' rode in carriages, the local assemblies carried banners calling for an eight-hour day. For although many Knights sought the respectable leisure options that were available to their middle-class counterparts, they first had to struggle to gain the time and resources required to enjoy such leisure.[24]

A closer look at the leisure events organized by the Knights suggests other significant differences from mainstream leisure activities. For instance, many of their dances were organized as benefits to help injured fellow Knights.[25] The mutuality of such events contrasts sharply with the colder charity dispensed by churches, municipal councils, and the middle-class organizers of charity concerts. One dance organized by the Thorold Knights was held to raise money for a library and gymnasium.[26] Given the presence in the community of a Mechanics' Institute and several sports clubs, this effort suggests that while the Knights sought manly self-improvement, they did not wish to achieve it on terms dictated by the town's middle-class leaders. Similarly, the Knights' strawberry socials and concerts were not only an assertion of working-class respectability; they were also evidence of a willingness among working-class women to organize for themselves, and in their own interests, events that were normally dominated by the town's middle-class women.[27]

Middle-class leaders certainly recognized that the Knights' respectability did not make them any less of a threat to middle-class social dominance.[28] This was very clear at Ingersoll's 1887 Dominion Day celebration, organized by the local Knights. The hostility of the Canadian Pacific Railway – symbol of the employing classes – was evident in its refusal to provide the excursion rates normally available for public holidays, thus limiting the number of Knights who could attend the celebration from out of town. The middle-class politicians who spoke at the event obviously feared the emergence of an organization that threatened the social harmony which they saw themselves presiding over. The local MPPs sought to assure themselves and their listeners that the Knights did not support strikes and did not reflect the emergence of a distinct working-class voice. These speakers cast the Knights' Dominion Day festivities in the mold of similar public holidays, pointing out that the celebration had done honour to the town and would not only help the working classes but would 'benefit ... the interests of all classes' In praising the local order, the mayor of Ingersoll noted, 'Here we have no strife, no strikes to cause disorder ... but we assemble as one people serving one Queen and one God.'[29]

Christianity and the Knights

Among the many banners flying at the St Catharines Knights of Labor parade was one calling for 'One day for God, five for labor, and one for humanity.'[30] Was this banner representative of the Knights' thought? What was their attitude towards Christianity, which was so central to dominant definitions of respectability? Kealey and Palmer have noted that religious zeal was part of the residual culture out of which the Knights of Labor fashioned their distinct 'movement culture.'[31] However, this religious legacy was treated very briefly in their study of the order. A closer look suggests that religion was more central both to the ideology of the order and to the lives of individual Knights than historians have acknowledged.

As was true of most fraternal orders, potential Knights had to declare their belief in God as part of the secret initiation ritual.[32] However, concern with religious issues went far beyond this. Christianity was often addressed in the Knights of Labor press, though the newspapers were careful to avoid sectarian controversy, noting that such conflict only served to divide the working class. The Hamilton-based *Palladium of Labor*, the Knights' primary paper in Ontario, regularly contained reports of various sermons, both supportive of and opposed to the labour movement, with appropriate editorial commentary. The churches were not irrelevant here: their attacks were responded to, and their support was applauded. Under 'Local News,' the *Palladium* periodically reported on the social and religious activities of various Hamilton churches, the working-class Primitive Methodist Church and the Salvation Army being most commonly featured.

In both Canadian and American labour papers, the journalists frequently expressed their hostility to the current economic system in terms of Christian belief, which they obviously assumed their readers shared. This approach was not new to the late nineteenth century. Teresa Anne Murphy demonstrates how, in early-nineteenth-century New England, labour leaders appropriated Christian religious language, using it to challenge the capitalist exploitation of workers. Herbert Gutman has shown that while many Gilded Age labour leaders had little respect for the church, their profound belief in Christianity fuelled their battles for social justice.[33] For example, a poem in the *Journal of United Labor* proclaimed:

> We'll fight in this great holy war till we die
> No longer in silence we'll whimper and sigh
> No longer we'll cringe at the proud tyrant's nod
> But defy him, and fight 'neath the banner of God ...
> King Labor is ruler of earth of God's word.[34]

The editor of the *Palladium of Labor* frequently adopted similar pro-labour religious rhetoric. He was particularly fond of arguing that true Christianity was allied with the workers' cause and that 'the doctrines of Jesus Christ, the carpenter – who would have been called a tramp and a Communist had he lived in these days – if applied to the present conditions would solve the question satisfactorily.'[35] Christ was also described as 'the greatest social reformer that ever lived. He had nothing but words of bitter scorn and scathing indignation for the idle and luxurious classes who oppressed the poor.'[36]

In assessing similar rhetoric in the Canadian labourist tradition, Craig Heron concludes that 'the crucial question remains whether working-class leaders got their politics from Christianity, or turned to a common cultural reservoir to express their politics.'[37] This question could be put less starkly. The oppression and material deprivation that workers experienced and saw around them no doubt provided the primary basis for their opposition to the capitalist system. However, the Knights' use of religious imagery does not reflect simply a routine acceptance of dominant cultural forms. It seems to have been based in some form of Christian belief. In the American context, Kenneth Fones-Wolf has argued that Christianity was at the core of the Knights' cultural system and that 'a deep religious inspiration and a commitment to Christian beliefs pervaded the Order's distinctly working-class program.'[38] The Knights' Christian beliefs probably did not kindle their anger against the capitalist system, but the disparity between the Christian message and nineteenth-century capitalism would have fuelled such anger.[39]

The institutional Christian churches were also used by the Knights to assert the order's claims to respectability. Kealey and Palmer have suggested that in certain small communities the Knights 'usurped the traditional role of the church,' but a close look at the small-town experience suggests that this was not the case.[40] In many communities, local assemblies attended special sermons on topics that were related to Christianity and the Knights of Labor. The attendance by the Knights in a body at services in Ingersoll and Merritton, for instance, parallels the annual attendance of Orangemen, Oddfellows, and other fraternal orders at their own special services.[41] The fact that many Knights of Labor leaders were also active in local fraternal orders certainly helps to explain the adoption of this ritual. The leaders of the Knights in Ingersoll, who requested that the town's Presbyterian minister preach a sermon on a labour topic, probably believed that, as with the fraternal associations, collective attendance at church would assert the order's position in the respectable culture of the town. An association with the local churches would certainly bolster the Knights' claims both to the manly breadwinner role and to womanly respectability. The limited evidence available for Ingersoll and Thorold suggests that these towns' male Knights were about as likely to be members of Protestant churches as other working-class men and that a few leading Knights were also active in the leadership of the local churches.[42] The forging of links with the churches may thus have been viewed as a way of reassuring potential Knights – or at least Protestant Knights – that involvement with the order would not conflict with their religious belief or involvement, and in fact would reinforce all that was most moral, upstanding, and family centred in their existing value system.

The Knights' march into the local church symbolized their links to the dominant respectable Christian culture. But like their dances, concerts, strawberry socials, and Dominion Day celebrations, all of which in external form were patterned on the standard components of respectable culture, the massed church visit may have meant something more.

Workers who were church members worshipped in churches that in most cases were dominated by the local elite. Those who were officials in fraternal orders shared these positions with local merchants and professionals. But when these men marched into church as part of the Knights of Labor contingent, they were not simply members of another fraternal order. They were part of an organization of working-class men and women who were asserting their class identity and their equal place in respectable culture. They did not want to reject Christianity, but they also no longer wanted to remain in the galleries of the local churches.

In proclaiming themselves full and equal members of respectable Christian culture, the Knights could then go on to assert their rights on this culture's own terms, as they did in Thorold and Petrolia. In 1888 the federal government permitted the Welland Canal to be opened on Sundays for a few hours in the morning and evening. Mountain Assembly no. 6798 of Thorold unanimously passed a resolution condemning this action, declaring 'that such order will conflict with both the social and religious liberty of many of our members who are the servants of the government and as such will be compelled to perform duties which their consciences cannot approve of.'[43] In Petrolia it was apparently common practice for certain companies to operate their oil wells on Sundays. Soon after the Knights of Labor arrived in town, they sent a letter to the offending companies requesting that they cease this practice because 'the laws of both God and man demand the due observance of the Lord's day, and the moral sentiment of the entire community.' They added: 'It is believed that it is only necessary to appeal to the respect and reverence which, living as you do in an enlightened and Christian community, you must feel for God's law ... in order to secure your unhesitating consent to this reasonable request of your fellow citizens.'[44] No mention was made of the men affected by this request. It was only the editorial in the *Petrolia Advertiser* (not a particularly pro-labour paper) which, in supporting the Knights' letter, stated: 'The most powerful reason why this should be done is that a large number of men, greatly against their wishes, in violation of conscience and in opposition to their sense of moral right, are compelled either to violate the laws of both God and man and desecrate the Lord's day, or be discharged from their situation and thus deprived of the means of earning an honest livelihood.'[45]

Why did the Knights press their demand against Sunday labour largely in religious terms? Was it simply a matter of tactics, a recognition that only an appeal to religious sentiment would be effective? This would certainly be part of the answer. Phillips Thompson, in the *Palla-*

dium of Labor, argued: 'It is only that sacred character [of Sunday] which has secured to the working men the invaluable boon of a respite from toil in one day out of seven ... Only the religious sanction was powerful enough to interpose this barrier between the insensate greed of the money power and the rights of the toilers.'[46] While tactical concerns no doubt played a role here, it is important to recognize that whether they were church members or not, most small-town Knights probably accepted dominant Christian values. However, in affirming that everyone had a right to the religious liberty and day of rest ordained 'by God's law,' they were using these values to affirm the dignity and worth of all in the context of communities that were characterized by hierarchy and inequality.[47]

Although the ministers allied themselves with the Knights of Labor in battles over Sunday observance, several of the sermons they preached to Knights audiences, or more generally on the topic of 'Capital and Labour,' reinforced the popular impression that the church was not sympathetic to the Knights' efforts to combat inequality. For instance, while the 'large number of knights' who went to the Pine Street Methodist church in the industrial village of Merritton to hear a sermon by the Reverend Mr Snider 'seemed very much pleased with the discourse,' their brother and sister Knights in neighbouring Thorold had much less to be pleased about in the sermon given by the Methodist minister, the Reverend Mr Lanceley. Lanceley preached a strongly anti-labour sermon. 'Let me warn you,' he thundered, 'against the cry of "our rights" it will spread like a fever ... It is an inflammation, a burning, that is set on fire of hell.' Lanceley said that capital and labour should make common cause together, and he warned against discontent and covetousness, telling his listeners that 'God will reward the meek and trusting spirit with its own reward.' Not all sermons were so extreme, but few provided whole-hearted support. The Reverend T. Atkinson of Ingersoll, while cautiously praising the aims of the Knights of Labor, talked of the interdependence of all classes and the need both for capitalists not to oppress labourers and for labourers to obey their masters.[48]

Those Knights in the congregation who subscribed to the *Palladium of Labor* might have pointed out to their sisters and brothers after the service that the minister preached this way because he was under the influence of the local elite, who paid his salary. The *Palladium* argued that unlike the Knights, most ministers had sacrificed their manhood to toady to the wealthy and that 'the paid teachers of Christianity dare not quote the Biblical denunciations of land grabbers, usurers and oppress-ers of the poor, and apply them personally to wealthy supporters of the church. If they did they would soon preach themselves out of their pulpit.'[49]

The *Palladium* certainly recognized that Ontario's increasing economic prosperity had led to the building of elaborate churches, which had strengthened the control of the monied classes in these churches. It protested: 'Many of our places of worship have become simply Sunday Clubs or opera halls, intended to attract rich congregations, where the poor are neither invited nor welcomed.' One social critic featured in the paper noted that 'if a man hasn't money to pay a high pew rent ... he ain't wanted in the church.' Another contributor sketched a picture of the contemporary churches with 'the rich man in the front seat,' while at 'the back of the church, or away up in the strangers gallery [you] will see the blacksmith, the machinist, or the carpenter.' A 'Canadian Girl' pointed to the material basis of church membership among the commercial classes, attacking a dry goods merchant for the terrible wages he paid his clerks and asserting that, for this man and others like him, their 'pretensions to Christianity [were] a blasphemy, their attendance at divine service a mockery, their [church] donations, an advertisement, or as they would be pleased to term it "a masterly stroke of business."'[50]

The hypocrisy of many wealthy churchgoers and the power the monied classes appeared to have in the churches may have led some labour activists not only to reject the church but to reject Christianity itself. The *Palladium* argued, 'There is no cause which has contributed in greater measure to the spread of rationalistic views and the indifference to popular religionism which paves the way for full blown Secularism, than the manner in which modern so-called Christianity has become identified with wealth, position and power.' There were certainly freethinkers in the order. Secularism was particularly common among German-American Knights.[51]

However, freethinkers were often middle-class men and were not associated with labour reform. Conversely, the Knights and labour reform cannot be too closely linked to secularism. Phillips Thompson, the editor of the *Palladium*, had flirted with free thought and certainly challenged the relationship between wealth and Christianity.[52] But when a member of the 'Social Club' featured in the *Palladium* said that he was starting to move towards free thought, since freethinkers 'are not always on the side of oppression and tyranny as religion is,' Freeman (who spoke for Thompson), while agreeing that many of the ministers were self-serving hypocrites, argued that the member was 'confounding two different things.' He explained: 'True religion is never on the side of tyranny.'[53]

Labour activists also denied that free thought was particularly common among workers. In explaining why increasing numbers of working people were staying away from the churches, the *Palladium* recognized that 'infidelity' might have something to do with it, but argued that their absence could be much more readily linked to the fact that workers did not feel welcome in elaborate churches dominated by the wealthy. A correspondent to the *Palladium* argued in a similar vein that workers were not becoming freethinkers: 'The muscle and sinew of Hamilton still pins its hope of emancipation to the doctrine preached from the cross.'[54]

A letter from 'Well Wisher' stated that he had once attended church regularly, but 'for want of that brotherly society and sympathy fell away.' He said he had found the 'human love and desire to help my fellow man,' which was missing from the churches, through his involvement in the Knights of Labor. Kealey and Palmer use this letter to buttress their argument that, for many workers, the Knights displaced the church. However, even 'Well Wisher' who had found brotherly love in the Knights still sought something more. He said that he would 'fain cry out with thousands of my fellow workmen, O for a warm kindly Christ like church, a common plane where we could all meet on an equality and be brothers in Christ in this world, even as we hope to be in the next.'[55]

At the local level, rather than replacing the churches, the Knights used them to legitimate the order's position in the respectable community. The labour press asserted that many Knights attended church on a regular basis. In response to a minister who preached against the labour movement, insisting that 'this democratic spirit scoffs at religion,' the *Palladium* responded, 'This is merely an assertion without any argument whatever to bear it out. Our churches are as well attended – with perhaps one exception (the Centenary) as they were before we had any organization among our work people.' And in describing the female Knights at the Dundas Cotton Mills, the reporter noted that they 'go to make up the well dressed congregation in some of the churches.'[56]

Assertions that the Knights did indeed go to church would have served to reinforce the respectability of female Knights and the domestic, family-centred manhood that was the Knightly masculine ideal. They may also have been intended to provide a potent counter-image to the common portrayal of labour activists as godless bomb-throwing anarchists. Regardless of their rhetorical purpose, such assertions do reflect a reality that labour historians have been reluctant to recognize. Workers were not isolated from the Christian-dominated world in which they lived. Many of them were church members. They were, however, less likely to be members than their middle-class neighbours, perhaps in part because of the barriers to working-class attendance created by the emerging association between material prosperity and definitions of true Christianity.

Through the Knights, workers could challenge the building of elaborate churches – in which ministers preached the gospel of Mammon and relegated working people to the galleries – as part of their broader challenge to the capitalist system that shaped these churches. This does not mean, however, that the Knights caused workers to abandon either Christianity or the churches. On special occasions Knights of Labor assemblies marched in a body to local churches, asserting their equal participation within them, and many individual Knights appear to have attended church regularly. Many, and perhaps most of those who no longer attended church still saw themselves as Christians. With their middle-class contemporaries, they shared a belief in many of the basic tenets of Christianity, but they reinterpreted much of this doctrine in the light of their own distinct working-class values and experience. The same Christian religion that middle-class Ontarians glorified in their many church-building projects fuelled a working-class challenge to the larger social and economic inequalities of Canadian society, as well as to the way in which these inequalities were increasingly embedded in the imposing Christian edifices of the day.

The Salvation Army and the Working Class

While the Knights of Labor sought an equal place for working-class Ontarians in the dominant respectable culture, another working-class movement of the 1880s gloried in attacking respectable norms, although from a most Christian perspective. When the freethinkers brought Charles Watts to speak at Thorold's Oddfellows Hall, the local ministers were not pleased. They wrote outraged letters to the paper and brought in Christian authorities to refute his arguments. The response of Thorold's Salvation Army detachment was more direct. In reporting on the lecture, the *Post* complained that 'it would be difficult to justify the salvation army in pursuing the tactics they did in disturbing the meeting by singing, shouting and playing their band to an extraordinary extent immediately in front of the hall for a considerable time during the early part of the lecture.'[57]

A willingness to challenge convention and respectability was integral to the appeal which the Salvation Army held for Ontario workers. Part of the Army's unconventional nature lay in its willingness to use emotionally charged methods of bringing 'the perishing' to salvation. The shouting, crying, and jumping up and down in the name of salvation that went on at Army meetings mirrored patterns in earlier revival movements. However, by the 1880s, 'emotionalism' had become anathema even among Ontario Methodists, who had once preached a 'fire and brimstone' message throughtout Upper Canada. By this period, middle-class Ontarians equated respectable religious observance with sedate church services. Conversion experiences associated with wild emotional excesses were rendered suspect. As the Reverend Mr Kay of Thorold's Methodist church noted in comparing his efforts to those of the Salvation Army, 'One conversion growing out of true Bible instruction [is] worth a dozen arising from the hot bed of undue excitement and the noise of unintelligent enthusiasm.'[58] The intensely emotional appeal of Army services was interpreted as a class-based challenge to respectable churchgoing by middle and working class alike.

The Salvation Army's 'blood and fire' revivalism was not all that distinguished it from respectable Christianity. The Army explicitly drew on working-class popular culture as a means of attracting converts. Like travelling circuses and variety shows, the Salvation Army paraded the streets of small-town Ontario with colourful banners and the music of brass bands, tambourines, and drums. Army hymns were set to the tunes of popular songs, while the uniforms worn by soldiers and officers offered an alternative to the regalia worn by fraternal orders, firemen, and bandsmen – an alternative that was available to women as well as men. Many Army events were advertised as religious alternatives to popular amusements. The officers hoped that Hallelujah Sprees would draw men out of the hotels and that Popular Matinees would attract theatregoers. When the Army first attacked, the Kingston officers competed directly with the visiting circus. They advertised all-night services in the new 'Great Free Salvation Tent' and announced: 'Superior to any show on earth. Free Salvation. Come and get it. Glorious experiences of Prodigal Sons. The Silver Band. Magnificant Choruses and Hallelujah Sing Song.'[59] Some Army officers – like 'Happy Bill' Cooper, who stood on his head and did cartwheels while preaching – certainly provided an entertaining alternative to circuses and variety shows. Other popular events included Hallelujah Pic-nics, Free and Easy Meetings, and Big Gos. Even the quintessentially respectable church tea meetings were transformed (and satirized) by the Army as Grand Tea Fights.

These events did not only appeal to the unchurched, whom the Army defined as their main target. The communion roll of Thorold's Presbyterian church contains the notation 'gone to "Army"' beside the names of several working-class communicants. In towns where the Army was more popular than in Thorold, the churches appear to have suffered considerable attrition from working-class churchgoers who found Big Gos more appealing than conventional church services. Small-town newspapers across the province noted that younger church members were particularly likely to abandon the churches at least temporarily for Army meetings.[60]

The Army's success among both church members and nonmembers attests to the efficacy of its unconventional methods. The fact that it emphasized the appeal of popular culture suggests that many Ontario workers – particularly the unskilled and the young, who were most attracted to Army services – were a long way from the more respectable culture to which the Knights' leadership sought to lay claim. The popularity of the Army does, however, in its own way demonstrate a distinct class identity among the many workers who chose a rowdy working-class religious alternative over the respectable mainstream churches. In a variety of other ways, the Salvation Army both promoted and reflected a certain form of working-class identity among Ontario workers.

The Army was willing to use any methods necessary to save souls because it believed the churches had failed in their responsibility to minister to all classes. Many Salvationists and their supporters were quite explicit in their opposition to the churches, providing a very trenchant class-based critique of mainstream Christianity, a critique which bears some similarity to that advanced by the Knights of Labor. In the first few years after the Army's appearance in Ontario, the newspapers were filled with letters both attacking and defending it. The defence of the Army frequently included an attack on the churches as middle-class institutions that had replaced Christ's true teachings with an emphasis on material glory and middle-class pride. The letter from 'Spectator' of Belleville is fairly representative in this respect:

Of all the denominations whose worship I have attended that which suffers least by comparison with the precepts and example of Christ is the Salvation Army ... As to the empty pews in the churches, they were so before the Army came to this

city, and why? Because Sunday after Sunday they serve out the dry bones of sectarianism for the living truths of Christianity ... I see the haughty 'Miss Shoddy'
sweep up the aisle and recoil in poorly concealed discomfort lest her costly robes
should touch the threadbare garments of some poor sinner who had the temerity
to enter therein. I hear the doctrine of Dives preached in the name of Christ ... I
see the Almighty blasphemed by the erection in His name of costly edifices,
wherein are exclusive and costly people who worship in a costly style, while
orphans cry for bread.[61]

'A Salvation Army Soldier' from Woodstock wrote in a similar vein,
defending the Army which, he said, 'reaches classes of people who have
precious souls but whose burden of sin the clergy will not touch with
even their little finger!' and he attacked the 'pew-renting and so-called
respectable congregations of town and country, whose very respectability has crushed many a bruised reed.' James Smith, a London Salvation
ist, wrote of 'the Salvation Army, who without money and without price
are nobly bearing their crosses, fighting the Lord's battles; while the
sluggish churches and overpaid ministry thereof have been asleep and
drunken in their opulence.' The complaints of Ingersoll churchgoers
make it clear that Captain Annie O'Leary preached a similar message,
frequently attacking the local ministers for being more interested in col-
lecting their salaries than in saving the souls of the poor.[62]
    The Salvation Army's class-based critique of the churches in some
ways echoes that of the Knights, particularly its attacks on the churches'
emphasis on money and appearance to the exclusion of both the true
word of God and the honest working man. However, for the Salvation
Army the true sin lay in the churches' neglect of the souls of the poor,
whereas for the Knights it was the churches' refusal to speak out for
workers' social and economic interests. An article by Commissioner
Railton in the Army's publication the *War Cry* makes explicit this focus
on spiritual rather than temporal concerns while at the same time drawing certain parallels between the two. Railton argued that as society was
moving away from an acceptance of 'the sight of poor creatures toiling
from early morning till late at night ... for a few cents,' religious society
would not 'tolerate the cold blooded existence of a Christian congregation, assembling twice or thrice a week for the worship of the Lord, and
making no effort to make known His Salvation to thousands who are
without it all around them.'[63]
    In fact, the Ontario Salvation Army of the 1880s was largely uncon-
cerned about the temporal welfare of the poor, but its emphasis on spiri-

tual equality appealed to many of the province's working men and women, tapping into or strengthening an emerging class-consciousness. The Army explicitly discouraged involvement in political movements, since its followers were expected to focus on the state of their own souls and the salvation of others. However, as historians such as E.P. Thompson and Bernard Semmel have argued in the case of other highly evangelical religious movements, the Army's message of spiritual equality may have spilled over into the secular realm, fuelling working-class anger at a society characterized by profound inequities.[64] At a minimum, this message would have reinforced a sense of self-worth among the Army's working-class adherents, who were increasingly subordinated and devalued in the larger society.

Some of the unorthodox methods employed by the Army appear to have been explicitly intended to validate working-class dignity and self-worth. The periodic 'Trades Meetings,' in which all soldiers marched in their workday clothes, visually demonstrated how the Salvation Army provided a space for workers to assert their distinct identity. So did advertisements that officers with names such as 'Billy the Tinker,' the 'Happy Shoemaker,' 'Wright the Printer,' and the 'Hallelujah Blacksmith' would be featured at various Army events.[65] Working-class pride was also evident among officers who flouted the middle-class standards of respectability that marginalized the language of working-class Ontarians. For example, Captain Hall of London East told his flock: 'We are accused of being illiterate and not using the Queen's English properly. Who cares for grammar. The Devil has his grammar, so has the Salvation Army. We have just been singing that good old hymn "Better and Better Every Day" let us change it, brothers and sisters, and sing "Gooder and Gooder every day" and it was sung.' The equal value of workers' language in the sight of God was similarly asserted by 'Hallelujah Jack' of Lindsay, who said, 'It is true I have not got the best of grammar, but I have got the love of God in my heart.' The primacy of salvation and the resultant irrelevance of mere earthly standards and social divisions was affirmed by 'Shouting Annie,' who proclaimed that 'there are no social distinctions in Heaven.'[66] Such class-based challenges can be seen as a harking back to an earlier era of evangelical Protestantism, when class divisions were less embedded in definitions of Christianity and the primary division was between the converted and the unsaved.

The appeal of the Salvation Army as a distinct working-class religious space is affirmed by the dominance of domestic servants in the movement, both as soldiers and officers. Servants were among the lowest on the social hierarchy and the least likely to be members of the mainstream churches. Rather than sitting in church, where she would be treated with disdain and watched closely by her mistress, the domestic servant was offered freedom from such control and a space where she would not be looked down on, a space where she could proclaim her equality in the context of her own distinct culture and language. The Army also provided these women with a unique opportunity to play active leadership roles, strengthening their sense of value and self-respect in a society that devalued them.[67] Such opportunities clearly appealed to many other workers, both women and men, skilled and unskilled.

Victor Bailey, a historian of the British Salvation Army, has argued that involvement in such a distinctively working-class organization reflected the emergence of class-consciousness. Roland Robertson, who also studied the Army in the British context, suggests that for many working-class Salvationists 'allegiance to the Salvation Army offered an opportunity of maintaining religiosity within the Protestant tradition but in opposition to the middle-class identified denominations.'[68] A similar dynamic seems to have existed in the Ontario branch of the movement. The decision to join the Army probably did not imply an active opposition to the middle-class-dominated churches among all soldiers, but it would certainly have reflected a sense of alienation from class-based institutions in which workers, particularly unskilled workers, were both subordinated and marginalized. The Salvation Army provided Ontario workers with a religious alternative that spoke to them in their own cultural terms and provided a separate religious space in which they could feel comfortable and in control. The popularity of the Army points to the existence of some form of distinct culture and class identity among Ontario workers in small towns as well as large cities, and the Army's activities would have reinforced this consciousness.

At the same time, the Salvation Army's success points not only to working-class consciousness but to working-class religiosity. The Army's message was delivered in working-class cultural forms, but it remained the message of evangelical Protestantism. As such, it was clearly familiar to those workers who were swept up in the Salvation Army. Some Salvation soldiers had been church members and had either drifted away from the churches or found the Army's 'blood and fire' methods more appealing than sedate church services. Many other Army soldiers and officers had never been church members, but they had had a Christian, very often a Methodist, upbringing.[69] Even those who had never even attended Sunday school lived in a society in which they could not avoid having some knowledge of basic Christian teachings. Many may have felt alienated from the churches while remaining committed to Christianity. The instant popularity of the Salvation Army certainly suggests that the basic message of evangelical Christianity was a familiar and welcome one to most workers when presented in a culture and language with which they could identify.

The Salvation Army did not, however, appeal instantly to all Ontario workers. Some, particularly those who were part of the male youth culture, were actively hostile to all religious practices. To these young men, Christianity was a feminine concept associated with the feminized spaces of church and home, which were considered antithetical to the rougher masculine world of street corners and hotel bars. Despite the Salvation Army's more flamboyant methods, many young working men viewed it as part of the same feminized world as the mainstream churches. In fact, the large number of female preachers in the movement may have further reinforced its generally feminine associations. Even the masculine military trappings would not have endeared it to young working men, since the Army conducted a full-scale offensive against their lifestyle. The Army's officers attacked drinking, loafing, gambling, and other popular pursuits of the male youth culture. And rather than preaching restrained sermons in the manner of the mainstream ministers, the Salvationists attacked sinful male practices loudly and directly, 'firing red hot shot' from public platforms and on the streets. In the first weeks of the Army's assault on Kingston, Captain Wass condemned the young men who came to the barracks to make fun of the proceedings and who 'frequently congregate at the corners and plot together and go hand in hand in doing that which is bad.'[70]

Salvation Army services proudly featured the public testimonies of men who had been rescued from the rough masculine world of street corners and hotels. In one typical testimony at an Army meeting in Toronto, a young man affirmed that 'the Lord had kept him from the use of tobacco and drink for over two years and a half.' Married men testified that the Army had converted them from drunken wifebeaters to responsible breadwinners, and provided heart-wrenching narratives of their former sinful ways.[71] The biographies of male officers published in the War Cry usually included stories of rough young manhood transformed. Captain Cicero Jones, for instance, had been born into a religious home in Uxbridge, Ontario, but had begun to 'go wrong' at an early age by reading novels and smoking tobacco. First working as a marble carver and then as a sailor, he 'went in for the devil with all [his] might' until he surrendered to God at a Salvation Army meeting.[72]

While Captain Jones may have believed that his surrender to God and his enlistment in the battle for souls had made him more of a man, unconverted young men viewed such surrenders with suspicion and scorn. Submission to the Lord may have been congruent with contemporary feminine images, but it was completely contrary to the tough, strong, masculine ideal of street corners and bars. As Pamela Walker has shown in the British context, men who abandoned rough male culture for the Salvation Army were despised as effeminate.[73] The same was true in Canada, where male converts faced considerable hostility and scorn from both workmates and friends. One Salvation soldier told of 'all the battles ... in the factory, for I had to acknowledge Him there ... as my Saviour.'[74]

The fact that the Salvation Army trumpeted its success in converting many of the young, unmarried working men who had previously remained aloof from the churches could only have increased the hostility of those who remained on the street corners and in the bars. These 'loafers' took their battle against the Army into the streets and the barracks, demonstrating their scorn for 'feminized' converts and their unhappiness with Salvationist attacks on their lifestyle. Groups of roughs frequently entered Army barracks to scoff and heckle. This behaviour mirrors the active response of working-class audiences to the performances of travelling troupes, but it was far more hostile. In some communities, young men assaulted the officers directly or threw rocks and rotten eggs at them. In other places, they resorted to more innovative tactics such as putting cayenne pepper on a stove during Army meetings or flooding the barracks.[75]

A major confrontation between the Army and unconverted men occurred in Ingersoll in December of 1883: 'During the parade of the Salvation Army on Monday evening an "indescribable" meeting took place between this and another body headed by a brass band composed of members of our town band and others. When the Salvationist started from the market square the other body, composed principally of working men to the number of several hundreds, also started from an opposite point, the band playing vigorously ... [when] opposite the Salvationists ... both bodies commenced to play with renewed vigour and to emit the most hideous yells.'[76] Catholic hostility to the Army's active Protestant revivalism may have fuelled some of the opposition, but undoubtedly much of it emerged out of rough culture. The young loafers may not have been particularly happy with the middle-class-dominated churches, but they did not see them as a threat. By contrast, the Salvation Army, which gloried in the testimony of converted former scoffers, posed a direct challenge to this youthful male subculture.[77] Of course, the Army's outrageous tactics certainly left it open to ridicule. Also, its working-class nature made it more vulnerable to attack.

The roughs and loafers were not the only Ontarians to attack the Salvation Army. In this battle if in no other, they were on the same side as numerous Protestant ministers and other respectable middle-class observers. Many ministers clearly saw the Salvation Army as competition and were unhappy that working-class church members and adherents were abandoning them for the Salvantionist movement.[78] Rather than acknowledging these concerns directly, most preferred to ridicule and denounce the Army's methods. These men assumed that the respectable trappings of the mainstream churches were integral to Christianity as they defined it. They frequently accused the Army of treating Christianity with vulgarity, levity, and frivolity, and disparagingly compared Army activities to popular working-class entertainments. A common, and telling, comparison identified the Army as being worse than 'a negro minstrel show.'[79] The adoption of the cultural forms of the marginal and the devalued, whether by class or race, placed the Army beyond the pale of true Christianity, which in the dominant discourse of the period was inextricably linked with respectability.

Like the local roughs, the ministers and other middle-class observers also challenged the masculinity of Salvationist converts. While the ministers were certainly not happy with the idea of female preachers, they reserved much of their hostility for the men who served under these women – who, 'weak-minded, ignorant, wilfully ... placed themselves under the government and control and teaching of a woman.'[80] The Salvationists were derided as 'calfish' men, and their overemotionalism was ridiculed. Unlike the roughs, the ministers and other respectable middle-class men who attacked the Salvationists believed that true men should be Christians, but their middle-class vision of ideal manhood did not include making a fool of oneself by marching in the streets or testifying in emotional terms on public platforms.[81]

The hostility to the Salvation Army was also fuelled by fears of disorder and loss of control. Respectable people frequently complained about the lack of order at Army meetings, and in particular at the Army habit of marching through the streets with drums and tambourines. In Ingersoll a letter to the editor complained of the 'infernal drum beating and parades' that forced ladies off the sidewalk into the gutter, and the *New-market Era* lashed out at the 'abominable nuisance of singing and howling ... after orderly people have retired to rest' and the 'drum and symball [*sic*] playing and singing, on the streets on Sunday.' Middle-class citizens frequently attempted to regain control over public space by petitioning town councils to pass by-laws prohibiting the Army from marching and beating their drums. In some cases, Salvationists were arrested for refusing to comply with such laws.[82] Supporters of the Army argued that their opponents were more eager to arrest Salvationists for praying in public than to arrest the drunken youths who normally loafed on the streets, but in fact the hostility to both groups appears to have stemmed from a common fear that the middle class was losing control of public space.[83]

Middle-class hostility towards the Army was gradually transformed, however, as the Salvationists converted more and more of these loafers. The Salvation Army was increasingly praised for its ability to bring Christianity to those who would never enter the mainstream churches. Middle-class observers were no doubt genuinely pleased by the Army's ability to save the souls of 'the perishing masses.' However, for these middle-class supporters 'getting religion' meant considerably more than accepting Jesus Christ. Through conversion, the Salvation Army was able to transform the lifestyle of young men – particularly working-class young men – which had so troubled respectable churchgoing folk. In newspapers across the province the Army was praised for reducing drunkenness, loafing, and crime, and for increasing the industriousness of working men. Middle-class Ontarians also lauded the Army for providing an alternative to the working-class movements that sought collective salvation on earth rather than individual salvation in heaven.[84]

This middle-class support was not misplaced. The Salvation Army did in many ways bring its followers more firmly into the respectable value system espoused by the evangelical churches. Former drunkards who described at Army meetings how they had been converted into reliable breadwinners may have been too rowdy and overemotional for middle-class tastes, but they were certainly much closer to the dominant ideals of respectable Christian manhood than they had been. An organization which, while denying that it provided strikebreakers, announced that if it had 'anything to say in reference to the strike and the strikers it would be get converted, strike against sin, and use the cash as God directs you after you have earned it,' would certainly appeal to middle-class Ontarians.[85] However, the Salvation Army cannot simply be dismissed as a manifestation of working-class false consciousness and middle-class social control. The Army was a working-class organization: while it did attract a minority of farmers and middle-class converts, the vast majority of both officers and soldiers were working class. The Army spoke to workers in their own language and from their own culture, and asserted the equal value of their souls to those that were ministered to in costly middle-class churches. It tapped into and reinforced a sense among working-class Ontarians of their own value and dignity in a society that was characterized by increasing inequality. The Army also provided the kind of space sought by 'Well Wisher' in the *Palladium of Labor*, where 'we could all meet on an equality and be brothers in Christ in this world, even as we hope to be in the next.'

Neither the Knights nor the Army retained the promise of the 1880s. The Knights declined rapidly towards the end of the decade as a result of poor economic conditions, external attack, and internal weakness; and although the Salvation Army remains active today, it is a very different movement from the one described in these pages. By the early 1890s, the Ontario Salvation Army had been transformed into a primarily social rescue organization along the lines of the British Salvation Army. With this change, growing class divisions developed in the Army itself, so that increasingly there were respectable officers ministering to the 'submerged tenth.' The loss of evangelical zeal that accompanied the shift to rescue work precipitated a major schism. It was led by Brigadier P.W. Philpott, who strongly opposed the Army's new emphasis on social work. Most tellingly, he also attacked the emergence of class divisions in the Army, pointing to the inconsistency of senior officers travelling first class while field officers often lived on less than a dollar a week – this despite the fact that 'we have always preached so much self-sacrifice and professed to the world to have all things in common.'[86]

The transformation of the Army and the decline of the Knights does not, however, negate their importance to Ontario workers of the 1880s. Thousands of workers throughout the province were influenced by these movements. Although each movement had greater appeal to different strata of the working class, for a brief period in the 1880s both the Knights and the Army revealed the existence of a working-class sense of identity and distinct class-based values, in small communities as well as large cities. Skilled working men who had bargaining power in the workplace and often a tradition of organized resistance more commonly turned to the Knights. The Knights sought to assert the place of working people in the dominant respectable culture. This place was not at the back of a hall or church, where they could be condescended to and 'improved'; it was a place where they would be recognized as manly, chivalrous men and respectable women who chose the nature and means of their own self-improvement. The Knights defined true Christianity quite differently from mainstream Christian discourse, asserting that Christ's true message was one of equality – an equality that challenged the oppression, materialism, and hypocrisy they saw around them. Their appropriation of the dominant religious language may have given the Knights' critique some broader social legitimacy, but they were not simply being strategic here. Most Knights shared the Christian beliefs which served to fuel their challenge to an increasingly hierarchical social order, both within the mainstream churches and in the larger social and economic sphere, and which also helped shape their alternative vision of a cooperative, egalitarian world.

Ontario's more powerless unskilled workers were more likely to be attracted by the individual heavenly salvation offered by the Salvation Army than by the earthly millennium envisioned by the Knights. The otherworldly emphasis of the Army negated the importance of a secular world where their lot was hard, their position lowly, and the prospects of material improvement slight. While many of the younger workers were drawn in by the excitement of Army meetings, the Army's popularity also revealed the significance of Christianity to their lives. More women than men were attracted to the Army, and many young working men mounted a spirited opposition to Army efforts to transform their rough lifestyle. While many of these hecklers did end up at least temporarily submitting themselves to the Lord at Army meetings, they were not transformed into carbon copies of middle-class manhood. For both the men and the women who joined the Salvation Army, piety neither undermined nor precluded working-class identity or consciousness.

In joining the Army, many Ontario workers were, at least temporarily, rejecting the mainstream churches, which embedded class divisions in elaborate edifices and rented pews. These workers had chosen instead a religious movement that attacked respectable middle-class Christianity, defining 'true' Christianity as that which ignored the social distinctions of the world and focused on the spiritual equality of all. The popularity of the Salvation Army – a religious movement that provided workers with their own space and spoke to them in their own language – points to the existence of distinct working-class beliefs and cultural forms among the unskilled male and female workers who made up the bulk of Salvationists.

Both the Salvation Army and the Knights of Labor demonstrate the significance of religion to working-class life in late-nineteenth-century Ontario. The religion of Ontario workers was in many ways not so very different from that of their middle-class neighbours. Many had worshipped with these neighbours in the same churches, especially in smaller communities. The coming of the Knights and the Salvation Army to these communities reveals, however, that working-class piety and even common church involvement did not guarantee shared values and class harmony. There was no single hegemonic definition of 'true' Christianity. Instead, as Kenneth Fones-Wolf has argued, religion 'was truly a contested terrain.'[87] In the Ontario of the 1880s, as in many other times and places, religion not only buttressed the social order but also challenged it.

7

Hallelujah Lasses: Working-Class Women and the Salvation Army

Some of the Salvation Army's activities were of particular interest to women. This was certainly true of the 'Hallelujah Weddings,' as the marriages of officers were popularly known. A Hallelujah Wedding that took place in Hamilton in the summer of 1884 attracted more than 1500 people, each of whom had paid fifteen cents to attend. The local press claimed that the event was 'the biggest display ever seen at a wedding in Hamilton.' The waving of banners, the banging of tambourines, and the frequent choruses of hallelujahs helped keep excitement at fever pitch throughout the ceremony. Afterwards, the couple rode in a carriage 'decked out with many coloured ribbons' as they paraded through streets thronged with curious onlookers. Apparently, women made up the majority and certainly the most interested portion of the crowd.[1]

While the ribbons, tambourines, and hallelujahs help explain the appeal of such events, the fact that at these weddings both groom *and* *bride* were public personages – active preachers of the Salvation Army message – increased public interest. Furthermore, the Hallelujah Lasses – the female officers – were major attractions in their own right at the most mundane Army events. In Thorold and many other communities, flagging interest in the Army was restored when one of these women turned up. The arrival of a new female officer in Kingston drew larger crowds than 'when the Governor General and the Princess were here'; the hall was 'jammed to the doors.'[2]

Such scenes were repeated in towns and cities throughout Ontario, for these female preachers were a common feature of the Salvation Army. In the 1880s more than half of all Salvation Army officers were women – a striking contrast to the exclusively male religious leadership of all other Canadian denominations. The majority of the Army's members – the soldiers – also were women. In this, the Army followed the same pattern as mainstream churches. However, the female soldiers (who, like the officers, were often called Hallelujah Lasses) played a more active role in the Army than their sisters did in the more established denominations. Like the Army's male soldiers, they were expected to stand up in crowded halls, give testimony to their faith in Jesus, and describe the sin and misery of their past lives. They also marched through the streets, beating drums or tambourines to attract attention to the cause.

As we have seen, the involvement of working-class men in the Salvation Army challenged, in very different ways, both rough culture's definitions of appropriate masculinity and the dignified ideals of middle-class manhood. How did the active testimony for Christ required of Hallelujah Lasses fit into the dominant ideals of femininity? And what can the female involvement in the Army tell us about working-class women's own definitions of appropriate womanly behaviour? We know much less about working-class women's understanding of femininity than we do about working-class masculinity. Working-class women lacked any equivalent to the public forums of street corner and hotel bar where rough male culture was expressed. As noted in chapter 5, a minority of younger working-class women became involved in cross-class temperance and literary societies, a fact that suggests some acceptance of dominant respectable values – and perhaps the paucity of other associational options. Many other working-class women, both single and married, joined local churches.

Contemporaries viewed churchgoing as particularly suited to women, given the dominant gender ideal of women as pious, passive, and frail, with higher moral natures and an exclusively domestic mission. Did working-class women's participation in the mainstream churches reflect their internalization of this dominant vision of femininity? Although working-class women were active in somewhat different spheres of church work than their middle-class sisters – preferring Sunday school work to the ladies' aid, for example – all such work took place in the context of subordinated, womanly Christian service. An examination of women's involvement in the Salvation Army can help determine the extent to which this ideal of pious true womanhood was relevant to the lives and the consciousness of working-class women.

Women's Position in the Salvation Army

Why did the Salvation Army offer more opportunities for women, including greater equality and more access to leadership roles than those available in the mainstream churches, or indeed in most other contemporary institutions, including the labour movement? Two reasons have been advanced to explain women's position in the Army. One was the lack of resources available to the early movement, a factor that increased the willingness to make use of all potential preachers, regardless of gender.[3] This explanation is inadequate in itself, since other religious movements have faced a shortage of workers, yet they have placed the preservation of patriarchal authority ahead of the saving of souls. This practical need for more workers may, however, have given more force to the arguments of Catherine Booth, co-founder with her husband William of the Salvation Army. Catherine Booth has generally been credited with establishing the relative equality of women in the Army.

The evangelical nature of the Salvation Army led to a focus on spiritual equality that could in itself justify female preaching (and had in fact provided some opportunities for female preachers in the early years of Methodism), but Catherine Booth went beyond this to provide what was in many ways an explicitly feminist critique of male religious domination.[4] In response to those who cited St Paul as forbidding female preaching, she pointed out that this argument was based solely on male interpretations of the Bible. She claimed that once women were able to interpret such passages themselves, the real truth would be forthcoming. For Catherine Booth it was not scriptural authority but male selfishness that relegated women to the private role of visiting the poor and sick while reserving the honour of the pulpit for men. She argued, 'Our Lord links the joy with the suffering, the glory with the shame.'[5]

Catherine Booth believed that there was nothing inherent in women's nature that made them incapable of preaching, and she maintained that women had been 'trained to subjection ... imbecile dependence on the judgement of others.'[6] In this she echoed the arguments of many feminists, from Mary Wollstonecraft on. However, like most nineteenth-century feminists, Catherine Booth did not believe that all gender differences were socially constructed. Women did have different natures from men, but this did not make them unfit to preach God's word. Booth maintained that rather than unsexing women, preaching 'exalts and refines all the tenderest and most womanly instincts of her nature.'[7]

The Salvation Army's rhetoric regarding women's equality was not always borne out in reality. Men certainly dominated the upper echelons of the Army. Nonetheless, the movement did provide real and unusual opportunities for women. Many female officers gained the rank of captain and were thus placed in charge of congregations – or corps, as they were known. The outraged response of middle-class critics underlines the extent to which this was a radical departure from dominant gender roles. For the Reverend A. Wilson of Kingston, the 'female preaching' when combined with 'fantastic dressing, the outrageous talk and singing of doggerel hymns' rendered the Army completely unacceptable. The more secular critics were also unhappy at seeing 'petty coats in the pulpit.'[8] Although many of these people were mollified by the Hallelujah Lasses' success in redeeming the rough and the disorderly, nonetheless, female preaching remained far beyond the norm of appropriate feminine behaviour.

Female Soldiers and Adherents

While the careers of female officers provided the clearest challenge to dominant gender roles, female soldiers also were expected to eschew familiar patterns. In some respects, the Salvation Army appealed to traditional female roles through its use of familial rhetoric, but in a variety of other ways it either required or provided the space for female soldiers and potential adherents to behave in a manner that ran counter to the conventional female roles of docility, passivity, and domesticity. The response of female soldiers to the unusual opportunities available in the Army provides an insight into the nature of working-class women's lives and can illuminate the distinct nature of working-class femininity.

The transformation of rough masculinity, for which the Salvation Army took much credit, had a major impact on working-class women. An 1885 Army report out of Ingersoll gloried in the fact that 'lots of families who used to be in sin, drunkenness, and misery ... now have homes like little Heavens,' and a saved drunkard's wife from Palmerston testified that 'she thanked God for the Army, as it had picked her husband up. She said it was the happiest Xmas she had spent for nine years.' Through the conversion of married men, the Army claimed to have transformed rough working-class homes into humbler versions of middle-class havens of domestic bliss. Ideal gender roles, with women as patient moral nurturers and men as reliable breadwinners, were featured in Army descriptions of families rescued from drunkenness.[9]

This rhetoric may be viewed as symptomatic of Army efforts to impose the dominant family ideology on the working class. However, male alcoholism created very real problems for working-class women, who had good reasons to seek to end or moderate male drinking, whether through cross-class temperance lodges or through the working-class Salvation Army. The statement by one female Salvationist that 'I'd rather have my husband beat the Salvation Army drum than beat me' may be apocryphal, but it probably reflected the feelings of many working-class wives.[10] These women would indeed have reason to be thankful for the conversion of their husbands – and to regret the transient nature of many such conversions.

The Salvation Army may have seen itself as shoring up the ideal Victorian family, but it also undermined the patriarchal nature of the family by requiring female soldiers and adherents to play active public roles. As well as performing their secular responsibilities in the home or the workplace, female soldiers were expected to spend weary hours going door to door selling the *War Cry* and trying to bring other townspeople to Christ. They also took part in the frequent noisy and flamboyant street parades. One such parade in London involved 'the backward jumping of the leading officers and the waving and swinging of the kerchiefs and streamers ... the drums and chorus [going] at their full beat.' At this parade, an elderly lady observed, 'There's a brave lot of lasses in the ranks, and they walk just as bravely as the men, and just take as big a step.'[11] The fragility and timidity of ideal Victorian ladyhood was not much in evidence here.

The female Salvationists were also expected to speak up in meetings to tell of their faith in God and to describe their past experiences. Women were not accustomed to speaking in public. Those who had internalized dominant gender roles may have been particularly reluctant to expose their private lives and spiritual beliefs to public scrutiny. It is therefore not surprising that although women made up the majority of those attending Army meetings, men predominated among those giving testimony. Women who did testify were sometimes inaudible. Because testifying to the impact that God had had on their lives was considered a religious responsibility, women who felt the urge to give testimony but failed to do so were seen as disobeying God's will. At least in certain corps, every effort was made to encourage women to testify. Some corps had 'sisters' meetings,' where only women gave testimony. In other cases officers, especially female officers, made a particular point of encouraging women to testify and to pray publicly.[12]

Many women were not at all reluctant to testify. Outraged middle-class observers complained of female Salvationists who testified loudly and joyfully, sometimes shouting, jumping up and down, and going into trances.[13] Ecstatic faith in God could overcome many inhibitions and had certainly been known to do so in earlier revivals.[14] But by this period, even appeals to God's spiritual power could not justify such behaviour for most Ontarians. Female piety was valued, but only in the context of sedate and ladylike church attendance. The behaviour of Salvation Army women therefore hints at the possibility that middle-class conventions of passive, pious femininity had little relevance to the lives of many working-class women. The Salvation Army provided these women with the opportunity to play a more public role, and it encouraged those who were more constrained by traditional gender roles to behave with greater confidence in public forums.

Women's responsibility to testify to God's love was assumed to supersede their responsibility to obey temporal authorities, such as husbands and fathers. In the London barracks, when a husband tried physically to stop his wife from kneeling at the penitent form and testifying, he was prevented from doing so by 'members of the Army, especially the females.' He was told that his wife was 'God's property now.'[15] For other married women, the Salvation Army could justify a rejection of traditional roles and responsibilities, despite the opposition of their husbands. One husband complained that his wife kept him awake at night by holding 'knee-drills' at all hours. The *Toronto World* reported a more extreme case of a husband who allegedly tried to commit suicide because 'his wife, who joined the Salvation Army last March ... has not been home, so he says, an evening since.'[16]

Men may have felt abandoned, but women believed that conversion gave them the responsibility to become more than domestic drudges. Drum Major Annie, an oil worker's wife from Petrolia, provides us with what appears to be the authentic voice of one such woman. In responding to a satirical attack on the Army she commented: 'Give us credit for the energy displayed in beating a drum, in playing a tambourine, in marching weary miles daily after attending to our domestic duties, the daily part of our unending toil, for while man's work is from sun to sun, women's work is never done ... We have willingly added to a toilsome, weary life much more of toil, and of weariness, of sorrow, of strivings, physical and spiritual, of anxious pleadings, of earnest exhortations, of willing self-sacrifice, that he and kindred wretches might be saved from the punishment they so richly deserve.'[17] Attempting to save the souls of these wretches may have added to women's traditional burdens, but it also offered a sense of mission and significance to the otherwise narrow and undervalued lives of working-class wives, as well as providing them with a justification for moving beyond the domestic sphere.

For the unmarried female soldiers, the Army provided a similar rationale for moving beyond parental authority. Concerns were expressed that young people were disobeying their parents by attending Army meetings far into the night. One particularly unhappy clergyman complained that the Army led young women 'from the shelter and duties of home and (if their sweet wills so decide) to disregard the wishes or even commands of parents.'[18] For many working women, involvement with the Army also justified defying employers. This appears to have been particularly true of servants. A number of newspapers echoed the complaint of Barrie's *Northern Advance* that 'a large number of the soldiers are domestics who should be at home at 10 o'clock at the outside, but who are often out until after midnight. It is impossible for them to attend to their duties properly the next day.'[19]

Sexuality and Salvation

While the evangelical emphasis of the Army could directly justify women's defiance of husbands, parents, and employers in the name of salvation, the Army also inadvertently provided space for those who sought to defy certain social conventions that were strongly upheld by the Army. The Army went to considerable effort to ensure that its meetings would be exclusively religious and would not be used as an excuse for any kind of sexual involvement. In Kingston, it forbade young men from walking young women home from meetings, though this was a common practice in the churches. In other towns, Salvation officers vigilantly tried to prevent the exchange of flirtatious looks or comments during religious meetings.[20] Despite this, the meetings provided an opportunity for young women and men – both soldiers and those who attended on a more casual basis – to meet and become romantically involved.

The late hours of Salvation Army meetings were justified by the need to struggle with those on the verge of a conversion experience. Many middle-class commentators, however, echoed the Anglican cleric who argued that 'excited meetings held up to late hours have led to licentiousness.' These commentators were horrified to report that, at the meetings, female officers kissed other women and hugged men in their efforts to bring them to salvation.[21] The fact that Salvation Army women played an active public role rather than remaining safe and pure within the domestic sphere may in itself have made them sexually suspect. The way that any perceived or actual sexual improprieties among Salvationists were hysterically denounced in the popular press suggests that the concerns went further than this, and that we may be observing a form of moral panic in which sexual fears were used as a scapegoat for deeper social fears – in this case, middle-class fears of working-class disorder and female autonomy.[22] It would therefore be unwise to take middle-class reports of Salvation Army sexual behaviour at face value.

Nonetheless, it does appear that the late hours and emotionalism of Salvation Army meetings could provide both the atmosphere and the opportunity for heterosexual contact among the many young people attending them. Army meetings also cast young women and men in an unaccustomed public light, which could increase their attraction to potential partners. A Salvation Army handbook cautioned: 'In selecting an individual for so important a relation as marriage, let no one be carried away with the mere appearance of a person in uniform, or their ability to speak or solo. A person who is all that can be desired on the platform may be entirely unsuitable as husband or wife.'[23]

Stories in the popular press suggest that male Salvationists made use of the Army to 'take advantage of' young women, but the nature of many of these relationships remains unclear. Some itinerant officers did exploit their public role to gain sexual access to women in the various corps where they were stationed. This was clearly the case with 'Happy Bob,' a former Thoroldite, who kept a photograph album titled 'The Conquests of Happy Bob of Canada ... The name and the age of some of my mashes while in the Salvation Army.'[24] A Lieutenant Adamson, who was found in the bedrooms of two different Hallelujah Lasses in one night, convinced no one with his explanation that he was there for the 'perfectly pure and noble purposes' of prayer and instruction.[25] The officers' responsibility for visiting converts and potential converts certainly gave them considerable opportunity for sexual adventure. However, women were not always passive victims. For some courting couples, the drive home from Salvation Army meetings provided the opportunity for a more consensual sexual relationship. Although the frequent accusations in the press of sexual looseness in the Salvation Army do reflect middle-class fears and prejudices, they also suggest that at the local level the Army may have provided a less constrained space for traditional courtship, a space that had at least a certain sanction of religious legitimacy.[26]

While many who used Salvation Army meetings as an opportunity for courtship were not Army members, a large number of members did deviate from official Army policy. This is also evident in the running battle in the pages of the *War Cry* over the wearing of uniforms. By the mid-1880s, all Salvationists were expected to wear a common official uniform. While the practice no doubt appealed to those accustomed to admiring the outfits of local firemen and bandsmen, the Army's clothing was considerably less elaborate than that favoured by most contemporary organizations. The plain navy blue uniform was intended to set Salvationists apart from the fashionable secular world and to proclaim their dedication to the saving of souls. While the *War Cry* denounced the many Salvation soldiers of both sexes who did not wear the uniform, most articles on this topic were aimed at women, who often subverted the uniform's purpose by adding lace, ribbons, or silk, or by wearing jewellery. Even though these women had a religious commitment to the Army, they were clearly not willing to renounce the world, as was expected of Salvation soldiers. They defined for themselves the nature of their involvement, which did not preclude participation in the contemporary young women's culture, with its emphasis on fashion and personal appearance.[27]

Not all Salvation soldiers were young. The female Salvationists included many older married women for whom the Army provided spiritual meaning, increased autonomy, and sometimes a transformed family life. The majority of the female Salvationists were, however, young working-class women. There were few associational or leisure avenues open to them, particularly in small-town Ontario, and the Salvation Army provided a space that was at least partly theirs – a space that provided excitement, spiritual significance, companionship, and the prospect of meeting interesting men.

There were also numerous young working-class women who attended Army meetings without becoming Salvation soldiers. For these women, many of whom were also involved in other churches, the Salvation Army offered excitement and entertainment without requiring any compromise with contemporary feminine interests. In some cases, young women attended Army services to laugh, heckle, and disrupt. Although such behaviour was far more common among young men, the 'giddy girls' reported in such incidents seem as far removed from the dominant feminine ideal as the women leading the services.[28]

Female Officers

The women who preached to the crowds that flocked to Army meetings to heckle, court, or be saved posed a major challenge to traditional gender roles. It is true that the Hallelujah Lasses were not the only women whom late-nineteenth-century audiences had seen on public platforms. Even small towns occasionally witnessed a travelling female temperance lecturer or spiritualist, and the presence of females on the public stage was even more common in the forms of popular entertainment that had been appropriated by the Salvation Army. For instance, travelling theatre companies often included women in starring roles in variety shows and melodramas, and female performers were frequent attractions in exhibitions of fancy skating at the roller rinks. In spite of such precedents – and certainly for the more respectable community, because of them – the Salvation Army's female officers, who not only appeared on public platforms but did so in the traditionally patriarchal role of religious leader, challenged the bounds of acceptable female behaviour.

Between 1882 and 1890, more than seven hundred Ontario women took up this challenge by becoming officers. These Hallelujah Lasses constituted more than 60 per cent of all Ontario officers. More than half of these women came from towns with populations of less than five thousand.[29] The officers were recruited from among the Salvation soldiers but, unlike the soldiers and adherents, they were expected to dedicate their entire lives to the salvation of others. Almost all female officers were involved in fieldwork, which meant that they worked with local corps. Two or three officers – a captain, a lieutenant, and sometimes a cadet – would be posted at each corps. They were expected to follow the directives issued by headquarters in Toronto and were subject to transfer at any time. However, their work required considerable initiative and effort, since field officers were responsible for all the tasks necessary to keep a local corps going. They had to organize and preach at a variety of services every night of the week as well as on Sunday. They were also responsible for the financial management of the corps, which involved organizing collections, paying local bills, and reporting on their financial situation to headquarters. During the day they visited both the converted and the unconverted, sold copies of the *War Cry* in the streets, and encouraged soldiers to do likewise. Officers also organized and led frequent street parades and were expected to plan innovative methods of drawing crowds.

In the early to mid-1880s, many of the female officers were sent to 'pioneer' the work in new towns. They faced a particularly daunting task, often preaching in the streets until they raised enough money to rent a hall. In order to gain an audience, these women had to be particularly imaginative. Before the development of standard Army uniforms, many deliberately exploited the particular interest shown in female preachers by wearing outfits designed to attract further attention to themselves and their cause. In this way, they certainly invited comparison with the flamboyant female performers of popular culture. For example: 'The three lassie officers who pioneered the work in Paris, Ontario, appeared in long red silk dresses reaching to within four inches of the ground. Six inches from the hem, in deep red letters, was the word "Hallelujah," and across the breast was boldly inscribed "The Salvation Army." Others wore red basques and blue shirts, red blouses or guernseys generously labelled with texts and declarations of faith. Immense straw hats draped with red bandana handkerchiefs were not uncommon.'[30]

Catherine Booth may have argued that preaching would exalt female officers' most womanly instincts, but the role of Salvation Army officer violated almost every facet of the dominant feminine ideal. Ladies were not expected to call attention to themselves, certainly not by marching in the streets in bizarre outfits that conjured up images of actresses and circus performers – or even more sexually suspect women. Respectable women were not supposed to abandon the domestic sphere for the public platform in any form, let alone by usurping the role of religious leader.

Who were the women who chose to take on this role, and why were they attracted to it? As noted in chapter 6, most female officers, like their male counterparts, were working class. The vast majority were unmarried, and both the city dwellers and those from smaller communities were much more likely to be employed than the average unmarried Ontario woman. Most had worked in traditional working-class female occupations (see table 29). Although the first Army officers were primarily English immigrants, most of the later ones appear to have been Canadian born.[31] Also, the officers were young – sometimes very young. Twelve per cent of female officers were less than eighteen when they became officers, and almost 80 per cent of officers of both sexes were less than twenty-five when they began their Army careers (see table 30).

The relative youth of most Salvation Army officers, both male and female, can be explained in a number of ways. It can certainly be linked

to the youthful nature of the Army congregations from which the officers were drawn. Younger people would also have been less burdened
with family responsibilities, and as a result would have been more willing to take up the itinerant role of Salvation Army officer. The officers
were transferred from place to place every three to six months, and for
many young people, particularly those from small towns, the opportunity to travel, especially to the larger cities, would have been appealing.
Another point is that youth was a period of spiritual introspection. For
those brought up in the evangelical tradition, this was generally the time
when they expected to experience conversion. The autobiographies of
female officers reveal that many of them were raised in Methodist
homes, where the conversion experience was 'closely associated with
the passage into adulthood.'[32] For these women, becoming an officer –
which required not only conversion but also a complete rejection of the
secular world and a commitment to assist in the conversion of others –
was congruent with the religious values they had learned in childhood.
In fact, the Salvation Army offered these women a more active role than
their own church in the spiritual work of salvation which Methodists
claimed to value most highly.

The weakening of the evangelical tradition in the mainstream
churches is underlined by the fact that Methodist parents were as
opposed as any other parents to their daughters' decision to dedicate
their lives to the salvation of others as officers in the Salvation Army.
The high proportion of female officers who were gainfully employed
may reflect the fact that these women would have been less constrained
by family opposition to their joining the Army. This would be particularly true for servants, who did not live with their own families. Working women who did live with their parents may have found that wage
earning provided them with some margin of independence in opposing
their parents' wishes. According to the autobiographies published in the
War Cry, many of the officers shared the experience of Captain Abbie
Thompson of Kingston, who on entering the Army, 'left home, dis-
owned and rejected.'[33] Some parents' opposition was based on a rejection of their daughters' religious beliefs. For others, religious commitment could not justify what was clearly viewed as a less than
respectable lifestyle. Lieutenant Nancy Maxwell's mother 'regarded her
as nothing better than a street singer' for choosing to become a Salvation
Army officer.[34]

While religious commitment did not mollify outraged parents, it
could justify a daughter's challenge to parental authority. One woman

whose parents would not allow her to become an officer threw [herself] 'at His feet and gave Him my life and my all ... After promising the Lord, I told my parents what I had done, and now that I must go without their consent if they would not grant it.'[35] Like other evangelical sects, the Army's emphasis on salvation left more scope for challenging traditional authority structures than more mainstream churches did.[36] Religious commitment, while sincere, could thus be used to carve out some autonomy for young women and could justify their escape from oppressive family situations.

For some women, escaping from parental supervision also gave them more freedom to meet potential marriage partners. On occasion, the Army was used for both purposes: 'Shouting Nelly, the Hallelujah lass from Toronto whose mother was recently compelled to invoke the authority of the police to compel her to remain at home, has returned to the city and has most effectually prevented the old lady from interfering with her liberty in the future by marrying one of the Army boys.'[37] Male and female officers, most of whom were single, had frequent contact and sometimes worked together. The Army was aware that a search for romance played a role in at least some enlistment decisions. An 1890 *War Cry* article asked: '[Do men] become officers to get wives? Girls come into the Army to find a man, get married and settled down? Perhaps some do ... The cap may fit some readers. Well, don't ask others to wear it.' The fact that the officers' manual stated that courting was forbidden during one's first twelve months as an officer and that flirting would result in dismissal is also telling.[38] The predominance of servants among the Hallelujah Lasses may in part be explained by the opportunities for contact with men that were available in the Army. These opportunities were generally denied servants through the conditions of their work, since they had only one evening off a week and were not permitted to receive 'gentlemen callers.'[39]

Although both senior Army officials and the popular press were most concerned about heterosexual involvement among officers, the Salvation Army provided female officers with a variety of social relationships. Many female officers developed the close relationships with other women that were apparently common among the middle class in the nineteenth-century.[40] Newspapers frequently commented on the warm friendships among female Salvation Army officers. For example, when Captain Nellie Ryerson, who had been working in Kingston with Captain Abbie Thompson, was to be sent to a new post, the two women 'were the objects of much attention as they walked about the waiting room with their arms around each others waists like two happy school girls, and this evidence of their affection for each other was supplemented by a hearty kiss.'[41]

The Salvation Army Training Home for Women provided an opportunity for young working-class women to live, work, and study together, at least briefly, in a manner that was generally only available to middle-class women who attended boarding school or university. The shared religious mission of female cadets appears to have fostered particularly close ties, as can be seen in various references to the sadness of having to 'break up our family' at the end of the Training Home course.[42] Relationships among female officers may also have been encouraged by the Army rule that single women must work in couples to avoid endangering their reputations. Thus, two or three women often ventured alone into a new town to set up a corps, sometimes facing hostility and persecution, conditions that were likely to develop close bonds among those involved. These relationships may have been sought particularly eagerly by servants, whose working conditions provided as little opportunity for socializing with their peers as they did for meeting potential marriage partners.

Some secular newspapers of the period put forward another, far more material, explanation for the motivations of Salvation Army officers. The *Toronto World* suggested that the Salvation Army

offers 'light' work, along with good clothes, good board, and a good time generally. What wonder then, that 'Captain Jacks' and 'Hallelujah Lasses' abound? They are simply trying to earn their living in this way, because situations in stores are difficult to obtain and they will not go on the farm ... The 'lass' ... wants to escape the drudgery of the kitchen, or the factory. More than that, it may be that opportunities for entering upon such drudgery may not very easily be found, to suit her. The 'hallelujah' door is open, and she goes in. Employment, wages and living make the main motive.[43]

The *World* was generally hostile to the Salvation Army, and the above passage has a clear class bias. Nonetheless, it may have reflected a reality for at least some potential officers. The Army officials were aware of this, and in their fervent appeal for candidates they stated that 'people who have anything in a material sense to gain by volunteering are not required.' Salvation Army wages were not high. Single male field officers appear to have received six dollars a week, single women five dollars, and married men ten dollars.[44] Since the wages were generally taken out of local collections, officers who had little local support earned much less. Nonetheless, for most women, the wages in the Army were at least equal to those they could receive in other employment.[45] This does not imply that women were joining the Army just to make a living, though this may have been true for some, especially those facing unemployment. But it does indicate that material conditions did not discourage women from entering the Army. If they were facing the choice between drudgery in a factory or someone else's kitchen or the life of a Salvation Army officer – with its sense of high spiritual calling, relative freedom, and male and female companionship – it is not surprising that many young women chose to become officers.

Hallelujah Lasses and Lady Knights: Working-Class Women and the Feminine Ideal

The public role offered by the Salvation Army provided a further attraction for potential candidates. While the circus or theatre may have given a small number of working-class women access to the public stage, there were certainly few opportunities for working-class women to play as active and powerful a public role as that available through the Salvation Army. The Army's official appeals for candidates reflect an awareness that the public nature of this role could draw both women and men. They pointed out to potential female candidates that 'the little lassie whom nobody knew when she was a servant at Mr. Grocer's, is welcomed by streets full of people.'[46]

How can one understand this apparent willingness of a significant number of Canadian working women to flout traditional gender roles? The example of female entertainment figures may have lessened the reluctance of working-class women to play a public role. Moreover, working-class women were more accustomed to working in the public sphere, albeit in humble positions, than their middle-class counterparts. But were working-class women's material and cultural experiences so different from those of middle-class women that they simply did not accept dominant definitions of femininity? Not necessarily. The constraints of conventional gender roles appear to have discouraged many working-class women from joining the Knights of Labor.

Leonora Barry, the organizer of women's work for the Knights, cited 'natural pride, timidity and the restrictions of social custom' as a barrier to women's organization.[47] Some women were able to overcome these concerns and joined the Knights. Certainly, Katie McVicar, who corresponded with the *Palladium* about the concerns of women workers and went on to organize the first woman's assembly in Canada, is a case in point. However, McVicar may have been unusual. The comments of a female co-worker suggest that this was so, for she stated: 'Organization ... was all very well, but how were girls to accomplish it; were they to advertise mass meetings, mount platforms and make speeches? If so, the Canadian girls, at least, would never organize.'[48] The fact that when McVicar died, the assembly petitioned Terence Powderly, the Knights' 'general master workman,' to appoint a man to chair their meetings points to the reality of such sentiments.[49]

What is one to assume then about the behaviour of Hallelujah Lasses, who were so willing to 'advertise mass meetings, mount platforms and make speeches'? Were middle-class conceptions of femininity less relevant to the young working women who became Salvation Army officers than to those who joined the Knights? There may be some truth in this, given the Knights' assertions of respectability, which involved a valorization of conventional family life and an acceptance of many aspects of the dominant gender ideology. (Remember those lady Knights riding in carriages at the St Catharines parade.)

However, there is something else going on here. Unlike the lady Knights, the Salvation Army officers were not mounting platforms, making speeches, and marching in parades in order to improve their own lives and their own working conditions. As the *War Cry* continually reminded them, by becoming Salvation Army officers, they had abandoned all self-interest and had dedicated their entire lives to Christ. In their autobiographies many women spoke of the complete self-sacrifice and the perfect obedience they were willing to give to God. Such self-sacrifice and submission, while expected of all officers, may have been particularly attractive to women, since it fitted so clearly with the contemporary feminine ideal. For some women, the public behaviour required of them as officers may have been justified as part of a most feminine and Christian submission to God's will. This was clearly the official Salvation Army position, as illustrated by a story in the *War Cry* of an officer's wife whose refusal to preach and testify publicly was presented as evidence of disobedience to God's will and a refusal to give herself completely to God.[50]

The bounds of acceptable feminine behaviour were certainly much narrower than the bounds of male behaviour. Mounting public platforms and marching in the streets placed women beyond respectable norms, and indeed by making them 'public' women it could threaten their sexual reputation. This may have contributed to the reluctance of many Knights of Labor women to play an active role in the movement. Salvation Army women could, however, justify their behaviour in the most feminine of ways, as obedience to God's will. But the question remains whether female Salvation Army officers flouted dominant gender roles reluctantly, as part of their submission to God, or whether they more consciously rejected these roles, which were not relevant to their own experience, while clothing this rejection in the conventional rhetoric of feminine passivity. An examination of women's role in Salvation Army rescue work provides some clues here.

In 1886 the Canadian Salvation Army followed the lead of the English Army by embarking on social service work. The first Canadian effort in this direction was the founding of a rescue home for prostitutes in Toronto. In 1890 other rescue homes were opened in a number of cities, as were a children's shelter and two homes for discharged prisoners. Social service work fitted the contemporary feminine ideal far more closely than preaching before crowds did. Appeals for volunteers for the social service division relied heavily on contemporary conceptions of femininity. The *War Cry* called for 'whole-hearted devoted women ... charged with a deep compassion for the lost' whose 'highest joy' was self-sacrifice. It appears that the response to this appeal to women's feminine nature was less than expected. In 1888 the *War Cry* called on 'officers and soldiers ... girls and women ... who from diffidence and possible lack of knowledge of the need have refrained from offering for service in this direction.' Since the rescue work was continually highlighted in the *War Cry* over the next two years, ignorance of the work could not explain why at the end of this period they were still appealing almost desperately for volunteers.[51]

In an article entitled 'How She Became a Rescue Officer,' one finds a candid confession of a reluctance to leave preaching for rescue work – though of course, once she was involved, the author claims to have come to love it.[52] But many women did not come to love this work. Half of all the women who were posted to rescue work left the Army immediately after their posting.[53] Most female officers clearly preferred an active public role as preacher to the more private self-denying and suitably feminine role of angel of mercy. This implies a certain rejection of or indifference towards middle-class norms of femininity among Army officers. However, the reluctance to enter social service work reflected not just an unwillingness to give up preaching, but a refusal to work with 'fallen' women and female alcoholics.[54] This suggests that most female officers shared certain contemporary attitudes about such women. Neither self-denying religious commitment nor sisterhood could overcome both a distaste for the 'fallen' and the fear of moral contagion instilled by the mores of the dominant culture.

Why Leave the Army?

While women who entered social service work were the most likely to leave the Salvation Army, turnover rates were high among all officers. The Army was rarely a lifetime commitment. More than one-third (35 per cent) of the female officers remained in the Army for no more than a year, and over 60 per cent stayed for three years or less. The male officers had even higher turnover rates, with 44 per cent remaining in the Army for no more than a year (see table 31). The relatively brief careers of most officers, as well as the rapid falling away of many soldiers, can be explained in part by the highly evangelical nature of the Army. Most emotional revivalistic religious movements that focus on conversion have similar difficulties in retaining members over the long term.

Salvation Army officers also faced various hardships that help to explain the high turnover rates. As mentioned earlier, the officers took their salaries from local collections, so when there was little or no local interest in the Army they could be reduced to near starvation.[55] As well, harassment from rowdy young men and persecution by local town councils may have provided a satisfying sense of martyrdom for a year or two, but a lifetime of persecution and harassment would ultimately lose its appeal.

Articles in the *War Cry* denouncing marriage to non-Salvationists suggest that these marriages, which were forbidden to officers, may also explain the relatively high turnover rates. While the Army stressed that officers who had committed their lives to God could live happy, holy, and useful lives if they remained unmarried, the dominant values, which viewed unmarried women as failures, were not so readily disregarded.[56] Among the minority of the female officers who made a commitment of more than ten years to the Army, almost half had married fellow officers within the first five years of their officerships.[57]

Despite these reasons, it is in some ways surprising that young women were almost as quick to leave the Army as young men were. Young men had many other options beyond the Army, options that in most cases did not require the rejection of the rough norms of youthful masculinity. But young working women had fewer alternatives, especially in small-town Ontario, and those that did exist certainly did not provide a space for the articulation of a distinctly assertive working-class femininity, as did the role of a Hallelujah Lass.

The Salvation Army was a male-dominated hierarchical organization that preached submission to God's will and idealized the dominant form of the family. Despite this, working-class women, who had few social outlets beyond the home or the middle-class-dominated churches, were able to use the Army to carve out more space for themselves. For many, especially younger women, the Army provided the justification to defy parents, husbands, and employers, the opportunity to create their own community, and increased freedom to meet potential marriage partners in that community. The Salvation Army also offered working-class women an unprecedented public voice. These women were certainly not speaking out for their own liberation, but by testifying in public or preaching before crowds, Salvationist women were far more audible and visible than the constraints of their lives usually permitted.

The fact that many women took up the opportunities made available by the Army suggests that the dominant ideal of passive, silent femininity may have had little reality for most working-class women. Nevertheless, its continued relevance in at least some form is seen in the reluctance of many women to speak out in public and in the fact that those who did so justified their behaviour as a most feminine submission to God's will. The fact that, for most, the role of Hallelujah Lass represented a fairly brief youthful stage demonstrates most clearly the continued value placed on conventional female roles, as well as the hardships and limitations of Army life. The opportunities made available through the Army were real, but for most women, particularly the officers, they were taken up only briefly in the years prior to marriage.

Many working-class women remained church members, or if they joined the Army as young women they later returned to the churches. On Sundays these women and their middle-class counterparts listened to middle-class male ministers preach of the value of women's role as pious, moral mothers, while during the week working-class women could play secondary roles in the female church associations, which exerted at best informal and occasional power in a male-dominated church structure. However, this vision of a cross-class pious and subordinated sisterhood is certainly not complete. The popularity of the Salvation Army among working-class women underlines the importance of Christianity to these women. At the same time, it also reveals that the dominant gender ideals of passive piety were at best an awkward fit for many working-class women, both within and beyond the mainstream churches.

8

'Safe in the Arms of Jesus': The Thorold Revival

Thorold, January 1893. The Salvation Army has departed years ago, and the tiny remaining Knights of Labor assembly will fold before year's end. Economic conditions, while bad throughout the country, are particularly grim here. There have been frequent bankruptcies among the local merchants, and many Front Street stores have been left vacant. No new industry has replaced the silverworks, which left Thorold three years ago, and in the fall of 1892 the owner of the casket factory died, precipitating the temporary closure of the establishment and prompting fears of permanent shutdown.[1]

In the fall of 1892 the leaders of Thorold's four Protestant churches joined together to invite the famous Canadian evangelists Hugh Crossley and John Hunter to visit the town. The evangelists arrived in mid-January and for four weeks preached daily to crowded churches. At the peak of the revival, many businesses, including the Welland House, a popular hotel, closed their doors for a few hours to permit employees to attend weekday services. The regular social life of the community came to a standstill. Even the band, no fan of the churchgoing community, postponed a planned concert in deference to the revival.[2]

The evangelists' efforts had impressive results. Almost four hundred people were converted in a community of approximately two thousand. It is no surprise that the *Thorold Post* called it 'The Great Revival.' Methodist church membership more than doubled, and both the Presbyterians and Anglicans also added to their numbers.[3] The converts came from all walks of life, including significant numbers of working-class people and young men. In responding to a revival that had clearly touched the entire Protestant community, Thorold's municipal council took the unusual step of passing a resolution 'to record their high appreciation of the noble work performed by [the evangelists], leading to the moral improvement of so many of our people.'[4] Crossley and Hunter were frequently able to effect large-scale conversions, but the Thorold revival ranks among their more impressive successes. Certainly, few of their 1893 visits to other Ontario communities came close to being as significant, at least when measured in the number of converts.[5]

How can one explain the evangelists' success among all classes in Thorold, a community whose working class had been sufficiently class-conscious to organize three assemblies of the Knights of Labor and to resort to strikes to solve a range of disputes? Thorold's dire economic situation of the early 1890s and the particularly gendered nature of the revival provide some answers here. At the same time, this unique event must be understood within the larger context of religious and leisure involvement in small-town Ontario. An understanding of this context also illuminates the postrevival period, when, with the emotional immediacy of conversion long past, male and female converts made decisions about whether to remain in the churches or to return to more familiar alternatives.

Revivals

While the Thorold revival was unusual in its scope and intensity, revivals were a common event for evangelical Protestant churchgoers in this period. An increasing number were interdenominational, though most churches continued to organize them separately. Local ministers often conducted their own 'special services,' though professional outside talent was increasingly called upon. The minutes of various congregations record that when finances were low and membership was decreasing, ministers and lay leaders often sought to engage the temporary services of a professional evangelist.[6] Through the revival services conducted by these men, the local leaders hoped to bring more souls to Christ, to increase membership numbers, and to restore the zeal (and generosity) of existing church members. For example, in 1887 the Reverend J.M. Kerr of Toronto preached in Campbellford's Methodist church for three weeks, and 'the church [was] crowded nightly.' The *Campbellford Herald* noted that through Kerr's services 'fifty to sixty persons have come into the light of a new day.'[7]

In a similar vein, every few years the Catholics brought in outside priests to conduct what were called parish missions. These missions were intended to reiterate the basic teachings of Catholicism, to strengthen the faith of the parishioners, and to bring any doubters back into the fold.[8] At these missions, efforts were made to reach all parishioners. Services were held several times a day for a week or more. At a mission which the Carmelite Fathers held in Thorold in early 1890, the first mass of the day 'for the working classes' was held at five-thirty in the morning. Other Catholic missions, or retreats, were aimed at particular groups within the congregations. For instance, a retreat for the young men of the Thorold parish was held in March 1886.[9] If the reports of local papers are to be believed, both retreats and missions were very popular. 'Large crowds' attended a mission in Ingersoll conducted by visiting priests in which 'the great truths of religion and the existence of Heaven and Hell, the mission of the Redeemer and a final judgement' were 'laid before the people in a clear and forcible light.' And later the same year, a mission service that involved 'the performance of acts of devotion, prayer, fasting and alms' attracted 'nearly the whole congre gation of the Sacred Heart Church.'[10]

Although there were parallels between the Catholic parish missions and the Protestant evangelical revivals, there were also significant differences. The main function of the revivals, and certainly the way in which their success was judged, was their ability to bring people to salvation through a conversion experience. Such an experience was necessarily intense and emotional. In some cases, the methods used to bring listeners to a recognition of their sinful, unsaved state were themselves exceedingly emotional, as in the case of the Salvation Army. However, by the late nineteenth century, the 'blood and fire' emotionalism and rowdy methods typical of the Salvation Army were not acceptable to the more mainstream Protestant evangelists. These evangelists sought to emulate the Army's success while jettisoning their 'objectionable' methods. For example, the 'Savage Band,' a group of young men and women who worked under the leadership of the Reverend D. Savage, held services which the *Ingersoll Chronicle* described as 'similar to those of the Salvation Army but without the offensive street parade and its noisy accompaniment.'[11]

Other evangelists, such as the famous Canadian revival team of Hugh Crossley and John Edwin Hunter, were even more careful to avoid the excesses of the Army. As the *Petrolia Advertiser* noted, Crossley and Hunter were 'not of the theatrical jumping jack order of evangelists.'[12] They were both Methodist ministers, appointed by the Methodist Church to act as professional travelling evangelists. As David Marshall and Kevin Kee have shown, Crossley and Hunter eschewed the more

complex intellectual approach popular among some evangelical ministers, promulgating instead a simple message of Christian faith and the
need for repentance and conversion. Their services 'were a mixture of
biblical exposition, hymn singing and exhortation,' which appealed to
people from all evangelical denominations.[13] Marshall suggests that the
evangelists focused more on the compassion than on the wrath of God,
but Crossley and Hunter's services did include spirited attacks on sin
and threats of hell-fire. The *Thorold Post* reported, 'Mr. Hunter is pugilis-
tic in his style, dealing sharp blows right and left. The bar room, the ball
room and the theatre are the special subjects of his attention and for
them he has no quarter.' While avoiding the Army's overtly emotional
approach, both evangelists did play on their listeners' emotions, including their terror of eternal damnation, sketching fearful pictures of young
men and women who died at dances before repenting of their sinful
ways.[14]

The Converted

According to the *Thorold Post*, Hunter and Crossely's efforts caused
many townsfolk to 'manifest anxiety about their spiritual safety,' and
large numbers responded to the evangelists' call for repentance and salvation. Who was converted in Thorold's Great Revival? The *Post* noted
that those who had 'acknowledged a change of heart' included 'many
heads of families and people of responsibility and position.'[15] While the
conversion of 'people of position' may have been most noteworthy, the
converts came from all classes. In fact, working-class people predominated – the proportion of working-class converts was far higher than
that of middle-class converts.[16] This was particularly true among married people. Working-class married women were much more likely to be
converted than their middle-class counterparts (see table 32). Similarly,
few middle-class married men were converted, but a significant number
of working-class 'heads of families' were brought into the churches.
Since relatively few of Thorold's working-class married men had been
church members before the revival, the ratio of revival converts to previous church members was about one to two (see table 32).

Among single people, working-class young men and women were
slightly more likely to be converted than their middle-class counterparts, but the revival precipitated the conversion of many young people
from all classes. The conversion of large numbers of young people was a
common pattern at revivals, but what was particularly noteworthy here

was the large number of single males who were converted. While women formed the majority of all revival converts, as they did of church congregations as a whole, single males made up almost two-thirds of all male revival converts in a startling reversal of normal patterns of male church membership. Among young working-class males, there were more than three times as many revival converts as there had been single male working-class church members before the revival. Among single middle-class males, there were twice as many revival converts as previous church members – still an impressive change (see table 32).

Some of the young male converts were very young indeed. In fact about 20 per cent of the converts of both sexes were thirteen years old or less. The majority of single male converts over thirteen were in their mid- to late teens, whereas the single female converts were more evenly divided between those in their teens and those in their twenties (see table 33). Most of the younger converts appear to have attended Thorold's Methodist Sunday school.[17] While Sunday school attendance may have created some understanding of Christian teachings and of the importance of salvation, it certainly did not guarantee conversion, as was witnessed by the concern among the mainstream churches that they lost most of their male students once they reached their teens.[18]

The revival brought young men into the churches who would normally have been lost to them, at least until marriage. This was true for both middle- and working-class young men, but were the patterns and meaning of conversion the same for the young men of both classes? For churchgoing middle-class families, the revival provided the opportunity to bring the young men, whom they feared they would lose, into the bosom of the Christian family as well as into the Christian church. More than 85 per cent of the middle-class converts belonged to families that already included at least one church member, usually either husband or wife, while half of the single middle-class converts were following in the path of both parents who were already church members (see table 34). For a very few middle-class families, the revival offered the chance to convert either husband or wife. This was, however, not the common pattern, as it may have been in earlier American revivals.[19] The Crossley and Hunter revival made it possible for many of Thorold's middle-class families to rejoice in the salvation of their daughters and, most surprisingly, of their sons as well.

The patterns among working-class families were rather different. This should come as no surprise, since working-class family members were far more likely to go their own way on Sundays than was the case in middle-class families. Almost 40 per cent of the working-class converts came from families that had no previous links to the churches (table 34). In a very few cases, an entire family – husband, wife, and children – was brought to salvation by the revival. This was true of the Manly family. Teamster Jack Manly, his wife Ann, and their children May and Walter all became church members for the first time through the efforts of Crossley and Hunter. The experience of Eliza Pound, wife of a Thorold labourer, who was the first member of her family to join the church and the only one to do so during the revival, was far more common, though in some nonchurchgoing working-class families two siblings, or a parent and child, were converted together. If the working-class converts did have a family member who already belonged to a local church, it was most commonly their mother. Only 15 per cent of the working-class converts came from families in which both parents were already church members (table 34).

Although a few working-class churchgoing wives and one husband had the joy of witnessing the conversion of a spouse, such occurences were rare, just as they were among the middle class. However, the reason they were rare among the middle class was that usually both partners had already been church members before the revival. This was not the case in most working-class families, and the revival did little to change the situation. Crossley and Hunter warned against marriage to the unconverted, citing Biblical authority: 'Be ye not unequally yoked together with unbelievers.'[20] Nevertheless, even though the evangelists did bring many more working-class Thoroldites into the churches, they did not bring many more working-class families, particularly husbands and wives, into shared church membership. Working-class mothers may have rejoiced in the conversion of sons and daughters, but in most working-class homes Christianity was no more the basis for a shared domesticity among all family members after the revival than it had been before.

Class, Gender, and the Revival

Even though the revival did not create working-class replicas of middle-class Christian family togetherness, it did bring into the churches many working-class Thoroldites, male and female, single and married. The popularity of the Salvation Army and the Knights of Labor demonstrated the significance of distinct working-class values and identity even at the small-town level. Why in Thorold, where the Knights were especially strong, were the working classes drawn so firmly into the churches through a cross-class revival? More particularly, why did Crossley and Hunter have so much success in converting working-class men, especially single men, who had been virtually absent from the churches prior to the revival?

In trying to explain the large-scale conversions brought about by Crossley and Hunter's revival, the concept of respectability is of little relevance. A concern with respectability may help explain why people join the church in staider times or why they remain there for years *after* a revival, but this concept is of limited value in helping us understand why certain individuals undergo a conversion experience in the highly charged emotional atmosphere of a revival. While spiritual reasons are no doubt significant – and are certainly central to the individuals experiencing a conversion – the fact that respectability is not important here does not deny the significance of other social factors in explaining the success of Thorold's Great Revival.

Given the extremely depressed economic condition of Thorold in the early 1890s, it is likely that anxiety about economic prospects played a role in many conversions.[21] By 1893 the prosperity of the early to mid-1880s, brought about by the building and deepening of the Welland Canal, was a distant memory. In 1891 at least 16 per cent of Thorold's working-class men were unemployed, and the economic situation worsened over the next two years.[22] An increasing number of merchants were going bankrupt, while others struggled to survive. Workers at the casket factory, one of the few relatively large-scale local employers, had recently been laid off and feared the permanent closure of the establishment. Despite occasional rumours, no new factories appeared to have any plans to set up shop in Thorold. Most of the young men faced the prospect of unemployment or of leaving for the West or the United States to search for a job.

The demise of the Knights of Labor had left many working-class Thoroldites without a distinct space of their own and without an organization that offered answers to their economic and social concerns. In an environment of economic uncertainty, many were searching for answers and for some source of stability in their lives. It may be symptomatic of larger patterns that while only five of the Thorold Knights who could be identified were church members before the revival, an additional four were converted by Crossley and Hunter. Some form of Christian belief may have been part of these men's lives before the revival, but at this time they and others sought the emotional commitment and certainty that religious conversion could provide.

In the American context, Curtis Johnson has argued that what he and other scholars call 'demand-side' issues – economic and social concerns beyond the churches – were not the only forces shaping the success of revivals. He argues that 'supply-side' issues – the nature of the revival itself and of the churches that sponsored it – were equally important.[23] Hunter and Crossley's particular approach was certainly crucial to the success of Thorold's Great Revival. While dominant gender roles were integral to contemporary mainstream Christianity, the particularly gendered nature of this revival is striking. Separate men's meetings were a common element of the revivalists' services in Thorold as elsewhere, and separate meetings for women were only occasionally featured.[24] The fact that women's meetings were less common than those for men is an indication of the evangelists' attitude to women. They certainly did not see women as playing an active role in the conversion of others as in the Salvation Army. When Hunter was asked whether women should preach and pray at public meetings, he responded by acknowledging that 'women should be heard, and God has blessed them in work,' but went on to state that he 'never could favour women preachers ... I would not want my wife to preach.'[25] For this evangelist as for most Ontarians, women's primary role was to be in the home.

Kevin Kee has found that Crossley's writings point to a somewhat more progressive attitude to women's role in the chruch, but Kee argues that in the revival work of the two men Hunter's approach prevailed, and 'opportunities to promote women in the church were frequently missed, even rebuffed.' Some American revivalists and even some Canadian ones countenanced women playing an active if subordinate role in spiritual work during a revival, for example, by going from door to door encouraging conversion. During a significant revival in Campbellford 'the ladies of the church [organized] with a view to carrying on Christian work throughout the village.' This sort of effort was rarely encouraged by Crossley and Hunter.[26] Moreover, their intense focus on the spiritual realm limited the more conventional roles that women had carved out for themselves in the church. They opposed the many 'questionable entertainments' that women customarily organized to raise money for the churches, maintaining that these events sullied the purity of the churches' spiritual focus. They argued that the only acceptable entertainments were non-fund-raising events that were intended to forge closer bonds among church members.[27] In Thorold the only active role for women sanctioned by the revivalists was that of encouraging young men to be sexually 'pure.' Crossley appealed to the young women of the community, asserting that 'soon men would be found as pure as women are required to be ... if women demanded of men the same exalted purity that men demanded of them when seeking wives.'[28]

Although flesh-and-blood women were not to play a role in the revival, Crossley and Hunter were certainly not reluctant to call on a range of feminine images of the divine. David Marshall has discussed the importance of hymns in the evangelists' services. Many of these portray Jesus in idealized feminine terms: as tender, soft, loving, and forgiving. Converts sang of being 'Safe in the arms of Jesus/ Safe on His gentle breast.' Heaven, as Marshall notes, was also depicted in welcoming, domestic imagery.[29] These feminine religious images may have been particulary evident in the services of these revivalists, but in fact they were becoming increasingly popular in late-nineteenth-century Protestantism. Thelka Caldwell has identified the use of similar feminized religious imagery during the American Third Great Awakening of the late nineteenth and early twentieth centuries. Caldwell argues that the contemporary idealization of women as pious moral mothers permitted the association of feminine virtues with Jesus while masculine sin became the focus of evangelist concern.[30]

In Thorold, as in many other Ontario communities, Crossley and Hunter focused much of their energy on the transformation of the men, who were far more likely than the women to be absent from church pews and to stray from the paths of righteousness. The evangelists attacked a range of sins that in contemporary discourse were associated primarily, if not exclusively, with men. Sexual 'impurity' was one of these sins. At revival meetings for 'men and boys only,' Crossley 'told the audience the things which many need to know concerning the laws of their physical being, and pointed out the terrible results of indulgences in secret vices.' While some may have been shocked by the subject matter, the *Post* assured its readers that Crossley's language was 'unmistakably plain and strong, yet so chaste that the most fastidious could take no exception to his mode of treating the delicate subjects which he handled.'[31] Others may have been less shocked, and indeed the large crowds at these men's meetings suggests that many sought titillation as well as salvation here. This was probably one of the first times that most of them had ever heard sexuality discussed from the pulpit, for the local ministers were unwilling to make more than oblique references to such topics.

While the evangelists' emphasis on sexuality may have been unfamiliar to Thorold churchgoers, the other typically masculine sins they denounced – including loafing, gambling, drinking, and using tobacco – were regularly featured in the local sermons.[32] Like the resident ministers, the evangelists aimed their words particularly at single young men. However, other elements of their message were intended for all men, whether single or married. Crossley and Hunter often appealed to men as workers, seeing men as united by their willingness to do 'honest work' rather than divided by class. Crossley 'besought all to learn trades or some useful business,' asserting that 'anyone who did not earn a living with his hands or his head or his means could not be a gentleman.' Both evangelists were ever ready to denounce the 'upper ten,' stating that these people were 'at the top ... for the same reason that froth is at the top.'[33] While such attacks were aimed at the supposed idleness of the very rich, they also focused on the fondness for dancing and other moral evils in 'high society.'

The evangelists had a particular message for married working men. Work was important, but for married men true Christianity also required a commitment to family responsibilities, in death as in life. Hunter 'recommended his hearers to make their peace with God, and also to invest in some life insurance. He had seen many widows left suffering because the husband had been too careless or too stingy to take out a policy of insurance; many a widow earning a living at the wash tub while the departed husband was singing hallelujahs in heaven.' In his chivalrous support of defenceless womanhood, Hunter argued that men should deal fairly with their wives and daughters in their wills and not leave all of their resources to their sons. Mindful of who controlled family resources, the evangelist also reminded men that 'the church of Christ should not be forgotten in the Christian's will.'[34]

Most of these messages were not new. Local ministers had encouraged men to support the church financially, to work hard, to be responsible breadwinners, and, most particularly, to eschew the life of bar rooms and street corners. Many married men tried to live up to such strictures, but most single men did not – staying away from 'feminized' churches, which they saw as the antithesis of true masculinity. When the Salvation Army had similarly attacked masculine vices and upheld the virtues of true Christian manhood, it had made many converts – but had evoked considerable hostility from young men. The more respectable cross-class appeal of Crossley and Hunter may have protected them from open challenge and ridicule. More importantly though, in Thorold at least, Crossley and Hunter's revival came at a very different time from the Salvation Army's attack of almost ten years before. In bad economic

times, men of all ages and classes were more willing to listen to denunciations of male sin and to seek solace at the breast of a 'feminized' Jesus.
For men who were uncertain about their economic future and were
seeking new meaning in their lives, the clearly defined masculine roles
offered by the evangelists may have had a significant appeal.

While an affirmation of masculine roles was important in itself, the
economic situation was challenging men's ability to fulfil such roles
successfully. In this context, Crossley and Hunter's message of the centrality of Christianity to all spheres of male endeavour would have been
particularly reassuring. The evangelists saw productive work and financial responsibility to family members as integral to true manhood.
However, they focused much less on the material rewards of hard work,
self-discipline, and ambition than many other ministers. Crossley and
Hunter were very clear that the world of work was of secondary importance, and could not be separated from sacred concerns. Crossley
argued:

We should not try to separate business and politics from religion. People say
'business is business' but business is religion. Christianity is not a department of
life, but life itself, and when this is thought out in full what a dignity it gives to
life ...

Whether we are weighing groceries, ploughing the land or any other occupation, it should all be done as to the glory of God. If one admits he cannot be a
mechanic or a trader and be a Christian, he admits his personal dishonesty, and
libels God.[35]

For workers, such a message obviously denied the significance of class
differences, since all men were working for the same end: the glory of
God. In better economic times, middle-class men might have resented
the suggestion that their business practices should be judged in any
other than 'practical' worldly terms. However, for unemployed workers,
bankrupt merchants, or young men facing an uncertain economic
future, the message could have been comforting. Despite their best
efforts, they could not ensure that they would make a living, which was
(and remains) so integral to notions of true manhood. The evangelists
stated that for Christians there was no separate secular sphere in which
men could be judged on their work performance alone. They stressed
instead the centrality of Christian belief – which was far more under the
control of their male audiences than the world of work. Such a message
could only have bolstered these men's sense of themselves and helped

to draw them into the churches. For working-class men, this message may have had a further appeal: by defining the meaning of being a Christian in purely spiritual terms, Crossley and Hunter may have temporarily obscured the newer meanings of being a Christian, which included both material requirements and material inequalities.

The evangelists implicitly addressed working-class concerns over the valorization of wealth in the churches. In a sermon entitled 'Excuses,' Crossley and Hunter examined the different reasons people gave for refusing to join a church. Hunter noted that 'some would not be Christians because there were hypocrites in the churches.'[36] Some of those who put forward this argument may have been echoing the Knights of Labor or the Salvation Army, who were always ready to point to middle-class churchgoing hypocrites who donated money to the church while living immoral lives. Other 'excuses' also pointed to the distance many saw between being good Christians and being church members. According to Hunter, some nonmembers asserted that they lived good moral lives and therefore did not need the churches, which were divided into so many denominations that it was clear that even they could not agree on the truths of Christianity.

The very articulation of these arguments suggests that many people accepted some form of religious belief while remaining beyond the institutional churches. Given the relative predominance of the middle class among church members, it seems likely that the majority of these generic Christians would have been working class. Many of them felt themselves sufficiently close to Christ to experience conversion during the revival. Even after conversion, however, some did not wish to join a church, insisting that 'they could live as good a life outside the church as in it.' Hunter denied such claims, stating that 'it was like saying they could live as good a Christian life disobeying the Lord.' He urged converts 'to join the church where he or she could be the most at home.'[37]

While not explicitly recognizing the existence of social distinctions in the churches, the evangelists acknowledged that workers might feel more comfortable in some churches than in others. However, they denied that true Christianity could exist beyond the institutional churches. During the revival many workers, seeking security and comfort in a world that offered little of either, were willing to overlook the social barriers that had formerly limited their church participation. Many asserted the primacy of their identity as Christian women – and even as Christian men – and joined their middle-class counterparts in the churches that offered solace in troubled times.

The Results

In early February 1893 the revival came to an end. The *Post* reported that at the last meeting, the Reverend Mr Hunter 'closed with the most remarkable prayer ever offered at Thorold, asking the divine blessing personally and particularly on all, mentioning the ministers, the ushers, the business men of Thorold ... the young men ...' The only woman mentioned was the evangelists' hostess. The next morning Crossley and Hunter left on the train for St Thomas. They were seen off by a large crowd, which sang the hymn 'Shall We Gather at The River?' as the train pulled out of the station.[38]

With the revival over, did the community simply revert to pre-revival patterns? Had anything changed? The emphasis during the revival on male sins, and particularly the sins of young men, prompted church people to do more than just complain about the behaviour of these men. At a union meeting of the Protestant congregations, the Reverend Mr Mitchell of the Presbyterian church 'referred to the many times which remark had been made concerning the street lounging habits of many young men ... It was now proposed to show them that the Christian people were willing to second their words with practical effort.' This practical effort resulted in the formation of reading rooms for young men. The money for the rooms was raised largely by a committee of 'young ladies,' while other women organized the furnishing of the rooms. These traditional roles were, however, the extent of feminine involvement in this attempted transformation of the lifestyle of Thorold's young men. The reading rooms were under the supervision of the Protestant ministers and male lay church leaders.[39]

At the opening of the rooms, the *Post* noted that in the front room there were pictures of Crossley and Hunter, which would 'remind callers that the present cozy rooms are one of the many happy results of their labors here.' The reading rooms included a parlour, where 'the young men will be afforded an opportunity of playing various standard [parlour] games.'[40] These games did not include billiards, although in other communities even strict churchmen had argued that billiards were harmless when not associated with drinking or gambling.[41] Despite the absence of billiards, the organizers of the rooms attempted to appeal to young men of all classes. They explicitly did not pattern themselves on the local Mechanics' Institute since, as the Reverend Mr Mitchell noted, 'he had never yet once ... seen a mechanics institute which was managed by, or was in the least degree a benefit to the class of people for whose benefit they were primarily intended – that is mechanics.'[42]

The reading room organizers appear to have succeeded in making the rooms welcoming to men of all classes, and certainly the influence of the visiting evangelists would have encouraged young men to eschew their formerly sinful ways. The *Post* noted soon after the rooms' opening that it was 'a pleasure to see the young men as well as the old men meeting nightly at the reading rooms instead of the hotels and street corners.' Most, or perhaps all, of these men would have been Protestant. Although the organizers claimed that the rooms were open to all, the Catholics naturally saw them as sectarian.[43]

While Protestant leaders focused on providing alternative leisure options for men in the wake of the revival, the appeal of certain forms of heterosocial leisure also declined among women. In reporting a sleighing trip to a dance in neighbouring Port Robinson, the *Post* noted that although 'plenty of invitations were extended ... only a very small party put in an appearance and among these the ladies were in the vast minority.' The paper suggested that perhaps 'the words of visiting evangelists on the subject of dancing have taken deep root.'[44] Similarly, the evangelists' attack on church fund-raising events and their endorsement of free church socials may explain why, just a month after their departure, Thorold's Methodist church took the unusual step of holding a social which the *Post* described as 'rather a novelty in its way ... it differed from other such socials [in] that there was no charge in connection therewith, everything being free.' The social was organized to welcome the many new church members drawn in by the revival. However, on most occasions, the financial realities of church management continued to overshadow purely spiritual concerns. In fact, the same week as the free social at the Methodist church, the Presbyterian ladies organized a more traditional entertainment, which was 'well attended ... [and netted] about $50 ... for church purposes.'[45]

Even successful evangelists did not have the power to proscribe pink teas and strawberry socials, but they did have a significant impact on the community. There was a general consensus that the behaviour of many townsfolk was transformed by the revival. One of the most impressive examples was that of Councillor A.E. Ripley, who apparently had lived an inordinately sinful life before conversion. After the revival he staunchly opposed liquor, attended church regularly, and struggled to overcome the habits of a lifetime.[46] Ripley was killed by a bolt of lightning before his resolve could weaken. But what of other converts?

Crossley and Hunter frequently sought to counter accusations that the conversions they effected were only temporary. They argued that in fact 90 to 95 per cent of their converts did not 'backslide.'[47] However, while they sought to avoid the excesses of the Salvation Army, even more sedate evangelistic revivals occurred in an overheated emotional atmosphere, and it was well known that once the emotion ebbed, spiritual resolve also could weaken.[48] Nonetheless, Crossley and Hunter do appear to have had some basis for their claim about the long-term nature of their conversions. The majority of the converts who joined Thorold's Methodist church seem to have remained church members for at least five years following the revival. Many are listed on the church rolls as having 'removed' from Thorold, but in doing so they would have taken with them their certificates attesting that they were church members in good standing. Only eighteen revival converts who could be identified were dropped from the church roll, usually for nonattendance at services (though some of these notations may have concealed more extreme deviations from evangelical Christian norms).

Given the small number of those 'dropped,' an analysis of the class and gender of these former converts can only be speculative. Nonetheless, it does suggest some interesting conclusions. Only three women were dropped from the church roll, and all three were working class. However, most female working-class converts, both single and married, remained in the church, as did their middle-class sisters. For many, the spiritual comfort they had found during the revival would have helped sustain them through the hard times that the community suffered throughout the 1890s. Although the spiritual ardour of some may have ebbed in the years following Crossley and Hunter's visit, church membership had other attractions for working-class women. As previously noted, the churches were one of the very few social outlets available to these women beyond the home. Moreover, church involvement granted some of the poorer women a claim to the limited material relief that was available through the churches and that was provided, more informally, by wealthier church members. For most working-class women, church membership was also an assertion of respectability in the face of poverty and continuing economic uncertainty.

Even shared church membership probably did not make many of these women fully respectable in the eyes of their middle-class counterparts. Scholars have suggested that revival converts were generally viewed as somewhat marginal in mainstream congregations; and, of course, financial barriers kept many of these women at the back of the church and away from women's church associations.[49] For many work-ing-class women, the distance from their middle-class sisters may have been exacerbated by their divergent visions of the proper nature of true Christian womanhood. Younger working-class women in particular may have chafed at the class-based restrictions of conventional feminin-ity. However, in Thorold in the 1890s, there was no alternative vehicle for working-class women. The Salvation Army was long gone, and although Crossley and Hunter may have provided spiritual solace in difficult times, they certainly did not endorse any role for women beyond the idealized vision of pure, pious, moral motherhood. None-theless, many working-class women, both single and married, joined the churches during the revival and remained there long after it. Their par-ticipation may not point to a cross-class Christian sisterhood, but it does suggest that like their middle-class counterparts, they found value and meaning in church involvement.

While most of the female revival converts remained in the churches, this was less true of the men. More than 80 per cent of converts who were dropped from the Methodist church roll were men, and more than 80 per cent of these men were working-class. Two-thirds of the dropped converts were single men,[50] and the only middle-class converts who drifted away from the churches were single men. There were, however, very few 'dropped' middle-class converts even among the single men. This suggests that family pressures were more successful in keeping young men in the churches once they had joined than in encouraging them to join in the first place.

The lack of shared church membership in most working-class families may help explain why working-class men, both married and single, were more likely to drift away from the churches than middle-class men. Working-class men were also more likely to leave the churches than their wives and daughters, because they had more alternative options available to them. While these men may initially have helped swell the numbers at the young men's reading room, two years later the institu-tion was less popular, which suggests that many younger working-class men had abandoned its 'wholesome' pleasures for the more appealing ones of street corners and hotels.[51] The excitement and spiritual ardour of the revival, the sense of being swept up in a community-wide event, and the revivalists' appeal to their common manhood may temporarily have dispelled the unwillingness of many working-class men to worship with their middle-class counterparts. However, as time passed, the social discomfort of worshipping with middle-class men and the greater appeal of an alternative lifestyle led some working-class men, particularly the unmarried ones, back out of the churches.

Many other working-class male revival converts did remain in the churches, however. Many of the married skilled workers who remained, especially the more prosperous and long-established ones, no doubt felt closer to the majority of middle-class churchgoers than to the street-corner loafers. Those unskilled workers and more poverty-stricken skilled workers who remained may have resented the social barriers that clearly existed in the churches, but like their sisters, wives, and daughters, they may have found spiritual solace there, as well as a means of asserting their respectability as workers and, in some cases, as members of Christian families.

In Thorold's Great Revival of 1893, Christianity served as a unifying force in the community. Catholics were obviously not part of this, and they would have felt more than usually marginalized during the weeks of high excitement and nightly services. For Thorold Protestants, however, Crossley and Hunter provided an extremely emotional religious experience that was shared by women and men, young and old, rich and poor. Such an experience was probably only possible in a small community. With hundreds of people attending the daily services, and businesses closing to accommodate employees who wished to attend, no one could have remained completely untouched. Even those who were usually far removed from the churchgoing community would have found it difficult to resist being drawn in by the excitement that gripped Thorold homes, streets, and workplaces.

Not all revivals drew the entire community together. When the Salvation Army came to Thorold, it attracted largely working-class audiences, and the visits of other evangelists to the mainstream churches usually brought only a few converts into the fold. Crossley and Hunter's style – emotional yet not 'excessive' – seems to have appealed to all. The fact that Thoroldites from all walks of life were converted in the Great Revival does not mean, however, that Thorold was a cosy organic community united by shared Christian beliefs. The popularity of working-class organizations such as the Knights of Labor and the Salvation Army – which appealed to those same Christian beliefs while defining 'true Christianity' rather differently from the mainstream churches – brought class differences into sharp relief.

Even during the revival, which seemed to bring townsfolk into the churches in an undifferentiated mass, class differences remained real. Divergent middle- and working-class attitudes towards Christian domesticity and family togetherness did not change. Middle-class single young people, and the occasional middle-class married convert, found themselves through conversion in the bosom of a Christian family, with many a mother rejoicing that her prayers had been answered for the conversion of her children, particularly the usually wayward sons. While the conversion of some working-class young people no doubt pleased their churchgoing mothers, many working-class converts were converted as individuals. Their subsequent efforts to remain faithful to evangelical norms would have received little support from their non-churchgoing families.

Despite such differences, Thorold's Great Revival did, in many ways, bring the community together. How are we to understand this? Why were so many more working-class townsfolk willing to worship with their middle-class counterparts than ever before? As we have seen in this study, and as other historians have increasingly recognized, our identities – our sense of who we are in the world – cannot be understood only in relation to one category, whether it be gender, class, age, religion, or any other. A broad range of categories of identity help us define ourselves, and help explain how we behave in the larger world.[52]

While the different facets of our identities are always with us, they are not at all times equally central to our sense of ourselves and to our manner of acting in the world. Christianity was part of the identity of most late-nineteenth-century Thorold men, but it was rarely central to how they defined themselves, either in work or in leisure. In Thorold in early 1893, the economic fears shared by the near-bankrupt merchant and the unemployed worker led both of them to take solace in a common religious faith. For these men, economic concerns were closely linked to their sense of themselves as productive working men, who ought to be able to provide for themselves and their families. Crossley and Hunter's appeal to their common manhood drew them in, as did the assurances of the evangelists that there was far more to life than the world of work. These men were ready to hear that salvation was of central importance and that, without it, mere worldly security and success were but dust and ashes. Working men were particularly attracted to definitions of Christianity in which the material inequalities of the world were of little relevance.

So for a brief moment, working men stood with their middle-class counterparts in Thorold's Protestant churches. They also stood with women of all classes, who found solace there too. Even in good times, however, these women had little access to and certainly little chance of success in the public world of work that had failed their men. For women, the churches offered options that were not available elsewhere, in good times as in bad. As the excitement of the revival died down after the departure of the evangelists, some intersection of class, gender, and age identities drew at least some working-class men out of the churches and back to a more appealing and perhaps more socially comfortable lifestyle. Most working-class women, however, remained in the churches. Church membership did not bring most of these women into a shared Christian sisterhood with their middle-class counterparts, but it was a space beyond the home that was open to them, unlike the many brotherhoods that welcomed only their men.

9

Conclusion

Sedate Sunday services, anti-Scott Act riots, roller rink crazes, Hallelujah Weddings, and strawberry socials ... Despite the stereotypes of dour Protestant small-town life, the religion and leisure activities of smaller communities in late-nineteenth-century Ontario were both complex and diverse. This in turn reflects the complexity of culture and identity in these communities and the danger of making facile assumptions about monolithic cultures, whether of Ontario Protestants, the working class, or women. To understand fully the nature of religious and leisure involvement and the larger social meaning of this involvement, we must weave together a range of intersecting issues.

First, to understand the extent to which Protestant culture was or was not hegemonic in these communities, it is essential to understand the meaning(s) of this culture in small-town Ontario. The culture needs to be understood at the level of faith and theology. But to the average small-town inhabitant, Protestant culture had other meanings as well, meanings that linked religion to the larger world in which these people lived. The class and gender meanings embedded in Protestantism were important here, as were the moral precepts which the Protestant churches expected their members to uphold, many of which they also tried to impose on those beyond the churches.

To understand not only the meanings of Protestant culture but the manner in which small-town inhabitants responded to it, we looked not just at religion but at the leisure options available to men and women in small-town Ontario. These leisure options could either complement a strictly Protestant lifestyle or could, to a greater or less extent, draw people away from the churches and their teachings.

Faith was central to Protestant culture. While each denomination had its own particular version of theological truth, successful revivalists such as Crossley and Hunter could draw Baptists, Methodists, Presbyterians, and even many Anglicans together in a shared evangelical faith. However, occurrences such as Thorold's Great Revival, when most Protestant townsfolk defined themselves first and foremost as believing Christians, were rare and fleeting. On a day-to-day basis, at most half of all small-town Protestant families included one or more church members. While church membership was about more than faith, the requirement that all members of evangelical churches experience conversion suggests that, for these women and men, belief was of ongoing importance. A small minority of townsfolk were far beyond the bounds of Christian faith, either rejecting God altogether or espousing a variety of heretical beliefs that ranged from spiritualism to Christian Science. Then there was the large number of people who told the census taker that they were Anglicans, Methodists, or Presbyterians but who never joined these churches. Some of these men and women were faithful Christians who may never have experienced conversion but who attended a church fairly regularly and donated money to it. Others went to church at Christmas and Easter at least, while many never darkened a church door. While it is difficult to assess the faith of nonchurchgoers, various hints (ranging from the excuses given to Crossley and Hunter to the rhetoric of the Salvation Army and the Knights of Labor) suggest that most nonchurchgoers shared at least some Christian beliefs. However, issues other than faith kept many people away from the churches. It is therefore crucial to look beyond questions of belief to other meanings that were part of being a good churchgoing Protestant in late-nineteenth-century Ontario.

In early-nineteenth-century Ontario, their shared faith may have bound evangelicals together and separated them from the things – and social divisions – of the world, but by the late nineteenth century all Protestant churches were far more integrated into the world. Churchgoing was a central sign of respectability in the larger society, and other elements defining respectability in the large culture, such as attaining at least a certain level of material prosperity, had entered into the churches' meaning of what it was to be a good Christian. This meaning was of course not stated explicitly in sermons or church journals, but it was increasingly inscribed in the very walls of the beautiful and imposing churches built in this period. The financial resources needed to build these churches could not help but bring the social and economic inequalities of the world more firmly into the churches, as those donating large sums to church-building projects were praised for their Christian commitment, while those unable to donate felt less a part of the religious community worshipping in these new edifices. A minority of middle-class Christians challenged the increasingly worldly emphasis of the churches, as did popular working-class movements such as the Salvation Army and the Knights of Labor, both of which in their own ways argued that the churches' acceptance of secular social distinctions pointed to their abandonment of Christ's authentic message.

The meaning of 'true Christianity' was contested in this period as in others, but the mainstream churches remained convinced that they reflected the true path. This path was not just about faith and respectability. The Protestant churches, and more particularly the evangelical denominations, defined a wide range of leisure behaviour as either godly or ungodly. Many nonchurchgoing small-town inhabitants indulged in ungodly behaviour that ranged from drinking and gambling to loafing idly on the streets, and they bitterly resisted churchgoers' efforts to alter their habits. What is perhaps more significant in tracing the degree of the churches' hegemonic power is that many people in the churches also rejected aspects of the churches' moral rulings, particularly regarding leisure activities. Female church members who listened to Sunday sermons attacking the sins of dancing and playgoing may have attended a 'hop' the previous evening and watched the performance of a touring theatre company the week before. The relationship of male church members to the churches' moral prescriptions was even more difficult. Most male church members were part of a masculine associational world, which even at its more respectable extremes accepted a certain amount of convivial drinking. This male world counterposed a masculine fellowship with its own manly rituals to those offered by the church community.

Many men, both church members and nonmembers preferred the masculine leisure and associational world to the churches. While the churches certainly did draw in many men, their appeal to men was limited in part by the feminized nature of late-nineteenth-century theology and the predominantly female congregations. Women attended church for a range of reasons, just as men did. The 'fit' between the ideal Christian and the ideal woman may have appealed to them; but, more negatively, most women had few other options beyond the home, for most of the rich leisure and association world of small-town Ontario admitted men only.

An exploration of the meanings of Protestant culture and the nature of involvement in the churches in the context of a range of complementary and alternative leisure options suggests that popular acceptance of the entire 'package' of Protestant beliefs, practices, and moral values was less common than the study of Protestant opinion leaders might suggest. The exploration of religious and leisure participation also reveals much about the nature and meaning of a range of individual and group identities in small-town Ontario.

Small towns did not reflect a seamless social harmony any more than they reflected a monolithic Protestant orthodoxy. Their social relations were different from those of the larger centres. Personal ties were more significant, and the more prosperous and long-settled skilled workers were viewed as the social equals of many of the middle-class townspeople. However, the popularity in many small-towns of working-class movements such as the Knights of Labor and the Salvation Army points to the significance of working-class identity among skilled and unskilled alike. The centrality of this identity for small town workers clearly varied over time. Similarly, the subterranean hostility between Catholics and Protestants, which was a constant feature of small-town life, erupted only occasionally, generally in response to broader conflicts and outside influences. At such times, religious identities could become primary, with former Knights of Labor joining the anti-Catholic Equal Rights Association.[1]

Other social divisions were more consistently visible in small communities. Gender was certainly key here. Concepts of masculinity were a potent force in small-town life, not only in excluding women from many associational and leisure activities but in defining the nature and meaning of these and other activities. Two competing definitions of appropriate masculinity coexisted in small-town Ontario. These definitions were related though not firmly tied to marital status. The first was clearly associated with respectability and could be linked to expectations surrounding the role of married men. Married men were breadwinners and household heads, and as such they gained a certain status in the community. They were expected to work hard in the public world to support their families, but they were also to enjoy the domestic environment created by their wives. Their commitment to a Christian family life was to be reflected in their presence in the family pew each Sunday. Ideally, they were also expected to live up to the same moral code, sexual and otherwise, demanded of their wives, and indeed to play an active role in promoting this code by taking up positions of leadership in the churches and the community. Although the younger single men could not aspire to such 'social fathering' roles, they could certainly go to church, work hard, and strive for intellectual, moral, and material self-improvement while waiting until marriage for the higher status conferred by the position of household head.

Some young men, primarily from middle-class families, did live the lives of eminently respectable breadwinners-in-waiting. Many others, both middle- and working-class, strayed to a greater or lesser extent from this ideal. They preferred a different version of masculinity, a version that was closely associated with young manhood and was most clearly represented by the street-corner loafer of small-town Ontario. These men preferred the male bonding of street corner and hotel bar to the domestic family circle. Prowess in drinking and gambling and the excitement of blood sports were part of this ideal of masculinity, as was scorn and hostility towards the 'feminized' world of the churches. This ideal was certainly linked more closely to unmarried youth than to married men. However, some married working-class men preferred this lifestyle to domesticity and church involvement. Middle-class mothers seem to have feared that any involvement in these so-called rough activities would lead their sons inexorably downward, but in fact most middle-class youths appear to have limited their involvement in this rough culture. Although they stayed away from the churches, sought the excitement of gambling at cockfights, and enjoyed the male companionship of the hotels, they were far less likely to be arrested for drunken brawling than young working-class men. This probably reflects not only the class bias of the local constable but the greater discretion of middle-class young men, who may have enjoyed these wild pursuits but seen them as merely a temporary phase in their life cycle. Nonetheless, the rowdiness of young men was certainly perceived as a cross-class problem, and it was of central concern to the respectable folk of small-town Ontario. Their big-city counterparts also worried about the immorality of young women, but in smaller communities these women were considered to be safely under their families' control. They could thus only be a positive influence on young men.

While the pursuits of young men were perceived as a challenge to respectability, the two conceptions of respectable breadwinner and 'wild' youth were not as clearly dichotomized as the parallel cultural concepts of 'good' woman and 'bad' woman. Certain elements of 'rough' masculinity can be identified in respectable male associational activities. The very popularity of these activities points to the appeal male bonding had among men of all classes and to a shared reluctance to spend as much time as might be expected in the family circle. This was the case even among churchgoing married men. Although the WCTU and individual wives and daughters looked askance at the drinking that went on even in the more respectable middle-class-dominated associations, these activities were certainly accepted by most men. It was only when rowdiness spilled onto the streets, as at the primarily working-class Orange Parade, that the bounds of respectable masculinity were perceived to have been truly breached.

The convivial masculine culture of lodge room and firemen's hall was shared by middle- and working-class men alike. However, conceptions of respectable manhood could and indeed were also appropriated by specifically working-class movements. The Salvation Army was less than successful here. While the Army trumpeted its success in saving young men from drink and idleness, and converting drunken wifebeaters into respectable Christian breadwinners, it suffered violent attacks from those it sought to reform and was ridiculed by the middle class. Emotional testimony to past sins and marching in flamboyant parades simply did not mesh with dominant images of respectable manhood. The Knights of Labor's ideals of chivalrous manhood were more in keeping with middle-class definitions of appropriate masculinity. However, the Knights redefined images of churchgoing respectable family men as emblems of class pride. Shared definitions of manhood asserted the respectability of working men in the face of the increasingly subordinated status of Ontario's working class and were intended to sharpen, not diffuse, the Knights' trenchant critique of capitalist injustice.

While conceptions of respectable masculinity could be appropriated by a particular class, they could also be used to draw different classes together. In Thorold, the revivalists Crossley and Hunter were able to bring single and married, middle- and working-class men into the churches through an appeal to a common vision of Christian manhood. The evangelists' use of a most feminized imagery of the divine, which in better times might have discouraged male involvement, seems to have offered solace in a difficult period. However, these feminized images of a gentle, forgiving Jesus limited the options of flesh and blood women. Conceptions of femininity so idealized as to be associated with the divine left little room for the kind of flexibility that was common to notions of masculinity. The feminine ideal prescribed for women included passivity, purity, and piety. True women were to find their fulfilment in the home, both as daughters and as wives, and in the churches as subordinated handmaidens to male church leaders.

Not surprisingly, many active churchgoing women did not fully adhere to this model. Although women's church associations ostensibly played the appropriately subordinate feminine role, the members of these associations often had ideas of their own about church matters, ideas that did not always mesh with those of male leaders. More subtly, the efforts of women's organizations to beautify the churches brought an increasingly feminine and domestic presence into the male-led churches. These changes were accepted and even welcomed by male leaders, who saw the improvements as redounding to their credit. However, the socials that women organized to raise money for the church improvements were regarded by many ministers as secular intrusions into sacred male-controlled space. These intrusions were conducted primarily by middle-class women, who could afford to pay fees and bake cakes to help build imposing new churches. Few working-class women joined these associations, but some sought alternative places in the churches through Sunday school teaching and young people's societies.

When the middle-class women of the mainstream churches asserted themselves, eschewing the passive role expected of them, their challenge was usually limited to spats over finances or to more subtle and sometimes unconscious flank attacks on male authority and male space. By contrast, some working-class women were more willing to challenge the dominant ideals of femininity. The Salvation Army's Hallelujah Lasses manifested a far more active and public vision of women's role than their counterparts in the churches. Their conceptions of femininity were not, however, completely distinct from those of the mainstream church-women, even though horrified observers may have thought so. Salvation Army women may have marched in parades and preached before crowds, but they justified their departure from conventional feminine behaviour in the name of a most appropriately feminine subordination to God's will. While these justifications may have been just that in the case of many Hallelujah Lasses, they may also demonstrate an unwillingness among working-class women to jettison completely the dominant feminine ideal. Young men could ignore the values of respectable manhood, living for a time by utterly different standards of masculinity, and then, on marriage, take up the respectable role of breadwinner. But although working-class women could reshape the dominant ideology of femininity to fit their lives and their experience more closely, they could not abandon it completely, for there was no alternative contemporary conception of womanhood – except for the image of the 'bad' woman who, once fallen, could never be redeemed.

Class and gender, as historians have shown in countless studies, are significant categories for dividing up the social world and for helping us understand it. But as Joy Parr has argued, the danger of dividing the world into distinct categories is that we can miss out on the intersections between categories and, indeed, on the way in which they are lived 'simultaneously' in the lives of working- and middle-class men and women.[2] These categories come together not only within individuals but also within families. By studying particular social variables in isolation or only at more aggregate and impersonal levels, scholars can ignore how they intersect at the level of family and household. In small-town Ontario, one cannot answer the question of who went to church simply by pointing to the higher levels of involvement among women or among the middle class. Age and marital status were also important categories of identity. When we look inside the family, it becomes clear that even middle-class respectability did not necessarily lead to church attendance by middle-class sons, some of whom may have been involved in very different leisure pursuits from the rest of the family. An understanding of the diversity of experience in middle-class families illuminates the motivations of middle-class women and men on a number of fronts. For example, middle-class women may have joined the WCTU not primarily to control working-class drinking but in the hope of safeguarding their own sons.

An exploration of religious and leisure involvement in the working-class family is even more revealing. Some members of working-class families were ardent churchgoers and were actively involved in various temperance associations, but brothers or sons of the very same families may have been arrested on 'drunk and disorderly' charges. While such patterns suggest differences between the lifestyles of male and female workers and between married and single working-class men, people's behaviour did not always break down this neatly. What is clear is that members of working-class families were far more likely to go separate ways than the members of middle-class families. Although the economic demands of the family economy may have united working-class families, the values of a shared Christian domesticity appear to have been far less significant in most working-class homes.

This study has explored some big issues in the context of three small communities. Questions of course can be raised about how representative Thorold, Campbellford, and Ingersoll were of larger patterns. The similarities in religious and leisure patterns within these communities, despite their distinct occupational and economic structures and histories of labour activism, suggest that the patterns found here were not confined to these communities. Studies of other small communities will further refine our knowledge of religion and leisure in small-town Ontario and may tell us more about the minority Catholic experience than has been possible here. An exploration of religious and leisure involvement in the large urban centres, while methodologically daunting, will reveal the extent to which the small-town experience was unique or was representative of broader Ontario patterns. Some urban experiences cannot help but have been different. For example, in the larger centres workers could and often did worship in predominantly or almost exclusively working-class congregations. As well, young men were not the central focus of respectable Christian concern; this concern was also extended to the single woman 'adrift' in the city. The greater ethnic and racial diversity of larger centres may also have made 'whiteness' an even more central category of identity for mainstream urban Christians than for their small-town counterparts. Other significant differences may well emerge as studies of urban religion and leisure are undertaken.

I have argued in this book that an integrated approach to the study of religious and leisure activities illuminates much that is missed when these activities are studied in isolation from one another. While this study has tried to integrate the study of religion and leisure, class, gender, and the family, it cannot claim to be 'total history.' The worlds of work and politics are as peripheral here as the exploration of religion and leisure have commonly been in earlier studies. Also, given the nature of the available sources, it has only been possible to explore activities that took place beyond the home. Inferences can be made about the nature of home life, but it remains very difficult actually to enter into the home and understand the religious and leisure activities that might have taken place there.

It is hoped that future researchers may be able to integrate fully the study of politics, work, religion, leisure, and home life. At the same time, this study's efforts at integration reveal the value of such an approach. Labour and social historians are beginning to recognize the need to incorporate religion into their work. Religion can no longer be ignored or be dismissed merely as a potential retardant of class-consciousness. Certainly, in some contexts religious faith did temporarily overcome class differences, but in other contexts religious beliefs were a potent force in challenging class inequalities. In either case, religion was part of how most Ontario workers saw themselves and their world. We can no longer allow our own more secular outlook to blind us to this reality.

Religion was particularly important to working-class women. Histori-

ans of working-class women's consciousness need to recognize that not
only were these women's lives defined in relation to work, home, leisure, and sexuality, but that religious ideas and practices were central to
many of them. A recognition of this fact can deepen our understanding
of other facets of working-class women's lives and of the interconnec-
tions among them.

In studying the lives of women and men together, this study has also
contributed to the growing field of gender history. By assessing the religious and leisure options of men and women in relation to each other, it
deepens our understanding of masculinities and femininities in late-
nineteenth-century Ontario and starkly reveals men's greater power and
privilege and the limitations of women's lives. This study also shows how
using gender as a way of analysing not just men and women, but also the
spaces and institutions they played and worshipped in, can further illuminate both the barriers faced by women and the choices made by men.

Some Canadian religious historians have in recent years argued that
the study of religious ideas, while important, is not in itself enough, and
they have called for an exploration of popular religious beliefs and practices.[3] This book shows that when the study of religion and leisure is
integrated, it becomes more possible to understand both the popular
appeal of mainstream Christianity and some of the counter attractions
that could weaken people's links to the churches or draw some of them
away entirely. Class and gender analysis are also essential to understanding popular religious practice. By class and gender analysis, I do
not just mean looking at how many men and women, middle- and
working-class people, were church members, although this is an essential first step. We must also explore how the analytical categories of class
and gender were embedded in the contemporary definitions of what it
meant to be a good churchgoing Protestant. In late-nineteenth-century
Ontario, the class assumptions that were part of such definitions created
real barriers that helped to keep many workers away from the churches
or led to a certain social unease among many who did attend. Similarly,
the feminine overtones of Christianity kept many young men away, and
they may help to explain the divided loyalties of many married men
who, on Sundays, asserted their respectability as church members but
who preferred to spend many of their nonwork hours in local lodge
rooms or firemen's halls.

A broadening of the focus of Canadian religious history is useful not
only in exploring questions of popular religious practice. The integration of class and gender, religion and leisure, can also assist in un-
tangling issues in Canadian religious history well beyond the bounds of

late-nineteenth-century small-town Ontario. For example, while the social gospel has long been studied by Canadian religious historians, the separation between religious and labour historians has ensured that the Knights of Labor have not been viewed as part of this topic. However, the Knights' Christian critique of social injustice is certainly a worthwhile subject of study for those tracing the origins of the social gospel, as scholars have recently noted in the American context.[4]

To give another example, secularization has been a much-discussed topic in English-Canadian religious history.[5] However, a gender analysis has never been part of the intense debates on this subject. Many of those studying this question have focused on the realm of ideas. A recognition of the gendered nature of particular currents of heretical new thought, from secularism to spiritualism, and the extent to which they would be more likely to attract either male or female support can only add depth to this interpretation. Gender analysis can be of particular value to the more material explanations for secularization that have been put forward. David Marshall has suggested that the emergence of new leisure options at the end of the nineteenth century contributed to secularization because these leisure activities provided counter attractions to church involvement.[6] This study has made clear, however, that Ontario men had access to a range of leisure and associational options before this period and that these activities did indeed draw them away from the churches or, at best, created divided loyalties for many of them.

Women had few other options at this time. A few commercialized leisure activities, such as roller skating, did exist in late-nineteenth-century Ontario and attracted many younger women. In the early twentieth century the range of commercialized leisure options available to women expanded greatly, particularly in the larger centres. They came to include not only the dance halls and roller rinks that appealed to single women, but amusement parks and movie theatres, which also attracted married women and their families.[7] Of course, the emergence of alternative leisure options for women does not in itself explain the declining interest in the churches of twentieth-century Canada. However, it may well have been a factor in reducing both women's own interest in the churches and the pressure they may have exerted to help keep their husbands there. Only future work that integrates the study of leisure and religion and incorporates an analysis of gender, class, and other relevant categories of identity into the exploration of the 'big' questions of Canadian religious history will allow us to begin to answer such questions.

Appendix A

Methodological Notes

Church Records

The small town focus of this study was based partly on the lack of historical work on smaller communities, but it was also dictated by methodological considerations. Since, in exploring church participation, I sought to identify both those townspeople with church affiliations and those without these affiliations, it was necessary to study communities where the records of all the churches had survived. Only in this way could it be assumed that individuals who did not appear in any church records had not been closely affiliated with any churches. Only in very small communities of two to three thousand people was it possible to assemble relatively complete church membership records for all the churches in the community. Even in towns of this size, many churches have at best only incomplete records for the late nineteenth century. Thus, while Thorold and Campbellford were chosen partly because of their very different occupational and economic structures, and histories of labour activism, the existence of relatively complete records from all their churches was also a major factor in the decision to study these towns. Ingersoll was studied primarily in qualitative and not quantitative terms because of the larger size of the community and the resulting greater number of churches: it was not possible to assemble complete church membership records for all Ingersoll churches for the late nineteenth century.

What can church records, even relatively complete church records, tell us about church affiliation? One could attend a church and donate money to it without becoming a church member, but among Baptists, Presbyterians, and Methodists church membership provides the clearest evidence of religious commitment and church affiliation. Church members are listed on membership rolls by the Baptists, on communion rolls by the Presbyterians, and in circuit registers by the Methodists. While some of these records provide more information than others, in all three denominations they record when the individual members joined the church and when (and how) they left.[1]

Becoming a member of a Baptist, Presbyterian, or Methodist church presupposed having some form of conversion experience, wherein one came to a strong recognition of one's sinful nature and felt a willingness to give oneself to Christ. Becoming a church member also involved making a formal undertaking to adhere to the religious and moral teachings of the denomination. At a minimum, church membership entailed fairly regular church attendance, especially attendance at communion services. The church minutes and membership records make it clear that nonattenders were dropped from the membership rolls in the churches of all three denominations.

Within these denominations, most of those who donated money to the church were also church members, but some clearly made the lesser commitment of donating money or attending periodically without becoming church members.[2] An analysis of the financial contributions to Thorold churches therefore provides a useful supplement to an understanding of the nature of church involvement. However, since the records of financial contributions are biased towards the more prosperous men, they were used with care and were separated from any analysis of church membership.

The records of financial contributions were particularly useful in studying Anglican and Catholic involvement. Since all Anglicans and Catholics in a parish are assumed to be part of their respective congregations, no clear distinction is made between members and nonmembers, as is the case among Methodists, Presbyterians, and Baptists. Among Anglicans, the closest equivalent is between communicants (those who take communion) and noncommunicants (those who do not). This distinction was more significant in High Anglican churches than in Low Anglican churches. Communicant records could therefore be more closely associated with Anglican church involvement in Campbellford, which was High Church, than in Thorold, which appears to have been more Low Church. In Thorold, the records of Anglican communicants end in 1886, which also limits their usefulness. In this case, the surviving records of church contributions, which extend into the 1890s, were a particularly valuable supplement.

It is more difficult to gain a sense of the nature of church involvement among Catholics than among Anglicans. Lists of those taking communion are very rarely available. Therefore I made use of the rare 'Status Animarum' for St Catharines. This register lists all of the members of St Catharines parishes by family, provides the occupation of those who were employed, and states whether or not each adult had taken communion at Easter and whether he or she regularly attended mass. This source provided valuable insights into the nature of Catholic religious participation by class and gender in an urban community that borders on Thorold. For Thorold Catholics themselves, the only existing records that provide evidence of church involvement are annual reports of financial contributions, which date from the late 1890s. These financial records are, however, particularly useful for Irish Catholic parishes. Since Irish Catholics appear to have had a particularly firm tradition of supporting the church financially, such records provide a more comprehensive sense of the patterns of church involvement than is the case with the records of Protestant church contributions.[3]

In studying the Thorold revival of 1893, the existing Protestant records were particularly useful, although a few points should be noted. In the case of Presbyterian converts, all those who joined the church immediately after the revival were listed in the session minutes as having done so, and consequently their status as revival converts was clear-cut. In the case of Methodist converts, all of those added to the circuit register in 1893 were assumed to be revival converts. Since the congregation more than doubled in the year after the revival, this was doubtless true of most new members, although a few would probably have joined even without the revival. In the case of Anglicans, in 1893 there were over forty candidates for confirmation, both adults and young people, while the norm was about twelve young people. It therefore seems justifiable to assume that the presence of the majority of those confirmed in 1893 can be attributed to the efforts of the revivalists.

Linkages

Data collected through the church records, the newspapers, and other sources regarding the names of church members, church contributors, the members and officers of various voluntary organizations, and so on were hand-linked with the Campbellford and Thorold manuscript census of 1891 and the Thorold assessment roll of 1886. The list of contributors to Thorold's Catholic church was linked to the 1901 Thorold manuscript census, since this list was only available from the late 1890s. The small size of the populations being studied made it feasible to make linkages simply on the basis of full names. This was often necessary in the case of members of voluntary societies, since no other information was provided in newspaper listings of society membership; but in the case of church membership, record linkages could also be confirmed with the information on denominational adherence provided in the census. The reading of local newspapers also increased familiarity with local families and individuals, and this too made linkages simpler. In the case of Campbellford records, all linkages were done by hand, using cards. With the more extensive Thorold data, however, once the initial linkage had been made by hand, each matching individual was assigned a discrete number and the relational data-base program *Knowledgeman* was then used to conduct a range of data analysis, which involved linking various membership lists both to one another and to the census and assessment roll data.

Occupational Classification and Class

Appendix B identifies the occupational groupings used in this study. Occupations were classified using a modified version of the vertical coding system developed by the Philadelphia project.[4] This system seemed most appropriate, since it was developed to study occupations in an industrializing economy.[5] Modifications to the occupational groupings used in the Philadelphia project included separating factory workers out as a distinct category rather than including them in the category of skilled or unskilled worker. As well, small employers were differentiated from larger ones. Most importantly, self-employed artisans were separated out as a distinct category. This distinction, as well as that between small and large employers, could not be made by scholars who worked with earlier manuscript censuses.[6] The 1891 census does, however, differentiate between employers, wage earners, and those who were neither, and it also provides information on the number of employees who worked for each employer.[7]

With this distinction, it becomes easier to group most occupations into either middle- or working-class categories. For the purposes of this study, employers were identified as middle class, as were supervisory and managerial employees and white-collar workers.[8] Blue-collar wage earners were identified as working class. The small group of skilled workers who were neither employers nor wage earners were not identified as either middle- or working-class but were categorized separately, as were farmers and widows.

As appendix B makes clear, I developed three levels of class/occupational classification for this study: a middle-class/working-class distinction and a broader and finer occupational classification system. The distinction I most commonly used was by class, although the broader occupational categories were also employed. Although I would have preferred to use the finer occupational categories, at this level of disaggregation the numbers involved were usually too small to permit meaningful conclusions to be drawn. This was particularly true of middle-class categories. One of the finer working-class categories – that of wealthy skilled worker – was sometimes of analytical value, since in certain analyses (particularly in relation to church membership) it demonstrated clear similarities to middle-class patterns and clear differences from other working-class ones. The general inability to use finer occupational categories is a problem that cannot be avoided when studying small communities, but it is offset by the methodological advantages that these communities offer to the study of religious participation.

Occupational data, while the primary means of identifying class/socio-economic hierarchies, were supplemented by sources on wealth or income. There are no surviving assessment rolls for late-nineteenth-century Campbellford. The 1886 Thorold assessment roll was, however, analysed for this study. The data on property holding available through the assessment roll provide some indication of wealth. This information was used primarily to identify wealthy skilled workers who, for the purposes of this study, were defined as those owning more than $800 worth of property.[9]

In the 1901 census, for the first time wage earners were required to state the amount of income earned over the previous year. In analysing Thorold Catholic records in relation to the 1901 census, it was therefore possible to provide two separate analyses: one based on occupational groupings and the other based on gradations of income.

Families and Household Heads

While recognizing that the concept of 'family' is a culturally constructed one, for the purposes of this study a family was defined as a group of related individuals living under one roof. Boarders and servants were therefore not included as part of a family but were defined as separate one-person family units. This categorization is an important one: unless otherwise indicated, aggregate family income was used to place an individual in a particular income group, and the occupation of the male household head was used to define the class/occupational grouping of all members of the family.[10] In the absence of a male household head, the occupation of the eldest male (or in the absence of employed males, eldest employed female) was used.[11] The category of widow was used only if no member of the family was employed.

Appendix B

Class and Occupational Groupings

Middle Class

Merchants/professionals
Merchants/hotel keepers
Gentlemen
Professionals
Managers/owners/manufacturers of workplaces with more than ten
  employees

Small employers/foremen
Employers of ten or fewer employees
Managers of workplaces with ten or fewer employees
Foremen/captains of boats

Clerks/agents
Lower-level salaried employees, e.g., clerks, agents, bookkeepers,
  salesmen, teachers
Very small-scale merchants

Artisans
Self-employed artisan

Working Class

Skilled workers
Wealthy skilled worker, wage earner
Skilled worker, wage earner

Lock tender/bridge tender, on canal
Seamstress/tailoress/dressmaker/milliner
Stone cutter/mason/quarryman

Semi-skilled/unskilled workers
Unskilled worker, wage earner
Miscellaneous
Teamster
Labourer

Factory workers
Factory worker, skilled
Factory worker, unskilled

Servants
Servant/washerwoman/laundress

Other

Farmers
Widows
Students (generally medical or legal)
Other (unknown/unclassified)

Appendix C

Tables

TABLE 1
Church membership, or communicant status, of Thorold Protestant families, by class, occupational group, and denomination, 1886–92[a]

Occupational group/class	Anglicans			Baptists			Methodists			Presbyterians			Total		
	Families with communicants		Total families	Families with church members		Total families	Families with church members		Total families	Families with church members		Total families	Families with church members		Total families
	No.	%	No.	No.	%	No.	No.	%	No.	No.	%	No.	No.	%	No.
Merchants/professionals	7	30	23	2	100	2	7	54	13	12	60	20	28	48	58
Small employers/foremen	5	36	14	1	50	2	9	64	14	2	67	3	17	52	33
Clerks/agents	3	38	8	–	–	–	5	42	12	5	71	7	13	48	27
Middle-class total	**15**	**33**	**45**	**3**	**75**	**4**	**21**	**54**	**39**	**19**	**63**	**30**	**58**	**49**	**118**
Artisans	4	44	9	1	33	3	1	17	6	5	50	10	11	39	28
Skilled workers	9	16	55	5	83	6	20	45	44	21	62	34	55	40	139
Semi-/unskilled workers	11	42	26	3	75	4	4	19	21	6	50	12	24	38	63
Factory workers	–	0	7	–	–	–	4	44	9	5	71	7	9	39	23
Servants	2	17	12	–	–	–	–	0	9	–	0	4	2	8	25
Working-class total	**22**	**22**	**100**	**8**	**80**	**10**	**28**	**34**	**83**	**32**	**56**	**57**	**90**	**36**	**250**
Farmers	2	50	4	–	0	1	–	0	1	–	0	1	2	29	7
Widows[b]	2	40	5	–	–	–	7	78	9	3	60	5	12	63	19
Other	–	0	1	–	–	–	–	0	1	–	0	1	–	0	3
Total	**45**	**27**	**164**	**12**	**67**	**18**	**57**	**41**	**139**	**59**	**57**	**104**	**173**	**41**	**425**

Sources: Thorold Protestant church records; National Archives of Canada (NA), Thorold manuscript census, 1891
[a] Families are counted as including church members if even one member of the family is a church member / communicant. 'Family' is defined as a group of related individuals living under one roof. Single unattached individuals are counted as separate families. The occupation used is that of father or husband, or of son or daughter in the case of a family headed by a widow with no occupation.
[b] This designation is used only for widows with no occupation and with no children employed.

TABLE 2
Church membership, or communicant status, of Campbellford Protestant families, by class, occupational group, and denomination, 1886–92[a]

Occupational group/class	Anglicans			Baptists			Methodists			Presbyterians			Total		
	Families with communicants		Total families	Families with church members		Total families	Families with church members		Total families	Families with church members		Total families	Families with church members		Total families
	No.	%	No.	No.	%	No.	No.	%	No.	No.	%	No.	No.	%	No.
Merchants/professionals	12	80	15	1	100	1	19	73	26	15	63	24	47	71	66
Small employers/foremen	1	50	2	1	100	1	9	82	11	17	85	20	28	82	34
Clerks/agents	7	88	8	1	50	2	4	40	10	3	27	11	15	48	31
Middle-class total	**20**	**80**	**25**	**3**	**75**	**4**	**32**	**68**	**47**	**35**	**64**	**55**	**90**	**69**	**131**
Artisans	1	20	5	4	100	4	13	72	18	4	67	6	22	67	33
Skilled workers	5	24	21	6	100	6	33	62	53	14	24	58	58	42	138
Semi-/unskilled workers	5	28	18	4	67	6	16	36	44	10	40	25	35	38	93
Factory workers	2	40	5	1	100	1	12	48	25	7	54	13	22	50	44
Servants	1	17	6	2	100	2	1	6	16	3	33	9	7	21	33
Working-class total	**13**	**26**	**50**	**13**	**87**	**15**	**62**	**45**	**138**	**34**	**32**	**105**	**122**	**40**	**308**
Farmers	2	100	2	–			2	40	5	6	60	10	10	59	17
Widows[b]	3	75	4	1	100	1	8	73	11	4	57	7	16	70	23
Other	3	43	7	1	100	1	2	15	13	3	30	10	9	29	31
Total	**42**	**45**	**93**	**22**	**88**	**25**	**119**	**51**	**232**	**86**	**45**	**193**	**269**	**50**	**543**

Sources: Campbellford Protestant church records; NA, Campbellford manuscript census, 1891
[a] Families are counted as church members if one member of the family is a church member / communicant. 'Family' is defined as a group of related individuals living under one roof. Single unattached individuals are counted as separate families. The occupation used is that of father or husband, or of son or daughter in the case of a family headed by a widow with no occupation.
[b] This designation is used only for widows with no occupation and with no children employed.

TABLE 3
Church membership by marital status, sex, and occupation of father and husband, Thorold Protestants, 1886–92[a]

	Married						Single					
	Female			Male			Female			Male		
	Church members		Total	Church members		Total	Church members		Total	Church members		Total
Occupational group/class	No.	%	No.	No.	%	No.	No.	%	No.	No.	%	No.
Merchants/professionals	20	49	41	19	43	44	12	33	36	6	23	26
Small employers/foremen	12	39	31	11	34	32	8	42	19	–	0	24
Clerks/agents	9	50	18	10	56	18	2	29	7	–	0	8
Middle-class total	**41**	**46**	**90**	**40**	**43**	**94**	**22**	**36**	**62**	**6**	**10**	**58**
Artisans	7	39	18	7	37	19	4	24	17	1	13	8
Skilled workers	41	40	103	23	23	101	24	30	81	7	11	66
Semi-/unskilled workers	13	30	44	6	14	43	7	29	24	1	3	37
Factory workers	4	25	16	5	29	17	4	25	16	–	0	10
Servants	–	–	2	–	–	–	2	10	20	–	0	2
Working-class total	**58**	**35**	**165**	**34**	**21**	**161**	**37**	**26**	**141**	**8**	**7**	**115**
Farmers	1	17	6	1	14	7	–	0	8	1	20	5
Widows	–	0	1	–	–	–	7	50	14	1	50	2
Other/unknown	–	–	–	–	–	–	–	0	2	–	0	1
Total	**107**	**38**	**280**	**82**	**29**	**281**	**70**	**29**	**244**	**17**	**9**	**189**

Sources: Thorold Protestant church records; NA, Thorold manuscript census, 1891
[a] Includes those fifteen years of age and older. Widows/widowers are not analysed as a category because their numbers are too small

TABLE 4

Church membership by marital status, sex, and occupation of father and husband, Campbellford Protestants, 1886–92[a]

	Married						Single					
	Female			Male			Female			Male		
	Church members		Total	Church members		Total	Church members		Total	Church members		Total
Occupational group/class	No.	%	No.	No.	%	No.	No.	%	No.	No.	%	No.
Merchants/professionals	36	72	50	29	56	52	7	41	17	3	13	24
Small employers/foremen	20	71	28	20	69	29	8	62	13	2	15	13
Clerks/agents	10	46	22	9	39	23	5	42	12	6	50	12
Middle-class total	**66**	**66**	**100**	**58**	**56**	**104**	**20**	**48**	**42**	**11**	**23**	**49**
Artisans	13	57	23	10	44	23	6	75	8	–	0	1
Skilled workers	38	46	82	27	33	82	23	44	52	10	21	47
Semi-/unskilled workers	21	25	84	22	26	85	15	40	38	6	14	43
Factory workers	12	48	25	10	40	25	8	44	18	2	15	13
Servants	–	–	–	–	–	–	5	20	25	–	0	3
Working-class total	**71**	**37**	**191**	**59**	**31**	**192**	**51**	**38**	**133**	**18**	**17**	**106**
Farmers	11	69	16	10	63	16	2	33	6	–	0	3
Widows	–	–	–	–	–	–	18	55	33	1	4	27
Other/unknown	–	–	–	–	–	–	11	39	28	–	0	9
Total	**161**	**49**	**330**	**137**	**41**	**335**	**108**	**43**	**250**	**30**	**15**	**195**

Sources: Campbellford Protestant church records; NA, Campbellford manuscript census, 1891
[a] Includes those fifteen years of age and older. Widows/widowers are not analysed as a category because the numbers are too small

TABLE 5
Church membership among unmarried Protestants, Thorold, by sex
and occupation, 1886–92[a]

| | Church members | | Total |
	No.	%	No.
FEMALE			
No occupation	48	30	161
Factory workers	7	39	18
Dressmakers/milliners	2	11	18
Servants	2	10	21
Clerks/teachers	11	52	21
Other	–	0	5
Total	**70**	**29**	**244**
MALE			
No occupation	2	6	35
Merchants/professionals	3	19	16
Clerks	4	16	25
Skilled workers	4	10	40
Semi-/unskilled workers	1	2	41
Factory workers	2	9	22
Servants	–	0	1
Farmers	–	0	3
Other	1	17	6
Total	**17**	**9**	**189**

Sources: Thorold Protestant church records; NA, Thorold
manuscript census, 1891
[a] Those aged fifteen and over. Occupation listed is their own
   occupation.

TABLE 6
Church membership among unmarried Protestants, Campbellford,
by sex and occupation, 1886–92[a]

| | Church members | | Total |
	No.	%	No.
FEMALE			
No occupation	40	38	105
Factory workers	31	46	67
Dressmakers/milliners	30	67	45
Servants	6	23	26
Clerks/teachers	2	29	7
Other	–	–	–
Total	**109**	**44**	**250**
MALE			
No occupation	5	12	42
Merchants/Professionals	3	23	13
Clerks	6	38	16
Skilled workers	11	21	53
Semi-/unskilled workers	2	5	42
Factory workers	2	9	23
Servants	1	33	3
Farmers	–	0	3
Other	–	–	–
Total	**30**	**15**	**195**

Sources: Campbellford Protestant church records; NA, Campbellford manuscript census, 1891
[a] Those aged fifteen and over. Occupation listed is their own
occupation.

TABLE 7
Financial contributors to Thorold Protestant churches, by sex, marital status, and occupational group, 1886–92[a]

Occupational group/class	Married						Single					
	Female			Male			Female			Male		
	Contributors		Total	Contributors		Total	Contributors		Total	Contributors		Total
	No.	%	No.	No.	%	No.	No.	%	No.	No.	%	No.
Merchants/professionals	15	39	39	29	69	42	8	24	33	10	45	22
Small employers/foremen	9	31	29	15	50	30	4	27	15	1	5	21
Clerks/agents	7	39	18	12	67	18	2	29	7	1	13	8
Middle-class total	**31**	**36**	**86**	**56**	**62**	**90**	**14**	**26**	**55**	**12**	**24**	**51**
Artisans	5	29	17	11	58	19	3	23	13	–	0	4
Skilled workers	30	30	99	22	23	97	11	14	78	3	5	64
Semi-/unskilled workers	10	24	41	5	12	41	2	10	21	1	3	32
Factory workers	4	25	16	7	41	17	1	7	15	1	10	10
Servants	–	0	2	–	–	–	–	0	20	–	0	2
Working-class total	**44**	**28**	**158**	**34**	**22**	**155**	**14**	**10**	**134**	**5**	**5**	**108**
Farmers	1	20	5	4	67	6	1	13	8	–	0	5
Widows	–	–	–	–	–	–	–	0	14	–	0	2
Other/unknown	–	0	1	–	–	–	–	0	2	–	0	1
Total	**81**	**30**	**267**	**105**	**39**	**270**	**32**	**14**	**226**	**17**	**10**	**171**

Sources: Records of Thorold's Anglican, Presbyterian, and Methodist churches; NA, Thorold manuscript census, 1891
[a] Includes those making either regular or one-time-only donations to various church funds; does not include Baptists, since there are no records of financial donations for Thorold's Baptist church

TABLE 8
Patterns of church membership among Protestant married couples, by occupational group, Thorold, 1886–92

Occupational group/class	Both spouses church members		Wife only		Husband only		Total
	No.	%	No.	%	No.	%	No.
Merchants/professionals	18	86	3	14	–	0	21
Small employers/foremen	8	53	4	27	3	20	15
Clerks/agents	8	80	1	10	1	10	10
Middle-class total	**34**	**74**	**8**	**17**	**4**	**9**	**46**
Artisans	6	75	1	13	1	13	8
Skilled workers	19	45	18	43	5	12	42
Semi-/unskilled workers	3	23	8	62	2	15	13
Factory workers	3	50	1	17	2	33	6
Working-class total	**25**	**41**	**27**	**44**	**9**	**15**	**61**
Total	**65**	**57**	**36**	**31**	**14**	**12**	**115**

Sources: Thorold Protestant church records; NA, Thorold manuscript census, 1891

TABLE 9
Patterns of church membership among Protestant married couples, by occupational group, Campbellford, 1886–92

Occupational group/class	Both spouses church members		Wife only		Husband only		Total
	No.	%	No.	%	No.	%	No.
Merchants/professionals	25	71	9	26	1	3	35
Small employers/foremen	16	70	3	13	4	17	23
Clerks/agents	9	90	1	10	–	0	10
Middle-class total	**50**	**74**	**13**	**19**	**5**	**7**	**68**
Artisans	8	53	5	33	2	13	15
Skilled workers	22	52	15	36	5	12	42
Semi-/unskilled workers	15	54	6	21	7	25	28
Factory workers	9	69	3	23	1	8	13
Working-class total	**46**	**55**	**24**	**29**	**13**	**16**	**83**
Total	**104**	**63**	**42**	**25**	**20**	**12**	**166**

Sources: Campbellford Protestant church records; NA, Campbellford manuscript census, 1891

TABLE 10

Financial contributions to the church among Thorold Catholic families, by occupational group and amount of annual donation, 1900[a]

	Amount donated yearly									Total no. of families
	$0		>$0, <$2		>$2, <$10		>$10			
Occupational group/class	No. of contributors	% of total	No. of contributors	% of total	No. of contributors	% of total	No. of contributors	% of total		
Merchants/professionals	2	17	–	–	1	8	9	75		12
Small employers/foremen	–	–	–	–	1	25	3	75		4
Clerks/agents	–	–	2	33	1	17	3	50		6
Middle-class total	**2**	**9**	**2**	**9**	**3**	**14**	**15**	**68**		**22**
Artisans	–	–	–	–	1	33	2	67		3
Skilled workers	7	16	2	5	7	16	27	63		43
Semi-/unskilled workers	7	21	5	15	7	21	14	42		33
Factory workers	3	30	2	20	2	20	3	30		10
Servants	3	50	2	33	1	17	–	–		6
Working-class total	**20**	**22**	**11**	**12**	**17**	**19**	**44**	**48**		**92**
Other	5	45	–	–	5	45	1	9		11
Total	**27**	**21**	**13**	**10**	**26**	**20**	**62**	**48**		**128**

Sources: Roman Catholic Archives, Archdiocese of Toronto (RCA, AT), annual financial reports, Holy Rosary Parish, Thorold, 1899–1902; NA, Thorold manuscript census, 1901

[a] The data are based primarily on those listed in the 1900 financial report; but those who were not listed in 1900 but did donate (or were at least listed) in 1899 or 1902 are also included. The table does not include intermarried couples who did not donate to the church.

TABLE 11
Financial contributions to the church among Thorold Catholic families, by family income and amount of annual donation, 1900[a]

Family income[b]	Amount donated yearly								Total no. of families
	$0		>$0, <$2		>$2, <$10		>$10		
	No. of contributors	% of total	No. of contributors	% of total	No. of contributors	% of total	No. of contributors	% of total	
<$360	14	36	8	21	1	3	16	41	39
>$360, <$600	2	10	2	10	7	35	9	45	20
>$600, <$1000	3	12	2	8	8	31	13	50	26
>$1000	–	0	1	5	3	15	16	80	20

Sources: RCA, AT, annual financial reports, Holy Rosary Parish, Thorold, 1899–1902; NA, Thorold manuscript census, 1901
[a] The data are based primarily on those listed in the 1900 financial report; but those who were not listed in 1900 but did donate (or were at least listed) in 1899 or 1902 are also included. The table does not include intermarried couples who did not donate to the church.
[b] Does not include all families, since data regarding income are available only for employees/wage earners.

TABLE 12
Thorold Catholics donating more or less than two-fifths of promised weekly
donation over the year, by sex and marital status, 1900[a]

Sex and marital status	Donating over 2/5 promised		Donating less than 2/5		Total
	No.	%	No.	%	No.
Married women	25	96	1	4	26
Single women	20	95	1	5	21
Widowed women	11	100	–	0	11
Total women	**56**	**97**	**2**	**4**	**58**
Married men	38	91	4	10	42
Single men	29	66	15	34	44
Widowed men	8	80	2	20	10
Total men	**75**	**78**	**21**	**22**	**96**

Sources: RCA, AT, annual financial reports, Holy Rosary Parish, Thorold,
1899–1902; NA, Thorold manuscript census, 1901
[a] While not definitive, whether or not one tended to pay the weekly contribution promised provides some indication of whether or not one was in church.

TABLE 13
Protestant male church officials, by occupational group and denomination, Thorold, 1886–94

Occupational group/class	Baptist		Anglican		Presbyterian		Methodist	
	No.	%	No.	%	No.	%	No.	%
Merchants/professionals	3	43	8	47	8	28	7	29
Small employers/foremen	1	14	3	18	2	7	6	25
Clerks/agents	–	–	–	–	4	14	4	17
Middle-class total	**4**	**57**	**11**	**65**	**14**	**48**	**17**	**71**
Artisans	–	–	–	–	2	7	1	4
Skilled workers	3	43	3	18	11	38	5	21
Semi-/unskilled workers	–	–	–	–	–	–	–	–
Factory workers	–	–	–	–	1	4	1	4
Servants	–	–	–	–	–	–	–	–
Working-class total	**3**	**43**	**3**	**18**	**12**	**41**	**6**	**25**
Farmers	–	–	3	18	–	–	–	–
Other/unknown	–	–	–	–	1	4	–	–
Total	**7**	**100**	**17**	**100**	**29**	**100**	**24**	**100**

Sources: Thorold Protestant church records; NA, Thorold manuscript census, 1891; Public
Archives of Ontario (PAO), Thorold assessment roll, 1886

TABLE 14

Protestant male church officials, by occupational group and denomination, Campbellford, 1886–94

Occupational group/class	Baptist		Anglican		Presbyterian		Methodist	
	No.	%	No.	%	No.	%	No.	%
Merchants/professionals	1	14	6	40	6	26	9	35
Small employers/foremen	1	14	1	7	6	26	3	12
Clerks/agents	1	14	4	27	3	13	1	4
Middle-class total	**3**	**43**	**11**	**73**	**15**	**65**	**13**	**50**
Artisans	2	28	–	–	–	–	–	–
Skilled workers	1	14	–	–	3	13	8	31
Semi-/unskilled workers	–	–	2	13	1	4	1	4
Factory workers	–	–	–	–	–	–	3	12
Servants	–	–			1	4	–	–
Working-class total	**1**	**14**	**2**	**13**	**5**	**22**	**12**	**46**
Farmers	–	–	2	13	2	9	1	4
Other/unknown	1	14	–	–	1	4	–	–
Total	**7**	**100**	**15**	**100**	**23**	**100**	**26**	**100**

Sources: Campbellford Protestant church records; NA, Campbellford manuscript census, 1891

TABLE 15

Members and executive of Protestant women's church organizations, by marital status and occupational group of father or husband, Thorold, 1886–94

	Anglican Women's Auxiliary					Baptist			
	Members				Exec.	Ladies Aid		Mission Circle	
						Members	Exec.	Members	Exec.
	Married[a]	Single	Total						
Occupational group/class	No.	No.	No.	%	No.	No.	No.	No.	No.
Merchants/professionals	7	5	12	39	5	1	1	2	1
Small employers/foremen	3	–	3	10	2	–	–	–	–
Clerks/agents	4	–	4	13	1	1	1	1	–
Middle-class total	**14**	**5**	**19**	**61**	**8**	**2**	**2**	**3**	**1**
Artisans	1	1	2	7	–	–	–	–	–
Skilled workers	6	1	7	23	2	4	4	2	2
Semi-/unskilled workers	–	1	1	3	–	1	–	1	–
Factory workers	–	–	–	–	–	–	–	–	–
Servants	–	–	–	–	–	–	–	–	–
Working-class total	**6**	**2**	**8**	**26**	**2**	**5**	**4**	**3**	**2**
Farmers	1	–	1	3	–	–	–	–	–
Widows	–	1	1	3	1	–	–	–	–
Other	–	–	–	–	–	–	–	–	–
Total	**22**	**9**	**31**	**100**	**11**	**7[b]**	**6[c]**	**6**	**3**

TABLE 15 (concluded)

Occupational group/class	Methodist Women's Missionary Society					Presbyterian Ladies Mite Society				
	Members				Exec.	Members				Exec.
	Married[a]	Single	Total			Married[a]	Single	Total		
	No.	No.	No.	%	No.	No.	No.	No.	%	No.
Merchants/professionals	4	1	5	26	2	3	3	6	22	1
Small employers/foremen	3	–	3	16	–	1	2	3	11	1
Clerks/agents	2	–	2	11	2	1	–	1	4	1
Middle-class total	**9**	**1**	**10**	**53**	**4**	**5**	**5**	**10**	**37**	**3**
Artisans	–	–	–	–	–	1	1	2	7	–
Skilled workers	3	1	4	21	1	9	2	11	41	3
Semi-/unskilled workers	–	–	–	–	–	1	–	1	4	1
Factory workers	1	–	1	5	–	–	1	1	4	–
Servants	–	–	–	–	–	–	–	–	–	–
Working-class total	**4**	**1**	**5**	**26**	**1**	**10**	**3**	**13**	**48**	**4**
Farmers	–	–	–	–	–	–	–	–	–	–
Widows	4	–	4	21	2	–	1	1	4	1
Other	–	–	–	–	–	–	1	1	4	–
Total	**17**	**2**	**19**	**100**	**7**	**16**	**11**	**27**	**100**	**8**

Sources: Niagara Diocesan Branch, Women's Auxiliary to the Domestic and Foreign Missionary Society of the Church of England, *Annual Report*, 1887–95; Women's Missionary Society of the Methodist Church of Canada, *Annual Report*, 1886–95; records of Thorold Protestant churches; NA, Thorold manuscript census, 1891

[a] Includes married women and widows
[b] Four married, three single
[c] Three married, three single

TABLE 16
Members and executive of Protestant women's church organizations, by marital status and occupational group of father or husband, Campbellford, 1886–94

Occupational group/class	Anglican Women's Auxiliary					Baptist Mission Circle		Methodist Women's Missionary Society				
	Members				Exec.	Members	Exec.	Members				Exec.
	Married[a]	Single	Total					Married[a]	Single	Total		
	No.	No.	No.	%	No.	No.	No.	No.	No.	No.	%	No.
Merchants/professionals	6	2	8	36	3	2	1	8	2	10	26	3
Small employers/foremen	–	1	1	5	–	–	–	4	–	4	10	1
Clerks/agents	3	–	3	14	–	–	–	1	–	1	3	–
Middle-class total	**9**	**3**	**12**	**55**	**3**	**2**	**1**	**13**	**2**	**15**	**39**	**4**
Artisans	–	–	–	–	–	2	2	–	1	1	3	–
Skilled workers	4	1	5	23	–	1	1	6	4	10	26	3
Semi-/unskilled workers	–	–	–	–	–	–	–	4	–	4	10	–
Factory workers	1	–	1	5	–	–	–	1	1	2	5	–
Servants	–	–	–	–	–	–	–	–	–	–	–	–
Working-class total	**5**	**1**	**6**	**27**	**–**	**1**	**1**	**11**	**5**	**16**	**41**	**3**
Farmers	–	–	–	–	–	–	–	–	1	1	3	1
Widows	–	4	4	18	4	1	–	4	2	6	15	2
Other	–	–	–	–	–	1	1	–	–	–	–	–
Total	14	8	22	100	7	7[b]	5	28	11	39	100	10

Sources: Toronto Diocesan Branch, Women's Auxiliary to the Domestic and Foreign Missionary Society of the Church of England, *Annual Report*, 1887–95; Women's Missionary Society of the Methodist Church of Canada, *Annual Report*, 1886–95; records of Campbellford Protestant churches; NA, Campbellford manuscript census, 1891
[a] Includes married women and widows
[b] Five married and two single women

TABLE 17

Members and executive of Presbyterian Young People's Society of Christian Endeavour, by sex and occupational group of father or husband, Thorold, 1891

Occupational group/class	Members				Executive			
	Male	Female	Total		Male	Female	Total	
	No.	No.	No.	%	No.	No.	No.	%
Merchants/professionals	1	7	8	16	–	3	3	18
Small employers/foremen	1	4	5	10	–	1	1	6
Clerks/agents	–	1	1	2	–	–	–	–
Middle-class total	**2**	**12**	**14**	**28**	**–**	**4**	**4**	**24**
Artisans	–	–	–	–	–	–	–	–
Skilled workers	10	16	26	52	4	6	10	59
Semi-/unskilled workers	1	3	4	8	–	1	1	6
Factory workers	2	3	5	10	–	2	2	12
Servants	–	1	1	2	–	–	–	–
Working-class total	**13**	**23**	**36**	**72**	**4**	**9**	**13**	**77**
Farmers	–	–	–	–	–	–	–	–
Widows	–	–	–	–	–	–	–	–
Other	–	–	–	–	–	–	–	–
Total	**15**	**35**	**50**	**100**	**4**	**13**	**17**	**100**

Sources: Records of St. Andrew's Presbyterian Church, Thorold; NA, Thorold manuscript census, 1891

TABLE 18
Those signing Campbellford temperance petition, by sex, marital status, and occupational group, 1890

	Married or widowed								Single[a]							
	Male				Female				Male				Female			
	Signatories		Total pop.		Signatories		Total pop.		Signatories		Total pop.		Signatories		Total pop.	
Occupational group/class	No.	%	No.	%	No.	%	No.	%	No.	%	No.	%	No.	%	No.	%
Merchants/professionals	7	10	52	16	7	10	50	14	–	–	13	7	–	–	–	–
Small employers/foremen	6	8	29	9	5	7	28	8	–	–	–	–	–	–	7	3
Clerks/agents	7	10	23	7	5	7	22	6	–	–	16	8	–	–	7	3
Middle-class total	**20**	**27**	**104**	**31**	**17**	**24**	**100**	**27**	**–**	**–**	**29**	**15**	**–**	**–**	**7**	**3**
Artisans	4	5	23	7	3	4	25	7	–	–	–	–	–	–	–	–
Skilled workers[b]	25	34	82	25	17	24	82	22	1	17	53	27	7	16	45	18
Semi-/unskilled workers	10	14	85	25	14	20	84	23	–	–	42	22	–	–	–	–
Factory workers	8	11	25	8	3	4	25	7	4	67	23	12	24	55	67	27
Servants	–	–	–	–	–	–	–	–	–	–	3	2	–	–	26	10
Working-class total	**43**	**58**	**192**	**57**	**34**	**48**	**191**	**52**	**5**	**83**	**121**	**62**	**31**	**71**	**138**	**55**
Farmers	2	3	16	5	3	4	5	1	1	17	3	2	–	–	–	–
Widows	–	–	–	–	12	17	45	12	–	–	–	–	13[c]	30	–	–
Other	5	7	–	–	2	3	–	–	–	–	42	22	–	–	105	42
Total	74	100	335	100	71	100	366	100	6	100	195	100	44	100	250	100

Sources: Campbellford municipal records, temperance petition, 1890; NA, Campbellford manuscript census, 1891
[a] Single men and women are listed by their own occupation.
[b] For single women's occupations, dressmakers/milliners are categorized as skilled; these occupations account for all single women so designated.
[c] Probably the majority of these women were middle class.

TABLE 19
Those signing Campbellford temperance petition, by family church
membership and occupational group, 1890

Occupational group/class	No church members in family		Total signatories[a]
	No.	%	No.
Merchants/professionals	1	7	14
Small employers/foremen	–	0	11
Clerks/agents	3	25	12
Middle-class total	**4**	**11**	**37**
Artisans	–	0	7
Skilled workers	15	30	50
Semi-/unskilled workers	5	21	24
Factory workers	11	28	39
Servants	–	–	–
Working-class total	**31**	**27**	**113**
Farmers	2	33	6
Widows	3	25	12
Other/unknown	5	25	20
Total	**45**	**23**	**195**

Sources: Campbellford municipal records, temperance petition,
1890; NA, Campbellford manuscript census, 1891
[a] Totals include eleven Roman Catholics; the remainder are
  Protestants.

TABLE 20
Officers of Royal Templars of Temperance and Sons of Temperance, Thorold, by sex
and occupational group, 1888–94

| Occupational group/class | Royal Templars of Temperance | | | | Sons of Temperance | | | |
| | Male | | Female | | Male | | Female | |
	No.	%	No.	%	No.	%	No.	%
Merchants/professionals	8		3		6		2	
Small employers/foremen	1		–		5		2	
Clerks/agents	4		–		2		–	
Middle-class total	**13**	**52**	**3**	**33**	**13**	**54**	**4**	**19**
Artisans	2		–		–		1	
Skilled workers	8		3		8		11	
Semi-/unskilled workers	1		–		3		3	
Factory workers	3		2		–		1	
Servants	–		–		–		1	
Working-class total	**12**	**48**	**5**	**56**	**11**	**46**	**16**	**76**
Farmers	–		1		–		–	
Widows	–		–		–		–	
Other	–		–		–		–	
Total	**25**	**100**	**9**	**100**	**24**	**100**	**21**	**100**

Sources: *Thorold Post*; NA, Thorold manuscript census, 1891

TABLE 21
Officers of Royal Templars of Temperance, Campbellford,
by sex and occupational group, 1888–94

Occupational group/class	Male No.	%	Female No.	%
Merchants/professionals	3		1	
Small employers/foremen	2		2	
Clerks/agents	1		–	
Middle-class total	**6**	**40**	**3**	**33**
Artisans	3		–	
Skilled workers	4		2	
Semi-/unskilled workers	–		–	
Factory workers	2		4	
Servants	–			
Working-class total	**6**	**40**	**6**	**67**
Farmers	–		–	
Widows	–		–	
Other	–		–	
Total	**15**	**100**	**9**	**100**

Sources: *Campbellford Herald*; NA, Campbellford
manuscript census, 1891

TABLE 22

Church membership of officers of Royal Templars of Temperance and Sons of Temperance, Thorold, by sex and occupational group, 1888–94

	Royal Templars of Temperance						Sons of Temperance					
	Male			Female			Male			Female		
	Church members		Total	Church members		Total	Church members		Total	Church members		Total
Occupational group/class	No.	%	No.	No.	%	No.	No.	%	No.	No.	%	No.
Merchants/professionals	4		8	3		3	6		6	–		2
Small employers/foremen	1		1	–		–	1		5	2		2
Clerks/agents	3		4	–		–	1		2	–		–
Middle-class total	**8**	**62**	**13**	**3**	**100**	**3**	**8**	**62**	**13**	**2**	**50**	**4**
Artisans	1		2	–		–	–		–	1		1
Skilled workers	5		8	3		3	2		8	4		11
Semi-/unskilled workers	–		1	–		–	–		3	1		3
Factory workers	2		3	2		2	–		–	1		1
Servants	–		–	–		–	–		–	–		1
Working-class total	**7**	**58**	**12**	**5**	**100**	**5**	**2**	**18**	**11**	**6**	**38**	**16**
Farmers	–		–	–		1	–		–	–		–
Widows	–		–	–		–	–		–	–		–
Other	–		–	–		–	–		–	–		–
Total	**16**	**59**	**27**	**8**	**89**	**9**	**10**	**42**	**24**	**9**	**43**	**21**

Sources: *Thorold Post*; NA, Thorold manuscript census, 1891

TABLE 23
Officers of fraternal orders by occupational group, Thorold, 1888–94

Occupational group/class	Orange Lodge[a]		OYB[b]		AOUW[c]		Masons		IOOF[d]		CMBA[e]		Other[f]	
	No.	%	No.	%	No.	%	No.	%	No.	%	No.	%	No.	%
Merchants/professionals	1	3	–	–	6	20	8	44	6	19	7	32	28	34
Small employers/foremen	2	5	3	14	7	23	–	–	5	16	2	9	17	21
Clerks/agents	3	8	–	–	2	7	4	22	2	7	1	5	3	4
Middle-class Total	**6**	**15**	**3**	**14**	**15**	**50**	**12**	**67**	**13**	**42**	**10**	**46**	**48**	**58**
Artisans	–	–	1	5	3	10	1	6	2	7	1	5	3	4
Skilled workers	15	39	6	27	8	27	5	28	10	32	6	27	23	28
Semi-/unskilled workers	9	23	7	32	4	13	–	–	5	16	3	14	6	7
Factory workers	6	15	2	9	–	–	–	–	–	–	2	9	2	2
Servants	1	3	–	–	–	–	–	–	–	–	–	–	–	–
Working-class total	**31**	**80**	**15**	**68**	**12**	**40**	**5**	**28**	**15**	**48**	**11**	**50**	**31**	**37**
Farmers	2	5	3	14	–	–	–	–	1	3	–	–	1	1
Other/unknown	–	–	–	–	–	–	–	–	–	–	–	–	–	–
Total	**39**	**100**	**22**	**100**	**30**	**100**	**18**	**100**	**31**	**100**	**22**	**100**	**83**	**100**

Sources: *Thorold Post*; NA, Thorold manuscript census, 1891
[a] There were two Orange Lodges in town, both of which are included under the Orange Lodge.
[b] Orange Young Britons, an order associated with the Orange Lodge
[c] Ancient Order of United Workmen
[d] International Order of Oddfellows
[e] Catholic Mutual Benefit Association
[f] The lodges listed under 'Other' include the Septennial Benefit Society, the Order of Canadian Home Circles, the Canadian Order of Chosen Friends, and the Canadian Order of Foresters. Individuals who belonged to more than one of these organizations are counted more than once.

TABLE 24

Officers of fraternal orders by occupational group, Campbellford, 1888–94

Occupational group/class	Orange[a] Lodge		AOUW[b]		Masons		IOOF[c]		Foresters		Sons of England/ Sons of Scotland	
	No.	%	No.	%	No.	%	No.	%	No.	%	No.	%
Merchants/professionals	2		2		2		2		2		4	
Small employers/foremen	1		2		4		1		4		5	
Clerks/agents	3		–		1		5		1		1	
Middle-class total	**6**	**22**	**4**	**40**	**7**	**70**	**8**	**36**	**7**	**64**	**10**	**53**
Artisans	3		1		–		3		–		3	
Skilled workers	5		2		1		8		2		3	
Semi-/unskilled workers	10		1		2		2		–		–	
Factory workers	3		2		–		1		1		2	
Servants	–		–		–		–		–		–	
Working-class total	**18**	**67**	**5**	**50**	**3**	**30**	**11**	**50**	**3**	**27**	**5**	**26**
Farmers	–		–		–		–		1		–	
Other/unknown	–		–		–		–		–		1	
Total	**27**	**100**	**10**	**100**	**10**	**100**	**22**	**100**	**11**	**100**	**19**	**100**

Sources: *Campbellford Herald*; NA, Campbellford manuscript census, 1891

[a] The Campbellford order of the Loyal True Blues is included under Orange Order

[b] Ancient Order of United Workmen

[c] International Order of Oddfellows

TABLE 25
Church membership among officers of fraternal orders, Thorold, 1888–94

Class	Orange Lodge			OYB[a]			AOUW[b]			Masons			IOOF[c]			Other		
	Church members		Total officers	Church members		Total officers	Church members		Total officers	Church members		Total officers	Church members		Total officers	Church members		Total officers
	No.	%	No.	No.	%	No.	No.	%	No.	No.	%	No.	No.	%	No.	No.	%	No.
Middle-class total	2	33	6	–	–	3	7	47	15	7	58	12	6	46	13	27	56	48
Working-class total	10	32	31	1	7	15	6	50	12	2	40	5	6	40	15	14	45	31
Total[d]	12	31	39	1	5	22	13	43	30	10	56	18	12	39	31	45	54	83

Sources: *Thorold Post*; Thorold Protestant church records; NA, Thorold manuscript census, 1891
[a] Orange Young Britons
[b] Ancient Order of United Workmen
[c] International Order of Oddfellows
[d] Totals include artisans, farmers, and others.

TABLE 26
Church membership among officers of fraternal orders, Campbellford, 1888–94

Class	Orange Lodge			AOUW[a]			Masons			IOOF[b]			Foresters			Sons of England/Sons of Scotland		
	Church members		Total officers	Church members		Total officers	Church members		Total officers	Church members		Total officers	Church members		Total officers	Church members		Total officers
	No.	%	No.	No.	%	No.	No.	%	No.	No.	%	No.	No.	%	No.	No.	%	No.
Middle-class total	3	50	6	3	75	4	5	71	7	5	63	8	6	86	7	7	70	10
Working-class total	–	–	18	3	60	5	3	100	3	6	55	11	1	33	3	4	80	5
Total[c]	3	11	27	6	60	10	8	80	10	12	55	22	8	73	11	12	63	19

Sources: *Campbellford Herald*; Campbellford Protestant church records; NA, Campbellford manuscript census, 1891
[a] Ancient Order of United Workmen
[b] International Order of Oddfellows
[c] Totals include artisans, farmers, and others.

TABLE 27

Officers and members of local sports clubs, by sports and occupational group, Thorold, 1888–94

Occupational group/class	Curling club				Football club				Baseball club, members		Other baseball teams,[a] members	
	Members		Exec.		Members		Exec.					
	No.	%	No.	%	No.	%	No.	%	No.	%	No.	%
Merchants/professionals	18		7		6		8		5		10	
Small employers/foremen	11		1		2		1		2		1	
Clerks/agents	–		–		–		1		2		2	
Middle-class total	**29**	**78**	**8**	**89**	**8**	**73**	**10**	**77**	**9**	**64**	**13**	**62**
Artisans	–		1		1		1		–		2	
Skilled workers	5		–		2		2		3		2	
Semi-/unskilled workers	1		–		–		–		–		1	
Factory workers	–		–		–		–		2		2	
Servants	–		–		–		–		–		–	
Working-class total	**6**	**16**	**–**	**–**	**2**	**18**	**2**	**15**	**5**	**36**	**5**	**24**
Farmers	2		–		–		–		–		1	
Other/unknown	–		–		–		–		–		–	
Total	**37**	**100**	**9**	**100**	**11**	**100**	**13**	**100**	**14**	**100**	**21**	**100**

Sources: *Thorold Post*; NA, Thorold manuscript census, 1891

[a] Includes members of various informal baseball teams formed in town who could be identified in the census. Although it includes a few members of factory teams, it includes more members from games between store clerks, or single versus married men, or thin versus fat men.

TABLE 28
Members of local sports clubs by sport and occupational group, Campbellford, 1890–92

Occupational group/class	Curling club		Baseball club		Cricket club	
	No.	%	No.	%	No.	%
Merchants/professionals	30		5		17	
Small employers/foremen	3		1		5	
Clerks/agents	6		2		3	
Middle-class total	**39**	**93**	**8**	**73**	**25**	**96**
Artisans	–		–		–	
Skilled workers	1		1		–	
Semi-/unskilled workers	2		1		1	
Factory workers	–		1		–	
Servants	–		–		–	
Working-class total	**3**	**7**	**3**	**27**	**1**	**4**
Farmers	–		–		–	
Other/unknown	–		–		–	
Total	42	100	11	100	26	100

Sources: *Campbellford Herald*; NA, Campbellford manuscript census, 1891

TABLE 29
Occupations of Ontario Salvation Army officers on becoming
officers, by sex, 1882–90[a]

	No.	%
FEMALE		
At home	137	28
Clerks	10	2
Nurses	7	1
Teachers	16	3
Dressmakers/tailoresses/milliners[b]	98	20
Factory workers	37	8
Servants	.186	38
Other	2	–
Total	**493**	**100**
MALE		
At home	2	–
Businessmen/professionals	14	4
Clerks	31	8
Teachers	4	1
Farmers	91	23
Skilled workers/artisans[c]	164	41
Semi-skilled workers	22	6
Factory workers	30	7
Labourers/unskilled workers	39	10
Servants	6	2
Total	**403**	**100**

Source: Salvation Army Archives, Toronto, officers' rolls
[a] This table does not include cases without data on occupation,
    and it includes only those officers who joined up in Ontario, not
    those transferred from England or from elsewhere in Canada.
[b] Some of these women probably worked in factories, but this is
    impossible to determine.
[c] Some of these men may have been self-employed, or even
    small masters, while many probably worked in factories. The
    roll provides only occupational titles.

TABLE 30
Ages of female and male Ontario Salvationists
on becoming officers, 1882–90[a]

Age	Female		Male	
	No.	%	No.	%
Less than 16	4	1	1	–
16–17	57	11	29	7
18–19	103	20	81	20
20–24	239	47	207	52
25–30	84	16	59	15
31–40	23	5	20	5
Over 40	3	1	4	1
Total	**513**	**100**	**401**	**100**

Source: Salvation Army Archives, Toronto,
officers' rolls
[a] Does not include cases without data on age.
Ontario Salvation Army officers are those who
joined up in Ontario.

TABLE 31
Length of tenure of Ontario Salvation Army officers,
by sex, 1882–90[a]

Years of Army service	Female		Male	
	No.	%	No.	%
1 year or less	238	35	236	44
More than 1 year, up to 3 years	208	30	143	26
More than 3 years, up to 5 years	115	17	67	12
More than 5 years, up to 10 years	85	12	53	10
More than 10 years	41	6	42	8
Total	**687**	**100**	**541**	**100**

Source: Salvation Army Archives, Toronto, officers' rolls
[a] Does not include cases without data on years of
service. Ontario Salvation Army officers are those
who joined up in Ontario

TABLE 32
Ratio of pre-revival church members to revival converts, by sex, marital status, and occupational group, Thorold, 1893

| | Single | | | | | | Married | | | | | |
| | Female | | | Male | | | Female | | | Male | | |
Occupational group/class	Revival converts	PRCM[a]	Ratio	Revival converts	PRCM[a]	Ratio	Revival converts	PRCM[a]	Ratio	Revival converts	PRCM[a]	Ratio
Merchants/professionals	12	12		4	6		1	20		–	19	
Small employers/foremen	4	8		7	–		3	12		3	11	
Clerks/agents	5	2		3	–		2	9		3	10	
Middle-class total	**21**	**22**	**1:1.1**	**14**	**6**	**1:0.4**	**6**	**41**	**1:6.8**	**6**	**40**	**1:6.7**
Artisans	2	4		–	1		1	7		–	7	
Skilled workers	29	24		22	7		13	41		12	23	
Semi-/unskilled workers	9	7		5	1		4	13		4	6	
Factory workers	6	4		2	–		5	4		3	5	
Servants	2	2		–	–		–	–		–	–	
Working-class total	**46**	**37**	**1:0.8**	**29**	**8**	**1:0.3**	**22**	**58**	**1:2.6**	**19**	**34**	**1:1.8**
Farmers	1	–		3	–		–	1		–	1	
Other/unknown	4	7		1	1		–	–		–	–	
Total	**74**	**70**	**1:0.9**	**47**	**16**	**1:0.3**	**29**	**107**	**1:3.7**	**25**	**82**	**1:3.3**

Sources: Thorold Protestant church records; NA, Thorold manuscript census, 1891
[a] Pre-revival church members

TABLE 33
Revival converts by age and sex, Thorold, 1893

Age[a]	Female		Male	
	No.	%	No.	%
6–13	23	22	16	22
14–17	26	24	26	35
18–28	24	22	7	10
29–40	19	18	14	19
>40	15	14	11	15
Total	**107**	**100**	**74**	**100**

Sources: Thorold Anglican, Presbyterian, and Methodist
church records; NA, Thorold manuscript census, 1891
[a] Age in 1893, calculated by adding two years to age
   given in 1891 census

TABLE 34
Revival converts by occupational group and pre-revival church membership patterns of family members, Thorold, 1893

Occupational group/class	No family links to church		Both parents church members		Father/husband church member		Mother/wife church member		Total	
	No.	%	No.	%	No.	%	No.	%	No.	%
Merchants/professionals	–	–	11	61	3	17	1	6	18[a]	100
Small employers/foremen	2	15	5	39	1	8	5	39	13	100
Clerks	3	33	4	44	1	11	1	11	9	100
Middle-class total	**5**	**13**	**20**	**50**	**5**	**13**	**7**	**18**	**40**	**100**
Artisans	–	–	–	–	–	–	1	100	1	100
Skilled workers	22	37	7	12	4	7	27	45	60	100
Semi-/unskilled workers	8	42	4	21	–	–	6	32	19[b]	100
Factory workers	4	29	3	21	2	14	5	36	14	100
Servants	3	100	–	–	–	–	–	–	3	100
Working-class total	**37**	**39**	**14**	**15**	**6**	**6**	**38**	**40**	**96**	**100**
Farmers	–	–	3	75	1	25	–	–	4	100
Other/unknown	2	40	2	40	–	–	1	20	5	100
Total	**44**	**30**	**39**	**27**	**12**	**8**	**47**	**32**	**146**	**100**

Sources: Thorold Anglican, Presbyterian, and Methodist church records; NA, Thorold manuscript census, 1891
[a] Includes three revival converts with Other family members who had earlier links to the churches
[b] Includes one revival convert with another family member who had earlier links to the churches

Notes

Abbreviations

ADA, DN   Anglican Diocesan Archives, Diocese of Niagara
ADA, DT   Anglican Diocesan Archives, Diocese of Toronto
CBA   Canadian Baptist Archives
CH   *Campbellford Herald*
IC   *Ingersoll Chronicle*
RCA, AT   Roman Catholic Archives, Archdiocese of Toronto
RR, WL   Regional Room Special Collections, Weldon Library
SAA   Salvation Army Archives
TP   *Thorold Post*
TPL   Thorold Public Library
UCA   United Church Archives

1: Introduction

1 See Bliss, 'Privatizing the Mind.'
2 More recently, feminist historians have shown that the home was also an important site for the development of class-consciousness. See, for example, Forestell, 'All That Glitters Is Not Gold,' and Frager, 'Politicized Housewives in the Jewish Communist Movement of Toronto.'
3 The extent to which gender analysis remains marginal in the recent work of 'mainstream' religious historians can be seen, for example, in Hatch's otherwise excellent *Democratization of American Christianity*. For a similar pattern in the history of leisure, see, for example, Rosenzweig, *Eight Hours for What We Will*.
4 For American studies, see, for example, Vandermeer and Swierenga, *Belief*

and Behaviour: Essays in the New Religious History, Hatch, *Democratization of American Christianity,* and Schantz, 'Piety in Providence.' Some Canadian religious historians have moved into social history, but as various commentators have noted, this area is still not a central focus of historical work. See Marshall, 'Canadian Historians, Secularization and the Problem of the Nineteenth Century,' and McGowan and Marshall, 'Introduction,' in *Prophets, Priests and Prodigals.* George Rawlyk's work includes much insightful social history, but Rawlyk focuses on the late eighteenth and early nineteenth centuries. See, for example, Rawlyk, *The Canada Fire* and *Ravished by the Spirit.* Much of the remaining work in the Canadian social history of religion has been in the field of women's history. See, for example, Brouwer, *New Women for God,* Mitchinson, 'Canadian Women and Church Missionary Societies,' and Muir and Whiteley, *Changing Roles of Women within the Christian Church in Canada.*

5 Grant, *A Profusion of Spires,* Westfall, *Two Worlds,* Gauvreau, *The Evangelical Century,* and Van Die, 'The Double Vision,' have argued most clearly that Protestantism retained its dominance in this period. For a critique of this focus on opinion leaders, see Marshall, 'Canadian Historians, Secularization and the Problem of the Nineteenth Century.'

6 Berger, *Science, God and Nature in Victorian Canada,* Cook, *The Regenerators,* McKillop, *A Disciplined Intelligence,* and Marshall, *Secularizing the Faith,* have noted the growing influence of secularizing forces in this period, but they still argue for the continued strength of Christian values and practices.

7 See Bocock, *Hegemony,* and Lears, 'The Concept of Cultural Hegemony,' for a discussion of hegemony. One recent doctoral dissertation has attempted to examine the nature of popular Christian practice (O'Dell, 'The Class Character of Church Participation in Late Nineteenth-Century Belleville, Ontario'). Very recently, there have been a few impressive historical studies that explore popular religious practice among Catholics (see Clarke, *Piety and Nationalism,* and Ferretti, *Entre voisins*).

8 See, for example, Palmer, *A Culture in Conflict.* In the American context, see Couvares, *The Remaking of Pittsburgh,* Steven J. Ross, *Workers on the Edge,* Rosenzweig, *Eight Hours for What We Will,* and Laurie, *Working People of Philadelphia.*

9 See Clarke et al., *Working-Class Culture,* and Thompson, *The Making of the English Working Class.*

10 This is unfortunate, since the few scholars who have studied working-class religious patterns have clearly demonstrated that Christianity could not only serve to integrate workers into the dominant culture but could also fuel a class-conscious critique of the capitalist system. See, for example, Corbin,

Life, Work and Rebellion in the Coalfields, Gutman, 'Protestantism and the American Labor Movement,' and Fones-Wolf, *Trade Union Gospel*. Also see Sutton, 'Tied to the Whipping Post,' for a recent critique of American labour historians' approach to religion.

11 See, for example, the articles in *Manliness and Morality*, ed. Mangan and Walvin; *Meanings for Manhood*, ed. Carnes and Griffen; and *Manful Assertions*, ed. Roper and Tosh. While the latter two works include a few articles on working-class masculinity, they focus primarily on masculinity among the middle class. For two recent Canadian dissertations that do examine issues of working-class masculinity, see Forestell, 'All That Glitters Is Not Gold,' and Rosenfeld, 'She Was a Hard Life.' See also Baron, 'Gender and Labor History: Learning from the Past, Looking to the Future,' in her *Work Engendered*.

12 Two articles that have recently examined aspects of the relationship between masculinity and religious involvement are Curtis, 'The Son of Man and God the Father,' and Walker, 'I Live But Not Yet I.' For work in the history of women and religion that does not address issues of class, see, for example, many of the articles in Muir and Whiteley's *Changing Roles of Women within the Christian Church in Canada*.

13 For some Canadian studies of women and religion that focus on the middle-class experience, see Mitchinson, 'Canadian Women and Church Missionary Societies in the Nineteenth Century,' Whiteley, 'Doing Just About What They Please,' and Brouwer, *New Women for God*. American scholars have provided an explicit discussion of the way religious involvement could nurture a distinctive 'women's culture'. See Cott, *The Bonds of Womanhood*. In *Women's Activism and Social Change*, Nancy Hewitt notes that women's religious culture was divided by class. However, she focuses on identifying different strata within the middle class and does not explore the issue of working-class women and religion.

14 See, for example, Peiss, *Cheap Amusements*, Stansell, *City of Women*, Benson, *Counter Cultures*, Baron, *Work Engendered*, and Strange, *Toronto's Girl Problem*.

15 Murphy, *Ten Hours' Labor*. Two studies that focus specifically on working-class women's religious involvement are Malmgreen, 'Domestic Discords,' and Valenze, *Prophetic Sons and Daughters*, while Higginbotham (*Righteous Discontent*) explores the experience of middle- and working-class women in the black Baptist church in the United States.

16 See Bock, 'Women's History and Gender History'; Tosh, 'What Should Historians Do with Masculinity?'; Scott, *Gender and the Politics of History* and 'The Evidence of Experience'; Valverde, 'Poststructuralist Gender Historians'; and Parr, 'Gender History and Historical Practice.'

17 Bennett, 'Feminism and History'; Hoff, 'Gender as a Postmodern Category of Paralysis'; Scott, 'Response to Gordon'; Gordon, 'Response to Scott'; and Sangster, 'Beyond Dichotomies.'

18 Baron, *Work Engendered*, 31. While on one level it may be true that there is no such thing as a separate material reality, since all is understood within various discourses, I believe that for historians the distinction between the discursive and the material remains useful. See also Weedon, *Feminist Practice and Poststructuralist Theory*, chap. 4; Ross, *Love and Toil*, 9–10; Strange, *Toronto's Girl Problem*, 12; and Sangster, *Earning Respect*, 8–10.

19 Davidoff and Hall, *Family Fortunes*. See also Ryan, *Cradle of the Middle Class*.

20 Suzanne Morton, *Ideal Surroundings*. See also Parr, *The Gender of Breadwinners*, and Forestell, 'All That Glitters Is Not Gold.'

21 See, for example, Davidoff and Hall, *Family Fortunes*, and Gordon, *Heroes of Their Own Lives*.

22 While 'low' Anglicans considered themselves evangelicals, other Anglicans did not. However, as William Westfall has noted, by the late nineteenth century, Anglicans and the more evangelical denominations such as the Methodists had much more in common than had been the case earlier in the century (Westfall, *Two Worlds*). See also Grant, *A Profusion of Spires*, 181, 194–5.

23 See, for example, Van Die, 'The Double Vision.'

24 See Brouwer, 'Transcending the "Unacknowledged Quarantine,"' and Van Die, *An Evangelical Mind* and 'A Women's Awakening.'

25 Johnson, *Islands of Holiness*. See also Rawlyk, *The Canada Fire*, and Grant, *A Profusion of Spires*, 167–8.

26 See Winks, *The Blacks in Canada*, 338, and Grant, *A Profusion of Spires*, 156.

27 The phrase 'small differences' is taken from Akenson, *Small Differences: Irish Catholics and Irish Protestants, 1815–1922*.

28 Parr, *The Gender of Breadwinners*, 245.

29 Thorold's population was 2,456 in 1881 and 2,273 in 1891, but it exceeded 3,000 in the mid-1880s with the influx of workers for the widening of the Welland Canal. See Canada, *Census of Canada*, 1881, vol. 1, table 1, and 1891, vol. 1, table 3. See also *Thorold Post* (hereafter *TP*), 9 September 1892.

30 In 1891, 16.0 per cent of Ingersoll's population was employed by industrial establishments, while the average among communities with populations from 3,000 to 5,000 was 16.7 per cent. In 1891, 17.0 per cent of Campbellford's population was so employed, as was 13.7 per cent of Thorold's population, while the average among communities with populations from 1,500 to 3,000 was 13.7 per cent (Canada, *Census of Canada*, 1891, vol. 4, table 8).

31 Poem entitled 'Thorold' by L.D. Brown, undated, in scrapbook of Mamie McBride Halliday, in private collection of Mrs Betty Millar.

32 Catholics, most of whom were Irish, made up 29.6 per cent of Thorold's population in 1881 and 28.1 per cent in 1891 (Canada, *Census of Canada*, 1881, vol. 1, table 2, and 1891, vol. 1, table 6). For a more detailed breakdown of the religious and occupational background of the populations of Thorold, Campbellford, and Ingersoll, see Marks's dissertation, 'Ladies, Loafers, Knights and "Lasses."'

33 See Orr, 'The Wrong Side of the Canal.'

34 Thorold Township was first settled by whites after the American Revolution. See *Jubilee History of Thorold Township and Town* and *Town of Thorold Centennial*. For a discussion of the Irish labourers on the Welland Canal in the 1840s, see Bleasdale, 'Class Conflict on the Canals of Upper Canada.'

35 See, for example, *TP*, 9 July 1886, 1 and 29 July 1892, 19 August 1892.

36 The Canadian average was less than 11 per cent (Canada, Dominion Bureau of Statistics, *Occupational Trends in Canada, 1891–1931*). Among Campbellford women who were gainfully employed in 1891, 41.9 per cent worked in the woollen factories (data calculated from Campbellford manuscript census, 1891, in National Archives of Canada [NA]).

37 The Methodists and Presbyterians were the largest denominations in the village. Canada, *Census of Canada*, 1881, vol. 1, table 2, and 1891, vol. 1, table 4.

38 *Campbellford Herald* (hereafter *CH*), 31 December 1885. See also *CH* 12 March and *CH* 30 April 1885, 20 August 1891.

39 The village went from a population of 1,418 in 1881 to 2,424 in 1891. It was not to grow much larger, however, and the population did not much exceed 3,000 in the twentieth century (Canada, *Census of Canada*, 1881, vol. 1, table 1, and 1891, vol. 1, table 3).

40 There were forty-five African Canadians listed in the 1881 census, making up about 1 per cent of the town's population. There were many more African Canadians in Ingersoll before the Civil War, when Ingersoll was a stop on the Underground Railway.

41 Catholics actually made up 12.9 per cent of Ingersoll's population in 1881 and 12.0 per cent in 1891 (Canada, *Census of Canada* 1881, vol. 1, table 2, and 1891, vol. 1, table 4).

42 See Bouchier 'For the Love of the Game and the Honour of the Town.'

43 See, for example, Katz, *The People of Hamilton*, 9–10, and Suzanne Morton, *Ideal Surroundings*, 5.

44 This means that even if people were found in both a church membership roll and the local newspaper, I have used a fictionalized name to refer to them (unless they were extremely prominent and their church membership would therefore be known from published sources).

2: Church Ladies, Young Men, and Freethinkers

1 See, for example, Grant, *A Profusion of Spires*.
2 Rubio and Waterston, *The Selected Journals of L.M. Montgomery*, 1:262. See also O'Dell, 'The Class Character of Church Participation in Late Nineteenth-Century Belleville,' 165-9.
3 See Semple, 'The Impact of Urbanization on the Methodist Church of Canada,' and S.D. Clark, *Church and Sect in Canada*.
4 Duncan, *The Imperialist*, 65; Rubio and Waterston, *The Selected Journals of L.M. Montgomery*, 1:262; *Ingersoll Chronicle (IC)*, 2 November 1882; *Stratford Beacon*, 2 April 1886.
5 Duncan, *The Imperialist*, 65; Rubio and Waterston, *The Selected Journals of L.M. Montgomery*, 1:262; C.S. Clark, *Of Toronto the Good*, 180.
6 Anglicans did not differentiate between members and nonmembers, since all Anglicans were considered part of the parish. However, Anglicans with a greater religious commitment were more likely to become communicants. In the context of this analysis, then, communicant status among Anglicans is equated with church membership in other Protestant denominations.
7 Presbyterians had a particular term for those who regularly attended without becoming church members. These people were adherents, and as regular attenders they were expected to contribute financially to the church.
8 From *Wesley's Doctrinal Standards*, xvi, cited in Airhart, *Serving the Present Age*, 26.
9 Nathaniel Burwash, 'Reminiscences of My Life,' 9-10, cited in Marshall, *Secularizing the Faith*, 32.
10 See, for example, Airhart, *Serving the Present Age*, Marshall, *Secularizing the Faith*, and Semple, 'The Impact of Urbanization.'
11 See appendix A.
12 *Campbellford Herald (CH)*, 31 May 1883; Grant, *A Profusion of Spires*, 197. Of course, if one-fifth of the village's inhabitants attended church in the morning, at least one-fifth probably also attended in the evening. However, considering the overlap in attendance at morning and evening services (which is usually calculated as about one-third of attendance at each service), the total does not look impressive and would certainly have been less than 45 per cent of the population.
13 *IC*, 18 January 1885, and *Thorold Post (TP)*, 17 August 1894.
14 The lower percentage of church members in Thorold can be at least partly explained by the fact that the existing list of Anglican communicants does not extend beyond 1886.
15 Not including the small congregation of Baptists for whom there are no

records of financial donations. Among Anglicans, Methodists, and Presbyterians, 239 out of 406 Thorold families included either church members or contributors, or both.

16 Of the 264 men who remained in Thorold between 1886 and 1891, 76 (29%) were church members. Of the 240 men who had left Thorold between 1886 and 1891, 22 (9%) had been church members. See the records of Thorold's Protestant churches; also Public Archives of Ontario (PAO), Thorold 1886 assessment roll; and National Archives of Canada (NA), Thorold 1891 manuscript census. For a discussion of geographical mobility in nineteenth-century Ontario, see Katz, *The People of Hamilton*. Only men can be traced in this way, as few women are listed on nineteenth-century assessment rolls.

17 Turnover could vary between 1 per cent and 20 per cent. Turnover fluctuated particularly greatly in Thorold with the shifts in the local economy. In looking at overall patterns of 'removals' by certificate in the communities that were included in the Hamilton and Paris presbyteries, between 4 and 6 per cent of all members in each presbytery tended to leave within a year (Presbyterian Church in Canada. *Acts and Proceedings of the General Assembly*, 1886-94).

18 For a discussion of working-class congregations in larger centres, see O'Dell, 'The Class Character of Church Participation.'

19 Doris O'Dell argues that in late-nineteenth-century Belleville, middle-class people were more likely to be involved in the church than workers, but at the same time she demonstrates that many workers were active church members. O'Dell's work is limited by the fact that she lacks membership records for some of Belleville's predominantly working-class churches (O'Dell, 'The Class Character of Church Participation').

20 This observation can be made only about Thorold. Assessment rolls, which are the source of these data, do not exist for Campbellford in this period. In Thorold, 13 out of 17 (77%) of the families of wealthy skilled workers included at least one church member. Families are defined as wealthy if they employed a servant, as demonstrated in the 1891 census, or owned at least $800 worth of property, as identified in the 1886 assessment roll. For a further discussion of occupational/economic classification, see appendices A and B.

21 For a discussion of the predominance of women in both American and Canadian Protestant churches, see Welter, 'The Feminization of American Religion, 1800-1860,' Douglas, *The Feminization of American Culture*, Rosemary Gagan, 'Women and Canadian Methodism' (report on work in progress presented to the Gender and Religion Group, Toronto, March 1990), and Lane, 'Wife, Mother, Sister, Friend.'

22 Women made up the majority of townspeople in both Thorold and Camp-

bellford. In 1891, 53.3 per cent of Campbellford's population was female and 53.1 per cent of Thorold's population was female (Canada, *Census of Canada*, 1881, vol. 1, table 1, and 1891, vol. 1, table 3). Nonetheless, women predominated much more heavily on church membership rolls than in the population as a whole.

23 In Thorold churches, the percentage of women church members was as follows: Anglican 66% (n=59), Baptist 62% (n=26), Methodist 68% (n=106), Presbyterian 65% (n=123); in Campbellford churches the percentage of women was as follows: Anglican 68% (n=60), Baptist 59% (n=27), Methodist 63% (n=212), Presbyterian 63% (n=158) (data from the records of Thorold and Campbellford Protestant churches).

24 See, for example, Caldwell, 'Revival and Chicago Working Girls,' and Curtis, 'The Son of Man and God the Father.' See Juster, *Disorderly Women*, 4–6 and chap. 2, for a discussion of the feminine nature of evangelical religion in an earlier period.

25 See Kee, 'The Heavenly Railroad,' 145–7, and Valverde, *The Age of Light, Soap and Water*, 30–1. The remaining work on the 'softening' of theology in the Canadian churches has focused primarily on attitudes towards children and on the shift away from the older, harsher vision of infant damnation towards a belief in childhood innocence, which scholars such as Ann Douglas see as an integral part of the feminization of American Protestantism (Douglas, *The Feminization of American Culture*, chap. 4). Neil Semple notes such a shift in the Canadian Methodist church, while Marguerite Van Die suggests that this shift was not uncontested and that some leading Methodists, such as Nathanael Burwash, opposed it (Semple, 'The Nurture and Admonition of the Lord'; Van Die, *An Evangelical Mind*, chap. 1).

26 *IC*, 30 April and 7 May 1885; also *TP*, 27 February 1891.

27 Chown, *The Stairway*, 7.

28 Van Die, 'A Women's Awakening.' See also Lane, 'Wife, Mother, Sister, Friend,' 116; Welter, 'The Feminization of American Religion'; and Davidoff and Hall, *Family Fortunes*, 107–8.

29 Mary Ryan's work is an important exception here, although she was focusing primarily on a revival situation (Ryan, *Cradle of the Middle Class*).

30 See, for example, Comacchio, 'Beneath the "Sentimental Veil,"' Gordon, *Heroes of Their Own Lives*, and Iacovetta, *Such Hardworking People*.

31 Laurie, *Working People of Philadelphia*. Recently Brian Clarke has noted that Catholic women were much more likely to be religiously active than the men in their families (Clarke, *Piety and Nationalism*).

32 Young women (age 15–29) were slightly less likely to be church members than women over 30, but this simply seems to reflect the fact that in certain

denominations many young women did not join the church until their late teens.

33 These patterns did not differ significantly by age. In Campbellford and Thorold, most unmarried men were under 30 (87 per cent in Campbellford and 89 per cent in Thorold) so the single males who were not church members were mostly younger men. However, older unmarried men were no more likely to join the churches. In fact, the reverse was true. In Campbellford, 17 per cent (28 out of 169) of single men aged 15–29 were church members, and 8 per cent (2 out of 26) of single men 30 or over were church members. In Thorold, 10 per cent (15 out of 154) of single men aged 15–29 were church members and 3 per cent (1 out of 35) of single men 30 or over were church members (records of Campbellford and Thorold Protestant churches; and NA, Campbellford and Thorold 1891 manuscript census).

34 The exception to this is Thorold, where skilled, semi-skilled, and unskilled working-class married men were only half as likely to be church members as married women of the same class. However, these men were still two and a half times as likely to be church members as their single counterparts (see tables 3 and 4).

35 Lane, 'Wife, Mother, Sister, Friend.'

36 See Davidoff and Hall, *Family Fortunes*, 108-13, and Curtis, 'The Son of Man and God the Father.'

37 See Rotundo, *American Manhood*, 132-3; and McClelland, 'Masculinity and the "Representative Artisan" in Britain.'

38 *TP*, 19 December 1890.

39 See Davidoff and Hall, *Family Fortunes*, and Valverde, *The Age of Light, Soap and Water*, 30–2.

40 See, for example, *Christian Guardian*, 22 September 1880, 297; 6 October 1880, 314; 20 October 1880, 330; and 23 February 1881, 58. See also Van Die, 'The Double Vision,' 260–1.

41 Rotundo, 'Learning about Manhood,' 38.

42 Pamela Walker discusses a similar pattern in the response of many working-class men to the British Salvation Army ('I Live but Not Yet I').

43 This was more likely to occur in Campbellford at 8 per cent (7 out of 90 two-parent families with children) than in Thorold at 5 per cent (3 out of 64 two-parent families with children) perhaps because there were more employed single women in Campbellford, who might have been more likely to go their own way regardless of family patterns (records of Campbellford and Thorold churches; and NA, Campbellford and Thorold 1891 manuscript census).

44 Among middle-class families in Thorold, there were no Catholic-Protestant marriages, and only 3 out of 90 (3%) Protestant couples had spouses of differ-

ent Protestant denominations. Among middle-class families in Campbellford, there was one Catholic-Protestant marriage (out of 127 married
couples), while 5 out of 100 (5%) Protestant couples had spouses of different
Protestant denominations (NA, Thorold and Campbellford 1891 manuscript
census).

45 Among working-class families in Thorold, there were 7 (3%) Catholic-
Protestant marriages out of 228 married couples, while 12 out of 161 (8%)
Protestant couples had spouses of different Protestant denominations.
Among working-class families in Campbellford, there were 7 (3%) Catholic-
Protestant marriages (out of 227 married couples), while 20 out of 191 (11%)
Protestant couples had spouses of different Protestant denominations (NA,
Thorold and Campbellford 1891 manuscript census).

46 Diary of Donald Mills (pseudonym), 1878-9, in private collection of Miss Dorothy Millar, Thorold.

47 IC, 5 November 1885. The Campbellford Herald also suggests that young men
'hung around' outside the churches (CH, 23 August 1883).

48 TP, 7 March 1884.

49 TP, 11 March 1892.

50 TP, 28 November 1890. Ministers across Ontario were concerned about the
churches' failure to attract youth. See Grant, A Profusion of Spires, 196.

51 See, for example, IC, 15 April 1886 and 6 March 1884, and TP, 27 January
1893.

52 Dorothy Millar collection, diary of Donald Mills, 8 December 1878. See also
TP, 31 March 1893 and 5 December 1890; IC, 14 April 1887 and 16 December
1886. Various articles in the Christian Guardian reflected a similar message
(for example, 13 October 1880, 322; 22 October 1880, 338; 24 November 1880,
370).

53 See Brian Clarke, 'The Parish and the Hearth.'

54 Hugh McLeod has certainly argued that for a 'hard core of parish stalwarts'
among New York's Irish Catholics, church involvement could reinforce a
sense of respectability, as it apparently did for Protestant churchgoers
(McLeod, 'Catholicism and the New York Irish,' 345). See also Brian Clarke,
Piety and Nationalism.

55 Nicholson, 'Irish Tridentine Catholicism in Victorian Toronto,' 434. See also
Akenson, Small Differences, and McLeod, 'Catholicism and the New York
Irish.'

56 Of Thorold Catholics, 60 per cent had fathers who had been born in Ireland,
and the majority of the additional 21 per cent with fathers who had been born
in Ontario would also probably have been of Irish origin (NA, Thorold
manuscript census, 1891).

57 *TP*, 18 December 1885.

58 *IC*, 19 March 1885, 18 March 1886.

59 *TP*, 24 June 1892.

60 This is argued by Miller in 'Anti-Catholic Thought in Victorian Canada.' For a discussion of the British roots of this strain of anti-Catholicism, see Best, 'Popular Protestantism in Victorian Britain.'

61 *CH*, 24 September 1885, 14 January 1886.

62 *IC*, 20 January 1887. See also, for example, *TP*, 12 April 1889; *IC*, 15 November 1883.

63 This is Miller's term for the Protestant Protective Association. ('Anti-Catholic Thought,' 492). See ibid., 483, for a discussion of the anti-Catholic message spread by ex-priests and nuns.

64 See Miller, 'Anti-Catholic Thought,' 483. For similar patterns in British anti-Catholicism, see Best, 'Popular Protestantism in Victorian Britain,' 127-36.

65 *CH*, 30 August 1894. For a description of other such lectures, see *CH*, 6 September 1894; *TP*, 29 September and 6 October 1893.

66 For a discussion of moral panics, see Weeks, *Sex, Politics and Society*, 14, 92.

67 *TP*, 6 and 13 October 1893.

68 Brian Clarke, *Piety and Nationalism*, 61.

69 The Catholic records on which the following discussion is based include a rare 'Status Animarum' roll, which provides detailed information on the spiritual state of Catholics in Thorold's neighbouring community of St Catharines. Lists of Thorold parishioners, including both contributors and noncontributors to church finances, are available for the late 1890s and early 1900s. The contributors and noncontributors listed in the 1899–1902 financial reports for the Church of the Holy Rosary, Thorold (Roman Catholic Archives, Archdiocese of Toronto [RCA, AT]) have been linked to the 1901 manuscript census (NA).

70 Eighty-one per cent of St Catharines Catholics took communion at Easter ('Status Animarum' for St Catharines, 1888–92, Family History Library, Toronto; and RCA, AT, annual reports of Holy Rosary Church, Thorold, 1884–8).

71 In St Catharines, parishioners from the families of semi- and unskilled workers were about 20 per cent less likely to attend mass or take communion at Easter than either middle-class or skilled working-class families (data calculated from St Catharines 'Status Animarum,' 1888–92, Family History Library, Toronto; see Marks, 'Ladies, Loafers, Knights and "Lasses,"' 517, for a detailed breakdown). In Thorold, not surprisingly, 36 per cent of families earning less than $361 a year contributed nothing to the church (see table 11).

72 Brian Clarke, *Piety and Nationalism*, 78.

73 Data calculated from St Catharines 'Status Animarum,' 1888–92, Family History Library, Toronto. See Marks, 'Ladies, Loafers, Knights and "Lasses,"' 517, for a detailed breakdown.

74 Lucia Ferretti found a similar pattern in an urban Catholic parish in late-nineteenth century Montreal (Ferretti, *Entre voisins*, 142, 155).

75 O'Dell, 'The Class Character of Church Participation,' 86, and McLeod, *Class and Religion in the Late Victorian City*. Thorold's Methodist Sunday school records reveal that 30 per cent of the 'core' Sunday school students had parents who were neither members nor contributors to the church. The available records do not include many of the more marginal students, who would have been more likely to have had nonchurchgoing parents.

76 In Thorold's Anglican church, between 1886 and 1894, 25 per cent of those who had their children baptized but were neither communicants nor financial contributors to the church were middle class, while 70 per cent were working class (n=40); 38 per cent of communicants or financial contributors who had their children baptized were middle class, while half were working class (n=48). In Campbellford's Anglican church between 1886 and 1894, 21 per cent of those who had their children baptized but were neither communicants nor financial contributors to the church were middle class, while 58 per cent were working class (n=19); 48 per cent of communicants or financial contributors who had their children baptized were middle class, while 31 per cent were working class (n=42). (Percentages do not add up to 100 because of those not classified as either middle or working class. Data from Anglican Diocesan Archives, Diocese of Niagara [ADA, DN], records of St John the Evangelist, Thorold; PAO, Thorold 1886 assessment roll; NA, Thorold 1891 manuscript census; Anglican Diocesan Archives, Diocese of Toronto [ADA, DT], records of Christ Church, Campbellford; and NA, Campbellford 1891 manuscript census).

77 *TP*, 30 December 1887. At the various services held on Christmas and Easter, Thorold's Anglican church drew between three and four hundred worshippers in the late 1880s and early 1890s. For regular services over the remainder of the year, the number attending services in Thorold's Anglican church was much lower. It was not much beyond the number of communicants and financial contributors (ADA, DN, service register, St John the Evangelist Anglican Church, Thorold).

78 Houston and Prentice, *Schooling and Scholars*, 240, 248.

79 See Cox, *The English Churches in a Secular Society*, 94. See also Williams, 'The View from Below.'

80 *TP*, 10 February 1893. This tendency to disregard denominational differences and focus on a basic belief in Christianity was becoming increasingly common in late-nineteenth-century Ontario, according to John Webster Grant (*A Profusion of Spires*, 181).

81 Most of those marked with an *X* in the 1886 assessment roll who were still present in Thorold in 1891 are described as Catholic in the census of 1891, where it seemed more obligatory to list a religion than in the assessment roll. In his study of New York Irish Catholics, McLeod has noted that the poorest were least likely to have had any links to the churches ('Catholicism and the New York Irish,' 344).

82 See Cook, *The Regenerators*.

83 Ibid., 52.

84 *TP*, 7 September 1883.

85 *TP*, 16 January 1885.

86 *TP*, 27 March and 10 April 1885.

87 *TP*, 13 March 1885.

88 *TP*, 20 March 1885.

89 O'Dell found that approximately the same proportion (82%) of Belleville councillors were active church members ('The Class Character of Church Participation,' 121).

90 Dorothy Millar collection, diary of Donald Mills, 6 January 1879.

91 *IC*, 12 June 1884; see also Brouwer, *New Women for God*, 85–67.

92 *TP*, 25 June 1886.

93 PAO, will no. 1243, Surrogate Court, Welland 1886.

94 *TP*, 10 December 1886.

95 St Andrew's Presbyterian Church, Thorold, session minutes, 13, 25 September 1889, 12, 19, 26 February and 21 April 1890, 24 June, 27 October, and 1 November 1891.

96 *Jubilee History of Thorold Township and Town*, 152. Thorold Public Library, minutes of Thorold Mechanics' Institute, 1 May and 4 September 1896. The executive of Thorold's Mechanics' Institute was dominated by upper-middle-class church members (see chap. 5).

97 *TP*, 29 December 1893.

98 *TP*, 5 October 1894; Cook, *The Regenerators*, 67, 83, 163.

99 Owen, *The Darkened Room*.

100 *CH*, 16 May 1895.

101 Cook, *The Regenerators*, 52.

102 *IC*, 21 September 1882.

103 *IC*, 2 October 1884.

3: Gender, Class, and Power

1 'Report on the State of the Denomination,' *Baptist Year Book*, 1894.

2 The Salvation Army did permit female preachers, but Salvation Army preachers were not formally ordained (see chaps. 6 and 7).

3 See Brian Clarke, *Piety and Nationalism*, and Grant, *A Profusion of Spires*.
4 In Methodism, the classes consisted of small groups of church members who met regularly to oversee one another's spiritual health.
5 Anglican Diocese Archives, Diocese of Toronto (ADA, DT), vestry minutes, Christ Church, Campbellford, 1886–91; Anglican Diocesan Archives, Diocese of Niagara (ADA, DN), vestry minutes, St John the Evangelist, Thorold, 1885–98.
6 Canadian Baptist Archives (CBA), congregational minutes, Thorold Baptist Church, 1893.
7 Colwell, 'The Role of Women in the Nineteenth Century Baptist Church of Ontario,' 13.
8 For a similar pattern in Belleville, see O'Dell, 'The Class Character of Church Participation,' 132.
9 See Parr, *The Gender of Breadwinners*, 188.
10 Thirteen of the twenty-six men who served on Thorold's municipal council between 1886 and 1893 held offices in local churches (*Thorold Post* [TP], and records of Thorold churches).
11 Cited in Grant, *A Profusion of Spires*, 197.
12 *Ingersoll Chronicle* (IC), 22 March 1883.
13 *Stratford Beacon*, 2 April 1886.
14 CBA, minutes of Campbellford Baptist Church, 29 September and 8 October 1892. Flagg was expelled from membership but was later reinstated. See Duncan, *The Imperialist*, 21, for a reference to the habit of not buying goods 'outside the congregation.'
15 See Paul E. Johnson, *A Shopkeeper's Millennium*, 116–35.
16 Belleville churches in this period reflected similar patterns. See O'Dell, 'The Class Character of Church Participation,' 160–1.
17 Obituary of George Grant, undated, in scrapbook of Mamie McBride Halliday, in private collection of Mrs Betty Millar.
18 See Curtis D. Johnson, *Islands of Holiness*, Grant, *A Profusion of Spires*, 58, Juster, *Disorderly Women*, and Marks, 'No Double Standard?'
19 See St Andrew's Presbyterian Church, Thorold, session minutes, 26 January 1885, 13 September 1888 and 24 June 1891.
20 CBA, minutes of Thorold Baptist Church, 8 April 1896. See also minutes of 3 January 1897 and 9 January 1895.
21 See Semple, 'The Impact of Urbanization,' and Curtis D. Johnson, *Island of Holiness*.
22 St Andrew's Presbyterian Church, Campbellford, session minutes, 27 November 1892; St Andrew's Presbyterian Church, Thorold, session minutes, 16 August 1889.

23 Sisters of St Joseph Archives, Thorold sisters' account book. The financial reports for Holy Rosary Church provide fairly detailed accounts of disbursements and do not list any expenditures on poor relief.

24 *TP*, 1 March 1889.

25 Pitsula, 'The Relief of Poverty in Toronto,' 61–2.

26 *Jubilee History of Thorold Township and Town*, 138; CBA, minutes of Thorold Baptist Church, 7 May 1893; Sisters of St Joseph Archives, Thorold sisters' account book.

27 This is generally mentioned in obituaries. See, for example, *Campbellford Herald (CH)*, 7 March 1895; *TP*, 13 August 1886, 27 February 1891, and 27 April 1894; *IC*, 5 June 1884.

28 *CH*, 9 May 1895; *TP*, 15 September 1882; 15 February and 12 December 1884. See also Marks, 'Indigent Committees and Ladies Benevolent Societies.'

29 Westfall, *Two Worlds*, 129.

30 *TP*, 24 March 1882.

31 ADA, DN, St John's Anglican Church, Thorold, vestry minutes, 1 May 1886 and 17 August 1891.

32 Westfall, *Two Worlds*, 138.

33 For discussions of the church leaders' attitudes towards progress, see Westfall, *Two Worlds*, 204 and Gauvreau, *The Evangelical Century*, 121–3.

34 *TP*, 24 March 1882 and 25 November 1892. See also Semple, 'The Impact of Urbanization,' 52 and S.D. Clark, *Church and Sect in Canada*, 332–4.

35 *TP*, 24 March 1882.

36 *TP*, 12 September 1890; *CH*, 13 May 1886.

37 Van Die, 'The Double Vision,' 263; Schantz, 'Piety in Providence.'

38 See also, for example, Van Die, *An Evangelical Mind*, 183.

39 Semple, 'The Impact of Urbanization on the Methodist Church in Canada,' 242.

40 Westfall, *Two Worlds*, 157.

41 Yeo, *Religion and Voluntary Organisations in Crisis*, 155, cited in O'Dell, 'The Class Character of Church Participation,' 134–5.

42 Regional Room Special Collections, Weldon Library (RR, WL), session minutes, Ingersoll Erskine Presbyterian Church, 1 July 1864.

43 See, for example, ADA, DN, St John's Anglican Church, Thorold, vestry minutes, 17 August 1891, 21 May 1888, 3 December 1891; and United Church Archives (UCA), Thorold Methodist Church Board of Trustees minutes, 10 September 1888.

44 Roman Catholic Archives, Archdiocese of Toronto (RCA, AT), letter of Father Sullivan to Bishop Lynch, 20 April 1886, papers of Holy Rosary parish, Thorold.

45 RCA, AT, financial statements of Church of Our Lady of the Holy Rosary, Thorold, 1898–1902.

46 Akenson, *The Irish in Ontario*, 215, cited in O'Dell, 'The Class Character of Church Participation,' 141; Stortz, 'The Catholic Priest in Rural Ontario,' 37.

47 Nicholson makes this point in relation to Irish Catholic church attendance. ('Irish Tridentine Catholicism').

48 UCA, Board of Trustees minutes, Thorold Methodist Church, 20 March 1882.

49 *CH*, 7 July and 1 September 1887.

50 ADA, DN, St John's Anglican Church, Thorold, vestry minutes, 6 May 1889, 12 April 1893, 13 August 1884.

51 Semple, 'The Impact of Urbanization,' 242.

52 See Brouwer, *New Women for God*, and Valverde, *The Age of Light, Soap and Water*.

53 See Mitchinson, 'Canadian Women and Church Missionary Societies,' and Strong-Boag, 'Setting the Stage.'

54 St Andrew's Presbyterian Church, Thorold, Ladies Mite Society minutes, 18 December 1895.

55 Whiteley, 'Doing Just About What They Please.'

56 ADA, DN, St John's Anglican Church, Thorold, Women's Auxiliary minutes, 28 April 1892, 27 January 1891, 29 March 1894.

57 Ibid., 15 May and 9 March 1895.

58 ADA, DN, Niagara Diocesan Women's Auxiliary, *Annual Report*, 1895.

59 Ibid.

60 CBA, Thorold Baptist Church, Ladies Aid minutes, 25 January 1895, 7 September 1894, 12 January 1894, 23 June 1893. St Andrew's Presbyterian Church, Thorold, Board of Managers minutes, 13 January 1886, and Ladies Mite Society minutes, 27 January 1896.

61 See, for example, ADA, DN, St John's Anglican Church, Thorold, vestry minutes, 1 May 1888; St Andrew's Presbyterian Church, Thorold, Board of Managers Minutes, 5 February 1895.

62 Whiteley, 'Doing Just About What They Please,' 298.

63 St Andrew's Presbyterian Church, Thorold, Board of Managers minutes, 12 June 1882, 12 January 1887, 11 February 1893, 3 December 1895, 10 February 1896.

64 Whiteley, 'Doing Just About What They Please,' 298.

65 St Andrew's Presbyterian Church, Thorold, Ladies Mite Society minutes, 15 May and 13 November 1895; ibid., Board of Managers minutes, 13 January 1886; ibid., Ladies Mite Society minutes, 12 March 1896; *CH*, 23 March 1882; *TP*, 6 April 1888; RCA, AT, *Souvenir Booklet Commemorating the Centennial of the Laying of the Cornerstone of Holy Rosary Church, Oct 8, 1887–1978*, 8; ADA,

DT, list of improvements, Christ Church Anglican Church, Campbellford, church records.

66 Duncan, *The Imperialist*, 66.

67 See also Whiteley, 'Doing Just About What They Please,' 292.

68 *TP*, 24 March 1882.

69 See, for example, Whiteley, 'Doing Just About What They Please,' and Mitchinson, 'Canadian Women and Church Missionary Societies.'

70 For a discussion of these issues in the American context, see Cott, *The Bonds of Womanhood*, and Hewitt, *Women's Activism and Social Change*.

71 St Andrew's Presbyterian Church, Thorold, Ladies Mite Society minutes; ADA, DN, president's address, Niagara Diocesan Women's Auxiliary, *Annual Report*, 1895.

72 Brian Clarke, *Piety and Nationalism*, 83. Lucia Ferretti has noted a similar pattern of cross-class involvement in Catholic devotional societies in late-nineteenth-century Montreal. (Ferretti, *Entre voisins*, 164).

73 CBA, Thorold Baptist Church, Ladies Aid minutes, 26 October and 7 December 1894.

74 ADA, ND, St John's Anglican Church, Thorold, Women's Auxiliary minutes, 27 January 1893. For similar occurences, see the Women's Auxiliary minutes for 25 January and 22 February 1894.

75 St Andrew's Presbyterian Church, Thorold, Ladies Mite Society minutes, 15 May 1895.

76 For similar patterns in Belleville, see O'Dell, 'The Class Character of Church Participation,' 144–5.

77 Whiteley, in 'Doing Just About What They Please,' saw these activities as alternatives to personal donations.

78 *CH*, 22 May 1890.

79 *IC*, 3 December 1885. See Bradbury, *Working Families*, for a discussion of the work required of working-class housewives in this period.

80 Anne Boylan has identified similar patterns in American Sunday schools in this period (*Sunday School*, 114–19).

81 The total numbers involved in the following discussion are small, so the results must be considered speculative. The Baptist numbers are very small, with two out of three of the teachers being working-class women. Thorold's Methodist Sunday school included twenty-nine teachers who could be identified. Eight were male, four of these men being from working-class homes. Among the twenty-one women teachers, twelve came from working-class homes (UCA, Thorold Methodist Church, Sunday school records; NA, Thorold 1891 manuscript census).

82 In Thorold's Baptist Sunday school three men and two women served on the

executive. In Thorold's Methodist Sunday school, the executive consisted of six men and three women. These women were all from working-class homes. (UCA, Thorold Methodist Church, Sunday school records; CBA, Thorold Baptist Church, Sunday school records; and NA, Thorold 1891 census). See also Boylan, *Sunday School*, 119-21.

83 St Andrew's Presbyterian Church, Campbellford, session minutes, 1 September 1893.

84 RR, WL, Ingersoll Methodist church (King St.), Epworth League minutes; St Andrew's Presbyterian Church, Thorold, YPSCE minutes. Grant, in *A Profusion of Spires*, 196, also notes the limited appeal of young people's societies.

85 St Andrew's Presbyterian Church, Thorold, YPSCE minutes, 6 November 1891. In Thorold's Presbyterian YPSCE, 7 of the 17 male members were 15 years old or younger, compared to 8 of the 39 female members who were 15 or younger (ibid., YPSCE minutes; and NA, Thorold 1891 manuscript census).

86 *CH*, 29 May 1890; NA, Campbellford 1891 manuscript census.

87 *IC*, 14 October 1886.

88 *CH*, 27 May 1886. See also *TP*, 5 July 1883. Both Dubinsky (*Improper Advances*, 116-17) and Ward (*Courtship, Love and Marriage in Nineteenth-Century English Canada*, 65) note that church socials were a common site for courtship in this period.

89 See the advertisement for the Thorold Catholic Mutual Benefit Association concert, which stated that although the concert was free, no 'hoodlums' would be allowed 'to disturb the proceedings' (*TP*, 9 November 1888). See also *TP*, 10 May 1889; *IC*, 9 November 1882; *CH*, 26 August 1886.

90 *TP*, 3 March 1882; *IC*, 31 December 1885.

91 *IC*, 31 March 1887.

92 Niagara Conference minutes, in Methodist Church of Canada, *Minutes of Conference*, 65. See also *CH*, 23 July 1891.

93 Marshall, *Secularizing the Faith*, 127-31; *TP*, 12 September 1890; *Welland Tribune*, 9 March 1888; *TP*, 1 May 1891.

94 Ann Douglas has noted a hostility among American Protestant ministers to women playing too active a role in church activities and thus encroaching on ministerial 'space' (Douglas, *The Feminization of American Culture*, 110-11). See Davidoff and Hall, *Family Fortunes*, 118-23, for a discussion of the gender ambiguities of the clergyman's role.

4: Rough and Respectable

1 *Thorold Post* (*TP*), 17 August 1894. See also *Campbellford Herald* (*CH*), 26 Octo-

ber 1882; *TP*, 21 December 1883, 13 March 1885, and 24 May 1889; *Ingersoll Chronicle* (*IC*), 13 January 1887.

2 For a discussion of such issues in the British context, see, for example, Bailey, 'Will the Real Bill Banks Please Stand Up?'

3 *IC*, 27 November 1884; *CH*, 26 October 1882. See also *TP*, 21 December 1883, 22 January 1892, and 20 May 1892; *IC*, 9 August 1883; *CH*, 26 October 1882; *TP*, 28 September 1883; *CH*, 7 June 1894.

4 *CH*, 7 June 1888; *TP*, 29 November 1889; *IC*, 19 September 1883, 10 May 1883; *TP*, 29 April 1889.

5 See, for example, *CH*, 18 November 1886, 17 November 1887.

6 See, for example, *Free Press* (London), 22 November 1876, 14 May 1877, 14 September 1880; *Citizen* (Ottawa), 12 November 1877, 30 September 1878. For British and American discussions of young male attitudes towards Christianity, see, Springhall, 'Building Character in the British Boy,' 55 and Curtis, 'The Son of Man and God the Father.'

7 *TP*, 14 November 1884; *CH*, 26 October 1884 and 23 August 1883.

8 See, for example, *CH*, 7 June 1883; *TP*, 24 May 1889; *IC*, 20 November 1884. For a discussion of middle-class efforts to control 'disorderly' working-class behaviour, see Rosenzweig, *Eight Hours for What We Will*.

9 *CH*, 13 July 1882 and 7 June 1883; *TP*, 13 May 1892. See also *TP*, 29 November 1889, 8 September 1893, and 17 August 1894. This was a common phenomenon in small American towns. See Blocker, *American Temperance Movements*, 74.

10 *IC*, 13 January 1887; *TP*, 8 September 1893.

11 Dubinsky, *Improper Advances*, 117.

12 *TP*, 8 July 1892.

13 See, for example, *CH*, 7 June 1883; *TP*, 8 July 1892.

14 *TP*, 3 March 1893.

15 *TP*, 7 June 1889, 26 February 1892, 1 January 1892.

16 See Rosenzweig, *Eight Hours for What We Will*. For a description of the tavern culture of a famous Montreal tavern of this period, see De Lottinville, 'Joe Beef of Montreal.' For examples of young men's involvement in local bars, see *TP*, 10 February 1882, 21 January 1887, 20 March 1891; *CH*, 1 December 1881.

17 *War Cry*, 18 June 1887. A similar pattern can be seen in other male Salvationist 'confessions'; see *War Cry*, 19 March and 1 October 1887. 'Confessions' may have been coloured by later conversions, but they do seem to reflect common social drinking patterns among young men.

18 *CH*, 24 May 1894.

19 *IC*, 12 November 1885.

20 *IC*, 14 January 1886.

21 The number of those arrested who could be linked to the manuscript census of 1891 or the assessment roll of 1886 was quite small (52 total), so these figures can only be considered suggestive.

22 Three of 52 men arrested on 'drunk or disorderly' or related charges were middle class, two being small employers or foremen and one being in the merchant/professional class. The remaining 48 (92%) were working-class men, including 27 skilled workers and 21 unskilled/factory workers. Seventeen of the 52 arrested on these charges were married or widowed (29%) while the remaining 35 (67%) were single men. (*TP*, Public Archives of Ontario [PAO] Thorold assessment roll, 1886; National Archives of Canada [NA] Thorold manuscript census, 1891.)

23 Warsh, 'Oh Lord, Pour a Cordial in Her Wounded Heart,' 89. Warsh estimates that about 16 per cent of all Victorian alcoholics were women.

24 *TP*, 11 August 1882, 26 June 1885, 28 June 1889.

25 See Dubinsky, *Improper Advances*, and Strange, *Toronto's Girl Problem*.

26 The lack of discussion about the sex trade in Thorold may mean that those seeking prostitutes took the streetcar down to nearby St Catharines. For a discussion of the sex trade in Campbellford and Ingersoll, see *CH*, 22 April and 16 September 1886; *IC*, 8 June 1882.

27 Dubinsky, *Improper Advances*. For examples of concern about single women in the urban context, see Peiss, *Cheap Amusements*, Stansell, *City of Women*, and Strange, *Toronto's Girl Problem*.

28 *TP*, 14 February 1890.

29 *TP*, 25 January 1889, 7 February 1890, 11 February 1892.

30 *TP*, 14 November 1890, 5 December 1884, 8 October 1887. See also *TP*, 18 and 25 September 1891, 20 January 1888; *CH*, 26 March 1885.

31 *TP*, 11 March 1892; *CH*, 14 March 1895.

32 *TP*, 15 April 1887, 13 February 1885; *IC*, 28 June 1883.

33 Most have studied this culture among either working-class or (more commonly) middle-class young men. See Kett, *Rites of Passage*, 92–3; Morgan, 'Languages of Gender in Upper Canadian Religion and Politics, 1791–1850'; and Rotundo, 'Learning About Manhood,' 40–3. For a discussion of how this culture could also be seen as a working-class culture among men living in predominantly male environments, regardless of age or marital status, see Forestell, 'All that Glitters Is Not Gold.'

34 Sturgis, 'The Spectre of a Drunkard's Grave.' For Fawkes, see Reading Room Special Collections, Weldon Library (RR, WL), Fawkes Family Collection, letter from T.F. Fawkes to Mrs. J. Fawkes, 11 October 1896.

35 Of the Protestant men arrested for being drunk and disorderly, 14 of 21 (67%)

had parents or wives who were church members/communicants; the figure was 13 of 20 for working-class men only (TP; PAO, Thorold assessment roll, 1886; Thorold manuscript census, 1891; and records of Thorold's Protestant churches).

36 CBA, membership records, Thorold Baptist church; *TP*, 5 August 1887 and 19 April 1889.

37 Gordon, *Heroes of Their Own Lives*, 251.

38 *TP*, 2 March 1888, 26 May 1893, 24 November 1893.

39 See Blocker, *American Temperance Movements*, 50–1. See also Decarie, 'The Prohibition Movement in Ontario, 1894–1916,' 8.

40 The following discussion analyses the executive members for the two temperance lodges in Thorold and the one in Campbellford. In these organizations, the officers were rotated four times a year to give members an opportunity to be on the executive. This suggests that this analysis does reflect the larger membership. Anstead's study of fraternal orders (including temperance lodges) in nineteenth century Ingersoll and Woodstock also shows that the class breakdown of fraternal officers reflects the class breakdown of lodge membership (Anstead, 'Fraternalism in Victorian Ontario,' 376). Nonetheless, the numbers in the following analysis are fairly small and can only be considered suggestive.

41 The Royal Templar officers included 21 men and 9 women who could be identified on the manuscript census. Among the Thorold Sons of Temperance, which attracted a younger membership, differences in marital status were less stark. Fifty-seven per cent of the 21 male officers were single, as were 91 per cent of the 21 female officers (*TP*; NA, Thorold manuscript census, 1891.

42 *TP*, 5 December 1890.

43 Cook, 'Continued and Persevering Combat,' 77. In the United States, many members of the Sons of Temperance were not church members (Blocker, *American Temperance Movements*, 50).

44 Graham, *Greenbank*, 91–2. and Cook, 'Continued and Persevering Combat,' 79.

45 Warsh, 'Oh, Lord, Pour a Cordial in Her Wounded Heart.'

46 In Thorold, although over half of the women on the executive of the Sons of Temperance and the Royal Templars of Temperance were church members, very few (17%) were also involved in women's church associations (*TP*; records of Thorold's Protestant churches).

47 See Graham, *Greenbank*, 75, and Cook 'Continued and Persevering Combat,' 84. In descriptions of county-level meetings of the temperance lodges, there are very few references to female executive officers. See, for example, *TP*, 6 October 1882, 19 February 1886, 12 March 1886, 21 May 1886.

48 *TP*, 8 April 1887, 18 September 1885. For other examples of excursions, see *TP*, 15 December 1882, 18 January 1884, 10 July 1885, 11 June 1886. Sharon Cook suggests that the temperance lodge might be considered a 'nineteenth century singles club' ('Continued and Persevering Combat,' 84). See also *TP*, 21 March 1890, and Graham, *Greenbank*, 75.

49 Cook 'Continued and Persevering Combat,' 84, 149; Mitchinson, 'Aspects of Reform,' 171, 201. In the U.S. context, Ruth Bordin recognizes that even at the local level the majority of WCTU officers were middle class. (Bordin, *Woman and Temperance*, 160, 173–4).

50 Of the 17 WCTU officers in Campbellford who could be identified, 4 were the wives of skilled workers, 8 were from the families of merchants/professionals, 3 from the families of clerks/agents, and 2 were widows (*CH*; PAO, Ontario WCTU annual reports, 1888–98; and NA, Campbellford manuscript census, 1891).

51 Of the 9 officers of Thorold's WCTU who could be linked to the census, 6 were from middle-class backgrounds. In Thorold's YWCTU, middle-class young women were even more dominant, making up over 80 per cent (13 out of 16) of those members and officers who could be identified (*TP*; PAO, Ontario WCTU annual reports, 1887–94; and NA, Thorold manuscript census, 1891).

52 Cook, 'Continued and Persevering Combat.' In Campbellford, 13 of 17 officers of the WCTU (between 1886 and 1895) were church members. In Thorold, the 10 officers of the WCTU who could be identified were all church members, while among the officers and members of Thorold's YWCTU who could be identified 12 of 17 were church members. At least some of those YWCTU members who were not church members were probably too young to have become members, while others were Anglicans, whose parents donated money to the church (PAO, Ontario WCTU annual reports, 1884–96; *TP*; *CH*; and Thorold and Campbellford Protestant church records).

53 This figure would undoubtedly be higher if the membership of Thorold's Methodist Ladies Aid were known, since many of the WCTU members were Methodists. Mitchinson notes the existence of close links between the WCTU and the Methodist Women's Missionary Society ('Aspects of Reform,' 186).

54 PAO, president's address, Ontario WCTU, *Annual Report*, 1891; president's address, Ontario WCTU, *Annual Report*, 1898; report of Parlor Meeting Department, Ontario WCTU, *Annual Report*, 1895; president's address, Ontario WCTU, *Annual Report*, 1904. See also *Woman's Journal*, June 1892; PAO, president's address, Ontario WCTU, *Annual Report*, 1908; *White Ribbon Tidings*, 15 March 1906.

55 Cook, 'Continued and Persevering Combat,' 119; 'How to Kill a "Y" Union,'
    in *Woman's Journal*, March 1892.

56 See Cook, 'Continued and Persevering Combat,' chap. 3, for a detailed
    description of WCTU departments of work.

57 PAO, reports of county presidents, Ontario WCTU, *Annual Report*, 1888; *TP*,
    23 November 1888. The Scott Act prohibited retailers from selling liquor but
    it did not prohibit people from drinking liquor.

58 *TP*, 18 June 1886. PAO, report of county presidents, Ontario WCTU, *Annual
    Report*, 1888; RR, WL, records of WCTU in Fawkes Family collection.

59 *IC*, 27 November 1884 and 21 May 1885. See also *TP*, 23 May 1884; *IC*, 28 Feb-
    ruary and 15 May 1884, 14 May 1885, 8 April 1886.

60 *Woman's Journal*, December 1885; PAO, corresponding secretary's report,
    Ontario WCTU, *Annual Report*, 1895. See also *CH*, 21 March 1895.

61 *Woman's Journal*, March and April 1892; *TP*, 18 October 1889, 14 February 1890.

62 PAO, report of county presidents, Ontario WCTU, *Annual Report*, 1888, and
    report of superintendent of Franchise Dept, Ontario WCTU, *Annual Report*,
    1891; *Woman's Journal*, March 1892. See also PAO, president's address,
    Ontario WCTU, *Annual Report*, 1894 and president's address, Ontario WCTU,
    Annual Report, 1901.

63 See Cook, 'Continuing and Persevering Combat,' 194; Epstein, *The Politics of
    Domesticity*, 61, 125; Decarie, 'The Prohibition Movement in Ontario,' 57–8.

64 Epstein, *The Politics of Domesticity*, 90, 101; Cook, 'Continuing and Persever-
    ing Combat",' 184–94.

65 See, for example, Decarie, 'The Prohibition Movement in Ontario,' 74, and
    Mitchinson, 'Aspects of Reform,' 202. In *The Age of Light, Soap and Water*, Mar-
    iana Valverde provides a more complex analysis of WCTU motivations.

66 Epstein, *The Politics of Domesticity*, 104–6. See also Bordin, *Woman and Temper-
    ance*, 162.

67 *Woman's Journal*, November 1885, January and February 1886, March, Octo-
    ber, and November 1890, January, April, and July 1891, and February 1892.
    In some stories about middle-class young men, the men are saved at the last
    moment by some timely advice or by the memory of their mother's expecta-
    tions.

68 *Woman's Journal*, December 1891. For similar appeals to middle-class moth-
    ers' self-interest (and guilt), see *Woman's Journal*, November 1885, November
    1890, and November 1891. Bordin raises the possibility that some women
    joined the WCTU from self-interest but does not focus on the particular ques-
    tion of concern for sons (*Woman and Temperance*, 160–1).

69 *TP*, 24 February 1888. See also *TP*, 17 November 1882, 13 February 1885; *IC*,
    28 June 1883.

70 *TP*, 26 June 1885.
71 *TP*, 17 March 1882. For descriptions of other Gospel Temperance meetings, see *TP*, 17 February, 14 April, and 16 June 1882.
72 For a discussion of the indifference of the mainstream churches to the temperance movement for most of the nineteenth century, see Decarie, 'The Prohibition Movement,' 28–30, and Cook, 'Continuing and Persevering Combat,' 76.
73 *CH*, 14 December 1893 and 22 March 1894; *TP*, 18 November 1887; *CH*, 16 October 1884 and 26 February 1885; *TP*, 22 December 1882; *CH*, 24 January 1895.
74 See *TP*, 29 July and 5 August 1887, 17 August 1883, 3 August 1888; *IC*, 22 October 1885.
75 *CH*, 12 October 1882. See also *TP*, 11 September 1885; *IC*, 7 September 1882.
76 *CH*, 27 July 1882; *TP*, 8 June 1883 and 23 April 1886; *IC*, 4 December 1884.
77 *TP*, 16 November 1888; *CH*, 23 April 1885 and 16 October 1884.
78 *IC*, 20 January, 3 February 1887, 9 June, 10 November, and 15 December 1887.
79 *TP*, 29 December 1893.
80 Decarie, 'The Prohibition Movement,' 31–2, and Brian Clarke, *Piety and Nationalism*, chap. 6.
81 *CH*, 25 January 1894. For a discussion of drinking among priests, see Stortz, 'The Catholic Priest in Rural Ontario,' 35–6.
82 *TP*, 5 December 1884, 7 March 1884, 11 February 1887.
83 Souvenir booklet, *The Centennial of the Laying of the Cornerstone of Holy Rosary Church, Thorold, 1887–1897*, 7.
84 Cook, 'Continued and Persevering Combat,' 222. Decarie, 'The Prohibition Movement,' 69.
85 See, for example, *IC*, 31 December 1885; *CH*, 14 March 1889; Graham, *Greenbank*, 83–4; *IC*, 28 May 1885, 21 January and 22 July 1886.
86 *IC*, 25 February 1886, 10 March 1887, 21 January 1886.
87 *CH*, 1 February 1894.

5: Mostly Male Worlds

1 *Thorold Post*, (*TP*), 1 May 1891.
2 Ibid. Joseph Peart, her son, was not a church member, but he had attended Sunday school. See United Church Archives (UCA), Thorold Methodist Church, church records.
3 See Clawson, *Constructing Brotherhood*, 162.
4 See Anstead, 'Fraternalism in Victorian Ontario,' chap. 4, for a detailed discussion of the various benefits provided by different fraternal orders.
5 Palmer, *Culture in Conflict*, 39–46. More recently, Palmer has argued that the

fraternal orders had more contradictory class implications, but he still suggests that they asserted working-class values of mutuality and co-operation (*Working Class Experience*, 95–7).

6 Clawson, *Constructing Brotherhood*, 176–7; Greenberg, 'Worker and Community: Fraternal Orders in Albany, New York,' 66–70; Houston and Smyth, *The Sash Canada Wore*, 178–9.

7 Clawson, *Constructing Brotherhood*, 256. See also Carnes, *Secret Ritual and Manhood in Victorian America*.

8 Brian Clarke, *Piety and Nationalism*, 236–8.

9 Anstead's study also shows that the class breakdown of fraternal officers reflects the class breakdown of lodge membership ('Fraternalism in Victorian Ontario,' 184, 188, 376).

10 Carnes, *Secret Ritual and Manhood*, 52–4 and 103. See also Clawson, *Constructing Brotherhood*, 82-3.

11 Cited in Newbury, 'No Atheist, Eunuch or Woman,' 73.

12 *TP*, 27 December 1889. See also *TP*, 8, 15 June, 18 January 1888, 21 February 1890; *Ingersoll Chronicle* (*IC*), 20 April and 7 December 1882, 14 February 1884. See also Anstead, 'Fraternalism in Victorian Ontario,' 144–6.

13 For examples of 'temperance dinners' see *TP*, 23 January 1885; and 15 January 1886. For examples of what appear to have been less temperate events, see *TP*, 18 January and 15 June 1888, 24 April 1891. For a discussion of efforts to make lodge activities temperate, see Carnes, *Secret Ritual and Manhood*, 26–7; Clawson, *Constructing Brotherhood*, 160–1, and Houston and Smyth, *The Sash Canada Wore*, 114–16. Anstead found that most late-nineteenth-century lodge suppers included alcohol ('Fraternalism in Victorian Ontario,' 173).

14 *TP*, 30 January 1885.

15 *Campbellford Herald* (*CH*), 16 July 1885. See also *TP*, 13 July 1883; *IC*, 26 July 1883.

16 *IC*, 6 September 1883. See also *TP*, 16 November 1883, 22 March 1889; *CH*, 25 March 1886; Clawson, *Constructing Brotherhood*, 186–7; Carnes, *Secret Ritual and Manhood*, 77–81; and Anstead, 'Fraternalism in Victorian Ontario,' 167.

17 *TP*, 3 December 1886. See also *TP*, 17 February 1888.

18 See, for example, *TP*, 13 February 1891 and 22 December 1882.

19 *TP*, 7 March, 20 June, and 21 November 1884. For examples of other fraternal orders' public socials, see *TP*, 6 February and 5 December 1885, 21 February 1890, 26 January 1894.

20 *CH*, 14 October 1886.

21 See Carnes, *Secret Ritual and Manhood*, chap. 2, and Houston and Smyth, *The Sash Canada Wore*.

22 *IC*, 25 June 1885. See also *TP*, 9 March 1888; *IC*, 27 April 1882 and 27 October 1887.

23 *TP*, 19 December 1890, 19 September 1890. See also *TP*, 9 March 1888; *IC*, 28 April 1887.

24 *TP*, 12 December 1890; *IC*, 28 April 1887.

25 Carnes, *Secret Ritual and Manhood*, 72–6; Anstead, 'Fraternalism in Victorian Ontario,' 151–2; *TP*, 14 March 1884.

26 See Wallace, *Rockdale*, 346, and Carnes, *Secret Ritual and Manhood*, 72–90.

27 *IC*, 28 April 1887. St Andrew's Presbyterian Church, Campbellford, minutes of session, 28 June 1891.

28 See also Carnes, *Secret Ritual and Manhood*, 74.

29 See, for example, *TP*, 19 December 1890, 29 April 1892; *IC*, 27 April 1882; *TP*, 19 December 1890.

30 *CH*, 14 July 1892, 12 October 1893; *TP*, 15 July 1892, 24 December 1886.

31 Although only officers are being studied here, it seems unlikely that the proportion of church membership would be higher among the rank and file.

32 As argued by Kealey in *Toronto Workers Respond to Industrial Capitalism* and by Palmer in *A Culture in Conflict*.

33 See also Anstead, 'Fraternalism in Victorian Ontario,' chap. 8.

34 See Grant, *A Profusion of Spires*, 84.

35 *TP*, 1 May 1891, 7 August 1885.

36 See Newbury, 'No Atheist, Eunuch or Woman,' and Clawson, *Constructing Brotherhood*.

37 See, for example, Laurie, *Working People of Philadelphia*, 54.

38 *IC*, 29 January and 9 July 1885, 1 July 1886.

39 Eleven of 31 (36%) of Thorold firemen worked in middle-class occupations. Nine of the 31 were church members in one of the Protestant churches, while 22 were either married (21) or widowed (1). See *TP*, and the records of Thorold's Protestant churches. See also *TP*, 26 February 1886.

40 See, for example, *TP*, 27 July 1883, 3 July 1885, 18 June 1886.

41 *TP*, 4 May and 10 August 1883.

42 Desmond Morton, *Canada and War*, 20–2.

43 Ibid., 9. This was also true in nineteenth-century Philadelphia (see Davis, *Parades and Power*, 51).

44 *IC*, 30 April 1885, 31 August 1882; *CH*, 28 May 1885.

45 *CH*, 30 July 1885.

46 *TP*, 10 April 1885, 30 July and 6 August 1886. See also *TP*, 10 June 1887 and 6 August 1886.

47 *CH*, 27 September and 4 October 1883. See also Desmond Morton, *Canada and*

War, 20; and Public Archives of Ontario (PAO), reports of 'work among soldiers' in Ontario WCTU annual reports for 1886, 1887, and 1889.

48 Of the nine members of the Thorold band who have been identified, six were skilled workers, one was an artisan, one was a factory worker, and one was from a middle-class background (*TP*; National Archives of Canada [NA], Thorold manuscript census, 1891). Among the twelve Campbellford band members who can be identified, half were employed in working-class occupations (*CH*; NA, Campbellford manuscript census 1891).

49 See, for example, *IC*, 11 August 1887; *CH*, 7 May 1883, 18 September 1884; *TP*, 3 August 1883; *IC*, 2 June 1887; *CH*, 31 May 1883, 6 December 1884; *TP*, 12 October 1883, 13 May 1892.

50 For an example of involvement in these competitions see *TP*, 8 October 1887.

51 *CH*, 14 December 1882; *TP*, 18 November 1887, 17 October 1890; *IC*, 9 March 1882; *TP*, 12 October 1888, 17 June 1892.

52 See, for example, *TP*, 15 March 1889.

53 *TP*, 5 and 19 July 1895.

54 See Howell, *Northern Sandlots*, chap. 5, for a discussion of attitudes towards women's involvement in team sports. See also Lenskyj, *Out of Bounds*. See *CH*, 8 May 1890, for an impassioned attack on Sunday ball playing.

55 See, for example, Bouchier, 'For the Love of the Game,' 11; Park, 'Biological Thought, Athletics and the Formation of a "Man of Character"'; and Howell, *Northern Sandlots*, 14–19. Such ideas had become even more popular by the early twentieth century. See, for example, Howell and Lindsay, 'Social Gospel and the Young Boy Problem,' and Barman, 'Sports and the Development of Character.'

56 Bouchier, 'For the Love of the Game,' 20. In the British context, see Springhall, 'Building Character in the British Boy.'

57 *IC*, 16 December 1886.

58 *CH*, 5 June 1884.

59 Bouchier, 'For the Love of the Game,' iv. See also Howell, *Northern Sandlots*, chap. 4.

60 In Campbellford 59 per cent of curling club members were married or widowed, while in Thorold 65 per cent were married or widowed (*TP*; *CH*; and NA, Thorold and Campbellford 1891 manuscript census).

61 Half of the men who were members of Thorold's curling club between 1888 and 1894 were church members (n=32), as were half of those who were members of Campbellford's curling club between 1890 and 1892 (n=37) (*TP*; *CH*; NA, Thorold and Campbellford 1891 manuscript census; and the records of the Protestant churches of Thorold and Campbellford.

62 See, for example, *TP*, 30 March 1883, 12 December 1884; *IC*, 22 February and 8 March 1883.

63 Metcalfe also notes that Ontario curling clubs were almost exclusively middle class in this period (Metcalfe, *Canada Learns to Play*), 41–3.

64 Bouchier, 'For the Love of the Game,' 258. Howell, *Northern Sandlots*, 40–2.

65 See, for example, *TP*, 14, 28 June, and 12 July 1889; also *TP*, 28 May 1886. For other cross-class games, see *TP* 23 and 30 August 1889.

66 Bouchier, 'For the Love of the Game,' 259.

67 Suzanne Morton makes a similar argument in *Ideal Surroundings*, chap. 6.

68 *CH*, 11 December 1884.

69 Fourteen out of 18 (78%) of the officers of Thorold's Mechanics' Institute were middle class, most being merchants or professionals. Only two were skilled workers. Twelve out of 18 (67%) of the officers were members of Thorold's Protestant churches (records of Thorold's Protestant churches; NA, Thorold 1891 manuscript census; and Thorold Public Library (TPL), minutes of Thorold's Mechanics' Institute).

70 *TP*, 8 October 1887.

71 See Vernon, 'The Development of Adult Education in Ontario.'

72 See, for example, *CH*, 18 November 1886; *TP*, 23 December 1887; *IC*, 8 December 1887. Among those men who joined the Mechanics' Institute between 1885 and 1893 for whom an occupation could be identified, 30 (71%) out of 42 were middle class, and only 8 (19%) were clearly working class. Of the 38 new members whose marital status could be identified, 33 were married, three were widowed, and only two were unmarried (NA, Thorold manuscript census, 1891; TPL, minutes of Thorold's Mechanics' Institute).

73 *IC*, 22 December 1887.

74 Among the members of Thorold literary societies 7 of the 10 male members whose marital status could be identified were married, and 16 of the 18 female members who could be identified were single (*TP*; NA, Thorold manuscript census, 1891).

75 Of the male members, 13 out of 15 (87%) were involved in middle-class occupations, while 9 of the 18 women were from working-class backgrounds (*TP*; NA, Thorold manuscript census, 1891).

76 Of the seven members of the managing committee of the Thorold Skating Rink who could be identified, three men were professionals or merchants, two others were engaged in other middle-class occupations, one was a skilled worker, and one was a farmer. All were members of a Protestant church. Four of the seven were involved in the Mechanics' Institute (*TP*; records of Thorold's Protestant churches; NA, Thorold manuscript census, 1891).

77 *TP*, 2 November 1883. See also *TP*, 31 January 1890.

78 *TP*, 5 January 1883. For a discussion of the political uses of masquerade, see Davis, *Parades and Power*, 73–111.

79 *TP*, 15 December 1882. See also Bouchier, 'For the Love of the Game,' 216.

80 See *CH*, 26 February 1885; *TP*, 16 January 1885; *IC*, 13 November 1884.

81 See, for example, *TP*, 27 March, 3 and 10 April, 12 June, and 5 December 1885; *CH*, 23 July, 8 October and 4 December 1885; *IC*, 11 December 1884; *TP*, 1 May and 23 October 1885.

82 *TP*, 10 April 1885. See also *TP*, 24 April 1885; *IC*, 4 December 1884, 3 September 1885.

83 *Petrolia Advertiser*, 17 April 1885. See also *IC*, 12 March 1885.

84 *CH*, 4 February 1886; *TP*, 24 April 1885. See also *IC*, 26 November 1885. See Faraday, 'The Debate about Prostitution,' 57 for a discussion of the fact that in big cities unchaperoned women who frequented ice rinks (or dance halls) were often labelled prostitutes.

85 See Dubinsky, *Improper Advances*, and Strange, *Toronto's Girl Problem*.

86 *TP*, 6 April 1883. See also *TP*, 27 January 1893; *CH*, 15 April 1886; and Davies, 'The Nineteenth Century Repertoire,' 92. Grant, *A Profusion of Spires*, 197, suggests that some members of evangelical churches did engage in such prohibited activities.

87 See, for example, *CH*, 23 November and 20 December 1883, 5 February and 30 July 1885; *TP*, 10 March 1882, 22 June 1883, 16 January 1885, 14 May 1886, 20 May and 23 September 1887; *IC*, 18 June 1885, 22 December 1887. See also Davies, 'The Nineteenth-Century Repertoire' and Brown, 'Entertainers of the Road.'

88 *CH*, 20 December 1883. See also *CH*, 6 December 1894.

89 O'Dell, 'The Class Character of Church Participation,' 250.

90 *IC*, 29 September 1887; *TP*, 23 January 1891.

91 *TP*, 26 December 1890; *CH*, 7 January 1886. See *TP*, 16 January 1885, for comments regarding 'vulgar' shows.

92 *TP*, 30 March 1894; *IC*, 17 January 1884. See also *TP*, 27 November 1884, and Davies, 'The Nineteenth-Century Repertoire,' 115.

93 *CH*, 18 November 1886.

94 *TP*, 3 October 1890, 13 January 1893, 9 April 1886. See also O'Dell, 'The Class Character of Church Participation,' 255.

95 See Rosenzweig, *Eight Hours for What We Will*, 200; Couvares, *The Remaking of Pittsburgh*, 39, and Wilentz, *Chants Democratic*, 258.

96 *TP*, 21 June 1889. See also *TP*, 13 September 1889.

97 *TP*, 5 February 1886, 14 March 1890, 27 May and 18 November 1892, 24 January 1884, 10 November 1887.

98 See, for example, *TP*, 4 August 1882, 7 August 1885. See Huskins, 'Public Celebrations in Victorian Saint John and Halifax,' for a discussion of the decline of large-scale cross-class public celebrations in the late-nineteenth-century Maritimes.

99 *TP*, 22 May 1891. See also *TP*, 25 August 1893; *CH*, 25 June 1886.

100 *TP*, 22 May 1891. See also *TP*, 25 August 1893.

101 See *TP*, 7 August 1885.

102 For similar patterns in the United States, see Ryan, *Women in Public*, 22.

103 *TP*, 15 July 1892. See also *TP*, 22 May 1891.

104 *CH*, 29 May 1884. See also *CH*, 5 and 12 June 1884.

105 See Bouchier, 'For the Love of the Game,' 179.

106 *TP*, 28 August 1885.

107 Ibid. See also *IC*, 26 May 1887.

108 See Bouchier, 'For the Love of the Game,' 152–3. For similar shifts in the Maritimes see Huskins, 'Public Celebrations in Victorian Saint John and Halifax,' chap. 8.

109 See Ryan, *Women in Public*, 19–37.

110 See *TP*, 11 August 1882, 28 May 1886.

111 *TP*, 12 and 19 August, 30 September 1892.

112 See, for example, *TP*, 8 February, 18 April, 6 and 13 June 1884.

113 Tosh, 'What Should Historians Do with Masculinity?' 186.

6: The Salvation Army and the Knights of Labor

1 *Welland Tribune*, 29 April 1887. See also *Thorold Post* (*TP*), 29 April 1887 and 10 April 1885.

2 Kealey and Palmer, *Dreaming of What Might Be*, 277–329.

3 The Salvation Army in fact emerged from an earlier organization known as the Christian Mission, which was founded by Booth in 1865.

4 The Salvation Army founded a rescue home in Toronto in 1886, but Salvation Army social work did not begin in a major way in Canada until 1890 (Moyles, *The Blood and Fire in Canada*, 65).

5 See *Daily British Whig* (Kingston), 26 March 1883; *London Advertiser*, 27 March 1883; *Newmarket Era*, 13 June 1884; *Northern Advance* (Barrie), 22 November 1883. A Salvation Army officer, Major Tackaberry, has gone through more than thirty Canadian newspapers for the first few years of the Army's presence in each town and has copied out all the references to the Army. This is the source used in chapters 6 and 7 in references to the mainstream press other than for the newspapers of Campbellford, Ingersoll, Thorold, and Petrolia.

6 Kealey and Palmer, *Dreaming of What Might Be*, 65; Sumner, *The New Papacy: Behind the Scenes in the Salvation Army by an ex-Staff Officer*, 7. Sumner, who denounced the Army in this pamphlet, would have had insider knowledge of Army figures. As well, he would have had no reason to make the Army look good.

7 For a detailed analysis of differences in the geographical basis of support for the Knights and the Army, see Marks, 'The Knights of Labor and the Salvation Army,' 95–6, 123–7.

8 *Sentinel Review* (Woodstock), 15 February 1884; *Petrolia Advertiser*, 28 June 1884; Kealey and Palmer, *Dreaming of What Might Be*, 82; *Belleville Daily Intelligencer*, 26 November 1883; *Sentinel Review* (Woodstock), 15 February and 4 July 1884; *Canadian Post* (Lindsay), 26 October 1883; *London Advertiser*, 8 January 1883. Between 1882 and 1890, 20 officers were recruited from the Belleville corps, 22 from Chatham, and 23 each from Lindsay, Seaforth, and Woodstock (Salvation Army Archives, Toronto [SAA], C roll).

9 *TP*, 23 March 1883 (letter from Kingston); *Daily British Whig* (Kingston), 12 March 1883; Kealey and Palmer, *Dreaming of What Might Be*, 347–8; *Belleville Intelligencer*, 15 October 1883.

10 Fink, *Workingmen's Democracy*, 13; Kealey and Palmer, *Dreaming of What Might Be*, 323.

11 *Toronto Mail*, 17 July 1882. In a few towns both middle- and working-class people appear to have been attracted to the Army. See, for example, Kingston's *Daily British Whig*, 17 July 1883.

12 For detailed tables of the occupations of converts, see Marks, 'The Knights of Labor and the Salvation Army,' 99.

13 In 1891 less than 11 per cent of the female population of Canada was engaged in paid employment. Most of those who were employed were unmarried. However, although the 1891 census does not provide a breakdown of female employment by marital status, we can be relatively certain that less that half of the unmarried female population was employed in this period, since in 1921, when more than 15 per cent of the female population was gainfully employed, only 49 per cent of unmarried women between the ages of fifteen and thirty-four were employed (Canada, *Census of Canada*, 1921; Canada, Dominion Bureau of Statistics, *Occupational Trends in Canada, 1891–1931*).

14 It is very difficult to gain specific information on the age and marital status of the Knights' leaders, but they do appear to have been among the more established skilled workers in each community. Certainly, in Thorold, eight of the ten male leaders of the Knights who could be linked to the census were married heads of households. For comments regarding the youthfulness of Sal-

vation Army congregations, see *Northern Advance* (Barrie), 22 November 1883; *Globe* (Toronto), 26 March 1884; *Welland Tribune*, 2 May 1884.

15 Fones-Wolf, *Trade Union Gospel*, 192.

16 Fink, *Workingmen's Democracy*.

17 In Thorold, 9 of the 36 male Knights who could be identified (24%) also held office in at least one fraternal order. Most of the male Knights who were identified were officers or were active on Knights committees that organized public events (*Thorold Post*). In Ingersoll, 13 of the 26 male Knights who could be identified (50%) also held office in at least one fraternal order (*Ingersoll Chronicle*). The overlap in participation in the Knights and the fraternal orders has been noted by other scholars who have studied the Knights. See Kealey and Palmer, *Dreaming of What Might Be*, 286, and Fink, *Workingmen's Democracy*, 55.

18 See Kristofferson, 'True Knights Are We.' See also Kealey and Palmer, *Dreaming of What Might Be*.

19 Dubinsky, 'Modern Chivalry,' and Kristofferson, 'True Knights Are We.'

20 *Petrolia Advertiser*, 19 November 1886. See also Dubinsky, 'Modern Chivalry,' and Levine, *Labor's True Woman*, 117–18.

21 *TP*, 11 February and 19 August 1887.

22 *TP*, 17 June 1887, 3 February 1888. See Levine, *Labor's True Woman*, 117–18, for a discussion of similar cultural activities among American female Knights.

23 *Palladium of Labor*, 20 November 1886; *Ingersoll Chronicle* (IC), 27 December 1883.

24 *TP*, 19 August 1887.

25 See, for example, *IC*, 20 January 1887; *TP*, 28 January 1887 and 3 February 1888.

26 *TP*, 6 May 1887.

27 See Kealey and Palmer, *Dreaming of What Might Be*, 293.

28 Fink, *Workingmen's Democracy*, 220.

29 *IC*, 7 July 1887.

30 *TP*, 19 August 1887.

31 Kealey and Palmer, *Dreaming of What Might Be*, 145.

32 Kristofferson, 'True Knights Are We,' 16–17.

33 Murphy, *Ten Hours' Labor*; Gutman, 'Protestantism and the American Labor Movement.' See also Corbin, *Life, Work and Rebellion in the Coalfields*.

34 *Journal of United Labor*, 25 May 1884.

35 *Palladium of Labor* (Toronto), 13 February 1886.

36 *Palladium of Labor*, 27 October 1883. See also *Palladium of Labor*, 22 May 1886, 20 March 1886, 14 March 1885, 29 December 1883, 8 September 1883.

37 Heron, 'Labourism and the Canadian Working Class,' 65.

38 Fones-Wolf, *Trade Union Gospel*, 79 and 84.

39 The disparity between the Christian message and social inequality has certainly fuelled oppositional consciousness in other contexts. See, for example, Thompson, *The Making of the English Working Class*, 431, 438; and O'Dea and O'Dea Aviad, *The Sociology of Religion*, 15.

40 Kealey and Palmer, *Dreaming of What Might Be*, 311.

41 See *TP*, 25 November 1887; *IC*, 20 and 27 May, 3 June 1886. *Stratford Beacon*, 16 April 1886; Anstead, 'Fraternalism in Victorian Ontario,' 201.

42 In Thorold 5 of the 16 Knights who could be identified as Protestant were church members (31%) before 1893. Three of these men held offices in their churches. After the Crossley and Hunter revival in Thorold in 1893, an additional four Knights became church members (*TP*; records of Thorold's Protestant churches). In Ingersoll 4 of the 26 Knights who could be identified appeared as church members in the surviving records of local Protestant churches (*IC*; records of Ingersoll Protestant churches).

43 *TP*, 13 July 1888.

44 *Petrolia Advertiser*, 24 September 1886.

45 Ibid.

46 *Palladium of Labor*, 10 January 1885.

47 For a discussion of the labour movement's role in the battle over Sunday streetcars in Toronto in the 1890s, see Armstrong and Nelles, *The Revenge of the Methodist Bicycle Company*. In *Trade Union Gospel* (47–52), Fones-Wolf demonstrates that Philadelphia workers sometimes used sabbatarian arguments to protect workers from Sunday labour but more often opposed sabbatarianism as an interference in working-class leisure.

48 *TP*, 21 and 28 October 1887; *IC*, 3 June 1886.

49 *Palladium of Labor*, 1 August 1885; *Palladium of Labor* (Toronto) 13 February 1886. See also *Palladium of Labor*, 27 October and 8 September 1883.

50 *Palladium of Labor*, 8 September and 27 October 1883, 14 March 1885, 29 September 1883. See also *Palladium of Labor*, 31 July and 16 October 1886.

51 *Palladium of Labor*, 20 December 1884; Fones-Wolf, *Trade Union Gospel*, 74–6.

52 See Cook, *The Regenerators*, 58, 157.

53 *Palladium of Labor*, 27 October 1883.

54 *Palladium of Labor*, 8 September 1883, 20 March 1886. See also Fones-Wolf, *Trade Union Gospel*, xviii.

55 Kealey and Palmer, *Dreaming of What Might Be*, 311–12. *Palladium of Labor*, 28 November 1885.

56 *Palladium of Labor*, 17 May 1884, 15 May 1886.

57 *TP*, 9 January 1885.

58 *TP*, 12 December 1884. See also Semple, 'The Nurture and Admonition of the Lord,' 172; Kee, 'The Heavenly Railroad,' 43–5; Airhart, *Serving the Present Age*, 34.

59 *Daily British Whig* (Kingston), 14 July 1883.

60 See, for example, *Northern Advance* (Barrie), 22 November 1883; *News Argus* (Stirling), 11 April 1884; *Stratford Times*, 6 August 1884; *Woodstock Sentinel Review*, 8 February 1884. Norman Murdoch suggests that in the British context the Salvation Army was more successful in converting former church members than in attracting those with no links to the churches (Murdoch, *Origins of the Salvation Army*, 134).

61 *Belleville Daily Intelligencer*, 5 December 1883.

62 *Woodstock Sentinel Review*, 6 June 1884; *London Advertiser*, 14 July 1883; *IC*, 1 November 1883, 10 January 1884.

63 *War Cry*, 27 August 1887.

64 Thompson and Semmel make this argument for early Methodism (Thompson, *The Making of the English Working Class*, 399, and Semmel, *The Methodist Revolution*, 193).

65 See, for example, *War Cry*, 25 June 1887; *Daily British Whig* (Kingston), 14 July 1883.

66 *Dumfries Reformer* (Galt), 24 April 1884; *Canadian Post* (Lindsay), 14 March 1884; *London Advertiser*, 16 November 1882.

67 Thompson makes a similar argument regarding the appeal of Methodism to English workers in *The Making of the English Working Class*, 44. See also Hobsbawn, *Primitive Rebels*, 132, and Colls, 'Primitive Methodists in the Northern Coalfields,' 326.

68 Bailey, 'In Darkest England and the Way Out'; Robertson, 'The Salvation Army: The Persistence of Sectarianism,' 94.

69 For some biographies of officers that mention their religious background, see *War Cry*, 4 December 1886; 19 February, 19 March, 18 June 1887. See also Murdoch, *Origins of the Salvation Army*, 134.

70 *Daily British Whig* (Kingston), 31 January 1883.

71 *War Cry*, 11 May 1889, 25 December 1884.

72 *War Cry*, 19 February 1887.

73 Walker, 'I Live but Not Yet I for Christ Liveth in Me.'

74 *War Cry*, 25 July 1885, 11 December 1886.

75 See, for example, *British Whig* (Kingston), 31 January and 3 October 1883; *Barrie Northern Advance*, 30 August 1883; *Renfrew Mercury*, 15 April 1887; *Woodstock Sentinel Review*, 14 December 1883; *Huron Signal* (Goderich), 13 February 1885; *TP*, 14 March 1884.

76 *IC*, 13 December 1883.

77 For similar behaviour among local roughs in the English context, see Bailey, 'Salvation Army Riots.'

78 See, for example, *London Advertiser*, 30 May 1884, and *Sarnia Observer*, 4 July 1884.

79 *St. Thomas Times*, 17 August 1883; *Toronto World*, 5 September 1884. See also, for example, *Daily British Whig* (Kingston), 30 April 1883; *London Advertiser*, 7 April 1884; *Sarnia Observer*, 16 May 1884.

80 *Daily British Whig* (Kingston), 30 April 1883.

81 *IC*, 23 July 1885; Walker, 'I Live but Not Yet I for Christ Liveth in Me.'

82 *IC*, 1 November 1883; *Newmarket Era*, 13 June 1884; *London Advertiser*, 7 April 1884. For a petition to pass a by-law against the Salvation Army, see *IC*, 27 March and 10 April 1884. See also *London Advertiser*, 19 and 20 June 1884.

83 For a detailed example of the attitudes of local authorities to the Salvation Army's 'disturbances' and the Army's response, see the transcript of the 1887 trial of Salvation Army officers for loitering and blocking the street in Lindsay, Ontario (transcript held at SAA)

84 For a discussion of the conversion of roughs to Christianity, see *Daily British Whig* (Kingston), 7 May 1883; *London Advertiser*, 3 March 1883; *Whitby Chronicle*, 4 April 1884. For comments regarding the reduction in drunkeness, see *London Advertiser*, 17 July 1883; *Belleville Daily Intelligencer*, 4 December 1883; *Hamilton Spectator*, 25 January 1884. For statistics pointing to a reduction in crime, see *London Advertiser*, 30 November 1882; *Northern Advance* (Barrie), 25 October 1883; *Hamilton Spectator*, 5 May 1884. For the testimony of businessmen regarding increased industriousness, see *London Advertiser*, 17 July 1883; *Petrolia Advertiser*, 28 June 1884, *Toronto World*, 17 December 1883. For a discussion of how the Army was preferable to revolutionary movements, see *Toronto Week*, 10 January 1884.

85 *War Cry*, 4 July 1885.

86 Philpott and Roffe, *New Light, Containing A Full Account of the Recent Salvation Army Troubles in Canada*, 17.

87 Fones-Wolf, *Trade Union Gospel*, xvii.

7: Hallelujah Lasses

1 *Hamilton Spectator*, 15 July 1884.

2 *Thorold Post (TP)*, 19 September 1884; *Welland Tribune*, 31 October 1884; *Daily British Whig* (Kingston), 1 October 1883.

3 Bramwell-Booth, 'The Call and Ministry of Women,' 89.

4 On female preachers in early Methodism see, for example, Anna Clark, 'The Sexual Crisis and Popular Religion in London, 1770-1820.' For more general

comments on the possibility of sexual egalitarianism in evangelical Protestantism, see Juster, 'Patriarchy Reborn,' 59–60.

5 Catherine Booth, 'Female Ministry,' 160, 152.
6 Bramwell-Booth, *Catherine Booth: The Story of Her Loves*, 395.
7 Catherine Booth, 'Female Ministry,' 135.
8 *Daily British Whig* (Kingston), 31 August 1883; *Mainland Guardian* (New Westminister), 29 February 1888.
9 *War Cry*, 10 and 24 January 1885; 25 December 1884.
10 *War Cry*, 2 August 1890.
11 *London Advertiser*, 18 April 1884.
12 *Canadian Post* (Lindsay), 1 February 1884; *War Cry*, 11 May 1889 and 1 December 1888; *Hamilton Spectator*, 27 June 1884; *War Cry*, 11 May 1889.
13 *Sentinel Review* (Woodstock), 14 December 1883; *World* (Toronto), 4 January 1883.
14 See, for example, Westfall, *Two Worlds*, 60–3; S.D. Clark, *Church and Sect in Canada*; Anna Clark, 'The Sexual Crisis and Popular Religion.'
15 *London Advertiser*, 3 March 1884.
16 *London Advertiser*, 30 March 1883; *World* (Toronto), 3 February 1885.
17 *Petrolia Advertiser*, 8 August 1884.
18 *Daily British Whig*, (Kingston), 7 May and 28 September 1883.
19 *Northern Advance* (Barrie), 18 Oct 1883; *Hamilton Spectator*, 26 March 1884.
20 *Daily British Whig* (Kingston), 20 March 1883; *Wiarton Echo*, 12 December 1884.
21 *Dominion Churchman*, 10 May 1883. See also *London Advertiser*, 30 May 1884; *Hamilton Spectator*, 25 January 1884; *Renfrew Mercury*, 8 April 1887; *Petrolia Advertiser*, 23 May 1884.
22 For a discussion of 'moral panics,' see Weeks, *Sex, Politics and Society*, 14, 92. Other 'disorderly' religious movements have sparked similar fears of sexual immorality (see Juster, 'Patriarchy Reborn,' 61). Other working-class women who ventured into the public world could also be defined as sexually suspect (see Strange, *Toronto's Girl Problem*).
23 General William Booth, *Orders and Regulations for Soldiers of the Salvation Army*.
24 *TP*, 25 February 1887.
25 *Stratford Times*, 13 August 1884; *Orillia Times*, 21 August 1884.
26 See Dubinsky, '"Maidenly Girls" or "Designing Women"?' For stories of sexuality and seduction in the Salvation Army, see *St Thomas Times*, 6 August 1883; *Newmarket Era*, 13 June 1884; *Renfrew Mercury*, 8 April 1887; *TP*, 11 April and 20 June 1884.
27 *War Cry*, 13 December 1884, 1 August 1885, 12 November and 24 December

1887, 25 May 1889. See Peiss, *Cheap Amusements*, 63-6, for a discussion of the role of fashion in the contemporary young women's culture of New York working-class women.

28 *Ottawa Free Press*, 4 April 1885.

29 Salvation Army Archives, Toronto (SAA), officers' rolls.

30 Moyles, *The Blood and Fire in Canada*, 16.

31 *Daily Sun* (Saint John, N.B.) 16 February 1886; Ashley, 'The Salvation Army in Toronto,' 24.

32 Gail Malmgreen, 'Domestic Discords,' 59.

33 *Daily British Whig* (Kingston), 29 January 1883. See also *War Cry*, 19 July 1890; 28 July 1888.

34 *British Whig* (Kingston), 5 February 1883.

35 *War Cry*, 1 August 1885.

36 See, for example, Henry Abelove, 'The Sexual Politics of Early Wesleyan Methodism,' in *Disciplines of Faith*.

37 *World* (Toronto), 17 May 1884

38 *War Cry*, 19 July 1890; General William Booth, *The Doctrines and Discipline of the Salvation Army*, 111.

39 Leslie, 'Domestic Service in Canada, 1880-1920.'

40 The extent to which some of these close emotional relationships had an explicitly sexual component has been debated in the lesbian/women's history literature. See, for example, Smith-Rosenberg, 'The Female World of Love and Ritual: Relations between Women in Nineteenth-Century America,' in her *Disorderly Conduct*; Faderman, *Surpassing the Love of Men*; Vicinus, 'They Wonder to Which Sex I Belong?'; Rupp, 'Imagine My Surprise.' I have not found evidence to suggest that there was a sexual element to women's relationships in the Salvation Army, although of course such evidence is difficult to find and to interpret, even among middle-class women, who were more likely to leave letters and diaries.

41 *Daily British Whig* (Kingston), 22 October 1883. See also *Daily British Whig* (Kingston), 22 September 1883; *London Advertiser*, 6 June 1884.

42 *War Cry*, 7 May 1887. Army training in this period ranged from three weeks to three months (Moyles, *The Blood and Fire in Canada*, 283–5).

43 *World* (Toronto), 3 July 1884.

44 *War Cry*, 19 November 1887; Sumner, *The New Papacy*, 61.

45 Working-class women's weekly wages seem to have ranged from $1.50 to $7.00 or $8.00. The average appears to have been less than $5.00 a week. See, for example, Dubinsky 'Modern Chivalry,' 25, and Acton et al., *Women at Work*, 48.

46 *War Cry*, 25 May 1889. See also Sumner, *The New Papacy*, 53.

47 Cited in Dubinsky, 'Modern Chivalry,' 141.

48 Quoted in ibid., 32.

49 Kealey and Palmer, *Dreaming of What Might Be*, 144.

50 *War Cry*, 1 December 1888. See also *War Cry*, 4 December 1886, 5 February 1887, 12 July 1890.

51 *War Cry*, 27 September and 2 August 1890, 24 November 1888, 27 September 1890.

52 *War Cry*, 2 August 1890.

53 Of the 36 women who entered the Army between 1882 and 1890 and were involved in rescue work, 18 left the movement after their first posting to rescue work. Most of these women had previously held several postings as field officers (preachers). Half of the 13 men who were involved in rescue work in this period also left the Army after their first posting to this work (SAA, C Roll, Officers' Rolls). In 'The Salvation Army in Toronto,' Ashley similarly argues that Army officers were reluctant to enter social service work (90).

54 See, for example, *War Cry*, 2 August 1890.

55 See, for example, *War Cry*, 9 July 1887 and 22 August 1885.

56 *War Cry*, 25 December 1886, 25 June 1887, 25 May 1889, 1 May 1897.

57 The 23 (out of 41) long-serving female officers who do not appear to have married were in most cases transferred to other countries, where some may have married. The Army may also have provided some of these women with a welcome alternative to marriage, since such alternatives were extremely limited for working class women (SAA, C Roll, Officers' Rolls).

8: 'Safe in the Arms of Jesus'

1 See *Thorold Post* (TP), 2 and 9 September, 4 November, and 2 December 1892.

2 *TP*, 3 February 1893.

3 Given Thorold's large Catholic community, these numbers are truly impressive, even assuming that some revival converts would have been from the countryside or from nearby communities. After the revival the Methodist congregation increased from 147 members to 338, and the Presbyterians added 28 members. In the case of the Anglicans, although fewer than 15 children were usually confirmed every year or two, in 1893 more than 40 people were confirmed, both adults and children (see the records of Thorold's Protestant churches).

4 *TP*, 17 February 1893.

5 Among the communities they visited in 1893 were Wiarton, Goderich, Berlin, Napanee, Port Elgin, and Lindsay (*TP*, 8 September 1893). An examination of Methodist church membership in these communities reveals that only in

Goderich did membership increase by more than 100 members. All of these
churches had more pre-revival members than Thorold's Methodist church
(Methodist Church of Canada, *Minutes of Conference*, 1893, 1894). Only in
Petrolia did Crossely and Hunter have a major success in 1893, converting
over 800 people in a town of about 5,000 (booklet of St Paul's United Church
Centennial, Petrolia, 1865-1965). Their successful services in Belleville in 1888
led to about 1,000 converts in a community more than four times the size of
Thorold (O'Dell, 'The Class Character of Church Participation,' 277). For a
discussion of other Crossley and Hunter revivals, see Kee, 'The Heavenly
Railroad.'

6 See, for example, Canadian Baptist Archives (CBA), minutes of Thorold Baptist Church, 22 December 1889 and 7 February 1892; and St Andrew's Presbyterian Church, Campbellford, session minutes, 1 December 1893 and
19 November 1894. See also Grant, *A Profusion of Spires*, 182, and Marshall,
Secularizing the Faith, 86–9.

7 *Campbellford Herald (CH)*, 10 and 17 February 1887

8 See Dolan, *The American Catholic Experience*, 226–7.

9 *TP*, 7 March 1890; *Welland Tribune*, 12 March 1886.

10 *Ingersoll Chronicle (IC)*, 4 February and 14 October 1886. For the popularity of
other missions, see *TP*, 26 September 1884, 7 March 1890.

11 *IC*, 26 February 1885.

12 *Petrolia Advertiser*, 8 September 1893.

13 Marshall, *Secularizing the Faith*, 90; Kee, 'The Heavenly Railroad,' chap. 4.

14 *TP*, 27 January 1893; *Petrolia Advertiser*, 29 September 1893.

15 *TP*, 3 February and 27 January 1893.

16 The data on converts are taken from the records of Thorold's Anglican, Presbyterian, and Methodist churches. For a further discussion of these data, see
appendix A.

17 Sixty-seven per cent of Methodist converts 15 years of age or less are
recorded as having attended the Methodist Sunday school in the previous
seven years. Another 14 per cent had siblings who are recorded as attending,
and since the Sunday school records do not appear to list all students, most
of these people were probably also involved at some point. Only 19 per cent
(10 converts) did not appear to have had any links to the Sunday school
(United Church Archives [UCA], circuit register and Sunday school minutes,
Thorold Methodist Church).

18 See, for example, *Onward* (journal of Epworth League), 3 January 1891, and
Boylan, *Sunday School*, 114–19.

19 See Epstein, *The Politics of Domesticity*, 51, and Johnson, *A Shopkeepers Millennium*, 108.

20 *TP*, 3 February 1893.

21 In *Transatlantic Revivalism*, Richard Carwardine notes that depressions were not the only potential cause of revivals, but he does acknowledge that poor economic conditions could in fact often be correlated with successful revivals (53–5).

22 National Archives of Canada (NA), Thorold manuscript census, 1891. The census appears to have underreported the extent of actual unemployment. See Baskerville and Sager, 'The First National Unemployment Survey,' 174–5.

23 Johnson, 'Supply-side and Demand-side Revivalism?'

24 See *TP*, 20 and 27 January 1893; *Petrolia Advertiser*, 8 September 1893.

25 *TP*, 3 February 1893.

26 Kee 'The Heavenly Railroad,' 143; *CH*, 24 February 1887. For female involvement in American revivals, see Ryan, *Cradle of the Middle Class*, 83–104, and Johnson, *Shopkeeper's Millennium*, 108. The Methodist Church by this period had even sanctioned the use of lay female evangelists. See Whiteley, 'Modest, Unaffected and Fully Consecrated.'

27 *TP*, 3 February 1893.

28 *TP*, 10 February 1893.

29 Cited in Marshall, *Secularizing the Faith*, 92–3.

30 Caldwell 'Revival and Chicago Working Girls.' See also Curtis, 'The Son of Man and God the Father.'

31 *TP*, 27 January 1893. Also see Kee, 'The Heavenly Railroad,' 149–53, for a discussion of Crossley and Hunter's focus on masculine sins.

32 Ibid., and 3 February 1893.

33 *TP*, 17 February 1893; *Petrolia Advertiser*, 29 September 1893; O'Dell, 'The Class Character of Church Participation,' 278.

34 *TP*, 10 February 1893.

35 *TP*, 17 February 1893.

36 Ibid.

37 *TP*, 3 February 1893.

38 *TP*, 10 February 1893.

39 *TP*, 3 March 1893.

40 *TP*, 31 March 1893.

41 *IC*, 22 December 1887.

42 *TP*, 29 March 1895.

43 *TP*, 29 September 1893, 1 and 8 November 1895.

44 *TP*, 24 February 1893.

45 *TP*, 24 March 1893.

46 *TP*, 4 May 1894.

47 *TP*, 10 February and 21 July 1893.

48 See Carwardine, *Transatlantic Revivalism*, 49–50, and Westfall, *Two Worlds*, 66–7.
49 For a discussion of the marginality of revival converts, see Juster, *Disorderly Women*, 8.
50 Men made up 15 of 18 of those 'dropped'; 12 of these 15 men were working class, and 10 of the 15 were single (UCA, Thorold Methodist Church records; NA, Thorold 1891 manuscript census).
51 *TP*, 29 March 1895.
52 See, for example, Parr, *The Gender of Breadwinners*, Baron, *Work Engendered*, and Suzanne Morton, *Ideal Surroundings*.

9: Conclusion

1 This occurred in Thorold. Three male Thoroldites who were identified as members of the Knights of Labor in 1887 and 1888 joined the local ERA branch in 1889. The recording secretary of Thorold's Mountain Assembly of the Knights was on the executive of the ERA. (See *Thorold Post* (*TP*); National Archives of Canada (NA), Thorold manuscript census, 1891; and Thorold Historical Society, membership list of Thorold branch of Equal Rights Association.
2 Parr, *The Gender of Breadwinners*, 245.
3 See, for example, Marshall, 'Canadian Historians, Secularization and the Problem of the Nineteenth Century'; Rawlyk, 'Kingston Methodists and Baptists and the Great Religious Revival of 1852 and 1853,' in his *Wrapped Up in God*, 96–8.
4 Fones-Wolf, *Trade Union Gospel*.
5 See, for example, Cook, *The Regenerators*; Marshall, *Secularizing the Faith*; Gauvreau, *The Evangelical Century* and 'Beyond the Halfway House'; and Marshall, 'Canadian Historians, Secularization and the Problem of the Nineteenth Century.'
6 Marshall, *Secularizing the Faith*, 127–8.
7 See Peiss, *Cheap Amusements*, and Strange, *Toronto's Girl Problem*.

Appendix A

1 They state whether the individual was 'dropped' for nonattendance or other lapses, or whether they had 'removed' to a church in another community.
2 Among Thorold Methodists, 67 per cent of those who donated money to the church were church members, while among Thorold Presbyterians 69 per cent of those donating were church members (Thorold Presbyterian and Methodist church records).

3 See McLeod, 'Catholicism and the New York Irish,' 345.

4 See Hershberg and Dockhorn, 'Occupational Classification.'

5 Although the Philadelphia project focuses on the 1860–80 period, the fact that Ontario industrialized later than the northeastern United States means that this classification would be appropriate for Ontario in 1891.

6 For a concern over the difficulty of differentiating between skilled workers and small masters, see Thomas Smith, 'Reconstructing Occupational Structures.'

7 Where possible, the employer/wage earner distinction appearing in the census was checked with town directories, which identified artisans who ran their own businesses. The two sources usually agreed on the status of particular individuals.

8 In this period, when (particularly in smaller communities) most male clerks could still aspire to managerial or employer status, their middle-class categorization seems less ambiguous than it was later to become.

9 Wealthy skilled workers were also identified as those employing a servant in the 1891 census. It was useful to identify wealthy skilled workers as a distinct category, particularly in small-town contexts, because they would be most likely to share the lifestyle and values of middle-class townspeople.

10 When single men and women are categorized by their own occupation or income for a particular analysis, this is specifically indicated.

11 While this practice may seem to reflect patriarchal assumptions, it recognizes that men had far more economic options than women and that the occupations of sons were more likely to reflect the class position of a family than the occupations of daughters.

Bibliography

PRIMARY SOURCES

Archival Collections

Anglican Diocesan Archives, Diocese of Niagara, McMaster University, Hamilton
  Records of St John the Evangelist Anglican Church, Thorold
Anglican Diocesan Archives, Diocese of Toronto, Toronto
  Records of Christ Church Anglican Church, Campbellford
Campbellford Town Hall, Campbellford
  Campbellford municipal records
Campbellford Public Library, Campbellford
  Local History Collection
Canadian Baptist Archives, Hamilton
  Records of Campbellford Baptist Church
  Records of Ingersoll Baptist Church
  Records of Thorold Baptist Church
Family History Library, Toronto
  'Status Animarum,' Roman Catholic parishes, St Catharines
Mrs Betty Millar, Toronto
  Private manuscript collection
Miss Dorothy Millar, Thorold
  Private manuscript collection
National Archives of Canada, Ottawa
  1891 manuscript census for Campbellford and Thorold
  1901 manuscript census for Thorold (by special permission)
  Powderly Papers, Knights of Labor

Public Archives of Ontario
  Assessment rolls, Thorold, 1885–8
  Woman's Christian Temperance Union, collection
Roman Catholic Archives, Archdiocese of Toronto, Toronto
  Records of Holy Rosary Parish, Thorold
Regional Room Special Collections, Weldon Library, University of Western
  Ontario, London
  Fawkes Family collection
  Records of Charles Street Methodist Church, Ingersoll
  Records of Erskine Presbyterian Church, Ingersoll
  Records of King Street Methodist Church, Ingersoll
  Records of Knox Presbyterian Church, Ingersoll
  Records of St Paul's Presbyterian Church, Ingersoll
  Records of St James Anglican Church, Ingersoll
St Andrew's Presbyterian Church, Campbellford
  Church records
St Andrew's Presbyterian Church, Thorold
  Church records
Salvation Army Archives, Toronto
  Converts' rolls for Feversham, Listowel, and Petrolia
  Corps records
  Court transcripts, Salvation Army cases, 1880s
  Manuscript collections: R. Braund, Gideon Miller
  Newspaper files for early years of the Salvation Army in Canada
  Officers' rolls: A roll, C roll, S roll
  Soldiers' rolls for Campbellford, Chatham, and Petrolia
Sisters of St Joseph Archives, Toronto
  Records of the Sisters of St Joseph, Thorold
Thorold Historical Society, Thorold
  Records of Thorold Equal Rights Association
Thorold Public Library, Thorold
  Local history files
  Records of Thorold Mechanics' Institute
United Church Archives, Toronto
  Records of Campbellford Methodist Church
  Records of Thorold Methodist Church

Newspapers and Periodicals

Campbellford Herald, 1882–95
Christian Guardian, 1880–1

Citizen (Ottawa), 1877–80
Free Press (London), 1876–80
Ingersoll Chronicle, 1882–7
Journal of United Labor, 1880–9
Palladium of Labor (Hamilton), 1883–6
Palladium of Labor (Toronto), 1885–6
Petrolia Advertiser, 1886–7
Stratford Beacon, 1886
Thorold Post, 1882–95
War Cry (Salvation Army), 1884–92
Welland Tribune, 1886–8
Woman's Journal (WCTU), 1885–1902
Woodstock Sentinel Review, 1886–8

Proceedings, Annual Reports, and Government Documents

Baptist Year Book. 1882–96
Canada. *Census of Canada*. 1881, 1891, and 1901
– Dominion Bureau of Statistics. *Occupational Trends in Canada, 1891–1931*. 1939
Canadian Advance, The. Salvation Army Report. Toronto, 1886
General Assembly of the Knights of Labor. *Proceedings*. 1880–96
Methodist Church of Canada. *Minutes of Conference*. 1884–96
Niagara Diocesan Branch, The Women's Auxiliary to the Domestic and Foreign Missionary Society of the Church of England. *Annual Report*. 1887–96
Ontario WCTU. *Annual Report*. 1887–1906
Presbyterian Church in Canada. *Acts and Proceedings of the General Assembly*. 1882–96.
Salvation Army in Canada. *Annual Report*. 1890
Toronto Diocesan Branch, The Women's Auxiliary to the Domestic and Foreign Missionary Society of the Church of England. *Annual Report*. 1887–96
Women's Missionary Society of the Methodist Church of Canada. *Annual Report* 1886–96

Directories

Campbellford Business Directory. 1893
Campbellford Business Directory. 1897
Farmers' and Business Directory for the Counties of Lambton, Middlesex, Norfolk and Oxford. Ingersoll 1889

St. Catharines Directory for 1881–1882, with Directories of Thorold, Merritton and Port Dalhousie. Toronto 1881

St. Catharines Directory for 1898, with directories of Thorold, Merritton and Port Dalhousie. St. Catharines 1898

Other Printed Sources

Archibald, Alexander. *Manual of Forms of the Presbyterian Church.* Philadelphia 1902

Booth, Catherine. 'Female Ministry.' In *Papers on Practical Religion.* London 1890

Booth, General William. *The Doctrines and Discipline of the Salvation Army.* Toronto 1885

– *Orders and Regulations for Soldiers of the Salvation Army.* London 1899

Clark, C.S. *Of Toronto the Good: A Social Study. The Queen City of Canada as It Is.* Montreal 1898

Duncan, Sara Jeannette. *The Imperialist.* 1904. Reprint, Toronto 1990

History of the Country of Welland, The. 1887. Reprint, Belleville, Ont. 1972

Philpott, P.W., and A.W. Roffe. *New Light, Containing a Full Account of the Recent Salvation Army Troubles in Canada.* Toronto 1892

Sumner, A. *The New Papacy: Behind the Scenes in the Salvation Army by an ex-Staff Officer.* Toronto 1889

SELECTED SECONDARY SOURCES

Books

Acton, Janice, et. al. *Women at Work, Ontario 1850–1930.* Toronto 1974

Airhart, Phyllis. *Serving the Present Age: Revivalism, Progressivism and the Methodist Tradition in Canada.* Montreal and Kingston 1992

Akenson, Donald Harman. *The Irish in Ontario: A Study in Rural History.* Kingston and Montreal 1984

– *Small Differences: Irish Catholics and Irish Protestants, 1815–1922. An International Perspective.* Kingston and Montreal 1988

Allen, Richard. *The Social Passion: Religion and Social Reform in Canada, 1914–28.* Toronto 1973

Armstrong, Christopher, and H.V. Nelles. *The Revenge of the Methodist Bicycle Company.* Toronto 1977

Bailey, Peter. *Leisure and Class in Victorian England.* London 1978

Baron, Ava, ed. *Work Engendered: Toward a New History of American Labor*. Ithaca and London 1991

Benson, Susan Porter. *Counter Cultures: Saleswomen, Managers and Customers in American Deparment Stores, 1890–1940*. Urbana 1988

Berger, Carl. *Science, God and Nature in Victorian Canada*. Toronto 1983

Blocker, Jack S., Jr. *American Temperance Movements: Cycles of Reform*. Boston 1989

Bocock, Robert. *Hegemony*. London 1986

Bordin, Ruth. *Woman and Temperance: The Quest for Power and Liberty, 1873–1900*. Philadelphia 1981

Boylan, Anne M. *Sunday School: The Formation of an American Institution, 1790–1880*. New Haven, Conn. 1988

Bradbury, Bettina. *Working Families: Age, Gender and Daily Survival in Industrializing Montreal*. Toronto 1993.

Bramwell-Booth, Catherine. *Catherine Booth: The Story of Her Loves*. London 1971

Brooks, Alan A. *Religion and Rural Ontario's Past*. Proceedings of the 5th Annual Agricultural History of Ontario Seminar. Guelph 1980

Brouwer, Ruth Compton. *New Women for God: Canadian Presbyterian Women and India Missions, 1876–1914*. Toronto 1990

Campbellford's Golden Jubilee History. 1956

Carwardine, Richard. *Transatlantic Revivalism: Popular Evangelicalism in Britain and America*. Westport, Conn. 1978

Carnes, Mark C. *Secret Ritual and Manhood in Victorian America*. New Haven 1989

Carnes, Mark C., and Clyde Griffen, eds. *Meanings for Manhood: Constructions of Masculinity in Victorian America*. Chicago 1990

Carrington, Philip. *The Anglican Church in Canada*. Toronto 1963

Centennial of the Laying of the Cornerstone of Holy Rosary Church, Thorold, 1887–1987. Souvenir booklet. 1987

Chown, Alice A. *The Stairway*. 1921. Reprint, Toronto 1988

Clark, S.D. *Church and Sect in Canada*. Toronto 1948

Clarke, Brian. *Piety and Nationalism: Lay Voluntary Associations and the Creation of an Irish-Catholic Community in Toronto, 1850–1895*. Kingston and Montreal 1993

Clarke, John, et al., eds. *Working-Class Culture*. London 1979

Clawson, Mary Ann. *Constructing Brotherhood: Class, Gender and Fraternalism*. Princeton 1989

Collins, Robert. *The Holy War of the Sally Ann: The Salvation Army in Canada*. Saskatoon 1984

Cook, Ramsay. *The Regenerators: Social Criticism in Late Victorian English Canada*. Toronto 1985

Corbin, David. *Life, Work and Rebellion in the Coalfields: The Southern West Virginia Miners, 1880–1922*. Urbana 1981

Cott, Nancy. *The Bonds of Womanhood: 'Woman's Sphere' in New England, 1780–1835*. New Haven 1977

Couvares, Francis G. *The Remaking of Pittsburgh: Class and Culture in an Industrializing City, 1877–1919*. Albany, N.Y. 1984

Cox, Jeffery. *The English Churches in a Secular Society: Lambeth, 1870–1930*. Oxford 1982

Danylewycz, Marta. *Taking the Veil: An Alternative to Marriage, Motherhood and Spinsterhood in Quebec, 1840–1920*. Toronto 1987

Davidoff, Leonore, and Catherine Hall. *Family Fortunes: Men and Women of the English Middle Class, 1780–1850*. London 1987

Davis, Susan. *Parades and Power: Street Theatre in Nineteenth Century Philadelphia*. Berkeley and Los Angeles 1986

DeCarrol, F.G.B., ed. *Reflections on Campbellford's Centennial Year*. 1976

Dolan, Jay P. *The American Catholic Experience: A History from Colonial Times to the Present*. Garden City, N.Y. 1985

– *Catholic Revivalism: The American Experience 1830–1900*. Notre Dame 1978

– *The Immigrant Church: New York's Irish and German Catholics, 1815–1865*. Baltimore 1975

Douglas, Anne. *The Feminization of American Culture*. New York 1977

Dubinsky, Karen. *Improper Advances: Rape and Heterosexual Conflict in Ontario, 1880–1929*. Chicago, 1993

Eisenstein, Sarah. *Give Us Bread but Give Us Roses: Working Women's Consciousness in the United States, 1890 to the First World War*. London 1983

Epstein, Barbara. *The Politics of Domesticity: Women, Evangelism and Temperance in Nineteenth Century America*. Middleton, Conn. 1981

Faderman, Lillian. *Surpassing the Love of Men: Romantic Friendship and Love between Women From the Renaissance to the Present*. New York 1981.

Ferretti, Lucia. *Entre voisins: La société paroissiale en milieu urbain Saint-Pierre-Apotre de Montréal, 1848–1930*. Montreal 1992

Fingard, Judith. *The Dark Side of Life in Victorian Halifax*. Porters Lake, N.S. 1989

Fink, Leon. *Workingmen's Democracy: The Knights of Labor and American Politics*. Urbana 1983

Fones-Wolf, Kenneth. *Trade Union Gospel: Christianity and Labor in Industrial Philadelphia, 1865–1915*. Philadelphia 1989

Foucault, Michel. *The History of Sexuality*. Vol. 1, *An Introduction*. New York 1978

Gagan, Rosemary R. *A Sensitive Independence: Canadian Methodist Women Missionaries in Canada and the Orient, 1881–1925*. Montreal and Kingston 1992

Gauvreau, Michael. *The Evangelical Century: College and Creed in English Canada from the Great Revival to the Great Depression*. Montreal and Kingston 1991

Gidney, R.D., and W.P.J. Millar. *Professional Gentlemen: The Professions in Nine-teenth-Century Ontario*. Toronto 1994

Gordon, Linda. *Heroes of Their Own Lives: The Politics and History of Family Violence*. New York 1988

Graham, W.H. *Greenbank: Country Matters in Nineteenth Century Ontario*. Peterborough 1988

Grant, John Webster. *A Profusion of Spires: Religion in Nineteenth-Century Ontario*. Toronto 1988

Gutman, Herbert G. *Work, Culture and Society in Industrializing America: Essays in American Working-Class and Social History*. New York 1966

Hatch, Nathan O. *The Democratization of American Christianity*. New Haven and London 1989

Heron, Craig. *The Canadian Labour Movement*. Toronto 1989

Hewitt, Nancy A. *Women's Activism and Social Change: Rochester, New York, 1822–1872*. Ithaca 1984

Higginbotham, Evelyn Brooks. *Righteous Discontent: The Women's Movement in the Black Baptist Church, 1880–1920*. Cambridge, Mass. 1993

Hobsbawn, E.J. *Primitive Rebels*. London 1959

Houston, Cecil J., and William J. Smyth. *The Sash Canada Wore: A Historical Geography of the Orange Order in Canada*. Toronto 1980

Houston, Susan E., and Alison Prentice. *Schooling and Scholars in Ninteenth-Century Ontario*. Toronto 1988

Howell, Colin D. *Northern Sandlots: A Social History of Maritime Baseball*. Toronto 1995

Iacovetta, Franca. *Such Hardworking People: Italian Immigrants in Postwar Toronto*. Kingston and Montreal 1992

Inglis, K.S. *Churches and the Working Classes in Victorian England*. London 1963

Johnson, Curtis D. *Island of Holiness: Rural Religion in Upstate New York, 1790–1860*. Ithaca and London 1989

Johnson, Paul E. *A Shopkeeper's Millennium: Society and Revivals in Rochester, New York, 1815–1837*. New York 1978

Jubilee History of Thorold Township and Town. Thorold 1897

Juster, Susan. *Disorderly Women: Sexual Politics and Evangelicalism in Revolutionary New England*. Ithaca and London 1994

Katz, Michael B. *The People of Hamilton, Canada West*. Cambridge, Mass. 1975

Kealey, Gregory S. *Toronto Workers Respond to Industrial Capitalism, 1868–1892*. Toronto 1980

Kealey, Gregory S., and Bryan D. Palmer. *Dreaming of What Might Be: The Knights of Labor in Ontario, 1880–1900*. Cambridge 1982

Kett, Joseph. *Rites of Passage: Adolescence in America 1780 to the Present*. New York 1977

Kingston, W.A. *The Light of Other Days*. 1967. (history of Campbellford)

Laqueur, T.W. *Religion and Respectability, Sunday Schools and Working Class Culture, 1780–1850*. New Haven 1976

Laurie, Bruce. *Working People of Philadelphia*. Philadelphia 1980.

Lenskyj, Helen. *Out of Bounds: Women, Sport and Sexuality*. Toronto 1986

Levine, Susan. *Labor's True Woman: Carpet Weavers, Industrialization and Labor Reform in the Gilded Age*. Philadelphia 1984

Lynd, Roberts S., and Helen Merrell Lynd. *Middletown: A Study in Contemporary American Culture*. New York 1929

McCann, Larry, ed. *People and Place: Studies of Small Town Life in the Maritimes*. Fredricton, N.B. 1987

McKillop, A.B. *A Disciplined Intelligence: Critical Inquiry and Canadian Thought in the Victorian Era*. Montreal 1979

McLeod, Hugh. *Class and Religion in the Late Victorian City*. London 1974

Mangan, J.A., and James Walvin, eds. *Manliness and Morality: Middle-Class Masculinity in Britain and America*. New York 1987

Marshall, David. *Secularizing the Faith: Canadian Protestant Clergy and the Crisis of Belief, 1850–1940*. Toronto 1992

Melosh, Barbara. *The Physician's Hand: Work Culture and Conflict in American Nursing*. Philadelphia 1982

Metcalfe, Alan. *Canada Learns to Play: The Emergence of Organized Sport, 1807–1914*. Toronto 1987

Milkman, Ruth. *Women, Work and Protest: A Century of Women's Labor History*. Boston 1985

Moir, John S. *Enduring Witness: A History of the Presbyterian Church in Canada*. Canada 1975

Moody, J. Carroll, and Alice Kessler-Harris. *Perspectives on American Labor History: The Problems of Synthesis*. DeKalb, Ill. 1989

Morton, Desmond. *Canada and War*. Toronto 1981

Morton, Suzanne. *Ideal Surroundings: Domestic Life in a Working-Class Suburb in the 1920s*. Toronto 1995

Mott, Morris, ed. *Sports in Canada: Historical Readings*. Toronto 1989

Moyles, R.G. *The Blood and Fire in Canada: A History of the Salvation Army in the Dominion, 1882–1976*. Toronto 1977

Muir, Elizabeth Gillan, and Marilyn Fardig Whiteley, eds. *Changing Roles of Women within the Christian Church in Canada*. Toronto 1995

Murdoch, Norman H. *Origins of the Salvation Army*. Knoxville 1994

Murphy, Teresa Anne. *Ten Hours' Labor: Religion, Reform and Gender in Early New England*. Ithaca N.Y. 1992

Murphy, Terrence, and Gerald Stortz, eds. *Creed and Culture: The Place of English-Speaking Catholics in Canadian Society, 1750–1930*. Kingston and Montreal 1993

Noel, Jan. *Canada Dry: Temperance Crusades before Confederation*. Toronto 1995

Noll, Mark A., David W. Bebbington, and George A. Rawlyk, eds. *Evangelicalism: Comparative Studies of Popular Protestantism in North America, the British Isles, and Beyond, 1700–1990*. Oxford 1994

Obelkevich, James. *Religion and Rural Society: South Lindsey 1825–1875*. Oxford 1976

Obelkevich, Jim, Lyndal Roper, and Raphael Samuel, eds. *Disciplines of Faith: Studies in Religion, Politics and Patriarachy*. London 1987

O'Dea, Thomas F., and Janet O'Dea Aviad. *The Sociology of Religion*. New Jersey 1983

Owen, Alex. *The Darkened Room: Women, Power and Spiritualism in Late Victorian England*. London 1989

Palmer, Bryan. *A Culture in Conflict: Skilled Workers and Industrial Capitalism in Hamilton, Ontario, 1860–1914*. Montreal 1979

– *Working-Class Experience: Rethinking the History of Canadian Labour, 1800–1991*. Toronto 1992

Parr, Joy. *The Gender of Breadwinners: Women, Men and Change in Two Industrial Towns, 1880–1950*. Toronto 1990

Peiss, Kathy. *Cheap Amusements: Working Women and Leisure in Turn-of-the-Century New York*. Philadelphia 1986

Rabinowitz, Richard. *The Spiritual Self in Everyday Life: The Transformation of Personal Religious Experience in Nineteenth-Century New England*. Boston 1989

Rawlyk, George. *The Canada Fire: Radical Evangelicalism in British North America, 1775–1812*. Kingston and Montreal 1994

– *The Canadian Protestant Experience, 1760–1990*. Burlington, Ont. 1990

– *Ravished by the Spirit: Religious Revivals, Baptists and Henry Alline*. Kingston and Montreal 1984

– *Wrapped Up in God: A Study of Several Canadian Revivals and Revivalists*. Burlington, Ont. 1988

Roper, Michael, and John Tosh, eds. *Manful Assertions: Masculinities in Britain Since 1800*. London and New York 1991

Rosenzweig, Roy. *Eight Hours for What We Will: Workers and Leisure in an Industrial City, 1870–1920*. Cambridge 1983

Ross, Ellen. *Love and Toil: Motherhood in Outcast London, 1870–1918*. New York and Oxford 1993

Ross, Steven J. *Workers on the Edge: Work, Leisure and Politics in Industrializing Cincinnati*. New York 1985

Rotundo, E. Anthony. *American Manhood: Transformations in Masculinity from the Revolution to the Modern Era*. New York 1993

Rubio, Mary, and Elizabeth Waterston, eds. *The Selected Journals of L.M. Montgomery*. Vols. 1, 2. Toronto 1985, 1987

Rutherford, Paul. *A Victorian Authority: The Daily Press in Late Nineteenth-Century Canada*. Toronto 1982

Ryan, Mary P. *Cradle of the Middle Class: The Family in Oneida County, New York, 1790–1865*. Cambridge 1981

– *Women in Public: Between Banners and Ballots, 1825–1880*. Baltimore and London 1990

Saddlemyer, Ann, ed. *Early Stages: Theatre in Ontario, 1800–1914*. Toronto 1990

Sangster, Joan. *Earning Respect: The Lives of Working Women in Small-Town Ontario, 1920–1960*. Toronto 1995

Scott, Joan. *Gender and the Politics of History*. New York 1988

Semmel, Bernard. *The Methodist Revolution*. New York 1973

Smith-Rosenberg, Caroll. *Disorderly Conduct: Visions of Gender in Victorian America*. New York 1985

Spelt, Jacob. *The Urban Development in South-Central Ontario*. Assen, Netherlands 1955

Stansell, Christine. *City of Women: Sex and Class in New York, 1789–1860*. Urbana 1987

Stephenson, Charles, and Robert Asher, eds. *Life and Labor: Dimensions of American Working-Class History*. New York 1986.

Strange, Carolyn. *Toronto's Girl Problem: The Perils and Pleasures of the City, 1880–1930*. Toronto 1995

Thompson, E.P. *The Making of the English Working Class*. New York 1963

– *The Poverty of Theory*. London 1978

Town of Thorold Centennial. Souvenir booklet. 1950

Valenze, Deborah. *Prophetic Sons and Daughters: Female Preaching and Popular Religion in Industrial England*. Princeton 1985

Valverde, Mariana. *The Age of Light, Soap and Water: Moral Reform in English Canada, 1885–1925*. Toronto 1991

Vandermeer, Philip R., and Robert P. Swierenga, eds. *Belief and Behaviour: Essays in the New Religious History*. New Brunswick, N.J. 1991

Van Die, Marguerite. *An Evangelical Mind: Nathaniel Burwash and the Methodist Tradition in Canada, 1839–1918*. Montreal and Kingston 1989

Waldron, John ed. *Women in the Salvation Army*. Oakville, Ont. 1983

Wallace, Anthony F.C. *Rockdale, The Growth of an American Village in the Early Industrial Revolution*. New York 1972

Ward, Peter. *Courtship, Love and Marriage in Nineteenth-Century English Canada*. Kingston and Montreal 1990

Warsh, Cheryl Krasnick, ed. *Drink in Canada: Historical Essays*. Kingston and Montreal 1993

Weedon, Chris. *Feminist Practice and Poststructuralist Theory*. Oxford 1987

Weeks, Jeffrey. *Sex, Politics and Society: The Regulation of Sexuality since 1800*. London 1981

Westfall, William. *Two Worlds: The Protestant Culture of Nineteenth-Century Ontario*. Montreal 1989

Wickham, E.R. *Church and People in an Industrial City*. London 1957

Wilentz, Sean. *Chants Democratic: New York City and the Rise of the American Working Class, 1788–1850*. New York 1984

Winks, Robin W. *The Blacks in Canada: A History*. Montreal 1971

Yeo, Stephen. *Religion and Voluntary Organisations in Crisis*. London 1976

Articles

Anderson, Cora. 'Shall Women Preach? Principles and Practices in the Salvation Army and in the Methodist Church in Ontario, 1882–1900,' *Conrad Grebel Review*, Fall 1990

Bailey, Peter. '"Will the Real Bill Banks Please Stand Up?": Towards a Role Analysis of Mid-Victorian Working Class Respectability.' *Journal of Social History* 12 (Spring 1979)

Bailey, Victor. '"In Darkest England and the Way Out": The Salvation Army, Social Reform and the Labour Movement, 1885–1910.' *International Review of Social History* 29, pt. 2 (1984)

– 'Salvation Army Riots, the "Skeleton Army" and Legal Authority in the Provincial Town.' In A.P. Donajgrodzki, *Social Control in Nineteenth-Century Britain*. London 1977

Barman, Jean. 'Sports and the Development of Character.' In Morris Mott, ed., *Sports in Canada*. Toronto 1989

Barrett, Michele. 'Words and Things: Materialism and Method in Contemporary Feminist Analysis.' In Michele Barrett and Anne Phillips, ed., *Destabilizing Theory: Contemporary Feminist Debates*. Stanford 1992

Baskerville, Peter, and Eric Sager. 'The First National Unemployment Survey: Unemployment and the Canadian Census of 1891.' *Labour/Le Travail* 23 (Spring 1989)

Bennett, Judith M. 'Feminism and History.' *Gender and History*, 1, no. 3 (Autumn 1989)

Best, G.F.A. 'Popular Protestantism in Victorian Britain.' In Robert Robson, ed., *Ideas and Institutions of Victorian Britain*. London 1967

Bleasdale, Ruth. 'Class Conflict on the Canals of Upper Canada in the 1840s.' *Labour/Le Travailleur* 7 (1981)

Bliss, Michael. 'Privatizing the Mind: The Sundering of Canadian History, the Sundering of Canada.' *Journal of Canadian Studies* 26, no. 4 (Winter 1991–92)

Bock, Gisele. 'Women's History and Gender History: Aspects of an International Debate.' *Gender and History* 1, no. 1 (Spring 1989)

Bradbury, Bettina. 'The Family Economy and Work in an Industrializing City: Montreal in the 1870s.' Canadian Historical Association, *Historical Papers*. 1979

Bramwell-Booth, Catherine. 'The Call and Ministry of Women.'In John Waldron, ed., *Women in the Salvation Army*. Oakville 1983

Brouwer, Ruth Compton. 'Transcending the "Unacknowledged Quarantine": Putting Religion into Canadian Women's History.' *Journal of Canadian Studies* 27 (Fall 1992)

Brown, Mary M. 'Entertainers of the Road.' In Ann Saddlemyer, ed., *Early Stages*. Toronto 1990

Bukowczyk, John J. 'The Transforming Power of the Machine: Popular Religion, Ideology and Secularization among Polish Immigrant Workers in the United States, 1880–1940.' *International Labour and Working-Class History* 34 (Fall 1988)

Clark, Anna. 'The Sexual Crisis and Popular Religion in London, 1770–1820.' *International Labor and Working-Class History* 34 (Fall 1988)

Clarke, Brian. 'The Parish and the Hearth: Women's Confraternities and the Devotional Revolution among the Irish Catholics of Toronto, 1850–1885.' In Terrence Murphy and Gerald Stortz, eds., *Creed and Culture*. Kingston and Montreal 1993

Colls, Robert. 'Primitive Methodists in the Northern Coalfields.' In Jim Obelkevich, et al., eds., *Disciplines of Faith*. London 1987

Colwell, Judith. 'The Role of Women in the Nineteenth Century Baptist Church of Ontario.' Canadian Society of Church History *Papers*, 1985

Commacchio, Cynthia. 'Beneath the "Sentimental Veil": Families and Family History in Canada.' *Labour/Le Travail* 33 (Spring 1994).

Condran, Gretchen A., and Jeff Seaman. 'Linkage of the 1880–81 Philadelphia Death Register to the 1880 Manuscript Census: A Comparison of Hand and Machine-Record Linkage Techniques.' *Historical Methods* 14, no. 2 (Spring 1981)

Curtis, Susan. 'The Son of Man and God the Father: The Social Gospel and Victorian Masculinity.' In Mark C. Carues and Clyde Griffen, eds., *Meanings for Manhood: Constructions of Masculinity in Victorian America*. Chicago 1990

Davies, Robertson. 'The Nineteenth-Century Repertoire.' In Ann Saddlemyer, ed., *Early Stages*. Toronto 1990

De Lottinville, Peter. 'Joe Beef of Montreal.' *Labour/Le Travailleur* 8/9 (Autumn/ Spring 1981/1982)

Dubinsky, Karen. '"Maidenly Girls" or "Designing Women"? Prosecutions for Seduction in Ontario, 1880–1929.' In Franca Iacovetta and Mariana Valverde, eds., *Gender Conflicts: New Essays in Women's History*. Toronto 1992

Faler, Paul. 'Cultural Aspects of the Industrial Revolution: Lynn, Massachusetts Shoemakers and Industrial Morality, 1826–1860.' *Labor History* 15 (Summer 1974)

Fink, Leon. 'The New Labor History and the Powers of Historical Pessimism: Consensus, Hegemony, and the Case of the Knights of Labor,' and 'Relocating the Vital Center.' *Journal of American History* 75 (June 1988)

Fones-Wolf, Kenneth. 'Religion and Trade Union Politics in the United States, 1880–1920.' *International Labor and Working Class History*. 34 (Fall 1988)

Frager, Ruth. 'No Proper Deal: Women Workers and the Canadian Labour Movement, 1870–1940.' In Linda Briskin and Lynda Yanz, eds., *Union Sisters: Women in the Labour Movement*. Toronto 1983

– 'Politicized Housewives in the Jewish Communist Movement in Toronto 1923–1933.' In Linda Kealey and Joan Sangster., eds., *Beyond the Vote: Canadian Women and Politics*. Toronto 1989

Fulton, John. 'Religion and Politics in Gramsci: An Introduction.' *Sociological Analysis* 48, no. 3 (1987)

Garrett, Clarke. 'Popular Religion and the Labouring Classes in Nineteenth-Century Europe.' *International Labor and Working Class History*. 34 (Fall 1988)

Gauvreau, Michael. 'Beyond the Halfway House: Evangelicalism and the Shaping of English Canadian Culture.' *Acadiensis* 20, no. 2 (Spring 1991)

Gordon, Linda. 'Response to Scott.' *Signs* 15 (Summer 1990)

Gray, R.Q. 'Styles of Life: The Labour Aristocracy and Class Relations in Later Nineteenth Century Edinburgh.' *International Review of Social History* 18 (1973)

Greenberg, Brian. 'Worker and Community: Fraternal Orders in Albany, New York, 1845–1885.' In Charles Stephenson and Robert Asher, eds., *Life and Labor: Dimensions of American Working Class History*. New York 1986

Gutman, Herbert. 'Protestantism and the American Labor Movement.' In *Work, Culture and Society in Industrializing America*. New York 1966

Gutmann, Myron P., et al. 'Keeping Track of our Treasures: Managing Historical Data with Relational Database Software.' *Historical Methods* 22 no. 4 (Fall 1989)

Harrison, Brian. 'Religion and Recreation in Nineteenth-Century England.' *Past and Present*, December 1967

Hauser, Robert M. 'Occupational Status in the Nineteenth and Twentieth Centuries.' *Historical Methods* 15, no. 3 (Summer 1982)

Heron, Craig. 'Labourism and the Canadian Working Class.' *Labour/Le Travail* 13 (Spring 1984)

Heron, Craig, and George De Zwaan. 'Industrial Unionism in Eastern Ontario, 1918–1921.' *Ontario History*, 77, no. 3 (September 1985)

Hershberg, Theodore, and Robert Dockhorn. 'Occupational Classification.' *Historical Methods Newsletter* 9, nos. 2 and 3 (March–June 1976)

Hillis, Peter. 'Presbyterianism and Social Class in Mid-Nineteenth Century Glasgow: A Study of Nine Churches. *Journal of Ecclesiastical History*, 1981

Hoff, Joan. 'Gender as a Postmodern Category of Paralysis.' *Women's Studies International Forum* 17, no. 4 (July–August 1994)

Howell, David, and Peter Lindsay. 'Social Gospel and the Young Boy Problem, 1895–1924.' In Morris Mott, ed., *Sports in Canada*. Toronto 1989

Johnson, Curtis D. 'Supply-side and Demand-side Revivalism? Evaluating the Social Influences on New York State Evangelism in the 1830s.' *Social Science History* 19, no. 1 (Spring 1995)

Juster, Susan. 'Patriarchy Reborn: The Gendering of Authority in the Evangelical Church in Revolutionary New England.' *Gender and History* 6 (April 1994)

Lane, Hannah M. '"Wife, Mother, Sister, Friend": Methodist Women in St. Stephen, New Brunswick, 1861–1881.' In Janet Guildford and Suzanne Morton, eds., *Separate Spheres: Women's Worlds in the 19th-Century Maritimes*. Fredericton, N.B. 1994

Lears, T.J. Jackson. 'The Concept of Cultural Hegemony: Problems and Possibilities.' *American Historical Review* 90, no. 3 (June 1985)

Leslie, Genevieve. 'Domestic Service in Canada, 1880–1920.' In Janice Acton, et al., *Women at Work, Ontario 1850–1930*. Toronto 1974

McClelland, Keith. 'Masculinity and the "Representative Artisan" in Britain, 1850–80.' In Michael Roper and John Tosh, eds., *Manful Assertions*. London and New York 1991

McKay, Ian. 'Historians, Anthropology, and the Concept of Culture.' *Labour/Le Travail* 8/9 (Autumn/Spring 1981/1982)

McLeod, Hugh. 'Catholicism and the New York Irish.' In Jim Obelkevich et al., eds., *Disciplines of Faith*. London 1987

Malmgreen, Gail. 'Domestic Discords.' In Jim Obelkevich et al., eds. *Disciplines of Faith*. London 1987

Marshall, David B. 'Canadian Historians, Secularization and the Problem of the Nineteenth Century.' CCHA *Historical Studies* 60 (1993–94)

Marks, Lynne. 'Indigent Committees and Ladies Benevolent Societies: Intersec-

tions of Public and Private Poor Relief in Late Nineteenth Century Small Town
Ontario.' *Studies in Political Economy*, Spring 1995
- 'The Knights of Labor and the Salvation Army: Religion and Working-Class
Culture in Ontario, 1882–1890.' *Labour/Le Travail* 28 (Fall 1991)
- 'No Double Standard? Gender and Sin in Upper Canadian Church Discipline
Records.' In Nancy Forestell, Kathryn MacPherson, and Cecelia Morgan, eds.,
Gender in Canada (in progress)
Miller, J.R. 'Anti-Catholic Thought in Victorian Canada.' *Canadian Historical
Review* 66, no. 4 (December 1985)
Mitchinson, Wendy. 'Canadian Women and Church Missionary Societies in the
Nineteenth Century: A Step towards Independence.' *Atlantis* 2, no. 2, pt. 2
(Spring 1977)
- 'The WCTU: "For God, Home and Native Land": A Study of Nineteenth Cen-
tury Feminism.' In Linda Kealey, ed., *A Not Unreasonable Claim: Women and
Reform in Canada, 1880s–1920s*. Toronto 1979
Nelson, Bruce C. 'Revival and Upheaval: Religion, Irreligion, and Chicago's
Working Class in 1886.' *Journal of Social History* 25, no. 2 (Winter 1991)
Nicholson, Murray. 'Irish Tridentine Catholicism in Victorian Toronto' Vessel
for Ethno-religious Persistence.' CCHA study session *Papers* 50 (1983)
O'Brien, Anne. '"A Church Full of Men": Masculinism and the Church in
Australian History.' *Australian Historical Studies* 25, no. 100 (April 1993)
Park, Roberta J. 'Biological Thought, Athletics and the Formation of a "Man of
Character": 1830–1900.' In J.A. Mangan and James Walvin, eds., *Manliness and
Morality*. New York 1987
Parr, Joy. 'Gender History and Historical Practice.' *Canadian Historical Review* 76,
no. 3 (September 1995)
Reynolds, David S. 'The Feminization Controversy: Sexual Stereotypes and the
Paradoxes of Piety in Nineteenth Century America.' *New England Quarterly* 53
(March 1980)
Robertson, Roland. 'The Salvation Army: The Persistance of Sectarianism.' In
Bryan Wilson, ed., *Patterns of Sectarianism*. London 1967
Rotundo, Anthony. 'Learning about Manhood: Gender Ideals and the Middle
Class Family in Nineteenth-Century America.' In J.A. Mangan and James
Walvin, eds., *Manliness and Morality*. New York 1987
Rupp, Leila J. '"Imagine My Suprise": Women's Relationships in Historical Per-
spective.' *Frontiers* 5 no. 3 (Fall 1980)
Sangster, Joan. 'Beyond Dichotomies: Re-Assessing Gender History and
Women's History in Canada.' *left history* 3, no. 1 (Spring/Summer 1995)
Scott, Joan. 'The Evidence of Experience.' In Henry Abelove, Michele Aina Barale,
and David M. Halperin, eds., *The Lesbian and Gay Studies Reader*. New York 1993

– 'On Language, Gender and Working-Class History.' In Scott, *Gender and the Politics of History*. New York 1988
– 'Response to Gordon.' *Signs* 15 (Summer 1990)
Semple, Neil. 'The Impact of Urbanization on the Methodist Church of Canada, 1854–1884.' Canadian Society of Church History *Papers*, 1976
– '"The Nurture and Admonition of the Lord": Nineteenth-Century Canadian Methodism's Response to "Childhood."' *Histoire Sociale/Social History*, May 1981
– 'Ontario's Religious Hegemony: The Creation of the National Methodist Church.' *Ontario History* 77, no. 1 (March 1985)
Smith, Thomas. 'Reconstructing Occupational Structures: The Case of the Ambiguous Artisans.' *Historical Methods Newsletter* 8 no. 3 (June 1975)
Speisman, Steven. 'Munificent Parsons and Municipal Parsimony: Voluntary vs. Public Poor Relief in Nineteenth- Century Toronto.' *Ontario History* 54, no. 1 (March 1973)
Springhall, John. 'Building Character in the British Boy.' In J.A. Mangan and James Walvin, eds., *Manliness and Morality*. New York 1987
Stortz, Gerald J. 'The Catholic Priest in Rural Ontario.' In Alan A. Brooks, ed., *Religion and Rural Ontario's Past*, Proceedings of the 5th annual Agricultural History of Ontario Seminar. Guelph 1980
Stout, Harry S., and Robert Taylor. 'Sociology, Religion and Historians Revisited: Towards an Historical Sociology of Religion.' *Historical Methods Newsletter* 8, no. 1 (December 1974)
Strange, Carolyn. 'From Modern Babylon to a City upon a Hill: The Toronto Social Survey Commission of 1915 and the Search for Sexual Order in the City.' In Roger Hall, William Westfall, and Laurel Sefton MacDowell, eds., *Patterns of the Past: Interpreting Ontario's History*. Toronto 1988
Strong-Boag, Veronica. 'Setting the Stage: National Organizations and the Women's Movement in the late 19th Century.' In *The Neglected Majority: Essays in Canadian Women's History*. Vol 1. Toronto 1977
Sturgis, James L. '"The Spectre of a Drunkard's Grave": One Family's Battle with Alcohol in Late-Nineteenth-Century Canada.' In Cheryl Warsh, ed., *Drink in Canada*. Kingston and Montreal 1993
Sutton, William R. 'Tied to the Whipping Post: New Labor History and Evangelical Artisans in the Early Republic.'*Labor History* 36 no. 2 (Spring 1995)
Thomas, John D. 'Servants of the Church: Canadian Methodist Deaconess Work, 1890–1926.' *Canadian Historical Review* 65 (1984)
Tosh, John. 'What Should Historians Do with Masculinity? Reflections on Nineteenth-century Britain.' *History Workshop Journal* 38 (Autumn 1994)

Valverde, Mariana. 'Poststructuralist Gender Historians: Are We Those Names?' *Labour/Le Travail* 25 (Spring 1990)

Van Die, Marguerite. 'The Double Vision: Evangelical Piety as Derivative and Indigenous in Victorian English Canada.' In Mark A. Noll, David W. Bebbington, and George A. Rawlyk, eds. *Evangelicalism*. Oxford 1994

Vicinus, Martha. '"They Wonder to Which Sex I Belong?": The Historical Roots of the Modern Lesbian Identity.' In Henry Abelove, Michele Aina Barale and David M. Halperin, eds., *The Lesbian and Gay Studies Reader*. New York and London 1993

Walker, Pamela J. '"I Live but Not Yet I for Christ Liveth in Me": Men and Masculinity in the Salvation Army, 1865–90.' In Michael Roper and John Tosh, eds., *Manful Assertions: Masculinities in Britain since 1800*. London 1991

Warsh, Cheryl Krasnick. '"Oh Lord, Pour a Cordial in Her Wounded Heart": The Drinking Woman in Victorian and Edwardian Canada.' In Cheryl Krasnick Warsh, ed., *Drink in Canada: Historical Essays*. Kingston and Montreal 1993

Welter, Barbara. 'The Feminization of American Religion, 1800–1860.' In Welter, *Dimity Convictions*. Athens 1976

Whiteley, Marilyn Fardig. '"Doing Just About What They Please": Ladies Aids in Ontario Methodism.' *Ontario History* 82, no. 4 (December 1990)

– 'Modest, Unaffected and Fully Consecrated: Lady Evangelists in Canadian Methodism, 1884–1900.' Canadian Methodist Historical Society *Papers* 6 (1987)

Williams, Sarah C. 'The View from Below: Working-Class Women and Religion in Late Victorian Britain.' *Crux* 10 (September 1994)

Theses and Unpublished Papers

Anstead, Christopher J. 'Fraternalism in Victorian Ontario: Secret Societies and Cultural Hegemony.' PhD thesis, Department of History, University of Western Ontario, 1992

Ashley, Stephen M. 'The Salvation Army in Toronto, 1882–1896.' MA thesis, Department of History, University of Guelph, 1969

Bouchier, Nancy Barbara. '"For the Love of the Game and the Honour of the Town": Organized Sport, Local Culture, and Middle Class Hegemony in Two Ontario Towns, 1838–1895.' PhD thesis, Department of History, University of Western Ontario, 1990

Caldwell, Thelka. 'Revival and Chicago Working Girls: The Transformation of Gender in the Third Awakening.' Paper presented at the Berkshire Conference on the History of Women, New Brunswick, N.J., 1990

Cook, Sharon Anne. '"Continued and Persevering Combat": The Ontario

WCTU, Evangelicalism and Social Reform.' PhD thesis, Department of History, Carleton University, 1990

Decarie, Malcolm Graeme. 'The Prohibition Movement in Ontario, 1894–1916.' PhD thesis, Department of History, Queen's University, 1972

De Zwaan, George. 'Elite and Society, Newmarket, Ontario, 1857–1880.' MA thesis, Department of History, Queen's University, 1980

– 'The Little Birmingham on the St. Lawrence: An Industrial and Labour History of Gananoque, Ontario, 1871–1921.' Department of History, Queen's University, 1987

Draper, Kenneth, L. 'P.W. Philpott and the Christian Workers' Church: Conservative Premillennialism in the Social History of Hamilton.' Unpublished paper, Department of History, McMaster University, 1988

Dubinsky, Karen. '"The Modern Chivalry": Women and the Knights of Labor in Ontario, 1880–1891.' MA thesis, Department of Canadian Studies, Carleton University, 1985

Ellis, Leonard Harry. 'Men among Men: An Exploration of All-Male Relationships in Victorian America.' PhD thesis, Columbia University, 1982

Faraday, Fay. 'The Debate about Prostitution: A History of the Formation and Failure of Canadian Laws against the Sex Trade, 1867–1917.' MA thesis, Department of History, University of Toronto, 1990

Forestell, Nancy. '"All That Glitters Is Not Gold": The Gender Dimensions of Work, Family and Community Life in the Northern Ontario Gold Mining Town of Timmins, 1909–1950.' PhD thesis, Department of History and Philosophy, OISE, University of Toronto, 1993

Holman, Andrew. '"Akenson's Wake": Irish Canadian Historiography and the Case of Corktown, Hamilton, 1832–1847.' Unpublished paper, McMaster University, 1987

Huskins, Bonnie. 'Public Celebrations in Victorian Saint John and Halifax.' PhD thesis, Department of History, Dalhousie University, 1991

Kee, Kevin B. 'The Heavenly Railroad: Ernest Crossley, John Hunter and Canadian Methodist Revivalism, 1884–1910.' MA thesis, Department of History, Queen's University, 1994

Kristofferson, Robert. '"True Knights Are We": Unity, Conflict and Masculine Discourse: The Knights of Labor in Hamilton.' Major research paper, York University, 1992

Levine, Gregory. 'In God's Service: The Role of the Anglican, Methodist, Presbyterian and Roman Catholic Churches in the Cultural Geography of Late Nineteenth Century Kingston.' PhD thesis, Department of Geography, Queen's University, 1980

Marks, Lynne. 'Ladies, Loafers, Knights and "Lasses": The Social Dimensions of

Religion and Leisure in Late Nineteenth-Century Small Town Ontario.' PhD thesis, Deptartment of History, York University, 1992

Mitchinson, Wendy. 'Aspects of Reform: Four Women's Organizations in Nineteenth-Century Canada.' PhD thesis, Department of History, York University, 1976

Morgan, Cecilia. 'Languages of Gender in Upper Canadian Religion and Politics, 1791–1850.' PhD thesis, Department of History, University of Toronto, 1993

Muir, Elizabeth. 'Petticoats in the Pulpit: Early Nineteenth Century Methodist Women Preachers in Upper Canada.' PhD thesis, McGill University, 1990

Newbury, Darryl Jean-Guy. '"No Atheist, Eunuch or Woman": Male Associational Culture and Working-Class Identity in Industrializing Ontario, 1840–1880.' MA thesis, Department of History, Queen's University, 1992

O'Dell, Doris Mary. 'The Class Character of Church Participation in Late Nineteenth-Century Belleville, Ontario.' PhD thesis, Department of History, Queen's University, 1990

Orr, Patricia. 'The Wrong Side of the Canal: Social Connections and Residential Land Use Patterns in Nineteenth-Century Thorold, Ontario.' MA thesis, Department of Geography, York University, 1984.

Pitsula, James Michael. 'The Relief of Poverty in Toronto, 1880–1930.' PhD thesis, Department of History, York University, 1979

Rosenfeld, Mark. '"She Was a Hard Life": Work, Family, Community, Politics and Ideology in the Railway Ward of a Central Ontario Town, 1900–1960.' PhD thesis, Department of History, York University, 1990

Schantz, Mark Saunders. 'Piety in Providence: The Class Dimensions of Religious Experience in Providence, Rhode Island, 1790–1860.' PhD thesis, Department of History, Emory University, 1991

Van Die, Marguerite. '"A Women's Awakening": Evangelical Belief and Female Spirituality in Mid-Nineteenth-Century Canada.' Paper presented at the Canadian Historical Association, Kingston, 1991

Vernon, Foster. 'The Development of Adult Education in Ontario, 1790–1900.' EdD thesis, University of Toronto, 1969

Index

Temperance; Woman's Christian
Temperance Union; Young
Woman's Christian Temperance
Union
theatre, 130, 131–3
Thompson, Capt. Abbie, 180, 181
Thompson, E.P., 7, 160
Thompson, John, 81
Thompson, Phillips, 152–3, 154
Thorold (setting), 16–17, 195, 198–9
Thorold revival (1893), 16, 43, 192–206;
cross-class appeal of, 198–9, 205–6;
emphasis on men, 197, 198; and
gendered meetings, 196
Tosh, John, 137
traditional sports, 136
Trent Valley Woollen Mills, 18
true Christianity, 12–13, 164, 167, 209–
10; Thorold revival and, 198–200.
See also financial contributions
Turner, George, 95

unorthodoxy. *See* Christian Science;
secularism; spiritualism

Van Die, Marguerite, 29–30
variety shows, 132
voluntary associations. *See* fraternal
orders
volunteer groups. *See* band; fire
brigades; militia
Vosper, John, 82, 83, 86, 119

Walker, Pamela, 163
Warsh, Cheryl Krasnick, 87
Watts, Charles, 44–5, 156
Welland Canal, 17
Wesley, John, 64
Westfall, William, 60
Whitely, Marilyn, 67

Wollstonecraft, Mary, 171
Woman's Christian Temperance
Union (WCTU), 95–102, 119,
282n52; and membership, 96–7
women: and church groups, 64–79,
214, 277nn81, 82; and employment,
144, 161, 291n13; and fraternal
orders, 110, 113; and Knights of
Labor, 147, 155; and lay leadership,
53–4, 57, 65–8; and leisure, 126–7,
128, 131–2, 137, 138; and religiosity,
29–30, 31, 34–5, 41, 46–7; and
religiosity of Salvation Army, 173–5,
178–9, 180–1, 184–5; and rough
culture, 82, 84–5, 87–8; and Salvation Army, 111–5, 169, 88, 214; and
temperance, 91–2, 93, 94, 95–102;
and Thorold revival, 192, 196,
203–4; and unorthodoxy, 46–7, 49,
51. *See also* femininity
women's groups, church-based, 64–9,
73–9, 214; barriers within, 70–2, 79,
203. *See also* Anglican Women's
Auxiliary; Ladies Aid; Ladies Mite
Society; missionary society
women's history, 7–8
women's suffrage, 99–100
working class, 14–15, 56, 132, 133, 134;
culture, 14–15, 115–16, 117, 141, 157–
8; fraternal orders and, 115–16; and
Mechanics' Institute, 127; and
religion, 27–9, 33–6, 41, 50; and
rough culture, 81–7; and sports, 123,
128, 129, 136; and temperance, 91–6,
106; and Thorold revival, 192–4, 200,
203–5, 206; and volunteer groups,
117, 121; and women's groups, 70,
71–2, 73–5, 79, 277nn81, 82. *See also*
Knights of Labor; Salvation Army;
working-class consciousness